OIL IN PUTIN'S RUSSIA

The Contests over Rents and Economic Policy

No sector has been as vital as oil to the Russian economy since Vladimir Putin came to power. The longest serving leader since Stalin, Putin has presided during a period of relative economic prosperity driven largely by booming oil windfalls. *Oil in Putin's Russia* offers an in-depth examination of the contests over windfalls drawn from the oil sector. Examining how the Russian leadership has guided the process of distributing these windfalls, Adnan Vatansever explores the causes behind key policy continuities and policy reversals during Putin's tenure.

The product of over ten years of research, including interviews with decision-makers and oil industry officials, *Oil in Putin's Russia* takes an innovative approach to understanding the contested nature of resource rents and the policy processes that determine how they are allocated. In so doing, it offers a comprehensive and timely account of politics and policy in contemporary Russia, and a significant contribution to research on the political economy of resource rents in mineral resource-rich countries.

ADNAN VATANSEVER is a senior lecturer at King's Russia Institute, School of Politics and Economics, King's College, London.

Oil in Putin's Russia

*The Contests over Rents
and Economic Policy*

ADNAN VATANSEVER

UNIVERSITY OF TORONTO PRESS
Toronto Buffalo London

© University of Toronto Press 2021
Toronto Buffalo London
utorontopress.com
Printed in the U.S.A.

ISBN 978-1-4875-0369-7 (cloth)   ISBN 978-1-4875-1853-0 (EPUB)
ISBN 978-1-4875-2281-0 (paper)   ISBN 978-1-4875-1852-3 (UPDF)

Library and Archives Canada Cataloguing in Publication

Title: Oil in Putin's Russia : the contests over rents and economic policy / Adnan
     Vatansever.
Names: Vatansever, Adnan, author.
Description: Includes bibliographical references and index.
Identifiers: Canadiana (print) 20200416898 | Canadiana (ebook) 20200416928 |
     ISBN 9781487522810 (paper) | ISBN 9781487503697 (cloth) | ISBN 9781487518530
     (EPUB) | ISBN 9781487518523 (PDF)
Subjects: LCSH: Petroleum industry and trade – Government policy – Russia
     (Federation) | LCSH: Russia (Federation) – Economic policy.
Classification: LCC HD9575.R82 V38 2021 | DDC 333.8/2320947–dc23

University of Toronto Press acknowledges the financial assistance to its publishing
program of the Canada Council for the Arts and the Ontario Arts Council, an agency
of the Government of Ontario.

Canada Council   Conseil des Arts
for the Arts   du Canada

ONTARIO ARTS COUNCIL
CONSEIL DES ARTS DE L'ONTARIO
an Ontario government agency
un organisme du gouvernement de l'Ontario

Funded by the   Financé par le
Government   gouvernement
of Canada   du Canada

Canada

For Sevi and Ayda

Contents

Acknowledgments

This book is product of over fifteen years of research. There are innumerable people to whom I owe my gratitude for their support, guidance, feedback, and assistance.

Starting in reverse chronological order, I would like to thank my colleagues at King's College London, who have been one of the main sources of encouragement during the past years. I am thankful to Marc Berenson, Samuel Greene, Alexander Kupatadze, and Gulnaz Sharafutdinova for providing an outstanding intellectual environment at the King's Russia Institute. Special thanks also to Gregory Asmolov, Jeremy Jennings, Natasha Kuhrt, and Simona Talani for their collegial support. I owe gratitude also to members of the International Political Economy working group at the university for their comments and critique of drafts that turned into book chapters. I have very much benefited from discussions with students, particularly in a post-graduate seminar on political economy of Russian energy.

Over the past decade, I presented pieces of this project at numerous panels and conferences, including those hosted by the Association for Slavic, East European and Eurasian Studies, the American Political Science Association, International Studies Association, the British International Studies Association, European Consortium for Political Research, the Moscow State Institute of International Relations (MGIMO), All Souls College at the University of Oxford, Economic Forum in Poland, and University of California, Los Angeles. I am particularly grateful for their stimulating questions, encouraging comments and constructive feedback to Anders Aslund, Andrew Barnes, Stephen Crowley, Scott Gehlbach, Vladimir Gel'man, Andreas Goldthau, Elizabeth Plantan, Douglas Rogers, Benjamin Smith, Laura Solanko, and Adam Stulberg, among many others. Fruitful exchanges at the 2015 Gaidar Forum and the 2017 April International Academic Conference on Economic and Social Policy helped to further enlighten me on key empirical aspects of this book. I have also grown grateful to Fatih Birol, Peter Charow, William Harwood, and James Henderson for sharing insights on the intricacies of Russian oil and energy industries. In addition, I am thankful to Thomas Remington for offering me valuable data on voting patterns within the State Duma, and Ben Noble, for sharing his research on Russian legislature.

I need to recognize the many institutions that have made an essential contribution to my research. As a researcher on Russian energy at Carnegie Endowment, I benefited from many opportunities to enrich my understanding of issues that turned out to be central for this book. Two separate panels on taxation of hydrocarbons and energy subsidies, put together at the Carnegie Moscow Center in 2011, were most helpful for building the basis of a chapter of this book project. Numerous trips to Moscow allowed me to benefit from a network of researchers and industry experts, whose input over the years has been invaluable for completing this project. Among many, I wish to thank Sergey Aleksashenko, Maria Belova, Vladimir Drebentsov, Sergey Drobyshevsky, Vladimir Feigin, Evsey Gurvich, Oleg Ignatov, Mikhail Krutikhin, Vladimir Milov, Andrey Movchan, Tatiana Mitrova, Nina Poussenkova, and Andrey Yakovlev.

The World Bank, where I was fortunate to be part of a research project on governance of mineral resources, provided me with valuable insights to put Russia's experience in a broader perspective. I am thankful to a team of highly dedicated experts, including Naazneen Barma, Alexandra Gillies, Kai Kaiser, and Tuan Minh Le. Thad Dunning, Alan Gelb, Anand Rajaram, Steven Ndegwa, Tina Soreide, Silvana Tordo from the World Bank, and Philip Daniels and Charles McPherson from the International Monetary Fund were kind enough to share their experience, allowing me to better understand not just the political economy of oil and other mineral resources in general, but the peculiarities of Russia's case as well.

I had the chance to be part of a highly stimulating learning environment at the Cambridge Energy Research Associates. I am deeply obliged to Thane Gustafson, who has been a role model, a mentor, and a main source of inspiration for my research on energy issues for over two decades. Matthew Sagers, with his immense insights into the Russian energy industry, has also had a lasting impact on me as a researcher.

A few lines will be too short to express my deepest and sincere gratitude to Bruce Parrott at the School of Advanced International Studies, the Johns Hopkins University. It has been a true privilege to develop academically under his supervision and invaluable mentorship. I have treasured every conversation with him, each one inspiring me not only intellectually, but also to be a better person. It has been also a distinct privilege to have received research guidance from Francis Fukuyama and William Chandler.

I wish to thank Alexei Bogaturov, Alexei Dundich, and Andrey Sushentsov for helping me stay productive while being hosted by MGIMO during one of my research trips to Russia. There are many people who helped me answer many of the questions explored in this book. I warmly thank Mihkail Deliagin, Miriam Elder, Lev Freinkman, Vladislav Inozemtsev, Peter Kaznacheev, Yulia Latynina, John Litwack, Valery Nesterov, Igor Nikolaev, Elena Panfilova, Vladimir Popov, Pavel Salin, Victoria Semerkhanova, Alexander Shitov, Mikhail Subbotin, Sergey Verezemsky, Vadim Visloguzov, Vladimir Voloshin, and Alexei Zudin for sharing their knowledge and wisdom with me.

I also owe much to Harley Balzer for inspiring me to follow an academic path. Starting an MA program with him at Georgetown University a week after the August 1998 financial crash in Russia was a steppingstone to an exciting career. I am thankful to Clifford Gaddy, whose course on the Russian economy at Georgetown was mind-opening, and his research most stimulating in developing my interest in Russia's rentier economy. Also, I would like to express my deep appreciation to Lowell Bezanis whose undergraduate course on Post-Soviet politics in 1995 triggered my interest in pursuing further studies on Russia.

I am indebted to Daniel Quinlan, the University of Toronto Press, for his utmost professionalism throughout this process. I am thankful to the three anonymous reviewers whose comments were essential in improving this book. Many thanks to Anna Laughlin for her editorial help, and to Barbara Porter for her guidance.

I owe my parents, Emine and Mumin Vatansever, for their love and support, and for encouraging me to pursue my dreams. Finally, I owe the most to my wife, Sevi Simavi, who has been with me since the very beginning of this journey as my most ardent supporter. It is to her and our daughter, Ayda, that I dedicate this book.

OIL IN PUTIN'S RUSSIA

The Contests over Rents and Economic Policy

Introduction

Oil has been vital for the economy in Vladimir Putin's Russia. No other sector has contributed as much to the nation's wealth. Natural gas may have put Russia more often in the spotlight, but it is oil that has delivered the largest revenues for the state and the economy as a whole.[1] In a historic turn, shortly after Putin was appointed as Russia's new prime minister in August 1999, oil prices entered an upward trend that lasted nearly a decade. An almost consistent growth in oil production further contributed to an increase in windfalls. By 2018, when Putin was elected as president for his fourth term, Russia's cumulative oil export revenues since 2000 amounted to nearly 3 trillion USD.[2]

In retrospect, it is clear that Putin has presided over oil windfalls of historic proportions. By contrast, his two immediate predecessors, Boris Yeltsin and Mikhail Gorbachev, faced considerably lower oil prices. Furthermore, their tenures did not last as long as Putin's. The last leader in the Kremlin to find himself with such vast oil windfalls was Leonid Brezhnev. It is remarkable that Putin and Brezhnev have been the two longest-serving leaders since Stalin.

As an oil-rich country, Russia is not alone in facing the various benefits and pitfalls commonly associated with having an economy heavily reliant on mineral resources. However, it offers an astonishing story to be explored. As Harley Balzer notes in regard to Russia today, "not since Spain in the 16th century has a major world power been based on mineral resources."[3] Understanding how Russia's leadership has perceived this reality and tried to address it is imperative.

This book provides an in-depth analysis of how Putin's Russia managed these historic windfalls. Not surprisingly, given the magnitude of the wealth, managing it has been an intensely contested area. One set of contests has revolved around who should be in the business of producing oil, taking charge of generating Russia's colossal oil windfalls. Another set of battles has occurred between the state and the oil companies on how to divide the windfalls between themselves. As the state has acted as the chief redistributor of the oil windfalls, the process of redistribution has also been the focus of vigorous political battles.

Finally, oil companies have also engaged in various forms of redistribution, often through informal channels, inviting further competition over the flow of wealth they generate.

The Russian leadership has been at the center of these contests, developing policies to steer the flow of oil windfalls. Both through formal and informal means, it has determined who gets their hands on Russia's oil fortune. Putin, quickly consolidating his power after 1999, could be described as the chief executive in this process.

This book explores one central puzzle. Throughout the period of the study, from 1999 till 2018, there has not been a change in the top leadership in a real sense. Putin, whether in his formal capacity as president or as prime minister, has stood at the helm of Russian politics. And yet, the approach of the Russian leadership on how to manage oil wealth has gone through periodic, sometimes rather dramatic, shifts. Namely, during the nearly two decades of the Putin era, many government policies developed to guide the contests on the oil windfalls have exhibited a considerable lack of stability, oscillating from one direction to another. Why such instability? In the meantime, the Russian leadership has maintained a rather consistent approach in some policy areas: it has adopted policies that have remained consistent in terms of their objectives and outcomes over time. What explains this variation? In short, the puzzle is: why have some of the government's policies endured over time while others have not?

To address these questions, it is important to clarify the key policy areas pertaining to the management of oil wealth. For this purpose, I introduce an innovative model to study the contested nature of oil as a mineral resource. Called the "rent allocation" model, it underscores the different processes and contests that lie behind the redistribution of resource windfalls.

In the following section I present a brief overview of some of the key outcomes with respect to rent allocation in Putin's Russia and summarize my main arguments. I develop the theoretical background of these arguments in the next chapter, which also elaborates on the methodology and the key contributions of this study.

The Contested Politics of Rent Allocation

Resource windfalls go through a complex process of redistribution, often involving numerous political battles. To describe this process, I introduce the term "rent allocation." Rent has been treated as a unique concept with respect to redistribution since the time of Adam Smith.[4] For the sake of simplicity, I define oil rents as the equivalent of industry profits: the difference between the total revenues generated within the industry and total costs that are considered "normal" for the industry.[5]

The process of "rent allocation" can be summed up in three continuous phases (figure 1.1). It starts with "rent generation," which is a precondition for any kind of rent allocation. Several points are significant to this phase. First, the size of the generated rents is important as it determines what is available

Figure 1.1. The Process of Rent Allocation

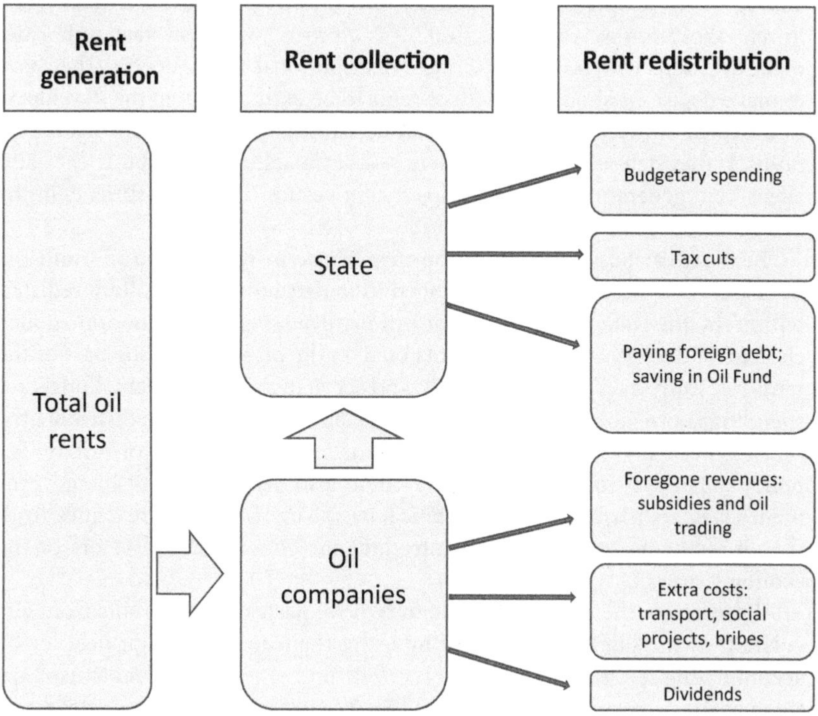

| Rent generation | Rent collection | Rent redistribution |

- Total oil rents
- State
- Oil companies
- Budgetary spending
- Tax cuts
- Paying foreign debt; saving in Oil Fund
- Foregone revenues: subsidies and oil trading
- Extra costs: transport, social projects, bribes
- Dividends

for allocation. This amount can fluctuate widely in relation to changes in the resource's output and its price.[6]

Second, who generates the rents is also significant. The type of ownership in particular could have numerous implications for how a resource sector functions and how its rents get redistributed.[7] In the case of the oil sector, this has traditionally involved local private oil companies, state-owned national oil companies (NOCs), or international oil companies (IOCs).

Third, governments can make decisions regarding rent generation with important distributional consequences. A new leadership in a resource-rich country would typically inherit a certain mode of rent generation comprising the size of the rents and the main players generating them. Its policies can determine how rent generation evolves further. For instance, a government can use policy tools such as licenses to determine how fast and in what particular locations companies extract the resources. Its leadership may also attempt to alter the ownership setup in the sector. There are multiple paths: a government can introduce new players, further empower existing ones, or eliminate those it dislikes. Finally, the leadership may take decisions that affect the scope of competition in the rent generation sector. Restricting or further encouraging competition may influence the level of profitability for the companies in the sector.

Once rents are generated, the question becomes how they will be allocated among the developers of the resources and the state. I define this next phase in rent allocation as "rent collection." It is a process whereby state authorities make decisions with potentially crucial distributional consequences. They have to make decisions about the share of rents to be extracted from the developers in the form of taxes or other fees. Such decisions are important for fiscal purposes, as they determine the amount of rents available to redistribute. They also affect "rent generation," as they shape incentives for future investments in the natural resource sector.

"Rent redistribution" involves the next phase in rent allocation. Both the state and the oil companies are engaged in redistributing rents. "Rent redistribution" by the state is a process that can involve several key economic policy choices: budgetary spending, tax cuts outside the oil sector, saving part of the rents for "rainy days" in special funds, and servicing sovereign debt. Budgetary spending is probably the most common means for the state to redistribute the rents. It necessitates determining numerous specific spending priorities. Tax policy outside the oil/resource sector could also become part of the government's rent redistribution. For instance, by raising additional revenues from the oil sector, a government can introduce tax cuts for select sectors or the economy overall.

Alternatively, the state can decide to remove parts of the oil rents from circulation in the domestic economy by using them to pay foreign debt, or by accumulating them in a special reserve/oil fund. The share of rents used for these purposes represents the amount that is "subtracted" from the "total rents" that are immediately available for the economy. In effect, the state forgoes redistributing a portion of the rents for the sake of additional economic objectives. While rents flowing into an oil fund may represent a forgone opportunity to redistribute, the accumulated revenues offer a government the possibility to spend more than what it manages to collect in a given year. An oil fund is a convenient policy instrument to have in case oil prices go down, though governments can opt to make use of it at other times as well.[8]

Oil companies can also act as agents of "rent redistribution." They typically pay a certain amount of taxes and are left with some after-tax profits. Yet, this is not where the story ends. Part of the pre-tax rents they generate and part of their after-tax profits are subject to further redistribution. While there are numerous ways oil companies engage in further redistribution, they can be summed up in three categories. Sometimes companies may forgo a portion of their revenues and allow other beneficiaries to get a hold of their rents. This would be the case when an oil company sells its commodity at subsidized prices or yields a chunk of its profits to a trading intermediary. An oil company could also redistribute rents by incurring some above-market costs. Gaddy and Ickes refer to such costs as "informal taxes" for the oil companies.[9] These could come in the form of bribes, overpriced contracts with providers of goods and services such as transportation, and payments made in the name of supporting various social, cultural, and local infrastructure projects. For instance, Surgutneftegaz, one of Russia's largest private oil companies, is known for its involvement in repairing a nuclear military submarine in Kamchatka – clearly an area that is not directly relevant to the oil business.[10] Finally, oil companies can redistribute a portion of their rents through dividend payments.

What is peculiar about rent redistribution by the oil sector is that it is a process that bypasses the state coffers. It requires oil companies to incur additional costs, which are equivalent to an extra tax, albeit not collected by the government itself.[11] It is also equivalent to subsidizing a set of beneficiaries who manage to get their hands on the oil rents. These may be state bureaucrats, city councils, various private and state-owned companies, nongovernmental organizations, sports teams, and so on.

Furthermore, while this type of redistribution is conducted by the oil sector, the sector itself is not necessarily the only decision-maker involved in allocating its rents. State officials at both the federal and regional levels can appear behind some of the oil companies' redistributive activities, such as picking the social and infrastructure projects that need funding. They can also decide the form and extent of the subsidies from the oil sector.

There are several additional points worth noting about the process of "rent allocation." First, all aspects of rent allocation occur *simultaneously* and are closely *interrelated*. The state collects oil rents and redistributes them, while the oil sector continues to generate the rents and engages in various forms of redistribution itself. In the meantime, the amount available for rent redistribution is contingent on the size of rents generated by the oil sector as well as on the extent of their taxation. Governments' specific policy choices about redistributing rents may also have far reaching repercussions. For instance, policy decisions expanding government spending may raise the tax pressure on the resource sector.

Second, if the leadership acquires the ability to influence the oil companies' redistributive activities, this widens the number of tools for rent redistribution at its disposal. Thus, the government may abstain from providing financial support (or limit the amount) to a select beneficiary, and instead get an oil company to step in to fill the gap.

Third, as both the state and the oil sector are focal points for rent redistribution, fundamental changes *within* each of these key sets of players can have important consequences for how rents are allocated. Transformative changes for rent allocation can take various paths. Sometimes they can originate within the state when the ruling elite is replaced with a new one. If the governing elite remains generally intact, however, intense struggles within the elite may also shift rent allocation policies from one direction to another. The ruling elite will need to find a way to resolve disagreements in areas such as how to conduct tax reform or where to allocate the spending priorities in relation to oil windfalls.

As the entities in charge of generating the rents, oil companies can also go through changes that become transformative for the allocation of their rents. There are multiple possibilities: a private oil company may be nationalized, a state-owned company may be privatized, and new management may take over the operations of either type of company. In each case, the transformation opens the prospects for rearranging the beneficiaries of the rents redistributed by a company.

Furthermore, fundamental changes within the elite and the resource sector may well be connected. Particularly in countries where the resource sector is not immune to political interference, changes in the ownership or the management of a resource company may be linked closely to competition within the political elites. As rents can be distributed both through the state and directly by the oil companies, the ultimate prize for a member of the elite is to acquire a role in both of these channels. In effect, both channels for redistributing rents are closely intertwined with the competition for power among elite members.

Finally, the potential scope of allocation may vary widely in terms of its beneficiaries. Some policies, such as subsidized fuel prices, may favor the population as a whole. Other policies may benefit only a particular sector of the economy, a company, and, in some cases, a designated person. As rents available to allocate are not limitless, decision-makers in the government need to constantly re-evaluate their choices regarding beneficiaries.

How political leaders govern the process of rent allocation and their political survival may be ultimately connected. This is because public support and the continuous backing of members of the political and economic elites may hinge on key policy choices. The entire chain of rent allocation is prone to policy decisions that can yield beneficiaries, but can also leave a significant part of society unsatisfied.

The Main Puzzle and Argument of the Book

As illustrated through the rent allocation model, a country's oil rents flow through a highly complex process. In each aspect related to rent allocation there is a wide range of possible outcomes. Oil-rich countries differ in terms of ownership in the oil sector, the way governments tax oil, the way they redistribute the wealth, and the extent to which political leaders try to guide how oil companies share their wealth with select beneficiaries.

Leaders of oil rich countries take, on a recurring basis, policy decisions affecting how rent allocation evolves. They may opt to maintain certain aspects of rent allocation while altering others. They may be dissatisfied with the status quo and launch a new policy to alter it. The policy may or may not succeed.

Each decision has distributional consequences, and some are more critical than others.

Looking at the Putin era, this book provides a detailed account of how rent allocation evolved and how the leadership tried to shape this process. It would be helpful to provide a glimpse of some of the key outcomes, and highlight what constitutes the main puzzle under discussion.

Putin's arrival at the helm of Russian politics brought some fairly rapid and drastic changes in rent allocation. During his first term as president, the number of changes he undertook is rather astounding. During the 1990s, a few privately owned Russian oil companies had managed to take over nearly the entire oil industry. By the time Putin was re-elected in 2004, the sector had been on a path to be partly nationalized and the main owner of Russia's largest oil company had been sentenced to prison. Rent collection went through similar transformations. The oil tax regime was entirely overhauled, allowing the state to finally collect the share it had failed to secure previously, despite all efforts under Yeltsin. The state's role in redistribution changed as well. A strong budgetary surplus and rapidly dwindling foreign debt replaced years of deficits and ballooning debt. The government adopted drastic measures to reform taxation for the rest of the economy as well. Also, for the first time, it put the management of the state's oil revenues under formal rules in a new institutional setting, the outcome of which was a special oil fund created in 2003.

What made these drastic changes possible? Why did the new leadership opt to make these profound changes? Even more importantly, how was it capable of engineering such a transformation in rent allocation? What does this say about the ability of the new leadership to launch critical reforms? And having altered the status quo in rent allocation profoundly, how committed was the new leadership to maintain it?

The last question in particular is key as it directs us to this book's main puzzle. At the time of writing, Putin is in his fourth term as president. And yet, looking back, many of the aspects of rent allocation he managed to transform at the start of his first tenure have remained distinctly unstable. By contrast, several key aspects of rent allocation have exhibited remarkable continuity over time, indicating that the Russian leadership has either valued the status quo or has not been able to do anything to change it.

A brief overview of the factual record on the key outcomes along the rent allocation model helps to illustrate the main areas of policy shifts and continuities. The question about who should generate Russia's oil rents has remained largely unsettled during the Putin era. Following drastic changes during Putin's first two-term presidency, ownership in the oil sector continued to fluctuate. This has been indicative of the government's frequently shifting approach on how to handle battles over who is in the business of producing oil – Russia's chief source of wealth. An outsider reading about Russia's oil tax regime might get the impression that the country has been in the midst of repeated attempts at another overhaul, with more to come. Furthermore, the Russian government has not always appeared committed to the tax rules it sets for the oil sector, reversing key decisions at will to secure more income for the state. Likewise, the government's budgetary policy has been similarly prone to major shifts. The leadership's approach has oscillated between remarkably fiscally conservative and highly expansionary policies. Moreover, such shifts cannot be explained by merely looking at changes in oil windfalls, which have generally tracked international oil prices. During the examined period, Russia went through two oil booms and two oil busts, and yet the budgetary response has been widely different each time.

In the meantime, a few aspects of rent allocation have exhibited notable continuity. For instance, following major reforms during Putin's first presidential term, the policy of taxation outside the oil sector has remained fairly steady. Likewise, the leadership has never stepped back from its approach to maintain a high tax burden on the oil sector – one of the highest in the world. Amid continuously changing tax rules, this is one area that has not changed in any significant way. The Kremlin's stance on Russia's sovereign foreign debt has constituted another major continuity. Foreign debt was lowered from the record level of 144 percent of the GDP in 1998 to barely 10 percent of GDP in 2005.[12] The newly acquired status quo of a low sovereign debt was never reversed despite major changes in the economic context. Another area of continuity relates to the organizational setup of Russia's oil industry. Amid major shifts in ownership, a few elements of this setup have remained resilient over time. For instance, foreign oil majors and independent smaller companies have never managed to make significant inroads in the Russian oil industry. Furthermore, the oil sector as a whole has retained its fairly competitive character whereby several big Russian players have managed to thrive. Finally, the Russian leadership has obstinately fought to maintain a role in how oil companies act as further redistributors of oil rents, relying principally on informal rules, and perpetuating conduct established in the early 1990s. The alternative would have been to let oil companies decide what to do with their revenues once they pay their tax dues.

In addressing the questions raised above, this book presents an approach that could serve as a helpful alternative to understanding resource-rich countries like Russia. The approach has several underlying goals. One is to capture the contested nature of the range of policies pertaining to rent allocation. Another is to avoid the determinism ingrained in many dominant paradigms on resource-rich countries. Namely, an approach examining rent allocation policies should ideally incorporate both structural constraints in policy-making and the role of agency in shaping policy outcomes. Finally, it should explain variations in policy outcomes in terms of their stability.

Developed in further detail in the next chapter, the approach presented here has one central concept defined as "executive power." I derive this concept from the "veto players" theory. The theory, espoused by the "New Institutionalist" school, has been commonly applied in the study of highly contested redistributive policies of governments. "Executive power" has multiple attributes that shed light on the executive branch in terms of its relative power to other institutional veto players in the political system, and in terms of its internal structure. Through its many attributes, the concept of "executive power" allows one to explain when the executive branch is capable of adopting a new policy and when it is more likely to remain committed to it. Echoing terminology from the veto players theory, here the executive's ability to launch a policy is defined as the "decisiveness" of the state, whereas its ability to commit to its policy is defined as the "resoluteness" of the state.[13]

This book examines the link between executive power and the outcomes of each of the four sets of battles on rent allocation in several steps. I start by evaluating the significance of the upsurge in executive power witnessed during the early years of the Putin era. The veto players theory suggests that, faced with weakened institutional veto players, the executive branch would likely emerge as more "decisive" in shaping the distinct aspects of rent allocation. Hence, this study portrays how the weakening of Russia's institutional players mattered for rent allocation policies. I illustrate that the drastic changes in the government's approach to rent allocation during Putin's first term can be explained via the enhanced "decisiveness" of the executive. Faced with weaker institutional veto players, the Putin administration was able to transform a range of rent allocation policies it inherited from President Yeltsin.

Yet, while Putin's first few years in the Kremlin can be seen as a transitional stage towards a more decisive executive power, one can regard the weakness of the institutional veto players outside the executive branch as constant during the following period. In the given context, what explains the variation in the stability of rent allocation policies? In other words, why have some of the policies kept fluctuating while others have exhibited a notable continuity?

To address this main puzzle, I take two additional steps. I look at the presence or lack of cohesion within the executive branch as a possibly critical attribute of executive power. Some areas of rent allocation clearly benefited from greater executive cohesion than others from the very start of the Putin era. I hypothesize that in policy areas where the executive remained more cohesive one can expect greater stability. Conversely, a lack of cohesion within the executive on how to handle a certain aspect of rent allocation is likely to yield policy instability (policy reversals) over time.

Next, executive cohesion needs to be evaluated along the leadership's perceptions about whether the status quo on a given rent allocation policy serves its objectives for staying in power. In order to explain policy stability across the distinct aspects of rent allocation, I hypothesize that the leadership will remain committed to a policy on rent allocation to the extent that it enhances or does not threaten its political survival. In effect, rent allocation, when guided in a particular direction by the incumbent, serves broader political purposes. In a way, this study aims to demonstrate how key policy choices with respect to the distinct aspect of rent allocation have also reflected the incumbent's considerations for political survival. In this respect, this book contributes to understanding the longevity of Putin's tenure.

Examining the factual record of the policy process on rent allocation in Putin's Russia, this book argues that policy achievements backed by a widespread consensus within the ruling elite and the public have been more likely to remain stable. Even then, the stability of a policy has depended on whether the policy status quo poses no risks for the political survival of the incumbent leadership. By the same token, frequent policy reversals along the entire chain of rent allocation in Russia can be explained by the lack of cohesion behind that policy and the leadership's wish to mitigate political risks.

Organization of the Book

The next chapter introduces the book's theoretical foundations. I start with the premise that natural resources, oil in particular, play a critical role in Russia's political economy. Illustrating some of the main approaches to studying resource-rich settings, the chapter establishes their key limitations in understanding Russia and addressing the main puzzles of this book. Relying on a theory that sets its focus on institutional veto players, I develop an alternative approach. Elaborating "executive power" as its central concept, I explain how this approach is beneficial to understanding the contested nature of rent allocation policies in resource-rich countries, including those with authoritarian regimes. The chapter specifies the methodology and sets out its key contributions for scholarship as well as the policy community.

In chapter 2, I start by documenting the upsurge in the executive's power in Russia after the late 1990s. To set the context for policy-making in Putin's Russia, the chapter focuses on how the executive managed to weaken the relative power of the other veto players: the two legislative chambers and the regional authorities. I demonstrate that it did not take long for Putin's Russia to make a transition from a setting with multiple veto players to one where the executive branch assumed a dominant role in policy-making. I also examine some of the broader sources of disagreements within the executive branch as early indicators of possible difficulties in securing cohesion. The relative power of the veto players and major attributes of the executive, such as its cohesion, appear as recurring themes with respect to distinct aspects of rent allocation examined in the rest of the book.

In chapter 3, I illustrate the extent of Russia's historic windfalls during the Putin era. Then, I shift my focus to the rather unique rent generation model that Putin inherited when he became president, and trace how this model was fundamentally altered over time. A key question I address is why one particular aspect of Russia's rent generation model – ownership – has gone through several phases of transformation, indicating a high degree of policy instability. The chapter presents a detailed narrative on Russia's contests over who should control the generation of the country's oil rents. Examining additional aspects of the rent generation model, which have proven resilient, I explain what has contributed to their tenacity.

Chapter 4 discusses rent collection in Russia's oil sector. Its main theme is the battle between the state and the oil companies on dividing the oil industry's rents. It provides an in-depth review of the financial relationship between the state and the oil industry, analyzing the discourse on taxation of this sector. My focus is on two particular aspects of Russia's evolving oil tax regime: the ability of the state to win and then retain the majority of the oil industry's rents, and the stability of tax rules over time. The key question explored in this chapter is what has made it possible for Putin's Russia to emerge and remain as the winner in this persistent battle over oil rents, and why its tax rules have been persistently unstable.

Next, I examine the role of the state as the chief redistributor of Russia's oil rents. Chapter 5 focuses on Putin's policy choices amid competing approaches for an economic strategy. It analyzes in detail Russia's budgetary process as the primary means for redistributing oil wealth. Here, I also look at tax cuts for the economy as an additional policy tool for redistributing oil rents. Chapter 6 looks at the government's other means to manage oil rents, namely through oil saving funds and foreign debt payments. These two chapters analyze how and why the Russian leadership has oscillated between remarkably fiscally conservative and highly expansionary policies of redistribution. I explore what has caused policy shifts over time, and specifically why the Russian leadership has responded differently each time to oil booms and busts. I underline key areas of continuity in the state's redistributive policies, providing explanations for the government's ability to stay committed to their outcomes.

Chapter 7 demonstrates that Russia's oil companies have also acted as agents of rent redistribution, apart from paying taxes to the state budget. It describes six distinct channels through which oil-producing companies have shared their wealth with a wider set of beneficiaries. The chapter notes that these additional rents have been a source of further competition, whereby the state leadership has actively strived to steer the flow of rents. Here I examine how the centralization of power under Putin has affected the rents redistributed by the oil companies, what enabled the state leadership to guide this process, and how the process itself has served further political functions. The central question is why the Russian leadership has promoted the primacy of informal rules to guide this segment of rent allocation, rules which have also delivered divergent results over time. The concluding chapter summarizes the key findings of this book, highlights some of its main lessons, and notes the applicability of its findings and its approach for further research.

1 Understanding Policy-Making in Resource-Rich Countries

Is having an abundance of natural resources a curse or a blessing for countries? Many economists and political scientists have been drawn to this question as more countries have started developing their resources in the past few decades. Scholars have sought to explain the role of natural resources in phenomena as diverse as weak economic growth, failure in economic reforms, regime breakdowns, failures in democratization, ethnic conflicts, corruption, and low levels of human development.

Much of the attention in this body of scholarly work, known as the "resource curse" literature, has been on the economic policy choices in resource-abundant countries.[1] This book addresses these policy choices, though its focus is more specific. It does not aim to explain how Russia's oil windfalls affected its long-term economic performance. Instead, it focuses on economic policy-making in a wide range of policy areas that are directly relevant to the allocation of rents. With an emphasis on policy change and policy continuity, the book sheds light on the Russian leadership's ability to undertake reforms in a broader set of areas, along with its likelihood to stick with them over time.

The chapter starts with a brief overview of some of the main approaches and arguments in the "resource curse" literature. Many of the arguments presented in this literature touch on the various distributional policy aspects of resource rents. Also, they underline some of the key implications of resource wealth for the state. This overview reveals a few important points. First, in many respects, Russia's experience as a country dependent on oil (and other mineral resources) is puzzling: many of its economic policy choices and outcomes cannot be explained through existing approaches discussed in the literature. Second, established approaches, while generally helpful, often appear to be highly deterministic. They do not adequately account for how and when a resource-rich country can abruptly deviate from established policy patterns. In other words, policy change (or policy continuity) in such resource rent-saturated contexts needs further explanation. These approaches also assign limited room for the role of agency in policy-making.

This brief literature review indicates that there is a need to develop an alternative approach. For the purpose, I introduce "executive power" as an alternative concept, and explain how this approach can better help us to analyze the contested nature of rent allocation policies.

Approaches to Understanding Resource-Rich Countries

Is Russia a "Rentier State"?

The "rentier state" is a concept that has been central to studying resource-rich countries. The term presupposes that resource-rich states are in some ways unique. As the focus of studies on "rentier states" has been particularly on oil-rich countries, it is worth introducing its main tenets, and start by asking: is Russia a "rentier state"?

Developed in the 1970s, the notion of the "rentier state" highlights several peculiar features of the state in heavily resource-dependent countries.[2] Such states receive a sizable portion of budgetary revenues from rents associated with the extraction of natural resources.[3] The government appears as the principal recipient of these rents, which are predominantly derived from sales abroad.[4] According to Luciani, the state's access to such rents liberates it from the need to develop a viable tax system for extracting income from the domestic economy. Instead, the principal function of "rentier states" is to allocate the resource rents rather than secure growth across the distinct sectors of the economy. Governments perform these functions typically through budgetary expenditures, but also through financing of vast patronage networks. The process of rent allocation is principally a means to enhance the position of those in power.[5]

On the surface, it is tempting to define Russia as a "rentier state."[6] After all, the country's budget and the economy at large depend heavily on the export of oil and other natural resources. However, as this book illustrates in detail, Russia's case is much more complicated. At best, the applicability of the "rentier state" concept to Putin's Russia is limited. In part, this is due to some peculiarities of Russia's case, but it also has to do with a few drawbacks related to the concept itself.

Russia is an odd case with respect to the classical understanding of a "rentier state." It exhibits some highly peculiar features in several areas. First, at the start of Putin's presidency, the state was not yet the principal recipient of the rents from the oil sector. William Tompson astutely notes that Russia's predicament in the late 1990s was not that it was receiving too much revenue from the oil sector, which would have made it easier to define it as a "rentier state." Instead, Russia was obtaining too little of these rents.[7] The situation changed over time, and eventually the state succeeded in becoming the principal recipient of the oil rents. One may argue that this has made Russia look increasingly like a "rentier state," though the share of resource revenues in the economy alone would not suffice to qualify the country as a typical "rentier state."

Second, thanks to years of industrialization during the Soviet era, Russia inherited a more diversified economy compared with the typical "rentier states" in the Persian Gulf, Africa, and South America that are examined in the literature. Third, its oil sector has presented some unique features when compared with other "rentier states." Typically, an oil industry in a "rentier state" would be either entirely state-owned or predominantly reliant on international oil majors to bring know-how, equipment, and capital. Russia inherited a well-developed, "homegrown" oil industry with its own expertise along an entire value chain, ranging from geologists to marketing specialists. By the time Putin took the helm of Russian politics, the oil industry had fallen almost entirely into the hands of private Russian, rather than international, owners. Despite several waves of nationalizations during the following years, ownership in the sector remained uniquely complex as private and state-owned companies continued to coexist. This peculiarity has the potential to shed new insights on the significance of the type of ownership in the Russian oil sector.

In the meantime, the "rentier state" as a concept has two main drawbacks that further constrain its practicality. It offers limited scope for examining how rents get allocated in a political entity. The concept focuses principally on the redistributive policies of the state. In reality, as this book illustrates, to study "rent allocation," one needs to examine a much more extensive and complicated chain of processes.

Additionally, the "rentier state" concept is fairly deterministic in nature. Its advocates have assumed that the nature of a state's revenues predetermines the fiscal behavior of the ruling elite. The state's redistributive activities create some beneficiaries, who, as Douglas Yates argues, emerge as sound supporters of the status quo. This helps to perpetuate existing policies of rent allocation.[8]

This determinism makes it difficult to explain major economic policy shifts unless there is a transformation in the nature of the state's revenues. For instance, in the past decade many oil-rich countries, including in the Middle East, have been increasingly inclined to experiment with groundbreaking new economic policies with significant distributional consequences.[9] When and why do some governments decide to abruptly change existing patterns of rent allocation? When do they implement new fiscal policies that allocate wealth differently, for instance, by adopting less generous social welfare policies? And a more fundamental question, to what extent are final outcomes determined by structural constraints and what is the role of agency?

Despite these drawbacks, the concept of the "rentier state" is crucial for understanding the political economy of resource-rich countries. Its emphasis on "allocation" as a principal function for a resource-rich state underlines the importance of looking at policies with distributional consequences. Its underlying assumption that certain states tend to perpetuate the status quo in rent allocation policies is particularly relevant to this book. In this respect, the concept's determinism provides a starting point to think about developing an alternative approach – one that provides a more elaborate explanation about when and how countries maintain the status quo in rent allocation and when they shift away from it.

Other Conventional Approaches in the "Resource Curse" Literature and Their Limitations

If, as I argue, Russia does not fit the classic example of a "rentier state," the substantial role of natural resources in its economy makes it necessary to evaluate some of the major approaches and concepts within the "resource curse" literature. These provide insights about possible factors and causal mechanisms behind policy outcomes in resource-abundant states.

According to Michael Ross, scholars have provided three types of explanations for a wide range of economic policy anomalies, dubbed as the "resource curse" in resource-rich states. He refers to cognitive, society-centered, and state-centered approaches.[10] Many authors have utilized a mixture of these approaches to study key economic policy choices and outcomes.[11]

The adherents of the *cognitive* approach have assumed that boom and bust cycles in oil-rich countries create myopia among policy-makers. During boom periods, abundant revenues from resources prompt policy-makers to significantly expand public spending and/or borrow internationally. Over time, these policies become unsustainable, often leading to financial and economic crises.

While this approach might have had some credence in the past, leaders of resource-rich countries have become more aware of the pitfalls of resource dependence over time. According to Alan Gelb, a leading economist in the study of the "resource curse," oil-driven myopia was much less common during the oil boom of the 2000s than in the boom the 1970s. Managing resource revenues remained a challenging task, but growing numbers of policy-makers had learned some helpful lessons from the past.[12] In essence, a lack of awareness about the "resource curse" is no longer a major problem. Instead, the main challenge is to adopt and successfully implement the right economic policies.

During the Putin era, the Russian leadership has clearly exhibited awareness of the pitfalls of the "resource curse." Yegor Gaidar, a prominent Soviet and Russian economist, has lauded the Putin administration for its proactive policies aimed at averting the "resource curse." By contrast, he has charged Soviet leaders for ignoring chronic economic problems associated with the dependence of the Soviet economy on oil exports, contributing to the USSR's ultimate collapse.[13]

The *society-centered* approach in the "resource curse" literature provides an alternative explanation. It assumes that the presence of natural resource rents empowers certain groups in the society whose policy preferences are aligned with maintaining the status quo of rent allocation. In effect, this approach presumes that resource-rich states have low capability to alter an existing policy status quo that perpetuates policy anomalies, such as excessive government spending that yields chronic deficits and debt. One problem with this approach is that it assumes that states will have weak leverage over societal actors. Yet, one could argue that the state's access to substantial rents could insulate it against societal pressures.[14] Also, there is no consensus on who should be blamed for policy anomalies: the resource sector or other beneficiaries in the society. Resource sectors, such as oil, with concentration of ownership and high entry barriers, could develop strong capacity for collective action, helping them to shape key economic policies in their interests.[15] Yet, non-resource sectors could also benefit from a policy status quo that is characterized by access to resource rents in the form of subsidies, tax breaks, or cheap government loans. They could also actively engage in the political process to maintain their privileges.[16]

The society-centered approach is also less helpful in explaining some of the more puzzling economic policy outcomes in Putin's Russia. For instance, Putin was quick to undertake drastic policy actions against some of the major economic beneficiaries of the 1990s. The oil sector suddenly faced sweeping changes in the oil tax regime, changes that ultimately resulted in the state being the chief beneficiary of Russia's oil wealth. Evidently, despite its heavy concentration in the hands of a few companies, the oil industry could not successfully exercise collective action in this critical policy area. Rather than having an active role in shaping economic policy preferences, Russia's oil oligarchs became a principal target in discussions about how to put the nation's oil wealth to better use. Likewise, many non-resource sectors also emerged as key beneficiaries, thanks to subsidies, tax breaks, and cheap loans during most of the 1990s.[17] Despite booming oil revenues, many of these privileges were lost during Putin's first term as president. The government opted for a conservative fiscal policy, drastically limiting access to state subsidies and tax breaks. Budget surpluses, unseen in post-Soviet Russia, and growing foreign currency reserves were the immediate economic policy outcomes.

The *state-centered approach*, probably the dominant one within the "resource curse" literature, underlines the state's central role in the management of the country's resource wealth. Its attention is focused particularly on various attributes of the state, such as its "power," "capacity," and "autonomy." Additional factors deemed to be important are the type of political regime and the institutional quality of a country. There are several principal questions raised within this approach: Could a "strong" state manage booms and busts more successfully than a "weak" one? Does the political regime matter for how resource-rich countries spend their wealth? How does the quality of institutions affect the way countries allocate their resource rents?

While this approach can shed some light on the critical role the state plays in addressing the various challenges associated with dependence on resources, it also has some limitations. The drawbacks are largely an outcome of the ambiguity inherent in the concepts describing a state's attributes. The limitations are exposed when these concepts are applied to explain economic policy-making in Putin's Russia.

As Joel Migdal has noted, scholars have hardly differed from one another in the way they define the state. Yet, nothing close to a consensus has emerged with respect to defining the state's key attributes.[18] Concepts such as state power, autonomy, and capacity have often been used interchangeably.[19] And, as Gabriel Almond has observed, the distinction between "weak" and "strong" states is not always clear in the literature.[20]

Furthermore, caution needs to be exercised when drawing conclusions based on specific attributes of the state. For instance, an appraisal of "state autonomy"[21] would not suffice as a way to understand policy outcomes. The impact of state autonomy on policy-making is not necessarily uniform across countries. A high degree of state autonomy might be a virtue in some cases, enhancing the state's effectiveness, but not in others.[22] A weak state autonomy may be indicative of the ruling elite's inability to formulate policies that are against the preferences of various social groups. Yet, as Ruschemeyer and Evans have claimed, under particular circumstances (such as in the case of predatory states), a higher degree of state autonomy may have mainly negative consequences for economic policies.[23] Thus, in the case of oil-rich countries, one can expect that it would be hard to associate state autonomy with a particular pattern in economic policies.

Another aspect of state autonomy that deserves attention is that its degree may vary from one policy issue to another. Eric Nordlinger points to different levels of autonomy, depending on the convergence of preferences between the state and the society.[24] Likewise, referring to state capacity, Stephen Krasner has noted that "there is no reason to assume a priori that the pattern of strengths and weaknesses will be the same for all policies."[25] Concurring with this argument, Theda Skocpol has emphasized that there is a large degree of "unevenness [of state capacity] across policy areas."[26] Thus, one can expect that a state will implement distinct rent allocation policies with a different degree of autonomy/capacity. The bigger challenge, however, is identifying the conditions under which a higher or lower degree of state autonomy will be translated into a particular policy pattern. This calls for identifying more specific causal relationships in explaining policy outcomes.

The "type of regime"[27] has also been a widely examined factor in search of patterns in governments' economic policy choices. Are democratic countries more likely to avoid the "resource curse"? Do authoritarian regimes have an advantage in implementing economic policies in line with the country's long-term economic objectives? Could some of the economic success stories in Putin's Russia be explained through the country's rising authoritarianism following President Yeltsin's departure from the political scene?

No clear correlation has been established between political regime and economic policies in resource-rich countries. Economic success and ruin are common, irrespective of the type of the regime. Norway and Indonesia under Suharto have both been lauded for implementing fiscal discipline and generally successful economic development policies. During the 1970s, both democratic Venezuela and authoritarian Nigeria had unsustainable expenditure policies, prompting deep economic troubles.[28]

In Russia, the type of regime can hardly account for major changes in economic policies. Shortly after Putin became president, he embarked on rent allocation policies that were markedly different from those of his predecessor. Although Russia moved towards an increasingly authoritarian regime under Putin, that would not fully explain the drastic shifts in economic policies. Furthermore, during Putin's long tenure, economic policies have shifted from one direction to another without a comparable change in the political regime.

The institutional quality of countries has been another factor studied in the "resource curse" literature. "Strong institutions" typically refer to the presence of an autonomous bureaucracy, a low degree of corruption, a high level of accountability by the governing elite, a high degree of rule of law and transparency, and strong property rights. Terry Lynn Karl, in her seminal work *The Paradox of Plenty*, has argued that resource rents can weaken state institutions.[29] Resource wealth can foster rent-seeking and corruption;[30] it can create incentives for lower transparency regarding government revenues;[31] it can weaken the accountability of the government by enhancing its autonomy from the rest of society;[32] and finally, due to its access to resource rents, the state may neglect taxation in other sectors, thus weakening its own "extractive capacity."[33] Karl argues it is possible to avoid these negative implications, if resource rents flow *after* a country has managed to develop "strong institutions."[34]

Despite its strengths in identifying possible pathways for the "resource curse," there is an inherent determinism in this approach, leaving limited scope for the role of agency. The institutionalist focus of this approach also makes it difficult to explain when one could expect a policy to endure over time or go through a major shift. This limitation is particularly exposed in a setting where weak institutional quality can be considered as constant. Russia's case is particularly puzzling in this respect. During his first term as president, Putin was able to enact and enforce a number of successful fiscal and economic policies, policies that were markedly different from those of many other resource-rich countries. Putin did not inherit "strong institutions" that could have contributed to this outcome. At the start of Putin's presidency, Russia ranked very low in terms of several institutional measures, such as voice and accountability, regulatory quality, rule of law, and control of corruption.[35] Over time, many of these measures have gotten even worse.

Given the above, what we need is an approach that avoids the determinism prevalent in previous studies and that balances the role of structural constraints and agency in policy-making.[36]

An Alternative Approach: Executive Power and Putting Politics Back In

I develop "executive power" as an alternative concept to studying how resource-rich countries manage their wealth and the key battles over redistribution. This new approach addresses the shortcomings inherent in the approaches examined above. First, it offers greater clarity in the analysis of economic policies (such as policies on rent allocation), particularly in terms of the key players and the potential causal mechanisms behind specific policy outcomes. Executive power is a considerably narrower and less ambiguous concept than its alternatives. Its emphasis is upon a country's executive, namely the president, in the case of a presidential system. Yet, it also takes into account the constitutional structure of the country, the actual political context of the period in question, the preferences of various political players, the extent of infighting within different branches and levels of the government when implementing policy, and public opinion. Second, by taking into account structural factors while incorporating the role of agency, this new approach is particularly useful in explaining policy continuity and policy change, and it helps to avoid deterministic conclusions. Finally, focusing on executive power in Putin's Russia helps to explain puzzling policy developments that cannot be unraveled through conventional approaches.

Introducing Executive Power

"Executive power" refers to the ability of a country's executive branch to adopt and implement policy decisions that reflect its own preferences. Strong executive power allows the executive branch to shape policies aligned with its own preferences, while a weak one yields results that are at odds with them.

What makes executive power strong or weak? To derive and measure executive power, I resort to George Tsebelis's veto players theory. The theory's underlining assumption is that in any policy area, the actual power of the executive is determined by its power relative to other veto players in the political system. This relative power is a product of a number of attributes pertaining to the executive branch and the remaining veto players (see below).

Developed by the "New Institutionalist" school, the "veto players" theory has been widely applied in a vast number of studies on economic policy. It has been particularly influential in explaining how changes in the relative power and policy preferences of various institutional stakeholders affect economic policies such as taxation and budgetary spending. With its focus on policies of redistribution, the theory can greatly facilitate an understanding of how governments in resource-rich countries run their economies and allocate their rents.[37]

The Fundamentals of the Veto Players Theory

Tsebelis defines veto players as individuals or collective actors whose consent is required for a change in the status quo.[38] For many economic policy areas a change in the status quo starts with passing legislation. To understand policy change, however, one also needs to look at policy implementation, as various agents may have the power to block legislative decisions from turning into action. For instance, as Alfred Stepan points out, it is common for some agents, such as regional governments, not to comply with federal laws following their adoption.[39] The result could be a failure in altering the policy status quo. Thus, to change the policy status quo, individual or collective actors would need not only to give their consent to pass the required legislation, but also to comply with its intended implementation.

Tsebelis assumes that there are two types of veto players: institutional and partisan.[40] Institutional veto players are determined by the constitution of each country, and include the president (in a presidential system) or the prime minister (in a parliamentary system) and the legislative chamber(s). In federal systems, regional governments can also be considered veto players.[41] Partisan veto players are generated from within the pool of institutional veto players during the political process. These are the political parties acting within certain formal institutions, namely, the legislative chambers.[42] Incorporating the partisan veto players is important. As Stoiber notes, the institutional veto players reflect the general political structure of a country prescribed by its constitution. Looking at partisan veto players allows the "political game" to be included in the picture.[43]

Tsebelis draws several key conclusions about veto players. First, the higher the number of veto players, the lower the potential to produce change in the status quo. He defines this lack of potential for a "significant departure from the status quo" as *policy stability*.[44] It is worth emphasizing that the "veto players" theory in general aims to explain the potential for change rather than the direction of such a change.[45] However, the theory also sheds light on the potential direction of policy change, provided that information is available on the identity and the preferences of the veto players.[46]

Second, beyond the number of veto players, the policy preferences of these players also matter. The similarity of the positions of the veto players on the given policy status quo determines the *level of congruence* among the players. The less congruence, the harder it is to produce policy change.[47] This is because, with a high degree of incongruence, the approval of a particular piece of legislation will require comparatively larger compromises across the spectrum of veto players.

The final observation has to do with the *cohesion within* each veto player. The emphasis here is on the similarity of positions among the members of each veto player. Tsebelis suggests that the more cohesive veto players the executive confronts, the harder it will be to change the status quo. Thus, a high degree of cohesion within the other veto players puts a limit on the opportunities for reaching compromises *across* veto players (provided that their positions differ in the first place). By contrast, cohesion within the executive branch can be an asset when it is directed towards a policy change.[48]

A particular strength of the veto players approach is that it adopts a dynamic rather than a static perspective on the political context. It considers policy-making as a chain of decisions involving repeated bargaining across, and often within, various veto players. The preferences of the veto players, the congruence across their preferences, and the cohesion within each of them constitute key elements in evaluating a dynamic political landscape. By focusing on these elements, this theory makes it possible to illustrate the conditions under which certain policy preferences are more likely to turn into actual policies.[49]

Furthermore, as the focus is on policy change, the veto players approach provides answers to a highly pertinent question in political science: what is the capacity of a political system to resolve problems when they arise?[50] Many scholars have focused on the role of institutions as a means to answer this question. The veto players approach recognizes the importance of institutions. Yet, as Tsebelis notes, it also considers actors that occupy these institutions as highly significant.[51] Thus, through its emphasis on the specific constellation of veto players – a function of their number, the congruence among their preferences, and the cohesion within them – the veto players approach is likely to provide a more straightforward explanation of specific government policies. The approach also provides a framework for understanding policy change over time and across diverse constitutional settings.

The Relevance of the Veto Players Approach to Studying Rent Allocation

As the veto players approach is well positioned for the analysis of policies with distributional consequences, it is surprising that it has not been widely adopted in the study of rents in resource-rich countries. In this respect, this book could pave the way to applying its key findings to broader comparative studies on resource-abundant states.

All aspects of rent allocation – rent generation, rent collection, rent redistribution by the state, and rent redistribution by the natural resource sector – can be analyzed through the elaborate framework presented by the veto players approach. In fact, numerous studies have already adopted the approach to examine a wide range of policy issues such as taxation, budgetary spending, and the rule of law. While their focus has not been specifically on the economic policies of resource-rich countries, these studies are highly relevant in such countries as well.

Empirical studies adopting the veto players approach have highlighted several key points that can also shed light on policies related to rent allocation. First, the number of *effective* veto players, which is determined by the constitutional setting as well as party politics, matters.[52] Tsebelis finds that countries with fewer veto players produce a larger number of significant laws and relatively few non-significant ones, while countries with many veto players produce few significant laws and many non-significant ones.[53] Others have elaborated on this finding by claiming that the increased number of veto players raises transaction costs, which may hinder the process of passing a significant law that affects the interests of large segments of the population.[54] Halleberg and Basinger look at taxation in the OECD countries and confirm that significant changes in taxation have been strongly correlated with the presence of fewer veto players. Moreover, they conclude that major transformations in the tax system have been possible only with fewer veto players.[55]

Cox and McCubins examine budget deficits across countries and discover a correlation between the number of veto players and the size of the deficit. They argue that in cases of a larger number of effective veto players, more agents are able to demand and receive "side payments" for their consent in reaching a compromise.[56] These side payments, also defined as "pork," can take various forms, such as subsidies and regulatory exceptions provided to particular regions or industries. As Samuels and Mainwaring note, in countries with a federal structure, regional governors emerge as additional veto players that tend to hamper budgetary discipline through their own demands for "side payments."[57]

The number of veto players is important for the rule of law as well. Analyzing thirty-five emerging democracies, Andrews and Montinola reveal that as the number of veto players increases, their ability to collude on accepting bribes goes down. Meanwhile, their incentive to vote on legislation strengthening the rule of law gets stronger.[58] Additionally, they find that countries with multiple veto players are more likely to create and reinforce independent agencies, those capable of implementing government policy impartially and checking the corrupt behavior of government actors.[59] Witold Henisz emphasizes that the presence of many veto players makes it more likely that a political system will "commit" not to alter the rules of the economic game.[60]

Second, the status quo with regard to a particular existing policy is significant. In the case of budgetary spending, Tsebelis claims that the presence of multiple veto players makes it more difficult to make any adjustments in the size of the deficit.[61] In other words, a higher number of veto players slows the adjustment process. Thus, having multiple veto players might be bad news for a country striving to end a budget deficit but it is likely to benefit a country where the status quo is a budgetary surplus. Franzese finds that having a higher number of veto players delays changes in budgetary deficits regardless of whether these deficits have been high or low.[62] Andrews and Montinola note the importance of the status quo with respect to the rule of law. They claim, "To the extent that establishing the rule of law requires policy change, then fewer veto players would be beneficial. But to the extent that it requires the prevention of expropriating behavior of government actors, then more veto players would improve the chances of establishing the rule of law."[63]

Third, it is also important to look at the preferences of the veto players in relation to the status quo, as well as the congruence among these preferences. Tsebelis and Chang examine the budget structure of nineteen OECD countries (1973–95).[64] As a measure of the preferences of veto players they rank each according to their "ideology." The study finds that the further the budgetary status quo is from the preferences of the veto players, the larger the departure from the status quo. Greater ideological differences between successive governments are associated with larger changes in budgetary spending. The study also confirms the importance of congruence *across* veto players. Considering each member of a coalition government as a veto player, Tsebelis and Chang discover that a government coalition is associated with more significant change in the budget if its members are less ideologically diverse.[65] Yet, as Carl LeVan finds, the presence of divergent preferences across veto players does not automatically lead to a veto. Having a divergent policy preference does not suffice. A veto player must also have the ability and the motivation to assert its preferences successfully.[66]

Finally, *cohesion within* veto players also appears consequential. In a cross-national study, Hagen and Harden look at the concentration in decision-making on budgetary matters as a measure for cohesion within the executive. Having multiple ministries or agencies in charge of the preparation of the budget is deemed to indicate a lack of cohesion within the executive. They find that budget deficits are less likely in countries where the process of budget-making within the executive branch is relatively centralized. They conclude that delegating power to a single ministry can be beneficial for fighting budget deficits.[67]

The Relevance of the Veto Players Approach to Non-democracies

The veto players framework has been applied overwhelmingly to countries regarded as democratic. In 1999, Freedom House rated Russia as "partly free." By 2005, Russia had already slipped to the "not free" category reserved for authoritarian regimes. Its ranking continued to deteriorate in subsequent years.[68] Therefore, it is fair to ask whether the veto players approach applies to Putin's Russia.

Indeed, democracies have a clear advantage with respect to the applicability of the veto players framework. There is far less ambiguity about identifying particular institutions as veto players in such regimes than in autocracies. Evidence of institutions blocking the will of the executive is more abundant in democratic countries, as the process typically occurs through formal means such as voting in the legislature.

Nonetheless, a growing number of studies have started applying the veto players framework to non-democracies.[69] In part, this has been due to the recognition, shared by Tsebelis, that most authoritarian regimes also possess multiple veto players.[70] Only in extreme cases do dictators govern unilaterally. As Hannah Arendt notes, in most regimes "power is never the property of an individual; it belongs to a group and remains in existence only so long as the group keeps together."[71] Decision-making in non-democracies is much more complicated than it may appear on the surface. Often autocrats need to delegate the task of developing policy proposals, finalizing legislation, and implementing policy decisions to lower-level agencies within the executive. Sometimes they are bound to do so by law.[72] Other times the technical nature of the policy matter necessitates the involvement of technocrats. Policies proposed by the autocrat may be subject to resistance and delays, effectively preventing a change in the policy status quo.

The veto players theory has several strengths that could enrich our understanding of non-democracies. As LeVan observes, the veto players framework generates tremendously helpful insights about how authoritarian regimes operate. First, it prevents over-simplifications about how such regimes function by underscoring that, in most cases, there is a degree of collective decision-making. Second, the veto players theory focuses on identifying various sources of checks on the power of the executive. It is less concerned with the type of political regime. Instead it aims to bring clarity about the key actors that hold some leverage over the policy process. Focusing on how such actors advance their policy preferences, the veto players approach sheds light on the actual process behind particular government policies. Third, the framework provides insights on how formal institutions operate in practice. For instance, as LeVan notes, even in authoritarian regimes with a rubber-stamp legislature, it is possible to witness parliamentarians successfully advancing the preferences of their distinct constituencies. Likewise, a pro-government party could go beyond providing support to the executive's agenda and engage in resolving intra-elite conflicts coming from within the executive.[73] Finally, the veto players theory also recognizes that informal institutions can play a significant role. While their preferences typically get "absorbed" by existing veto players, the veto players framework underscores the need to trace how they work in the political system.[74]

Measuring Executive Power

One of the key areas examined in this book is how changes in executive power affect policy outcomes. For instance, Putin's early tenure witnessed a major upsurge in executive power. To what extent did it shape the leadership's rent allocation policies? Thus, how do we know that executive power has changed, and how can it be measured?

I rely on the veto players framework to establish a measure for executive power. One of the main strengths of the veto players approach is its capability to capture a whole set of characteristics in a country's policy-making process. Attributes of veto players such as their number, their preferences on the policy status quo, and their internal cohesion provide invaluable information.

Though each of the attributes of veto players has been the subject of extensive study, they have not been brought together theoretically or empirically. I develop an all-encompassing measure for executive power as applied to Russia's constitutional framework. Adjusting to a different constitutional context, the proposed method may ultimately serve to test how changes in executive power affect policy performance in other case studies and larger comparative studies.

One needs to recognize that the methodology for determining the precise number of institutional veto players remains unsettled. In part this is due to differences in how to define a veto player.[75] Also, the number of veto players is not necessarily constant across policy issues. For instance, the legislature may act as an institutional veto player with regard to passing a particular tax law, but it may not have any authority to nationalize a private company.

While the number of veto players is significant, taking into account additional attributes is essential. This is particularly true in non-democracies where an authoritarian leader might "absorb" other veto players to the extent that he or she emerges as the sole veto player in the political system. And yet, a range of policies, particularly those of a more technical nature that require delicate elaboration, would provide opportunities for various participants to have an input. There is also the possibility that the sole veto player would face some resistance when implementing a policy.

To develop a measure of executive power, looking at the constitutional structure of a country is a good start. This makes it possible to identify the institutional veto players, though not necessarily their actual relative power in the policy process. In Russia's case, the 1993 Constitution prescribes four institutional veto players: the executive (led by the president), the lower chamber of the legislature (the Duma), the upper chamber (the Federation Council), and the subnational governments. All these veto players are generated electorally, which distinguishes them from other potential institutional veto players, such as the courts.[76] It is essential to note that while oil companies are an important

Table 1.1. Determinants of Executive Power

President	Lower Chamber	Upper Chamber	Regional Governors
Change in the number of institutional veto players	Size of the "party of power" and its internal discipline	Degree of centralization of power	Degree of centralization of power
Constitutional powers of the president relative to other veto players	Congruence of the preferences of the "party of power" vs. other parties		Economic and political peculiarities of each region
Degree of cohesion within the executive	Party discipline outside the "party of power"		
Congruence of executive's preferences vs. other veto players			
Level of public support			

player in the narrative of this book, they are not a veto player because they need to go through one or more of the institutional veto players in order to influence policy.

Executive power is a function of several attributes of the executive itself and the remaining veto players in Russia (table 1.1).[77] Looking from the perspective of the executive, the study proposes five measures that shed light on the power of the executive relative to other institutional veto players. First, potential changes in the number of veto players would constitute a key indicator. While such a phenomenon is uncommon, it may occur as a result of constitutional or major legislative reform affecting the authority of a veto player to block a policy change.[78]

Second, the constitution prescribes certain formal powers for the executive. Shugart and Carey identify two dimensions in which to assess a president's formal powers: a legislative dimension, comprising six legislative areas, and a non-legislative dimension, comprising four additional areas. The authors scaled each of these powers to estimate the overall presidential power across countries.[79] Their categorization serves as a helpful indicator of a president's formal power. These formal powers and any changes in them are significant. However, executive power comprises much more than that. The political context is also significant as it has implications for the relative power of the executive. Furthermore, the formal powers need to be assessed relative to the constitutional powers assigned to the remaining institutional veto players.

The level of cohesion within the executive serves as another indicator. Cohesion here is about the similarity of policy preferences of members of the executive who have some authority in the policy process: the more similar their policy preferences, the higher the degree of cohesion. Following Tsebelis, lower cohesion within the executive would imply greater difficulty in reaching decisions, potential coordination problems, higher transaction costs, and hence a weaker executive. An important sign for weak cohesion would be the presence of major disagreements within the executive on a given policy. In Russia's constitutional setting, such disagreements may appear in various forms: within the presidential staff, within the cabinet, or between the cabinet and the presidential staff. A major indicator of lack of cohesion, for instance, would be the presence of competing pieces of legislation (on the same policy issue) drafted by different agencies within the executive. A lack of cohesion may also resurface during debates on a legislative bill.

Looking at cohesion within the executive is particularly important in nondemocracies, hence I return to this concept below. It is common in such settings to witness a powerful executive, one that faces weak veto players or none at all, dominating the entire policy process. Yet, disagreements within the executive could have repercussions on the policy outcome. A focus on cohesion also allows incorporating informal practices that shape how the executive branch reaches a decision.

The level of congruence between the position of the president on a particular policy area and the position of the remaining veto players is an additional indicator. The veto players theory suggests that under a higher degree of congruence, the president is more likely to secure the approval of a policy proposal. High congruence expands executive power on the particular policy area.

Finally, the level of public support for the president could also affect executive power. A high degree of public support for the executive could enhance its bargaining power against other political representatives, such as the legislatures and regions. Low support, on the other hand, has the potential to disrupt or delay the legislative process and the implementation of a policy.[80] To measure public support, it is worth looking at both electoral outcomes and popularity/approval ratings. The latter measure is useful especially in the case of a political system where the president does not belong to a party, as there may not always be an identifiable pro-presidential victory in parliamentary and regional elections.

Looking at the remaining veto players helps to provide a more complete picture of the relative power of the executive. The purpose here is to assess whether the remaining power can be distinguished as "weak" or "robust." The basic assumption is that if other veto players can be defined as weak, this translates into strength for the executive. And conversely, the more "robust" the remaining veto players are, the lower the relative power of the executive.

As for the lower chamber, the Duma, several attributes determine its relative strength. If a cohesive pro-executive partisan majority dominates this chamber, it is considered a "weak" veto player. This is the case when a pro-executive party ("party of power") with a high degree of party discipline[81] holds a sufficient number of parliamentary seats to pass legislation.[82] When the "party of power" has no majority, the number of missing seats required to pass legislation is indicative of the chamber's power as a veto player. The chamber will tend towards being a "robust" veto player if opposition parties hold the majority sufficient to block legislation. The most extreme case would be if the seats they occupy let them override a presidential veto. Meanwhile, cohesion within the parties outside the "party of power" is also a significant factor. It could be determined by looking at parties' voting discipline. The lower the cohesion in such parties, the higher the likelihood for the "parties of power" to find allies from these parties to pass legislation supported by the executive.[83]

The level of congruence between the preferences of the party of power versus the remaining parties in the chamber appears as an additional indicator. The higher the congruence, the greater the opportunity to find allies and build a pro-executive alliance that will secure the votes to pass legislation. Thus, high congruence would contribute to the "weakness" of the legislature as a veto player. Distinct factors could create political cleavages across political parties in a chamber. Some of them could be ideological, which could allow placing the parties on a continuum ranging from political left to political right. In such instances, the ideology of the "party of power" would be highly significant. The closer it is to the political center, the more likely it is that its position would be congruent with the remaining parties. Political cleavages, however, could arise for other reasons as well, including struggles over redistributive policies that do not necessarily reflect a particular ideology. Thus, congruence in policy preferences is best examined on a case-by-case basis.

Determining the relative power of the upper chamber, the Federation Council, is somewhat complicated by the fact that it is not composed of political parties. As Thomas Remington observes, such a setup is not unique to Russia. It is typical for members of the upper chamber to have weak or no party affiliations, and to form coalitions on an ad hoc basis in order to support or oppose policy proposals.[84]

Yet, constitutional (formal) powers assigned to the president and the upper chamber can serve as a guide for executive power. Namely, the extent of centralization of power would be a key indicator and can be traced by examining the executive's authority in the selection and dismissal process of the members of the upper chamber. A president's ability to select who gets a seat at the upper chamber, or to dismiss such officials, would indicate a major weakness for the latter. Likewise, the extent of fiscal centralization would also be indicative of the upper chamber's powers. A higher degree of revenue centralization would empower the executive, as it gets the upper hand in bargaining about how to spend these revenues. As centralization prescribed by law may change over time, such changes might be essential in terms of their consequences for executive power.

Regional governors constitute an additional veto player in Russia's context. While regions are already represented in the legislature, regional governors' potential importance comes primarily during the implementation stage of major policies affecting rent allocation. For instance, regional governors may significantly hamper objectives defined by the central authorities, such as tax reform (e.g., via authorizing tax breaks) and government spending (e.g., via running budget deficits).

Assessing the balance of power between the executive and the regional governors is highly cumbersome, given the large number of regions. The bargaining process is affected by numerous factors, which may differ significantly from one region to another.[85] Nonetheless, as in the case of the upper chamber, centralization of power appears as a significant indicator for the level of constraints faced by the executive when dealing with regional governors overall. Various legislative changes could be indicative of an upsurge in the power of the executive versus that of the regions. These include legislative changes that expand the president's authority in the selection and dismissal of regional governors, laws that enhance the supervisory functions of the central executive over the regions, and laws that explicitly limit the scope of decision-making delegated to the regional governments. A shift in the revenue distribution in favor of the center would also signify weakening of regional governors as veto players.

In summary, adhering to the veto players theory, I derive executive power as a factor that could explain major policy shifts and continuities. Given the theory's heavy emphasis on policies with distributional consequences, a focus on executive power appears to be particularly conducive to the study of such policies in the context of resource-rich countries.

The Link between Executive Power and Policy Stability/Change

The veto players approach points out a major trade-off in policy-making. According to Cox and McCubins the trade-off is between the capability of a state to enact and implement a new policy[86] and its ability to commit to that policy.[87] Enacting a policy that alters the status quo is commonly defined as "policy change," whereas the lack of significant departure from the policy status quo is known as "policy stability." States capable of enacting and implementing a new policy are considered to be "decisive," whereas states that commit to maintaining a policy are called "resolute."

In their analysis of policies in settings with multiple veto players, Cox and McCubins illustrate that the actual number of veto players is at the center of this trade-off. States with more veto players tend to be less "decisive" but more "resolute." The underlining logic here is that with more veto players, there are higher transaction costs to reach an agreement. And as costs are high, this causes delays both for the process of enacting a new policy and the process of shifting away from an existing one.[88] Tsebelis has further elaborated on this trade-off by suggesting that policies are likely to be more stable ("resolute") in a political setting marked by a greater number of veto players who are cohesive and who hold preferences that diverge. In such settings, it is more difficult to enact a policy (i.e., the state is less "decisive").[89]

Tsebelis succinctly emphasizes why it matters whether it is difficult or easy to change the policy status quo:

> [O]ne way of conceiving policy stability is like a credible commitment of the political system not to interfere in economic, political, or social interactions and regulate them. Another way is to conceive policy stability as the inability of the political system to respond to changes occurring in the economic, political or social environment. Both these aspects are intrinsically linked, and inseparable. Some analysts may prefer one way of thinking to the other, until the moment that institutional structure praised for its ability to make credible commitments is unable to respond to some shock, or the political system with admirable decisiveness was not able to make credible commitments.[90]

Thus, if a country experiences a shift from multiple veto players to a political setting characterized by weakened veto players outside the executive branch, this transformation is expected to have major repercussions for the state's decisiveness as well as its ability to commit to a new policy. The first few years of the Putin era corresponds to such a shift in the political setting. Hence, I analyze how the upsurge in executive power during Putin's early tenure affected rent allocation policies. In line with the theory, I illustrate that, as the executive branch became much less constrained by other veto players, it turned into a more decisive, yet less resolute, actor.

Explaining Policy Change and Policy Stability When "Weakness" of Non-executive Veto Players Is Constant: A Focus on Executive Cohesion

Explaining policy change and (in)stability gets much more complicated once executive power is assumed to be strong and when it remains constant – a setting that has characterized the rest of the Putin era. Here, strong executive power refers to a setting where any institutional veto players outside the executive are too weak to exercise their veto power.[91] In such a setting, a state would be expected to be more decisive and less resolute in the policy-making process. And yet, it is safe to suggest that when one takes a policy-by-policy approach, there will typically be differences in the state's decisiveness and resoluteness from one policy to another. What would account for the variations?

The veto players approach has remained obscure in terms of identifying the precise mechanism that contributes to policy change and instability in contexts with strong executive power.[92] This obscurity is particularly relevant to non-democracies, where it is typical for the executive to emerge as the only institutional veto player that matters. So, how does policy change emerge and what makes policy instability more or less likely in such settings?

This book suggests that *cohesion within the executive*, as one of the key attributes of the veto players approach, requires closer examination. Among the many attributes of executive power, cohesion (or lack thereof) is particularly crucial to understanding the policy process and outcomes. This is because in the context of strong executive power, especially in non-democracies, decision-making on significant policies moves nearly exclusively into the executive branch. Other attributes related to the executive itself, such as constitutional powers, are also significant, but possibly less helpful in explaining how policies evolve over time if they remain constant. Likewise, particularities related to the other veto players are less important in such settings, though should not be discounted as entirely irrelevant, even in the non-democracies. The legislature and regional governments, for instance, may still perform useful roles such as legitimizing the regime, serving as a channel to communicate social grievances through opposition figures,[93] co-opting opposition leaders,[94] and providing elites with institutionalized access to rents[95]. Examining such institutional players may even reveal helpful clues about cohesion within the executive branch itself.[96]

There are multiple potential causes for a lack of cohesion within a country's executive branch, even within a non-democracy. First, when power is delegated to the executive's lower-level agencies and bureaucrats, there is the inevitable principal-agent problem that could weaken cohesion. The agents can be tempted to enact or implement policies that are closer to their own preferences, which may not always overlap with those of the principal.[97] For a principal, monitoring each single decision adopted within the entire executive branch is a monumental task. This gives agents room to enact or implement a policy differently than their principal would expect. In part, this latitude could arise owing to the technical nature of the policy in question. It may also arise when the distributional consequences of a policy proposal are hard to predict ex ante.

Second, executive cohesion may suffer from splits within the ruling elite caused by factors such as differences in ideology, professional backgrounds, and patronage networks. From the standpoint of political leadership, there are no easy solutions to problems with cohesion caused by such differences. One possibility is for a leader to embrace a lack of cohesion and strive to balance the divergent interests of elite members by bringing their representatives to key executive positions. Conversely, in authoritarian settings, a leader may entertain the option to build a bureaucracy based entirely on loyalty and shared objectives.[98] However, members of the bureaucracy may still disagree on the means to attain the desired outcome.

Third, problems with cohesion may arise when different parts of the executive branch compete to influence a policy. Institutional redundancies in particular are likely to foster competition and potential intra-executive disagreements. Yet the presence and extent of competition varies across policy issues. Policies that have more pronounced distributional consequences are likely to be more susceptible to competition as well as disagreements. Likewise, the scope of involvement of executive agencies is significant. Some policy areas necessitate the involvement of numerous executive agencies. For instance, enacting the annual budget typically involves nearly every ministry and agency within the executive branch. Other policy areas, such as reforming taxation in a select industry, tend to have a narrower scope in terms of bureaucratic engagement. The broader the scope of engagement, the greater the number of agents that strive to align their input with their own preferences, making it more difficult to maintain cohesion.

How is cohesion within the executive linked to policy change and policy (in)stability in the context of strong executive power? It is important to look at whether a given policy is backed by executive cohesion. If the leadership opts to alter the policy status quo, and enjoys executive cohesion for this policy shift, the new policy status quo is likely to remain stable. In other words, a state can prove that it can be both "decisive" in launching a new policy and "resolute" by committing to maintain it. The policy can be expected to last as long as there is executive cohesion to back it. Over time, such cohesion may break down, thus allowing the possibility for a new policy shift.

By contrast, the executive may lack cohesion from the very start on a policy that has proven to be more controversial. Whether it adopts a new policy, however, would depend on the political process, namely, whether decisions are made collectively or the chief executive decides on her or his own.[99] In a setting with collective decision-making, the state is likely to be less "decisive": lower cohesion will translate into difficulties in reaching a decision, coordination problems, and higher transaction costs. Alternatively, if the chief executive takes action on her or his own – more likely in non-democracies – this will yield a more "decisive" state. A similar outcome can occur if the chief executive grants support to a selected executive agency to move forward. Yet, once a policy is undertaken with no executive cohesion to back it, its stability will suffer. The chosen policy will leave some members of the executive disgruntled, unless the decision was taken through numerous compromises that satisfied each member of the executive involved.[100] In a setting whereby some members of the executive are left dissatisfied, policy instability is more likely.

The rationale proposed here leads to two further questions. If a policy benefits from executive cohesion, when can one expect a policy shift? Alternatively, if executive cohesion is lacking with respect to a certain policy, can there still be policy stability?

I argue that the incumbent leadership's desire for political survival is a particularly significant factor, one that also determines policy stability over time. In other words, the executive will prefer a policy that enhances its chances to stay in power. Leadership that overlooks opportunities to enhance its political survival may not last long. A policy status quo brought through executive cohesion is likely to remain if it continues to advance the incumbent's political survival. Over time, however, cohesion within the executive may break down if its members believe that the status quo threatens political survival. This would prompt a policy shift, because insisting on maintaining the status quo may pose political risks, particularly if it generates widespread dissatisfaction within the ruling elite (the executive branch) that mirrors public discontent as well. By contrast, a policy that does not enjoy executive cohesion may remain stable for a prolonged period if the chief executive perceives that the status quo poses fewer risks for political survival than proposed alternatives.

One may suggest additional motives determining a leadership's adherence to a policy. For instance, ideological beliefs about the value of a particular policy choice may also be important. This book acknowledges such additional factors, but considers political survival as essential for policies that have "critical" distributional consequences. The latter point about the critical nature of the policy under consideration needs particular emphasis. By implication, the explanations proposed here are likely to be valid for a range of economic and other policies as long as they are of critical nature. There is no simple criterion to assign a level of significance to a government policy. Yet, this study assumes that rent allocation policies will be of critical importance due to their wide-reaching economic and political repercussions in countries highly dependent on resource rents. The direct involvement of a country's leader in a given policy should also attest to the critical nature of that policy. For instance, in examining the distinct aspects of Russia's climate policy, Anna Korppoo reveals that the extent of Putin's involvement varied depending on the significance of the issue. Expert agencies, rather than Putin, acted as de facto veto players in areas that did not constitute a national priority.[101]

Overall, the extent of executive cohesion is expected to vary from one policy to another. A lack of cohesion can be described as a condition that detracts from executive power, and can cause either a delay in adopting a new policy or eventually prompt policy instability. Hence, one can witness more executive power on some policy issues than on others. Correspondingly, the state's decisiveness and resoluteness will vary across policy issues, even when weak veto players (outside the executive) remain as constant. Yet, the presence or lack of cohesion alone does not suffice to explain the evolution of a policy. Instead, cohesion needs to be evaluated in light of the leadership's own perceptions of whether the policy status quo serves its objective of staying in power.

Can Russia's Oil Wealth Explain Putin's Long Tenure?

A subset of the "resource curse" literature has explored the link between resource wealth and the political survival of incumbent leaders or regimes.[102] A common assumption has been that resource wealth equips the political leadership with funds that can be used to increase the likelihood of their remaining in office.[103] Michael Ross argues that resource-rich governments tend to take strategic action to increase the probability of remaining in power.[104] In an extensive study covering 120 countries between 1984 and 2009, Bjorvaten and Farzanegan further elaborate on the link between resource wealth and survival of the ruling elite. Their findings suggest that resource rents are positively associated with the stability of a powerful incumbent, while they have a destabilizing effect on a less powerful incumbent. In other words, resource wealth can promote political stability and the survival of the incumbent only when political power is "sufficiently concentrated" in and around the executive.[105]

In another comparative study, Andreson and Aslaksen find that oil wealth and political survival are correlated in non-democracies only.[106] Robinson et al. put an emphasis on the quality of institutions. According to their study, in countries with institutions capable of limiting the ability of the incumbent to engage in patronage and clientelism, resource wealth is less likely to help with extending the incumbent's stay in power.[107] Other scholars, however, have drawn attention to a different possibility that incumbents need to take into account: resource wealth invites political struggles. Prospects for control of the resource wealth give the challengers a strong incentive to bring down the existing government.[108]

While a systematic examination of the relationship between Russian oil wealth and Putin's tenure in power is beyond the scope of the present study, its findings can shed light on how Putin's policy choices on rent allocation have helped him stay in power. First, it demonstrates how the fading role of Russia's institutional veto players (outside the executive branch) has enhanced the incumbent's ability to develop strategic action with respect to rent allocation.

Second, recognizing that Putin's policies on rent allocation may provide only a partial explanation of his long tenure, this book looks at political survival as an underlying motive that has shaped the incumbent's policy choices. Through a detailed account of distinct aspects of rent allocation, the study examines how Putin steered the flow of rents, driven in large part by considerations for political survival. Electoral concerns, constitutional term limits for the president, and worries about public backlash feature as significant areas associated with political survival.

Third, an important question addressed in this book is how Putin's approach to rent allocation expanded (or reduced) the state's resources to mitigate political risks. The underlying assumption is that if political survival is about mitigating political risks, then the resources available to do so will be of critical importance. One can suggest that the leadership will prefer rent allocation policies that help to expand the availability of such resources. Having more resources does not predetermine the direction of a policy. Instead, it helps to widen the leadership's policy choices, potentially weakening the need for accountability.

Overall, the incumbent's desire for political survival appears influential in determining whether the policy status quo with respect to rent allocation is maintained or altered. By taking into account such considerations, this study highlights the broader political functions of different aspects of rent allocation.

The Approach and Methodology

Using a process-tracing method, this book examines key developments and turning points in policy-making with respect to historic oil windfalls in Russia. It links executive power to major rent allocation policy outcomes from the early days of Putin's appointment as prime minister in 1999 until his re-election for his fourth term as president in 2018.

The period examined has two significant advantages from a methodological standpoint. First, during the nearly two decades following Putin's rise to the helm of Russian politics, the oil windfalls flowing into Russia have gone through several cycles. Putin's Russia has witnessed two major oil booms and two relatively shorter phases characterized by a drastic decline in the flow of oil rents. Booms and busts can create different challenges, necessitating different policy responses. The book looks into how these cycles have mattered with respect to the approach of the Russian leadership to rent allocation. It is particularly important to look into continuities and shifts in the policy response during similar oil price trajectories. For instance, why does a policy shift in the middle of a boom, and why is the policy response different during the next oil boom?

Second, examining the entire Putin era allows drawing a link between variations in executive power and rent allocation policies. It is possible to distinguish between two periods: Putin's early years in the Kremlin and the rest of his tenure. During the early period, Russia transitioned from a political setting with several relatively strong veto players to one marked by a strong executive power. It was also during this period that Russia witnessed a major transformation with respect to many rent allocation policies. In essence, an analysis of Putin's early years shows how this transition towards strong executive power affected policy-making and policy choices on rent allocation. Comparisons with the Yeltsin era are particularly helpful.

An analysis of Putin's early years in the presidency can offer insights in several respects. By examining the roles of various veto players in rent allocation, this book explores how the power balance shifted decisively in favor of the executive, while the role of other veto players waned over time. It is also important not to understate the extent of policy debates in Russia, especially with respect to some of the fundamental reforms and policy decisions affecting rent allocation during Putin's first few years in the Kremlin. I illustrate that the Duma in particular had significant input in areas such as overhauling the oil tax regime and transitioning towards a balanced budget during this period. I analyze voting results in Russia's legislative chambers and public statements by their members to assess policy preferences relative to the executive.[109] I also evaluate how policy preferences of such veto players differed, and whether they got "absorbed" by the executive over time. A detailed review of this initial period helps to trace the origin of Putin's approach to rent allocation, shedding light on the foundations of some of Russia's principal economic policies.

If executive power was transformed during Putin's first term as president, how was policy made in this new setting and how can we explain the stability or shifts of rent allocation policies over time? Weak institutional veto players outside the executive branch have remained a constant feature of Russia's political setting in this new (second) period. Thus, my emphasis for this period is primarily on the executive branch.

And yet, executive power cannot be considered as entirely constant for the remainder of Putin's tenure. I argue that, as the executive branch emerged as the single most important veto player, policy stability depended largely on Putin's own policy preferences as well as the extent of cohesion within the executive. A primary area of interest is how cohesion within the executive affected the evolution of distinct rent allocation policies over time. One can expect that executive cohesion may vary from one policy area to another, not least because some policies go through the oversight of a larger segment of the executive branch than others, triggering potential coordination problems. Hence, with respect to any given rent allocation policy, I address several main questions: What was the scope of involvement of executive agencies and who were the main players vying to shape the policy? How cohesive was the executive in regard to that policy? How did cohesion evolve over time?

Cohesion within the executive branch is challenging to measure or quantify.[110] I treat signs of lack of cohesion as a factor that tends to detract from strong executive power. To assess the extent of cohesion I examine statements by key policy-makers within the Kremlin and the Russian government. Official documents indicating the policy position of the Kremlin, and key ministries such as the Finance Ministry and the Ministry of Economic Development, are helpful for the assessment of policy preferences of key actors.[111] I compare their policy positions and examine Putin's role in supporting or rejecting a particular position. I also look at whether the final outcome reflects the chief executive's (Putin's) original policy preferences. Competing economic policy proposals are particularly worth analyzing. Some of these proposals have come up in the form of policy drafts, legislative bills and economic programs, while others have been reflected in public statements. They often indicate diverging views on the role of the state in how to manage Russia's resource wealth. Interviews with public officials and policy experts have also been employed to determine policy preferences. Additionally, I examine Putin's choices in filling key government posts as possible indicators of his preferences as well as of potential changes in executive cohesion.

As this book explores the link between executive power and rent allocation in Putin's Russia, it is worth noting how I further operationalize rent allocation. I analyze rent in three interrelated phases. The first phase – rent generation – is fairly straightforward to examine. Total rents are a function of two main parameters that benefit from ample statistical data: Russia's oil output and the price of Russia's Urals-blend oil. What also matters in this phase is who generates the rents. Thus, I explore the key features of the rent generation model that President Putin inherited at the end of the 1990s. I then examine how the model evolved over time in terms of its ownership.

Rent collection refers to the state's ability to acquire a share of the rents generated by the oil sector. Using Russian statistical sources, I illustrate how the government was able to engineer a major reversal in terms of the state's share in Russia's oil windfalls at the start of Putin's tenure. Next, I examine the government's evolving approach to the oil tax regime in terms of the burden it imposed on the oil sector as well as the stability of the tax policy itself.

Rent redistribution by the state is a comprehensive theme involving a range of economic policies. I look into four specific policy areas: Russia's general (consolidated) and federal budget, tax reforms outside the oil sector, payment of foreign debt, and accumulation of oil revenues into specially designated oil funds. In each case, my main emphasis is on the role of oil rents within these policy areas. As in the case of rent collection, I illustrate that rent redistribution by the state was subject to a similarly radical overhaul during the early years of Putin's presidency. I examine the rest of his tenure in terms of continuities and shifts in the redistributive policies of the state. Depending on the price cycle for oil, the key measure for these policies is their degree of cyclicality.[112] The data on these policy areas are acquired from open sources primarily through Russia's Finance Ministry, the International Monetary Fund, and the World Bank.

One of the challenges in studying rent redistribution by the oil sector is the limited availability of data. This aspect of rent allocation consists of various outlays by oil companies such as expenses for social (responsibility) projects and overpriced contracts, forgone revenues through trading companies, payments of bribes, dividend payments, and costs incurred due to fuel subsidies. Save for the latter two areas and, in part, for social responsibility spending, data are sparse and accurate estimates are not possible. Yet, there is sufficient evidence confirming the significance of this particular type of rent redistribution. I look at the "rule of law" and "property rights" in Russia as proxy measures that affect rent redistribution by the oil sector. Russia's evolution in these particular areas has been reported regularly by international agencies. The focus of my research is primarily on discovering the main channels of rent redistribution employed by oil companies, rather than on building an extensive list of the main beneficiaries. This approach makes it possible to replicate the book's methodology in studies of other countries.

In each chapter exploring a distinct aspect of rent allocation, I begin by outlining the key outcomes of Russia's rent allocation policies from the start of Putin's first presidency until his reelection in 2018. Following this, I shift to a detailed narrative explaining what led to these outcomes. The narrative examines the various policy battles that have determined the outcome of rent allocation by putting them in the context of executive power.

Contributions of the Study

I present an in-depth study of how Putin's Russia managed its historic oil windfalls. The book fills an important gap by providing a comprehensive account of Russia's rent-driven political economy, deepening our understanding of Russia as a country rich in mineral resources, and contributes to an extensive literature dedicated to the study of such countries. By examining key aspects of Russia's economic policy-making, it also helps to identify the sources of resilience as well as the vulnerabilities of Russia's economy today.

As this book provides an account of decision-making in Putin's Russia, it contributes to the scholarship on authoritarianism as well. Presenting a case study on Russia, where a historical boom in oil revenues coincided with a rise in authoritarian leadership, this study demonstrates how the concentration of power in and around Putin shaped the way his administration managed Russia's resource wealth. Its exploration of how the incumbent leadership resolved distinct contests on the oil windfalls also sheds light on Putin's ability to maintain his long tenure at the helm of Russian politics. In showing how Putin's policy choices have aided his political survival, this book can inform future studies on the link between oil and consolidation of an autocracy.

Through its innovative approach to analyzing the contested nature of resource rents as well as the policy process that shapes the allocation of these rents, this book makes a substantial theoretical contribution. My starting point is that the scholarship on resource-abundant countries is in need of greater clarity on the object of analysis (the dependent variable) as well as on its precise causal patterns. Examining economic growth or economic reforms, as has been the predominant focus of studies on the economies of resource-rich countries, does not necessarily capture the true level of contests over resource rents. Likewise, causal mechanisms often remain fuzzy when economic policy outcomes are merely associated with broadly defined political categories and factors.

In order to capture the contested nature of resource rents, I introduce the term "rent allocation." The focus of this term is unambiguously on economic policies that are directly relevant to the distributional aspects of a country's mineral wealth. I provide a systematic way of studying how resource windfalls flow to various destinations, necessitating a policy response. I identify several distinct, yet interrelated, phases of rent allocation: generation of rents by resource developers, collection of a portion of these rents by the government, and engagement by both players in various forms of redistribution. Each phase comprises various battles over the resource rents. Studying how these battles are shaped and resolved through the policy-making process raises fundamental questions about how policies are made in a resource-rich country and how the country is governed. Looking at each phase of rent allocation also constitutes a new way of examining institution-building in a resource-rich country. Thus, reforming taxation, setting new budgetary rules, establishing special funds to save windfalls for the future, and developing practices that impact on the rule of law represent not only battles on the resource rents but also political struggles over building institutions that direct how these rents flow.

As rents are contested, a key question is: What determines the outcomes of these contests? In other words, as these contests represent various policy areas, what determines policy performance in resource-rich settings? Dominant paradigms point to factors such as state power, type of regime, and institutional quality. Adhering to a well-established theory on veto players, this book offers an alternative approach based on the concept of "executive power." This approach has a number of advantages. Its vigor derives from its clarity in identifying the key players with leverage on a given policy, their preferences, and their strengths (e.g., internal cohesion). Executive power incorporates structural constraints in policy-making while emphasizing the role of agency in shaping outcomes. This, in part, helps to avoid the determinism that is prevalent in the "resource curse" literature. With its focus on what preserves or prompts a change in the policy status quo, and how a policy change is enacted and implemented, the approach based on executive power helps explain the durability of policy decisions. This is of particular interest in terms of its implications for the policy community in resource-abundant countries.

Furthermore, the concept of "executive power," along with the criteria that I develop to measure it, has the potential to enhance the applicability of the veto players theory in studying policy performance on a wider scale. The concept brings together all critical attributes of the veto players theory – the number of veto players, their relative policy preferences and internal cohesion – to offer a theoretical understanding of what ultimately shapes policy outcomes. Existing studies adhering to the veto players theory have generally examined the importance of individual attributes. Hence, "executive power" as a summative concept fills a significant conceptual gap. Meanwhile, through its emphasis on the multiple attributes of veto players, "executive power" highlights the extent of bargaining and negotiations that eventually shape policies, including in authoritarian settings.

While the concept of "executive power" brings together various attributes of veto players, the book's emphasis on one particular attribute – cohesion within the executive – can further enrich the veto players theory, particularly in settings where the executive branch has emerged as the dominant or the only veto player. Looking at the extent of cohesion on a given policy can help elucidate what the veto players theory has dubbed as the state's "decisiveness" (its ability to enact a policy) and "resoluteness" (the ability to commit to a policy). This work shows how policy shifts from one direction to another are more likely in case of splits within the executive, particularly if the policy status quo is perceived as a threat to political survival. Throughout, I provide detailed case studies of how the presence/lack of cohesion within the executive has been accompanied with continuities and shifts in Russia's rent allocation policies.

Finally, the value of the veto players theory is yet to be recognized in studying governments dependent on mineral resources. Offering a case study of Russia, this book's methodological approach can be adapted for future research on how changes in executive power affect battles over rents and, therefore, economic policies in other resource-rich countries.

2 The Upsurge in Executive Power under President Putin

To understand how the Russian leadership settled a series of contests on oil, the country's primary source of wealth, it helps to start with a brief overview of the context for policy-making. If Putin managed to transform distinct aspects of rent allocation while Yeltsin failed to do so, what explains this capability? And if some of Putin's policies endured, while others, including some key achievements, were reversed over time, what explains that variation?

This chapter highlights two major changes in Russia's policy-making context following Putin's ascent to power. First, Russia quickly shifted from a political setting characterized by several effective institutional veto players to one where the executive branch acquired an overriding role. The executive headed by the new president experienced an upsurge in power, one not seen since the collapse of the USSR. Much of this change occurred during Putin's first term as president. In Aslund's words, Putin created a "true masterpiece" of power consolidation.[1] This chapter emphasizes the extensive nature of centralization of power undertaken by Putin. To provide context, I offer a brief overview of the evolution of Russia's four institutional veto players after 1999: the executive branch, the two legislative chambers, and regional governors. To document the upsurge in executive power, I examine key changes in voting patterns and several legislative developments.

Second, President Putin took action to ensure greater cohesion within the executive branch. Decision-making became largely confined to the executive branch during his first term as president and remained there ever since. Thus, it is important to look at executive cohesion when analyzing the Putin era.

The weakened veto players (outside the executive) and the steps taken to bring greater cohesion within the executive point to a defining development of the Putin era. The Russian state emerged as more "decisive" than it was in the 1990s. It became much more capable of launching new policies and transforming rent allocation to suit its preferences. Furthermore, it could do so while keeping other institutional veto players formally engaged in the process.

And yet the distinct rent allocation policies in the aftermath of this upsurge in executive power exhibited great variety. One explanation for this can be found by looking at the extent of executive cohesion on respective policies. Ultimately, one can expect cohesion to vary from one policy to another. I identify several significant factors that put substantial constraints on Putin's efforts to bring about greater cohesion.

The Rise of the Executive and the Decline of Other Veto Players under Putin

The President as a Veto Player

Adopted in 1993, the Constitution of the Russian Federation established a rather complex executive branch that comprises the president with his administration and the cabinet led by the prime minister. Focusing on the president as the head of Russia's executive branch, I examine five areas that are likely to affect executive power (table 1.1). The first two are determined by the country's constitution, while the rest are products of the political process.

How powerful is the Russian president in constitutional terms? There is a considerable lack of consensus on this question. The disagreement among scholars is reflected in their failure to find a commonly accepted view of the constitutional design of Russia's political system on the continuum ranging from presidentialism to parliamentarism. According to Tiffany Troxel, this disagreement has arisen largely because scholars focus on different aspects of the Russia constitution.[2] Stephen Holmes[3] and Eugene Huskey,[4] for instance, describe Russia as a "super-presidential" system, largely due to the president's power to rule by decrees, which effectively dilutes the separation of powers. According to Arendt Lijphart's typology of constitutions, which puts an emphasis on how the executive is selected and whether it depends on the legislature's vote of confidence, Russia has a "presidential" system.[5] Matthew Shugart, on the other hand, contends that the powers of the Russian president are not "excessive" and Russia's political system is better identified as "semi-presidential."[6]

Applying a comprehensive methodology on presidential power developed by Shugart and Carey,[7] Troxel finds that the Russian president has substantially high legislative and non-legislative powers compared to most presidents worldwide. In fact, historically, only six presidents have had more constitutional powers than the Russian president.[8] Nevertheless, when the same methodology is applied to compare the president's power relative to the legislature, the findings are highly revealing. Evidently, while the 1993 Constitution assigned substantial powers to the president, it also granted almost correspondingly large powers to the legislature.[9] Hence, the balance of constitutional powers has been only slightly tilted in the president's favor.

This relative balance of constitutional powers between the president and the legislature has opened the possibilities for political stalemates. That is, it has compromised the state's ability to act "decisively" and initiate policy change. Such stalemates were a frequent phenomenon under President Yeltsin. To end a deadlock and modify the policy status quo, Yeltsin frequently had to rely on instruments that allow bypassing the legislature.[10] As detailed below, Russia's first president frequently opted to issue decrees, and used his power to veto bills coming from the legislature. By comparison, Putin has resorted to such instruments much more sparingly, something which merits explanation.

In assessing the constitutional powers of the president, it is essential to look at whether and how these powers have changed over time. In this respect, there was a striking continuity between the presidencies of Yeltsin and Putin following the succession in 2000. There was no change in the constitution that would affect the formal status of Russia's institutional veto players. The four institutional veto players active under Yeltsin were maintained. The Duma, in particular, witnessed no legal changes to its status. Major changes regarding the Federation Council and regional governors were accomplished through legislative bills and presidential decrees rather than constitutional reform.

This continuity underlines that Yeltsin (after 1993) and Putin operated under similar constitutional terms. And yet, while Yeltsin's confrontation with the remaining veto players frequently led to deadlocks in his legislative and policy initiatives, this was hardly the case under Putin. Thus, to assess changes in executive power under Putin we must look beyond constitutionally determined powers.

Looking from the standpoint of the executive branch, one can refer to three additional determinants of executive power, each going through significant changes in favor of the president after Putin succeeded Yeltsin. First, the executive branch emerged as a more cohesive entity overall. Some factors, however, continued to put a limit on its cohesiveness. Given the centrality of the concept in understanding policy-making in the context of strong executive power, I analyze it at further length below.

Another area that helped to enhance executive power was the growing congruence between the overall policy preferences of the president and those of the remaining veto players. The extent of congruence varied across policy areas but Russia's political landscape shifted in a direction such that Putin faced veto players who were more likely to support his policy choices compared to those of his predecessor. Specifically, the increasingly loyal legislative chambers and regional governments allowed for greater congruence.

Finally, public support for Russia's president underwent a major turnaround following Yeltsin's departure, further helping to enhance executive power. In marked contrast to his predecessor, Putin enjoyed high levels of public support, both in terms of electoral outcomes and his approval ratings. Unlike Yeltsin during the 1996 presidential elections, Putin managed to get elected in the first round in March 2000. Subsequent presidential elections through 2018 had a similar outcome. As McFaul has observed, "riding the wave of support for the Russian military intervention into Chechnya [in the autumn of 1999]," Putin enjoyed the highest approval ratings of any Russian prime minister during his first months in office.[11] Putin's approval rating was already above 60 percent as early as October 1999, only two months following his appointment as prime minister.[12] Putin has managed to maintain high approval ratings throughout his tenure. Polling data from the Yuri Levada Analytical Center indicate that Putin's approval rating never dropped below 60 percent in the entire period examined in this study.[13] By contrast, Yeltsin's approval ratings had fallen to single digits towards the end of his time in office.[14] Moreover, no other political figure in the Russian Federation generated as much public trust as Putin during his first presidency.

As Steven Fish points out, the high level of public support for Putin cannot be equated to a high level of legitimacy for the political regime. Based on a number of measures, legitimacy remained low even by post-communist standards.[15] Nor was Putin's public support purely based on merit, as state control over the media outlets expanded under his rule, and elections often involved interference.[16]

Yet, strong public support gave Russia's new president significant political capital. As early as the summer of 2000, Putin decided to transform the relationship of the federal executive with two traditional opponents, the regional governors and prominent large business magnates known as oligarchs. While Yeltsin had often relied on their support (especially prior to the 1996 elections) in exchange for various favors (secured particularly via presidential decrees or special agreements), Putin did not hesitate to confront them.[17]

The Duma

The 1993 Constitution bestowed the Duma, the lower house of the legislature, with extensive powers, designating it as a potentially critical veto player in Russia's legislative and policy processes. The president has the authority to largely bypass the Duma by resorting to the office's decree powers, though there are certain limitations. Statute laws passed by the Duma have constitutional supremacy over presidential decrees. In addition, decrees are easier to reverse than laws. Decrees can be overturned either by the legislature or the president himself. By contrast, reversing laws passed by the Duma is a more cumbersome process.[18] This is consistent with the veto players theory: if passing a law requires the consent of a comparatively larger number of agents, reversing it is harder as well. As presidential decrees are more liable to reversals, they are less credible in the eyes of bureaucrats and private agents. Thus, the president has an incentive to pursue a policy agenda through laws approved by the legislature.[19]

Chaisty and Schleiter assert that laws passed by the Duma have been "better suited to promote successful regulation, compliance and enforcement" than presidential decrees.[20] Examining the Duma's legislative work during the Yeltsin era and Putin's first two years, they find that, despite the president's constitutional powers, Russia's lower chamber shared sovereignty with the executive in a significant way. The Duma had a critical role in passing legislation on some of the most pressing areas, such as economic and legal policies. Meanwhile, it vetoed many legislative proposals, occasionally leading to a deadlock in the policy process. Thus, Russia's executive branch has a stake in cooperating with the Duma to enact important legislation.[21]

Nonetheless, securing the cooperation of the Duma, especially under Yeltsin's presidency, was often cumbersome, owing in large part to a particular understanding of separation of powers embedded in the 1993 Constitution. The government of the Russian Federation is not formed on the basis of a parliamentary majority.[22] This constitutional arrangement often led to a lack of a stable base of support for the executive in the legislature during Yeltsin's presidency. Both in the 1993–5 and the 1995–9 legislative periods, the Duma was dominated by parties opposed to the executive's economic reform agenda. In both periods, there were "parties of power" represented in the Duma, but they managed to capture only a modest share of seats.[23]

President Yeltsin's own choices were also partly responsible for his difficulties in securing the Duma's cooperation. He not only never identified himself with a political party, he abstained from openly and consistently supporting the "party of power." Instead, for each legislative proposal, he had to rely on the support of constantly shifting alliances within the Duma. The bargaining process between the executive and the legislative branch frequently led to deadlocks, prompting Yeltsin to rule by decree and use his power to veto bills coming from the legislature.[24]

During Putin's first presidential term, the executive branch was finally able to secure a stable voting bloc within the Duma. Starting with the surprisingly successful result involving the newly created "party of power," Unity, during the December 1999 Duma elections, a major step was taken towards securing a loyal legislature.[25] Garnering 23 percent of the votes, Unity trailed by only one percentage point behind the Communist Party of Russia (the KPRF) – still the largest party in the 1999 elections. Unlike his predecessor, Putin took direct interest in this new project of creating a "party of power." As a sign of open support, he endorsed the party in November 1999, shortly before the Duma elections.[26]

However, the process of building stable legislative support was gradual, and its success hinged upon a number of choices and tactics adopted by Putin and his team. For instance, election results accorded Unity only 72 of the seats, far from the required 226 seats for a legislative majority. Building cooperative relations with other parties in the lower house remained critical.

Regina Smith has aptly described the important choices, as well as the political conditions, that ensured successful cooperation between the new "party of power" and the other political factions in the Duma. First, Unity appeared as a "centrist" party on a range of issues. Its position was typically closer to that of the median voter than was the case with previous "parties of power," most of whose policy preferences on economic reform were deemed by the public as too radical.[27] This facilitated its task of building a winning coalition on a given policy issue.

Second, political polarization had already subsided towards the end of the 1990s. Many confrontations during the 1990s related to the legitimacy of the new post-Soviet regime. By the time Putin took the helm of Russian politics, rifts remained deep, but they were predominantly on matters of redistribution. This shift towards redistributive issues provided a fertile ground for the further development of a centrist party. Conversely, it made the position of formerly powerful parties, such as the KPRF and the Agro-Industrial Group, susceptible to accusations of being "too extreme."[28]

Third, Unity adopted a deliberate strategy on the composition of the list of Duma candidates, one that eventually ensured comparatively high party discipline. In contrast with other parties whose subnational candidate lists were based on administrative boundaries, Unity amalgamated its regional lists. Because of this, the Duma candidates belonging to Unity were more dependent on the party leadership and less able to rely on the support of popular regional governors.[29] Additionally, officials in the Presidential Administration and within the leadership of Unity took a direct interest in the discipline of voting along party lines, occasionally expelling defectors.[30]

Finally, under the guidance of Putin, Unity orchestrated several tactics that ensured a winning coalition in the Duma. Soon after the December 1999 elections, Putin struck a deal between Unity and the KPRF, resulting in a split of the Duma committee chairs that sidelined other factions.[31] While this deal secured KPRF's support on key pieces of legislation, it was a temporary tactic, as Unity eventually (in April 2001) stripped the KPRF of its committee leadership positions.[32] Meanwhile, during the first two years of the Third Duma, an increasing number of deputies were lured to join Unity. The "party of power" secured the support of several other factions as well.[33] Most importantly, the rival centrist party, Fatherland All Russia (OVR) gradually disintegrated, leading to the merger of the two centrist parties into United Russia towards the end of 2001. As OVR was in effect the "party of regional powers," built around the support of many regional governors, this merger was influential in attracting support to the policies of the federal executive.

Putin's ability to secure a docile Duma was further reinforced following the December 2003 elections. United Russia won a sweeping victory, obtaining 37.6 percent of the votes, which eventually translated into a comfortable majority.[34] Building a winning coalition in the Duma to support the executive's policies became a simpler task. Convening in the period between 2004 and 2007, the Fourth Duma was increasingly described as a rubber stamp for President Putin.[35] This was reinforced in subsequent years following the 2007, 2011, and 2016 Duma elections, as United Russia maintained its powerful position.

There is strong evidence that the Duma turned gradually into a weak veto player, and the period of the Third Duma (2000–3) was critical for this transition. There was a sharp drop in the share of bills vetoed or returned by the president after the Duma elections in 1999. President Yeltsin had opted to veto or return over a quarter of the bills approved by the Second Duma. Putin's rise to the presidency marked an abrupt change to this pattern. During his first year as president, the share of vetoed/returned bills dropped sharply to only 7.2 percent. By 2003, the corresponding figure was down to a mere 1.7 percent. During the subsequent convocations of the legislature, presidential vetoes became a rare phenomenon. In 2016, President Putin vetoed only one bill out of 2,200 (see table 2.1). This outcome can be attributed to the fact that bills passed by the Duma were more in line with the preferences of the president over time.

Haspel et al. find additional evidence for the gradual demise of the Duma as a significant veto player after 1999.[36] Owing to the president's enhanced ability to avoid a stalemate with the Duma, there was a significant drop in the number of presidential decrees starting with the beginning of the Third Duma legislative period.[37] In other words, apart from vetoing fewer bills, the president was inclined to exercise his decree powers less frequently. This trend was particularly noteworthy during the months preceding a presidential election. Yeltsin had tended to intensify his reliance on decrees in order to garner public support prior to the 1996 presidential elections. By contrast, the number of presidential decrees issued during the three months preceding the 2000 and 2004 presidential elections was actually lower than during other months.[38]

Additionally, starting with the Third Duma, a growing proportion of bills began to originate from within the executive branch. In the meantime, Putin approved a larger proportion of Duma-sponsored bills than Yeltsin. These outcomes can be attributed to a variety of factors, such as the executive's enhanced ability to control the agenda within the Duma through the dominant role of United Russia.[39] They are also indicative of the higher degree of congruence between the preferences of the president and the increasingly docile Duma.

There are several important conclusions to draw from the above. Faced with the Duma as a robust veto player, the state inevitably suffered from a lack of "decisiveness" during the Yeltsin era. President Yeltsin was partly able to compensate for this weakness of the executive branch and regain "decisiveness" for the state by resorting to his decree powers. Indeed, Yeltsin ushered in some of the most radical economic reforms of post-Soviet Russia through presidential decrees. The liberalization of prices and the privatization of state property were

Table 2.1. Duma Bills Vetoed/Returned by the President or the Federation Council (1995–2016)*

	Second Duma	Third Duma				Fourth Duma	Fifth Duma	Sixth Duma
	1996–9	2000	2001	2002	2003	2004–7	2008–11	2012–16
Number of bills approved by the Duma	1045	166	238	221	180	1087	1608	2200
Number of bills vetoed or returned by the president (in % of total approved by the Duma)	300 (28.7)	12 (7.2)	16 (6.7)	4 (1.8)	3 (1.7)	10 (0.9)	4 (0.2)	1 (0.04)
Number of bills vetoed or returned by the Federation Council (in % of total approved by the Duma)	254 (21.3)	14 (8.4)	28 (11.8)	14 (6.3)	17 (9.4)	30 (2.8)	16 (1.0)	23 (1.0)

*Some bills are vetoed by both the president and the Federation Council, while others are vetoed by only one of these institutional veto players.

Source: Compiled from www.duma.gov.ru

two historic phenomena triggered by decrees.[40] Yet, by using his veto power, the president often hampered the "decisiveness" of the state. In theory, policy change could be initiated by both the executive and the legislature. When the legislature took the upper hand and tried to move the policy status quo in a direction not favored by the president, his power to veto often prevented a change in policy.[41]

By contrast, Putin was able to regain the "decisiveness" of the state by creating a loyal legislature. He felt less and less the need to issue decrees that would circumvent the legislature in his pursuit of policy change. Resorting less frequently to his veto power could be regarded as further evidence of the state's "decisiveness." Presidential efforts to prevent a policy change by the exercise of veto powers steadily receded from Russia's political scene as the legislature's significance in launching a new policy faded.

The Federation Council and Russia's Regions

Putin inherited Yeltsin's legacy of what could be described as administrative chaos in Russia's center-periphery relations. This chaos was a product of Yeltsin's nearly decade-long bargaining with regional leaders, involving numerous compromises by the federal government. In the early 1990s, in exchange for their support, Yeltsin encouraged regional leaders to grab "as much autonomy as they could swallow." Eventually, more than half of Russia's then 89 regions signed special agreements securing for themselves additional autonomy from Moscow. In violation of the constitution, many regions adopted local legislation that contradicted federal laws. As well, regions were often reluctant to transfer revenues designated to go to the federal budget.

It is not surprising that one of Putin's earliest efforts to consolidate power involved Moscow's relations with Russia's regions. Often dubbed as building the "vertical of power," this process had two targets: the regional governors and the Federation Council.[42] Right after his victory in 2000, Putin took three steps. First, the Federation Council was fundamentally restructured.[43] Hitherto, the upper chamber had been composed of the heads of the executive and the legislative branch in each of Russia's 89 regions. A new bill, approved by both chambers, determined that two nominees from each region, one for each branch, would represent the regions at the Federation Council.[44] Evidently, the president managed to exercise considerable influence in the selection process of these nominees. About 75–80 percent of the nominations for the upper chamber were either recommended by, or cleared with, the Presidential Administration during the first two years of the law.[45] Furthermore, these nominees had little chance to acquire the same political weight as that held by regional governors or the speakers of regional legislatures.[46] This likely led the Federation Council to lose strength as a veto player. Finally, the bill also fundamentally affected regional elites. Governors and speakers of regional legislatures could no longer enjoy the parliamentary immunity they had while sitting in the upper chamber during the 1990s. This made them increasingly vulnerable to judicial assaults, whereby the federal executive could demand loyalty.

Second, Putin signed a bill that granted him the right to dismiss governors under investigation for violating federal law. The bill gave significant leverage to the president to sideline disloyal governors.[47] This newly acquired leverage, as well as the president's administrative resources, helped to lure a growing number of regional governors to support Putin and his "party of power."[48] By the fall of 2003, almost all of Russia's governors were expressing support for Putin and United Russia. Many of them joined United Russia and hoped to benefit from Putin's popularity in upcoming elections.[49]

To further centralize power, Putin issued a presidential decree that created seven federal super-districts, headed by his representatives.[50] These representatives were given the task of overseeing the implementation of federal laws and budgetary policies in their districts. The decree was clearly intended to reduce the autonomy of regional governors and to ensure compliance of regional laws with federal legislation.[51]

The autonomy of regional leaders was further restricted through reforms that brought about fiscal centralization. By the end of the 1990s, Russia's regions had managed to secure an increasing share in the total revenues collected by the state. This trend was decisively reversed under Putin (see chapter 5). As the federal government started to capture a growing share of the total state revenues, regions became increasingly dependent on the goodwill of the federal executive on transfer of funds.

Finally, Putin took a further step in political centralization in December 2004, when new legislation was passed that allowed the president to directly nominate all regional governors.[52] This occurred despite the fact that, by 2004, the president enjoyed a loyal upper chamber whose members readily approved bills. Putin's move further ensured that the executive could rely on the continuous support of the Federation Council.

Putin's approach to establishing a loyal upper chamber was significantly different from his strategy to subdue the lower chamber. The upper chamber had never been based on political parties. Instead of bringing together deputies around the "party of power," Putin's administration opted in favor of completely prohibiting the formation of partisan caucuses within the Federation Council. This prohibition was secured through standing orders adopted at the beginning of 2002. According to Remington, this move ensured that informal relations between the executive and the deputies of the upper chamber remained decisive in shaping their voting preferences.[53]

The centralization of power around the federal executive quickly transformed the voting patterns in the Federation Council. As early as 2000, the first year of reforms curbing the power of the regions, there was a drastic drop in the number of bills vetoed or returned by the upper chamber. The upper chamber had vetoed or returned about one-fifth of all bills approved by the Second Duma. This rate dropped to 8.4 percent in 2000 and remained comparatively low throughout the Third Duma period (see table 2.1).[54] The ratio of rejected bills remained at around 1 percent between 2008 and 2016. It is noteworthy that some of these rejections were in line with the preferences of the president, and did not necessarily reflect disagreement between the executive and the upper chamber.

The Rise of Executive Cohesion and Its Limits

There is one element of executive power that deserves further attention in regard to policy-making in Putin's Russia: cohesion within the executive branch. As decision-making became consolidated within this branch, looking at the extent of cohesion can say much about the "decisiveness" of the executive and the "stability" of its enacted policies. The degree of cohesion should vary across policy issues and may change over time. How cohesion translates into policy will also vary from one policy to another depending on the scope of involvement of the executive branch. Yet, it is worth outlining the key changes in the broader political context that followed Putin's ascent to power. These changes made a cohesive executive more likely. However, several factors remained as likely constraints on the overall cohesiveness of the executive branch.

Putin's Efforts to Build a Cohesive Executive Branch

Policy-making under President Yeltsin was conducted in the context of widespread intra-executive disagreement. Putin laid the foundations of an executive branch that was much more likely to be cohesive. His presidency, particularly during its early years, broke with the past on several levels.

The selection process of cabinet members changed radically under Putin. Yeltsin often engaged in compromises when forming the cabinet. Under pressure from the Duma, he frequently included personalities that were favorable to the opposition. For example, Yeltsin yielded to the Duma and installed Yevgeny Primakov as the new prime minister in the fall of 1998, even though his preference had been former prime minister Viktor Chernomyrdin. Following this appointment, Primakov, with input from the Duma, endorsed several ministers that were clearly at odds with Yeltsin.[55] Such compromises became far less common as soon as Putin took over. As described by Holmes, Putin initiated a process of "subordinating all federal ministries and executive agencies, including the office of the prime minister, to the will of the Kremlin."[56] Thus, the possibility of major disagreements between the president and the prime minister or key cabinet members was minimized. However, as Holmes acknowledges, it became more difficult to understand the inner workings of the Kremlin under Putin, and spotting actual disagreements became harder.[57]

Putin differed from his predecessor in terms of his relations with the cabinet. Partly owing to health issues, but probably also as a matter of personal choice, Yeltsin had been notorious for his distance from the cabinet's daily affairs. He often surprised cabinet members by extending his support to alternative policy proposals coming from Duma deputies, and scolded government officials for economic policies that became unpopular. By contrast, at least during his first few years as president, Putin reinforced the ties of his administration with the government. Sokolowski notes, "Putin has stood by his government more closely that Yeltsin did. There have been far fewer instances of harsh public criticism of the government by the Russian president. Putin has made fewer attempts to shift responsibility for economic policy shortcomings onto the government."[58]

Additionally, Putin took deliberate action to reduce intra-agency squabbles, enhancing cohesion within the executive. During Yeltsin's presidency, ministerial staffs often faced overlapping jurisdiction, leading to a lack of coordination and conflicts. Holmes notes: "They concealed useful information from their counterparts … They worked at cross purposes, lobbied for clashing interests …, and pursued disparate policies, while paying only occasional lip service to the ostensible common purposes weakly articulated by the Kremlin." On many occasions, "different ministries, under Yeltsin, negotiated with each other as if they were foreign countries."[59]

As one of its first tasks following Putin's victory in the March 2000 presidential elections, the government issued an order demanding that no agency or department submit bills or proposals to the Duma without first clearing them with the official representative of the cabinet in the Duma. This measure aimed to improve coordination among agents and undercut the individual initiatives of ministers (or other agents) to raise support within the Duma for their self-serving proposals.[60]

Securing greater coordination within the executive required more than one initiative, and it took some time to move towards this objective. Some of the major government reshuffles in the following years were likely driven in part by Putin's dissatisfaction with the degree of policy coordination within the executive branch. For instance, in 2004, Putin unleashed a wave of reorganization within the state administration. The cabinet was considerably streamlined and nearly half of the ministries were eliminated.[61]

Overall, from the very start of his presidency, Putin brought greater cohesion to the executive branch. The intense intra-executive squabbles of the Yeltsin era were left behind. Disagreements within the cabinet, however, were common, a situation which indicates some of the limits on cohesion within the executive branch.

The Limits on Cohesion

According to the 1993 Constitution, the executive branch is composed of the Presidential Administration and the cabinet. The two entities are institutionally separated and each has its own sizable administrative staff, often in charge of the same policy. Huskey has described a long tradition of institutional redundancy in Russian and Soviet politics. Leaders in the Kremlin have found it convenient to have multiple institutions in charge of similar policies. They have preferred to maintain or even encourage such redundancies.[62] According to Colton, the "dual executive" created by the Constitution has inevitably been a source of competition within the Russian ruling elite for "the ears and the signature" of the president.[63]

As Putin preserved this "dual executive" system, it remained ripe for redundancies whereby different parts of the executive competed to influence policy. In theory, redundancies are not necessarily equated with a lack of cohesion within the executive. Policy preferences of people representing different institutions may converge. Likewise, redundancies may matter less for policy-making, at least in the short term, if members of the executive branch do not enjoy autonomy in decision-making and are obliged to stand behind the decisions of the chief executive.[64] However, the factual record indicates that representatives of the executive branch often came up with competing policy proposals. Squabbles across government agencies were never entirely eradicated despite measures to improve coordination within the executive branch. Different ministries may not always agree on policy solutions. On the other hand, the autonomy of the Russian state bureaucracy remained limited with respect to critical policies on rent allocation. In effect, Putin was the single most important principal whose policy preferences were ultimately decisive. A change in Putin's official status – from president to prime minister and back to president in 2008 and 2012 – did not alter his decisive role in decision-making.

Ideological cleavages associated with the heavily distributional nature of rent allocation policies also emerged as potential constraints on executive cohesion. Putin inherited spirited ideological divides on issues ranging from who should generate the oil rents to how much of the rents should be spent and where. Policies on rent allocation turned into battles of ideas. Several leading members of the executive, often dubbed as economic liberals, advocated fiscal discipline, while urging the leadership to continue the predominantly market-driven approach of the 1990s. However, as Zweynert notes, liberal economic ideas were not deeply rooted or well understood in post-Soviet Russia.[65] Many members of the elite demanded more intervention by the state in the economy. These demands were further reinforced as the oil windfalls kept swelling.

In this context of ideological differences, Putin's policy preferences and his choice of key personalities were major factors shaping cohesion within the executive branch. As we will see in chapter 5, President Putin's initial choice was to entrust the economy to economically liberal-minded elites. In effect, this represented a continuity rather than a change from the Yeltsin era. However, Putin's support for economic liberals was not unequivocal. He maintained a policy of balancing conflicting demands by shifting his support occasionally from one group to another. This was reflected in his cadre choices over time, as he opted to include more proponents of state-led development in key positions to take charge of economic policy-making. Inevitably, some of the policies proposed by members of the executive branch reflected a lack of cohesion. Putin's own ambivalence on some key economic policies over time also fostered problems with cohesion.

Broader shifts within Russia's ruling elite also need to be taken into account in terms of their impact on executive cohesion. For instance, the rise of the *siloviki* – individuals with a background in intelligence, the military, and the police – was a major development in the Russian political establishment following Putin's assumption of power.[66] The origins of this shift go back to the final years of President Yeltsin's administration.[67] The roots of this shift go even deeper. Post-Soviet Russia, unlike many countries in Eastern Europe, had never experienced a "de-KGBization" process after the end of the Cold War. Yeltsin had splintered the KGB into several intelligence organizations, but he never tried to dismantle the old *Chekist* system, nor did he dishonor its former leaders and collaborators or prevent them from participating in politics or key economic sectors.[68]

The *siloviki* survived the Yeltsin era as a silent force waiting in the wings of Russian politics. They constituted a large pool of elite members available for the chief executive to bring into the ruling circles. If they were brought into the executive branch, it was likely that this could weaken cohesion on a variety of issues ranging from economic policy to relations with the West. Putin reinforced the policy of Yeltsin's final years in the Kremlin of filling key positions within the executive with *siloviki*, with whom he had much in common in terms of professional background. This advancement of the *siloviki* became another source of competition within the Russian elite, not least because the *siloviki* were also intent to have an impact on how oil rents were allocated. Yet, as this book illustrates, the rise of the *siloviki* did not always equate to growing problems with cohesion. Their impact on cohesion depended largely on their ability to be part of the decision-making process and on the extent to which their policy preferences converged with the rest of the ruling elite.

Finally, it is important to recognize that cohesion within the executive could be compromised in a context characterized by the prevalence of informal rules and networks. Alena Ledeneva describes the active role of informal rules of governance in Soviet and Russian politics, which have often acquired primacy over formal institutions. The informal networks have combined members of the executive as well as the business elite.[69] "Political clans" within these networks have competed to shape policy outcomes in line with their preferences.[70] William Tompson suggests that it has been common even for Russia's high-ranking state officials to describe competition and conflicts around the president in terms of competing clans and networks.[71] The availability of such networks to shape policy outcomes, as opposed to a strict requirement to make decisions through formal institutions, is a further cause for problems with executive cohesion. Informal rules have had a significant effect in shaping some aspects of rent allocation examined later in this book.

Conclusion

The end of the Yeltsin era signified a major transformation in the broader political context. Russia made a rapid transition towards a political setting in which the executive branch was far less constrained by other institutional veto players. The Federation Council and regional governors were the first to emerge as weakened veto players. The Duma experienced a similar fate, as the Kremlin built a majority around a "party of power." The state acquired an ability to act "decisively" to an extent not seen previously. But this also raised the possibility that it could become less committed to its own policies. As decision-making moved so clearly to the executive branch, cohesion within the branch and the policy preferences of the chief executive became key elements of policy-making in Russia.

It was in this context that the many battles over Russia's oil rents took place. As I turn to each of these battles, I analyze in depth how the upsurge in executive power shaped Russia's rent allocation policies, and what drove policy outcomes throughout the Putin era. In each case, my analysis starts with an overview of the key outcomes with respect to rent allocation policies and then shifts to an explanation of these outcomes.

3 Russia's Historic Oil Windfalls and the Contest over Who Will Generate the Rents

Putin presided over oil windfalls that brought an unprecedented flow of wealth to the Russian economy. As oil revenues poured into the country, they were inevitably accompanied by unforgiving political battles. One set of battles transpired between the state authorities and the oil industry over the division of rents. No less intense were the political fights over how the state should redistribute these rents. This chapter begins by analyzing a battle revolving around a fundamental question with major distributional consequences: who should generate Russia's oil rents, and no less important, who should not? This relentless contest for control over the oil industry's rent-generating assets has been a fight for power and property.

I examine this contest by identifying several key aspects of Russia's oil rent generation model. The analysis highlights one central puzzle. In a way, the rent generation model has gone through profound and continuous transformations under Putin: ownership in the oil industry has been in flux. Russia has witnessed the takeover of the country's largest private oil company by one of the smallest state-owned players in the field. It has also witnessed the partial privatization of its emerging national oil champion. Yet, other aspects of the rent generation model have endured over time. For instance, foreign oil majors and smaller independent oil companies have never managed to make significant inroads in the Russian oil industry. Instead, the sector has been overwhelmingly under the control of a handful of vertically integrated Russian-owned oil companies. Competition among these companies has constituted another enduring feature of the model. Why has ownership in the rent generation model gone through major transformative changes, and why have other aspects of the model persisted over time?

I begin by illustrating the astounding boom in oil windfalls that Russia witnessed during the Putin era. Next, I focus on the unique oil rent generation model Putin inherited, and the key developments that fundamentally transformed this model over time. Finally, I look at the evolution of Russia's rent generation model within the broader institutional and political setting. This leads to the chapter's central argument: the "instability" in ownership over oil assets has been facilitated by the lack of robust veto players and by weak rule of law that has fostered competition within the executive and the ruling elite over-all. In this context, the "instability" has brought significant political dividends for the Russian leadership at minimal economic cost. By contrast, key aspects of the rent generation model that have endured over time have been less prone to competition and disagreements within the executive. Maintaining the status quo has been the safer choice.

The Historic Oil Windfalls under Putin and What They Meant for the Russian Economy

For over a century Russia has boasted one of the largest oil industries in the world. At the end of the nineteenth century, tsarist Russia emerged as the world's leading oil producer, overtaking the United States.[1] In the Soviet Union, despite major setbacks following the October Revolution, the oil sector continued to thrive. It was not until the 1970s, however, that a massive spike in Soviet oil output, coupled with the peaking of oil production in the United States, brought the Soviet Union once again to its leadership position in the world.[2] The Soviet Union retained its top spot until its collapse, which saw a drastic contraction in the oil industry. By 2007, Russia was once again the world's leading producer, this time overtaking Saudi Arabia. Since then, Russia and Saudi Arabia, and more recently, the United States, have vied for the status of being the world's leading oil producer.

Soviet and Russian leaders have presided over windfalls that have varied substantially in size. Oil price cycles and developments in the oil industry have generated some notable similarities and contrasts during the past five decades. The Putin era could best be compared to the Brezhnev era. Brezhnev presided over a colossal oil boom. During the 1970s the Soviet oil industry went through a major geographic shift. The heartland of the industry moved from the traditional Volga Urals region to West Siberia, which has remained the primary source of oil for post-Soviet Russia as well. Oil production in West Siberia alone rose tenfold between 1970 and 1980.[3] Coincidentally, two oil shocks – the OPEC crisis in 1973 and the Iran Revolution in 1979 – brought oil prices to new heights.

Remarkably, Brezhnev and Putin, the two big beneficiaries of oil windfalls, are also the longest-serving Soviet/Russian leaders since Stalin. On 12 September 2017, Putin overtook Brezhnev in terms of the length of his tenure.[4]

Brezhnev's successors were not so fortunate. The Soviet oil industry was already in crisis by the early 1980s, preparing for an imminent peak in production. Both Gorbachev and Yeltsin presided during periods of relatively low oil prices. This further exacerbated the economic predicament they faced. For Gorbachev, the collapse of world oil prices overlapped with his launch of *perestroika*. According to Gaidar, this severely magnified Gorbachev's challenge as the new general secretary.[5] In Yeltsin's case, the price of oil remained low through most of the 1990s, while the economy kept contracting.

How large has the windfall of oil rents in the Russian economy been under Putin? A precise estimate of oil rents, even if defined in simple terms as the difference between the total revenues of the oil industry and its "normal" costs, is a forbidding task. The complexity of the Russian oil industry, built on hundreds of oil fields, a massive transport network, and over two dozen refineries, makes it methodologically difficult to determine industry-wide "normal costs." Instead, looking at Russia's oil export revenues provides a simpler, yet effective, indicator of the extent and trends in oil windfalls. Estimates by the Russian Central Bank indicate that Russia's cumulative oil export windfalls between 2000 and 2018 stood at 3.027 trillion USD (figure 3.1). This made oil by far the most indispensable sector for the Russian economy. Cumulative export revenues from natural gas, Russia's second most important export item, stood at 819 billion USD during this period – equivalent to barely more than a quarter of the windfalls from oil exports. Russia's total oil windfalls have certainly been higher once domestic sales are taken into account. The annual share of such sales has ranged from 23 percent to 36 percent of the total output. Domestic sales, however, have on average generated fewer revenues per barrel, because of lower prices.

Given the duration of Putin's leadership, the price of oil and the size of windfalls have fluctuated significantly over time. Thus, it is possible to refer to two periods of booming oil windfalls. The first period lasted from the start of Putin's presidency until 2008, when the Great Recession sparked a drastic drop in the price of oil. During this period, when oil prices remained on an almost consistent upward trend, Russia's oil windfalls amounted to 921 billion USD. The next oil boom, condensed within only four years (2011 to 2014), was even bigger in nominal terms, generating 1.1 trillion USD in export revenues. Technically, oil prices have remained relatively high for the remainder of the Putin era examined in this book. But, the periods between 2009 and 2010, and subsequently between 2015 and 2018, could qualify as oil "busts," owing to the sharp drop in oil prices and export revenues, and to the immediate burden this brought to Russia in terms of adjusting to the new reality.[6]

Four factors have helped Russia benefit from a vast increase in oil windfalls under Putin. First, the price of oil has appeared as the most critical element. Coincidentally, oil prices bottomed out shortly before Putin became Russia's new prime minister. After dropping to as low as 9.89 USD/barrel in January 1999, the export price of Russian oil entered a sustained upward trend. Despite some minor fluctuations, oil prices remained substantially higher in the 2000s than in the Yeltsin era. The average (nominal) price for the 1991–8 period stood

Figure 3.1. Russia's Export Revenues from Crude Oil and Petroleum Products (billion USD)

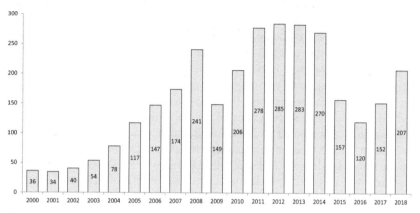

Source: RF Central Bank

at 16.8 USD/barrel. It rose to 41 USD/barrel during the 1999–2008 period. The price of Urals crude oil reached an even higher level during the 2011–14 boom, averaging about 106 USD/barrel. Even during the relatively brief periods of "busts," oil prices were markedly higher than during the 1990s (figure 3.2).[7]

Second, Putin's rise in politics also overlapped with a turnaround in the Russian oil industry. A nearly decade-long contraction was just coming to an end. By 1998, Russia's oil output was almost half of the peak amount it reached in 1987.[8] While oil prices were rising, output grew by 52 percent, or 8.7 percent per year on average, between 1999 and 2004. By 2005, the oil sector's output had recovered above its 1991 level. The pace of growth declined sharply in 2005 and went down even further after this. Yet the oil industry managed to ramp up production every year, except for 2008 and 2017, until 2018. By 2018, Russia was producing 82 percent more oil than in 1999 (see figure 3.2).[9]

Another source of growing oil windfalls was the continued rise in Russia's oil exports relative to its oil output. Exports of crude oil and petroleum products doubled in volume between 2000 and 2015.[10] While crude exports grew, refined product exports rose even faster.[11] By 2015, the share of oil taken out of Russia rose to 77 percent, up from 63 percent of the oil output in 2000. Unlike other aspects of the oil boom under Putin, growing oil exports represented a high degree of continuity with the Yeltsin era. Starting in the early 1990s, there was a consistent drive among Russia's oil producers to export more. It was simply more lucrative to focus on exports, as domestic prices remained relatively lower. Furthermore, Russia's oil exports gradually shifted away from the former Soviet republics, where prices on average remained below the international

Figure 3.2. Russia's Crude Oil Production and Oil Prices (1991–2018)

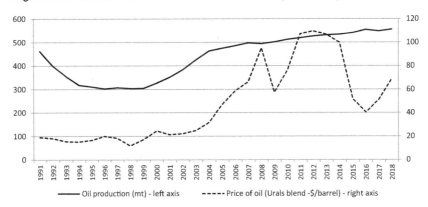

Source: RF Central Bank

level. This further ensured that Russia would capitalize on more windfalls in case of an oil boom.[12]

Overall, higher oil prices, an expanding oil industry, and growing oil exports account for most of the dramatic increase in oil windfalls during the Putin era. By 2014, Russia's annual oil export windfalls were eightfold above the level in 2000 – Putin's first year as president – securing the country 270 billion USD (figure 3.1).[13] By comparison, oil export revenues were merely 14 billion USD in 1998, when the annual average of oil prices reached its post-Soviet nadir. This was equivalent to less than a month of oil export windfalls during the boom years of 2011–14.

One additional factor has affected the true magnitude of the oil windfalls for the Russian economy. Fluctuations in the value of the ruble have been critical for both the oil industry and the government as the primary recipients of these windfalls. Changes in international oil prices have been strongly correlated with the value of the Russian ruble.[14] Sudden drops in the price of oil have typically triggered depreciation of the ruble. Russian oil companies have benefited from a weaker ruble; most of their costs have been denominated in local currency, while most revenues have accrued in US dollars. Thus, for instance, the oil industry received a major boost in the aftermath of the 1998 financial crash when the ruble lost about three-quarters of its value.[15] The oil companies benefited twice more from ruble depreciation: first in the aftermath of the Great Recession in 2008, and subsequently in 2014 following Russia's annexation of Crimea. The favorable implications of a weaker ruble have partly accounted for the Russian oil industry's continuous growth even when faced with setbacks in international prices. Likewise, the Russian government's finances have also benefited during these three major cases of ruble depreciation. By shielding the oil sector, ruble depreciation has helped the federal budget as well. This mechanism has been crucial in moderating the impact of oil price busts on the Russian budget.

As oil windfalls increased after 2000, so did the importance of oil for the Russian economy. For instance, the share of hydrocarbon revenues in the federal budget rose rapidly during the first oil boom. Hydrocarbon revenues accounted for 17.9 percent of the federal budget revenues in 2002. This share rose to 47.3 percent in 2008. During the next oil boom between 2011 and 2014, hydrocarbon revenues accounted for approximately half of the federal budget.[16] As the Russian government has tended to report its budget by lumping oil and gas together under a single category of hydrocarbon revenues, the precise importance of oil for the budget has often been clouded. One estimate put the oil sector's share at 88 percent of the government's hydrocarbon revenues amid high oil prices in 2013.[17] In other words, oil has been vastly more significant than gas as a source of revenue for the state.

Similarly, as oil production and prices boomed during the 2000s, the oil industry's role in Russia's total exports expanded. In 2000, crude oil and petroleum products accounted for slightly more than a third (36.4 percent) of Russia's export revenues. This share rose to 51.7 percent in 2008, and further to 54.2 percent in 2014.[18] The actual importance of oil for the Russian economy has been even more pronounced than these headline figures would indicate. Oil revenues have not only driven up the government's ability to spend but have also trickled down to other sectors, spurring their growth.[19]

The Unique Rent Generation Model Putin Inherited

There is considerable variation in how countries generate rents from their oil reserves. The ownership of the companies engaged in producing the oil, the extent of involvement of foreign investors, and the scope of government intervention in day-to-day activities of the oil businesses provide a distinctive character to a country's oil industry. It is possible to identify a few broadly distinguishable rent generation models. One of the models is characterized by the predominant role of state-owned "national oil companies" (NOCs) tasked with developing the nation's oil reserves. Sometimes a single NOC has dominated a country's entire oil sector, limiting competition over its resources. This model spans a wide area geographically, from the Middle East to Latin America to Africa. In other instances, NOCs have established partnerships with international oil companies (IOCs), while still maintaining a dominant role. Sometimes a handful of IOCs have managed to dominate a country's entire oil business. A few countries – the United States, the United Kingdom, and Canada – have offered a further alternative. Their model has been characterized by the dominant role of *privately owned* companies, along with a greater degree of competition over who generates the rents.

In this respect, Putin inherited a rather unique rent generation model. Three major features stood out. First, unlike in many oil-rich developing countries, Russia's oil sector had gone through a full-scale privatization during the 1990s. Second, amid privatization, it was indigenous, Russian-owned companies that emerged as the new owners. The involvement of IOCs or any foreign companies in Russia's oil sector had remained relatively negligible. This particular aspect distinguished Russia's oil industry from those in other former Soviet republics as well. For instance, IOCs succeeded in acquiring substantial stakes in Kazakhstan and Azerbaijan. One may be tempted to liken Russia's model at the end of the 1990s to the Anglo-American one, where privately owned oil majors dominate the field. However, there was a major difference in this regard. As Aslund notes, the state remained heavily involved, and its role was "both greater and more arbitrary than the Anglo-American model would permit."[20]

Understanding the peculiarities of the oil rent-generating model Putin inherited is significant in several respects. The model's features have impacted its tenacity as well as the direction in which it evolved under Putin. Additionally, as examined in the next chapter, this model has had implications on how the process of rent collection was eventually transformed. Also, the model itself and the transition towards a new one during the 2000s brought distinct opportunities for rent redistribution by the oil industry (see chapter 7).

The Predominance of Privately Owned Oil Companies

A large-scale reorganization in the oil sector began shortly before the collapse of the USSR. The Soviet leadership approved the creation of several vertically integrated enterprises in leading sectors as a means to enhance their productivity.[21] The oil major Lukoil and the gas behemoth Gazprom, for instance, were the products of this experiment.

The reorganization of Russia's oil industry into several vertically integrated enterprises, operating an extensive value chain ranging from oil exploration and production to refining and petrol stations, remained as a dominant theme in the first years of Yeltsin's presidency.[22] Rather than going through a potentially lengthy legislative process, the reorganization was set in motion through a presidential decree in November 1992.[23] The decree called for rearranging most of Russia's oil industry into three large entities, soon to be converted into joint stock companies: Lukoil, Yukos, and Surgutneftegaz.[24] The rest of the assets were entrusted to a newly created entity, Rosneft. The government's intention was to privatize all these companies eventually, though it planned to maintain its majority share in them.[25]

Initially, the privatization process in the oil sector proceeded slowly. The government took gradual steps to lower its stake in the three holding companies. A major impetus for speeding up the process emerged at the end of 1995. Upcoming presidential elections and the country's precarious financial position prompted the Yeltsin administration to negotiate a special deal with some of the country's leading businessmen. The Russian government agreed to give away its shares in several oil companies (along with those in other sectors) in exchange for loans.[26]

As a result of the various privatization schemes, by the end of the decade, the oil sector was predominantly in the hands of private owners. While the government lacked majority ownership in only two major oil companies in 1995 (Surgutneftegaz and Yukos: see table 3.1), its ownership control was limited to only a handful of relatively minor players by 1999.[27] Putin did not immediately interrupt the privatization process. When he became president, selling the state's remaining assets in the oil sector was still a key item on the agenda.

Along with privatization, there were two other significant developments during this period. Smaller players were never given a chance to go beyond having a very modest role in Russia's oil business. Instead, the field remained in the hands of less than a dozen vertically integrated companies (VICs). Meanwhile, the presence of multiple VICs ensured intense competition within the oil industry. The oil majors that rose to dominate the sector differed in many ways, including in their geological assets and corporate culture. Some VICs, such as Lukoil and Surgutneftegaz, were led by veterans of the Soviet oil industry. Others, Yukos, Sibneft, and TNK, fell into the hands of financial barons who carved themselves a decisive role in Russia's oil industry.[28] By contrast, the gas sector evolved in a very different direction: Putin inherited a sector that remained almost entirely under state-controlled Gazprom.

Limited Role of Foreign Companies

The collapse of the USSR prompted a growing number of international oil majors to set their sights on Russia. The country's reserves were massive and a mature oil industry had developed during the previous decades in isolation from foreign companies. Foreign majors saw an opportunity to conquer this new frontier for the global oil industry.[29] Other former Soviet republics also presented appealing opportunities. Yet, with the largest reserves in the former Soviet Union, Russia was the real prize. As early as 1992, there were already 30 foreign companies working in Russia's oil industry, and another 150 in the process of negotiating to enter the country.[30] Joint ventures with Russian oil businesses mushroomed throughout the 1990s.

By the end of the decade, however, international oil majors succeeded in acquiring only a marginal role in Russia's oil sector. Instead, private Russian

Table 3.1. Government's Shares in Russia's Major Vertically Integrated Oil Companies, 1993–9* (%)

	1993	1994	1995	1999
Lukoil	90.8	80.0	54.9	16.9
Yukos	100.0	100.0	48.0	0.1
Sidanko	–	100.0	85.0	0
Surgutneftegaz	100.0	40.1	40.1	0.8
Tyumen Oil Co. (TNK)	–	–	100.0	49.8
Eastern Oil Co. (VNK)	–	100.0	85.0	36.8
East Siberian Oil and Gas Co. (VSNK)	–	100.0	85.0	1.0
Orenburg Oil Co. (ONAKO)	–	100.0	85.0	85.0
Rosneft	100.0	100.0	100.0	100.0
Slavneft	–	83.0	83.0	75.0
Sibneft	–	–	100.0	0
Komi-TEK	–	100.0	100.0	1.1

* Historical information on ownership for Tatneft and Bashneft is lacking. Both companies went through privatization in the early 1990s, but the regional government maintained its controlling stake.

Source: Infotek, No 11, 2000

companies rose to dominate the country's entire oil sector chain, from the oil wells to the gas stations. Such a development stood at odds with the broader tendencies in the oil industry around the world. During the 1960s and 1970s, governments in many oil-producing nations had opted to assert control over their oil sectors. By the 1990s, however, the mood had changed, as oil-rich countries appeared in a rush to attract foreign investors. IOCs had made substantial advances around the world, adding new sites to their portfolio through a variety of contractual arrangements such as joint ventures, production sharing agreements (PSAs), concession agreements, and service contracts.[31]

In Russia's case, joint ventures involving foreign oil companies accounted for merely 6.6 percent of the oil output in 1999. This share had not risen in any significant way since the mid-1990s.[32] Furthermore, joint ventures were confined primarily to smaller oil fields.[33]

PSAs provided an alternative means for international majors to get involved in Russia's oil sector, but resulted in a similar disappointment. The initial approach of the Yeltsin administration had been supportive of engaging foreign oil majors through PSAs. Hoping to revive the rapidly declining oil sector, the Russian government already authorized three PSAs – known as Sakhalin-I,

Sakhalin-II, and Khariaga – before the Duma approved a law on PSAs at the end of 1995. Yet, no significant progress was recorded through the end of the decade. To a large extent this outcome was the product of lobbying and resistance from Russia's emerging oil majors in response to the rise of IOCs as potential competitors at a time when the industry was in the midst of consolidation.

Overall, when Putin came to power, the oil sector was firmly in the hands of several Russian-owned private companies. This development in itself was remarkable. The oil industry had not been taken over by IOCs even when it urgently needed investment. Instead, starting in 1998, Russian oil companies began appearing in the headlines mainly for their involvement in the acquisition of various assets abroad.[34] Rather than being taken over by foreign investors, they emerged as likely competitors to foreign majors on the international stage.

An Interventionist State

State regulation in the oil sector is a common phenomenon worldwide, including in countries with no state ownership in the oil industry. However, in countries where private companies dominate, state intervention is typically confined to the non-competitive segments of the oil sector, such as transportation, and environmental and safety-related issues.[35] In Russia's case, even when the state rapidly reduced its stake in the oil industry during the 1990s, it maintained an extensive set of tools to guide the players in the industry.

A distinctive feature in the evolution of the Russian oil industry during the 1990s was the government's determination to maintain state ownership in the country's oil pipeline network. Right after the Presidential Decree (No. 1403), which brought the reorganization of the oil industry, the government established the oil pipeline company Transneft as the successor to the Main Production Department for Oil Transportation and Supplies of the USSR Ministry of Oil Industry (Glavtransneft).[36] The Russian state never relinquished its control over Transneft, while also securing the company's de facto monopoly status over the entire oil pipeline network. The importance of an oil pipeline network can hardly be exaggerated, especially in Russia's case, where the size of the country and the distances between oil deposits and seaports make pipelines the primary means of transportation.

The Russian government's control over the oil pipeline network proved beneficial. It secured government control over the flow of crude oil, providing it with significant leverage in dealing with oil companies. Throughout most of the 1990s, the government failed to develop clear rules to regulate oil companies' access to the pipeline network. The arbitrariness and lack of transparency in accessing the network were somewhat reduced by the late 1990s. However, the government was still able to discriminate in favor of certain companies (such as state-owned Rosneft), while also using its leverage to meet additional goals.[37] For instance, access to the network was occasionally linked to companies' tax compliance or their willingness to follow government-set priorities, such as delivering subsidized fuels to designated consumers.

Unlike governments adhering to the Anglo-American model, the Russian government remained inclined to regulate prices in the oil sector during the 1990s. When the Russian leadership took one of its most radical economic measures and decided to liberalize prices in January 1992, the energy sector was treated as a major exception. When the liberalization of prices finally took effect in the middle of the decade, the Russian government employed numerous policy instruments to keep domestic prices lower. Export taxes, export quotas, and compulsory delivery requirements[38] to the domestic market helped to maintain domestic prices below world prices.[39] Transneft aided the government in enforcing its goals.

Licenses for oil development provided an additional tool for government intervention in the oil business. While their use is common in international practice, the way Russian authorities employed licenses was often controversial. The threat of withdrawing an oil company's license was commonly utilized to secure various government objectives, such as collecting tax dues and promoting faster (or alternatively, slower) development of particular fields.[40] A lack of clarity about how and when licenses could be suspended and the arbitrariness of authorities had often proven worrisome for oil companies operating in Russia during the 1990s.[41]

Licenses in Russia's context also exhibited a significant difference from those in many other resource-rich countries. Traditionally, licenses are a key source of revenues for the state in that they entail one-time fees for the right to operate a field. They can also establish a helpful guideline on how to tax a company operating within a particular field. By contrast, licenses in Russia never became a major source of revenue. Nor were they designed to set the precise fiscal terms for oil businesses. Instead, government revenues from oil had been predominantly determined in a burgeoning set of tax codes that evolved during the 1990s. To a large extent, the way Russia's licenses evolved was predetermined by the fact that the country inherited a highly mature oil industry. Getting into the oil business, for most players, happened through privatization or acquisition of a stake in another company, instead of a bidding process for a prospective new field. Still, the process of acquiring a license could be as controversial as the process of having it suspended. The Yeltsin administration developed a "two keys principle" for granting a license, which necessitated approval at both the federal and regional levels.[42] In effect, oil companies had to actively lobby at both levels for their licenses.

Finally, state intervention in Russia's oil business could take even more arbitrary and non-traditional forms. It was common for government officials to request oil companies to step in and finance various state liabilities, such as payments of overdue government wages and the construction of schools and roads. While oil majors worldwide commonly assume social expenses, they typically do it on a voluntary basis. The practice that evolved in Russia during the 1990s and remained deeply entrenched afterwards was more controversial.

In sum, Putin inherited a unique model to generate oil rents. It was unlike the one found in many developing countries where NOCs dominate the scene. It was also unlike the Anglo-American model, as the Russian state had maintained a highly interventionist approach with a large set of tools to guide the oil companies.

The Transformation of the Rent Generation Model under Putin

What Putin inherited as a rent generation model for the oil sector was unique, but it did not take much for it to be fundamentally transformed. The transformation was gradual, but also full of developments that sent shockwaves through the entire industry and the economy as a whole. When Putin was re-elected for the fourth time in March 2018, Russia's oil rent generation model looked very different from the one in place in 1999. The ownership of the main players, and their respective rankings, had changed substantially. Remarkably, state-owned Rosneft, one of the smallest VICs of the late 1990s, transformed itself into a national champion for oil akin to NOCs in many oil-rich developing countries. In effect, the state had reasserted itself in the oil industry.

While Putin transformed Russia's rent generation model, there were a few notable elements of continuity in the leadership's approach. At the time of his re-election in 2018, several of the key private oil players of the late 1990s were still intact. The share of privately owned companies receded substantially. However, the coexistence of private and state-owned oil majors, and a degree of competition within Russia's oil industry, were maintained. Likewise, the involvement of foreign oil majors in the oil business remained limited, as Russian-owned companies continued to dominate. Additionally, small and medium-size oil players were never given the chance to rise to the task of addressing Russia's emerging geological challenges. A handful of large VICs maintained their dominance within the Russian oil industry. How did Putin's Russia end up with this new status quo, one that combined fundamental changes in ownership with certain key features inherited from the late 1990s?

Much of the transformation in Russia's oil sector involved Rosneft. At the end of the 1990s Rosneft stood as one of the few oil-producing companies not yet privatized. Over the next few years, it went from being nearly overtaken by private oil majors to emerging as the oil industry's dominant player. This reversal in its fortunes, as Poussenkova has observed, has left many hints about the state of Russia's oil industry as well as the leadership's approach to the sector.[43]

From the mid-1990s till Putin's ascent to power, the political discourse on Rosneft had oscillated between two vastly different alternatives. At the one end, Rosneft could turn into the next Russian oil major to be privatized. At the other end, it could form the basis of a larger NOC and integrate the remaining state-owned assets in the oil industry under the aegis of its management. Many Russian officials actively promoted the latter possibility, but private oil majors successfully prevented it from happening. Rosneft was repeatedly sidelined from major auctions for the government's stakes in state-owned oil companies.[44] In 1999, amid an intensified discourse within the Russian government to promote Rosneft's standing in the oil industry, private oil majors Yukos, Lukoil, and TNK managed to convince the leadership to step back. A planned merger of state-owned assets under Rosneft's umbrella was suspended.[45]

When Putin succeeded Sergey Stepashin as Russia's new prime minister in August 1999, he opted against reviving the idea of creating a national oil company as a competitor to the existing private ones. In fact, Putin showed no signs of favoring a reversal in the ownership structure of the sector. Privatization in the oil sector continued full speed as the government auctioned most of its remaining stakes in oil companies.[46] When Slavneft was privatized at the end of 2002,[47] Rosneft (and to a limited extent Tatneft and Bashneft, in which regional governments held key shares) remained the only state-owned VIC. Rosneft remained on the radar of Russia's private oil majors seeking to grow through acquisitions.

Putin's third year in the presidency proved eventful. First, in February 2003, as a possible sign of a turnaround in the involvement of foreign companies in Russia's oil sector, British Petroleum (BP) decided to put 6.75 billion USD into a joint venture with TNK, one of Russia's largest private oil companies, buying half of its shares.[48] Yet, in retrospect, BP's endeavor turned out to be the first and last foreign acquisition of a large Russian oil company in the Putin era.[49] Likewise, there was no breakthrough for foreign oil majors with respect to their pursuit of PSAs in Russia. After years of discussions, the Russian legislature finally adopted a new bill on PSAs during 2003. However, Russia's oil majors, Yukos and Sibneft in particular, had lobbied aggressively against turning PSAs into a mechanism for foreign players to make inroads into Russia.[50] The new law limited the scope of opportunities for PSAs, guarding the Russian majors' comparative advantage in the country's oil industry.[51] Leading government officials had also expressed doubts about the need to follow the model of other oil-rich countries with respect to PSAs. Even major proponents of economic reform, such as ministers Kudrin and Gref,[52] believed that Russia needed neither PSAs nor the involvement of IOCs for the development of the country's oil industry.[53] Overall, what Putin inherited – a sector with limited involvement of foreign oil majors – remained strikingly unchanged.[54]

Second, the Russian oil industry went through a major shock in the fall of 2003, when Mikhail Khodorkovsky, the owner of Yukos, was sent to prison on fraud charges. By 2003 Yukos had emerged as Russia's largest oil producer, while Khodorkovsky had come to be known as the country's richest individual. The company's shares were frozen following charges of underpaid taxes. At the end of 2004, the government auctioned Yukos's main subsidiary, Yuganskneft-egaz.[55] Two state-owned companies, Gazprom and Rosneft, set their sights on this asset. The latter emerged as the winner. Rosneft's victory was telling: it was Russia's second smallest VIC before the acquisition, but was able to take over the country's largest one.[56] This unleashed a major rearrangement of owner-ship in Russia's oil sector. Yukos had been the biggest prize in the industry and it was effectively nationalized. Henceforth, state-owned oil companies were on the rise. A year after the sale of Yuganskneftegaz, Gazprom successfully pur-chased the country's fifth-largest oil producer, Sibneft.[57] By the end of 2005, oil companies with majority state ownership (including by regional governments) accounted for 41.5 percent of Russia's oil output, up from 15.4 percent two years earlier.[58]

Rosneft's rise as Russia's oil champion continued for over a decade after its acquisition of Yukos's assets. In 2013, Rosneft bought TNK-BP, the country's third-largest oil producer. This was a major move towards further consolidat-ing Rosneft's role as a national oil champion.[59] In fact, with this acquisition, the company became the world's largest publicly traded oil company, surpassing the international oil giant ExxonMobil.[60] Three years later, it made an addi-tional purchase when the government auctioned a stake in Bashneft. Following this takeover, state-owned companies were now responsible for more than half of Russia's oil output.[61]

The rise of state ownership in the oil sector, however, was a far more compli-cated process than a steady expansion of Rosneft's holdings. On the one hand, oil industry insiders had to keep guessing who would be the next target for Ros-neft after its consolidation of Yukos's assets. On the other hand, privatization did not entirely recede from the agenda. In fact, after Medvedev became president in 2012, the privatization of state assets in key industries, including oil, emerged as a major area in policy discussions.[62] In 2016, after a delay of several years, the government followed through on its promise to privatize oil assets by reduc-ing its stake in Rosneft to 50 percent.[63] Formally, even Rosneft's acquisition of Bashneft was part of this privatization drive. State-owned Rosneft ended up purchasing Bashneft, but the proceeds went to the state coffers.[64] In the mean-time, privately owned players survived. Key private players such as Lukoil and Surgutneftegaz remained intact during this process of transformation.

In sum, there has been enduring instability in Russia's rent generation model during the Putin era. The first cases of nationalization in 2004 and 2005 were not the final ones. State-owned Rosneft became central to the transforma-tion of Russia's rent generation model. Yet, Rosneft itself was eventually sub-ject to partial privatization. In the meantime, the co-existence of private and state-owned players, along the limited inroads made by foreign majors into the Russian oil industry, indicate that at least some aspects of the leadership's approach to rent generation were maintained.

Explaining the Evolution of the Rent Generation Model under Putin

The evolution of Russia's rent generation model under Putin, particularly the ongoing instability in the model itself, represents a complex process that calls for explanation. The complexity, in part, derives from some of the unique aspects of the rent generation model as well as how it was transformed. Russia's efforts towards nationalization have targeted mainly private oil companies owned by Russian oligarchs, rather than foreign investors. Also, each case of nationalization has differed vastly from the other. Meanwhile, some elements of the Russian model have remained unchanged, which has added further to the complexity of this process.

The intricate evolution of Russia's rent generation model raises important questions: What made the model Putin inherited untenable and why did it evolve the way it did? What can explain the sweeping changes in the ownership of Russia's main oil-producing companies? Why has Russia's rent generation model been subject to such instability? What role have contests within the ruling elite played in the evolution of the model? Where does the incumbent's drive for political survival and the success in reaching this goal fit into these contests? And what explains some of the elements of continuity in Russia's rent generation model?

In addressing these questions I follow several steps. First, I start by situating the evolution of Russia's oil rent generation model within its broader institutional and political setting. My primary focus is on the instability of the model itself. I employ the veto players framework to explain the decisiveness of the state to undertake periodic transformative changes in the rent generation model. Next, to avoid a deterministic explanation, I examine Putin's position as the chief executive in terms of his preference for the model he inherited from Yeltsin. The analysis highlights some early signs indicating that the model was bound to go through some fundamental changes over time. Third, I argue that there have been broader political motives behind the executive's choice to alter an existing rent generation model. This is particularly the case when it involves nationalization of private property, though the same motives may apply with respect to other major changes in the rent generation model. The diverse fate of Russia's private oil companies points to the complex set of factors that drove the evolution of the model. Fourth, I provide a detailed analysis of two cases of nationalization, examining how this process was linked to the broader competition among Russian elites over the country's largest source of rents. In effect, the rent generation model represents a case that has lacked executive cohesion from the very start of the Putin era. Finally, I explain why, amid this major instability in ownership, some aspects of the rent generation model have remained notably unaltered.

Transforming Rent Generation with Weak Veto Players

Five key moments shook the setup of the rent generation model of the Putin era. Three involved the nationalization of private oil companies by Rosneft, another case of nationalization of a private company by Gazprom, and finally the partial privatization of Rosneft. These fundamental changes can be interpreted as a persistent *instability* in Russia's rent generation model. They engulfed large parts of Russia's oil industry, creating new owners of oil assets and prompting the departure of some existing ones. In effect, the winners of the rent generation model that Putin inherited were subject to a process of continuous rearrangement.

The veto players approach adopted in this book provides a helpful framework for understanding these periodic shifts in Russia's rent generation model. As the power of the executive branch expanded under Putin, the ability of various institutions to exercise oversight over the executive was substantially curbed. It is noteworthy that neither the legislature nor the regional governments were able to play even a minimal role in the process of the nationalization of Russia's leading oil companies. The decisions were taken and implemented through the executive branch. No approvals by the legislature were needed to transfer key private assets to state companies. The weakness of regional governments during this process was epitomized during Sibneft's nationalization. Roman Abramovich, Sibneft's main shareholder, was in fact a governor of Chukotka Autonomous Okrug at the time his company was taken over by Gazprom. His position provided him no basis to resist the ongoing nationalization process. Overall, given the weakness of these veto players, oil companies lacked the institutional basis to resist such major changes in the rent generation model.[65] The executive branch had the upper hand and the "decisiveness" to initiate a transformation in the status quo without being in any significant manner constrained by other veto players.

A comparative study by Henisz suggests that having multiple veto players helps to create a credible commitment for non-interference with property rights. When such veto players are weakened, the ability of the political system to "commit" not to alter the rules of the game is compromised.[66] Indeed, how Putin launched the transformation of the rent generation model delivered a severe blow to property rights and the rule of law: the takeover of Yukos and the imprisonment of its main owner represented a major setback in terms of these aspects of institutional quality. It is unclear whether Putin could have avoided such a setback and still transform the model of rent generation. Arguably the process was easier to accomplish if the rule of law was not upheld.

While there is a likely connection between weakened veto players and the rule of law, a decisive state is not predetermined to weaken the latter. By implication, such a state does not necessarily have to modify its rent generation model, especially through violating the property rights of a company. In this respect, two points help to explain the instability in Russia's rent generation model.

First, the status quo ante and the policy preferences of the executive regarding the rule of law are highly significant. The status quo ante determines the possible direction for change in a given political and institutional context. For instance, according to Andrews and Montinola, having fewer veto players might actually be beneficial in a context where some policy action is required to secure improvement in the rule of law.[67] However, such an improvement is not assured, as it would depend on the preferences of the key veto player – the executive branch in Russia's case. A key question is whether the executive intends to uphold the rule of law.

President Putin inherited weak rule of law to start with. In theory, the fading role of veto players should have enhanced the executive's ability to produce major changes in Russia's rule of law. This change could have been in either direction – an improvement or further erosion. Evidently, Putin was not committed to strengthening property rights and the rule of law in the oil sector. Instead, he was clearly willing to alter the setup in the rent generation model and he opted to take action more than once throughout his tenure. Many fundamental changes in the model represented a setback for the rule of law in the oil industry. Having weak rule of law to start with and an executive branch open to its further erosion facilitated these changes.

Second, the extent of cohesion within the executive branch, the only veto player that has mattered in this case, needs some attention in terms of its potential significance. Weak rule of law and a lack of cohesion in the executive's approach on whether the status quo in the rent generation model should be upheld can be mutually reinforcing. Weak rule of law can expand the possibilities of rearranging the beneficiaries of the rent generation model, contributing to a rivalry within the executive, and possibly within the ruling elite overall. In turn, members of the executive branch may find weak rule of law beneficial to their purposes. They may even strive to weaken it further. In such a context, a rent generation model can be expected to be inherently unstable, mirroring changes of balance of power within the political elite.

The executive branch under Putin could be described as inherently incohesive with respect to the rent generation model, yielding instability for the model. The detailed cases of the nationalization of Yukos and Sibneft, analyzed below, depict the intense rivalry within Russia's ruling elite in reshaping the rent generation model. This rivalry and the continuous instability in the model have allowed Putin a crucial role in balancing what one may define as competing patronage networks. He has acted as an arbiter among the competing members of the elite, distributing rewards as a means for creating political elite networks dependent on him. This pattern of behavior fits Henry Hale's description of Russia as "patronal presidentialism," whereby the president exercises his authority by selective distribution of resources, often ignoring formal rules and institutions.[68] Such behavior is largely facilitated by the lack of effective institutional veto players outside the executive branch.

Putin's Stance on the Rent Generation Model He Inherited

Even before becoming president, Putin showed a strong interest in Russia's natural resources. He published two academic works that provide some early hints about his thinking. About two years before he was appointed prime minister, he defended a doctoral dissertation (*kandidat* thesis) at the St. Petersburg Mining Institute[69] titled "The Strategic Planning of Regional Resources under the Formation of Market Relations." The main focus of his thesis is on the role of natural resources in the development of the regional economy of St. Petersburg and Leningrad Oblast. A related theme elaborated on in the thesis is the application of strategic planning to natural resource development.[70]

In 1999, Putin published an article in the journal of the St. Petersburg Mining Institute in which he further articulated his views about the potential role of natural resources in Russia's future.[71] The article made three key points that eventually became central topics in Putin's speeches following his ascent to power. First, he emphasized that Russia needed to grow at least twice as fast as the advanced economies in order to reduce its developmental gap.[72] He considered Russia's resource wealth as critical to its future economic development, particularly to ensure the targeted pace of economic growth.[73] Third, Putin emphasized that the state needed to enhance its role in the country's natural resources:

> At the beginning of market reforms in Russia the state let strategic management of the natural resource complex slip from its hands ... But now the market euphoria of the first years of economic reform is gradually giving way to a more measured approach, allowing the possibility and recognizing the need for regulatory activity by the state in economic processes in general and in natural resource use in particular.[74]

Putin was evidently not satisfied with the status quo in terms of the ownership of the natural resource sectors in Russia. He appeared to be in favor of maintaining a mixed form of property ownership but remained obscure about what constituted the optimal role of the state versus the private sector. This vague approach has continued throughout his tenure.

Putin's public speeches following his move to the Kremlin often reflected the ideas set out in his academic writings. His emphasis on the resource sectors and the wealth they generated helped to keep the oil sector in the spotlight. His numerous speeches on the Russian economy and the oil sector were strong indications that one could expect changes in the rent generation model.

President Putin was quick to set ambitious economic growth targets,[75] and to stress the crucial role for the natural resource sector in meeting them. Addressing energy executives in Surgut in March 2000, he noted the significant role of Russia's oil and gas sector in the future economic development of the country. He remarked, "In the last few years the natural resources sector was a factor stabilizing the economy of Russia. In the next decade it has to become a factor for [economic] growth."[76]

While recognizing the importance of natural resources in the economy, however, Putin was blunt in expressing his dissatisfaction with the way Russia generated its oil rents. His public statements often reflected his resentment that the state-owned oil assets had been transferred to the private companies virtually for free during the preceding decade.[77] Putin's discontent was not solely related to the dominant role of the private oil companies in the oil sector. The president was highly critical that these companies were not paying their dues (see chapter 4). He also accused them of "abusing" their licenses and criticized them for using suboptimal techniques in developing their reserves.[78]

Putin's stance was widely shared by the public as well as by parts of the ruling elite. Public animosity against Russia's private oil companies was apparent; government polls illustrated strong support for nationalization of the country's leading sectors in general[79] and the oil sector in particular.[80] Similarly, many members of the ruling elite were clearly unhappy with the way the oil rents generation model had evolved during the 1990s. It is important to note that privatization of the oil industry was largely accomplished through decrees during the early 1990s, and had never acquired widespread support within the legislature or among the frequently changing members of the executive.

Political Motives to Alter Russia's Rent Generation Model

Understanding what drives the instability in Russia's rent generation model is complicated by the diversity of cases representing change in the model's status quo over time. Russia witnessed several cases of nationalization, as well as the partial privatization of Rosneft. The cases of nationalization are equally diverse, particularly with respect to the fate of former winners of the status quo ante. For instance, in the case of Yukos, its nationalization was preceded by the imprisonment of its chief owner, Mikhail Khodorkovsky. The company's assets were frozen and subsequently sold to Rosneft, and its owners were not compensated. Khodorkovsky remained ten years in prison. A slightly different outcome emerged with respect to Bashneft. Vladimir Yevtushenkov, the chairman of the conglomerate AFK Sistema that owned Bashneft, was put under house arrest in 2014, but was released shortly thereafter.[81] The company's assets were seized by the state and sold to Rosneft. Following a decision by Moscow's Arbitration Court, AFK Sistema was only partly compensated for its losses.[82] By contrast, the nationalization of Sibneft and TNK-BP was accompanied by hefty compensation to their owners, while no lawsuits were brought against them.[83] These two cases diverged on one particular dimension, however. Sibneft was fully acquired by a state-owned company (Gazprom), and its owner relinquished control over the company. British Petroleum, one of the co-owners of TNK-BP, has continued to operate in Russia. It was awarded a major stake in state-owned Rosneft in exchange for ceding its shares in the Russian private oil major.[84]

In essence, the transformation of Russia's oil rent generation model under Putin has taken a divergent path with respect to the private oil company owners. It has been possible to have a company nationalized, and its owner imprisoned, without any compensation. Yet, evidently private company owners have had other options: exiting the market with compensation has clearly been one of them. Likewise, for some companies, Lukoil and Surgutneftegaz in particular, it has been possible to avoid nationalization altogether. Thus, some of the "winners" of the privatization of the 1990s have lost out during this process, while others have continued to be on the winning side.

This complexity indicates that no single explanation will suffice. In regard to nationalization in the oil sector, Philip Hanson notes that multiple motives have been in play, acknowledging that the exact balance of any motives may not be known.[85] Many of these motives are political in nature, meaning that they serve some key function from the standpoint of the leadership. According to Hanson, a possible objective for the ruling elite has been to ensure its political survival by weakening any potential centers of independent power. Nationalizing the assets of oligarchs has served this goal. For instance, Khodorkovsky, Yukos's head, had been well known for his support for opposition parties and civil society movements, presenting a potential threat to Putin.[86] According to former prime minister Kasyanov, interviewed shortly after he left the cabinet in 2004, Russia's large business owners lost their opportunities to support opposition parties after Khodorkovsky's arrest. This undercut their leverage over Putin.[87]

In a comparative study, Luong and Weinthal offer a comprehensive review of what accounts for differences in ownership within the oil sector across a number of countries.[88] The study provides an explanation of why Russia ended up with a privatized oil sector during the 1990s in the first place. The authors argue that two factors have generally shaped the type of ownership in the oil sector across countries: the level of political contestation faced by the leadership, and the availability of alternative sources of revenues for the state (other than the export of natural resources). Their underlying assumption is that political leaders are driven by a desire to maximize the sovereignty of the state over the country's natural resources and to maximize their ability to stay in power. Based on this, the political realities of the 1990s shaped the way ownership in Russia's oil sector evolved. The Yeltsin administration faced powerful opposition threatening its political survival. It engaged in privatization as a means to maintain support among economic and political elites. The transfer of assets from state to private hands helped to bolster patronage networks for the administration. In the meantime, there was no urgency to expand oil production for the sake of securing revenues for the state. There were alternative ways to achieve this, such as a potential improvement in tax collection across the economy. Thus, unlike the situation in many other oil-rich countries, in Russia there was no rush to invite international oil majors to develop its oil assets. In fact, Russia's private owners in pursuit of oil assets clearly preferred less competition with international majors. In effect, the oil rent generation model evolved in line with the preferences of these Russian private actors, whose support for the leadership remained essential.

Applying Luong and Weinthal's reasoning to the Putin era leads us to the observation that following the upsurge in executive power after the end of the 1990s, a glaring mismatch emerged between the new political reality and the state of affairs in Russia's rent generation model. The extent of political contestation diminished rapidly during Putin's first presidential term and yet the oil sector remained overwhelmingly in private hands. This mismatch was largely alleviated when Russia's two leading oil companies, Yukos and Sibneft, were nationalized. The main owners of these two companies, Mikhail Khodorkovsky and Roman Abramovich, had been among the key beneficiaries of the privatization in the oil sector at a time when Russia's ruling elite faced a genuine threat to its political survival. With the two oil majors taken over by state-owned companies, the process of maximizing the state's sovereignty over the oil sector had begun.

The nationalization process also potentially helped maximize the leadership's ability to stay in power. Russian economist Andrey Yakovlev notes that following the state's takeover of Yukos and the imprisonment of Khodorkovsky, collective action within Russia's oil sector, as well as within the country's large businesses altogether, was effectively weakened.[89] Noting the far-reaching changes in the Russian oil industry in the aftermath of the Yukos Affair, these private oil companies have been described by an oil industry insider as "quasi-private." They were no longer different from state companies in letting the state guide key strategic decisions. Their owners were no longer as autonomous as they once were. The Yukos takeover clearly demonstrated the government's leverage over these private owners.[90] Another Russian analyst has suggested that without major steps in nationalization, oil companies, as the single most important source of

Russia's revenues, would have remained critical players in deciding the winner of subsequent national elections. Putin removed this possibility. Following the Yukos takeover, Russia's oil industry had only state-owned and "potentially state-owned" companies, as the threat of nationalization loomed over the latter category.[91]

Yet, major changes in the rent generation model need not be restricted to nationalization in order to maximize the leadership's goals of political survival. There are plenty of other possibilities at the disposal of the leadership that allow rearranging the set of beneficiaries. For instance, the executive could instigate the privatization of a state company, engineer a change in the ownership of a private company through a new trusted owner, or change the management team of a state company. Each of these paths to shift the status quo is prone to create new losers and winners. For the chief executive, this would entail the possibility of punishing disloyal members of the political and business elite, while rewarding loyal ones.[92] Thus, it is no surprise that the nationalization of Yukos and Sibneft did not constitute the final point in the evolution of Russia's rent generation model.

A few additional motives need to be taken into account to fully explain the instability in Russia's rent generation model. Luong and Weinthal point to the possible link between changes in ownership and rent-seeking. Nationalization, when taking place in the context of a lack of transparency, opens up possibilities for personal gain. The new management may benefit from exclusive access to information on the flow of rents and from misdeeds pertaining to these rents.[93] By the same token, a political leader could create a new set of winners by privatizing state assets. If the process is accompanied by a lack of transparency, the winners may well be pre-selected in line with the executive's choice.[94] These outcomes presuppose a context, which Douglas North describes as "limited access orders." In such settings, there is a competition over rents; however, access to these rents is not open to all. Instead, the leadership is capable of ensuring privileged access to select members of the elite.[95]

Also, one should not discount alternative explanations, although they could be ultimately linked to the leadership's desire to advance its objectives for political survival. For example, some of the policy choices on ownership in Russia's oil sector under Putin might have been driven by deeper ideological considerations. Thus, for instance, the privatization of the oil sector during the 1990s coincided with the rapidly diminishing role of the state in the economy – a policy choice driven by the then ruling elite. As we will see in chapter 5, by the middle of the 2000s, the tides had turned: proponents of state-led development had grown more vocal over time. Oil was not the only sector witnessing the "return" of the state. Russia's response to the global financial crisis in 2008 paved the way for further state intervention in the economy. The takeover of TNK-BP and Bashneft by Rosneft could be regarded as a reflection of this broader trend in the oil sector. Overall, developments with respect to ownership in Russia's oil sector have mirrored developments in the rest of the economy. Still, it is possible to argue that ideological shifts and the leadership's concern for political survival are closely interconnected. Not adapting to the changing ideological mood could be detrimental for a political leader.

Additional potential benefits gained through enhanced state ownership over oil assets may help to explain some of the major changes in Russia's rent allocation model. Karen Stegen argues that consolidating the state's control over resources such as energy is a key condition if the leadership aspires to utilize it as a source of leverage in its foreign relations.[96] While this argument is likely to be more appropriate for the gas industry than for oil, it is noteworthy that Putin has considered Russia's mineral resources an asset of critical importance.[97] He has referred to Russia's raw materials as the "basis for the country's military might" and as a key to raising the country's international status.[98] Thus, in the early 2000s, when Yukos began negotiations with partners from China to build an oil pipeline that would be independent from the state-owned Transneft's network, this could not have fit well with Putin's strategy to secure the primacy of the state on such projects of strategic importance.[99]

It also important to note what has *not* had a role in the evolution of Russia's rent generation model. States can be engaged in nationalization in order to secure more tax revenues from a company or a sector. In Russia's case, however, this was not a valid motive. As examined in the next chapter, before the launch of Yukos's nationalization, Russia accomplished a major overhaul of the tax oil regime, securing an ever-growing share of rents for the state. Nationalization for the sake of collecting more revenues was essentially not required in Russia's case.

The Executive Branch as a Battleground for Asset Redistribution: The Cases of Yukos and Sibneft

Changes in Russia's oil rent generation model could hardly happen without intense political battles. The executive branch emerged as the battleground for several competing camps. Some fought to preserve the status quo; others were determined to displace existing oil players with new ones. I examine these competing groups within the Russian ruling elite with respect to two cases that were closely linked: the nationalization of Yukos and that of Sibneft.[100]

An overview of how competing camps fought over Russia's oil assets is helpful in several respects. It highlights the lack of cohesion within the executive branch. The analysis allows us to take account of the wide spectrum of motives of those involved in the process of nationalizing oil companies. It also helps to underline the significant role played by informal networks in Russia's contest over oil rents.[101] These cases reveal Putin's important place in this contest.

A key challenge in analyzing elite competition lies in identifying members of the elite as part of distinct political clans or networks. There is inevitably a degree of arbitrariness in distinguishing between elite networks. The composition of such informal groups can shift over time and across issues. For the period surrounding the nationalization of Yukos and Sibneft, Bremmer and Charap have observed, the number of elite factions (aka "clans") in Putin's Russia ranged between two and ten, depending on how one defines them.[102]

It is helpful to identify competing political factions with respect to a specific issue, provided there are distinct policy preferences that unite members of such factions around them. Accordingly, I identify four informal factions in terms of their position with respect to the nationalization of Yukos and Sibneft. The purpose is not to identify every significant member of the faction. Instead, the analysis aims to underscore how divisions within the executive and the resulting shift in the balance across competing factions were aligned with the ongoing transformation of Russia's rent generation model.

First, there was the "old Kremlin elite." Its key members had belonged to the inner circle of President Yeltsin. Known also as the "Family," they actually had a major role in selecting Putin as Yeltsin's successor.[103] Putin retained some of them at highly senior positions for a while. For instance, Alexander Voloshin, who had served as the head of Yeltsin's Presidential Administration, remained in this position until October 2003.[104] Mikhail Kasyanov, a long-time bureaucrat working for Gosplan during the Soviet period and for the Ministry of Economy and the Finance Ministry during the 1990s, was elevated to the position of prime minister at the start of Putin's first presidential term.[105] He retained this position until almost the end of Putin's first term. Putin launched a war against some of the "Family" members early on.[106] However, his confrontation had not yet engulfed the entire faction.

A distinctive feature of the members of this faction was their support for oil oligarchs who had benefited greatly from the privatization deals of the 1990s. On various occasions they lobbied on behalf of some of Russia's leading oil companies, namely Yukos, Sibneft, and TNK. They not only shared the idea that *private* oil companies should maintain their leading role in Russia's oil sector, but also tried to help them to further expand their assets in the sector. For instance, Prime Minister Kasyanov effectively helped Sibneft to take over Slavneft and to compete against Rosneft during its privatization in 2002.[107]

This faction stood as the lone defenders of the rent generation model Yeltsin left as a legacy.[108] When Khodorkovsky found himself behind bars in the fall of 2003, Kasyanov and Voloshin came to his defense. They criticized the prosecutor's office for using "excessive" measures in handling the Yukos case. Kasyanov warned that rising concerns about property rights in Russia could have disastrous repercussions on the investment climate.[109]

The old Kremlin elite paid dearly for their approach. During the summer of 2003, rumors emerged about the dismissal of Voloshin and Kasyanov in regard to their close ties to Yukos.[110] It did not take long for this to happen. Voloshin resigned only a few days after Khodorkovsky's arrest and hours after the prosecutor's office decided to impound a major stake in Yukos.[111] In less than four months, Kasyanov was dismissed. By the time Putin was sworn in for his second term as president, the vestiges of the old Kremlin elite were removed from Russia's executive branch.

"Economic liberals," also known as liberal reformists, constituted another key faction within the executive branch. This group included prominent officials in charge of the economy, such as Minister of Finance Alexei Kudrin, Minister for Economic Development and Trade German Gref, Deputy Prime Minister Viktor Khristenko, and presidential economic advisor Andrey Illarionov. Putin made a conscious decision to assign this group a critical role in decision-making about the flow of oil rents in the economy. Kudrin and Gref engineered a major overhaul of the way Russia collected the oil rents. They were also put in charge of the redistribution of rents, determining the priorities for budgetary policy, paying Russia's sovereign debt, and accumulating savings for "rainy days." This group also regulated access of oil companies to the export infrastructure (via an entity commonly known as the Khristenko Commission), determined transportation tariffs, and oversaw production sharing agreements.

Despite their critical role in the flow of oil rents, this faction remained rather peripheral in the ongoing struggle for the redistribution of assets in the oil sector. They had leeway to engage more actively in this process, but evidently opted to stay aloof. First, many members of this faction held important positions in the boards of state companies, including in the oil sector, such as Rosneft and Transneft.[112] Yet, there is no evidence that they used this privilege to have a say in the struggle over the future of Yukos and Sibneft. Second, known for their leading role in liberal economic reforms, Kudrin and Gref could have demonstrated a resolve to defend property rights and the rule of law. Instead, it became increasingly evident that the "liberalism" this faction adhered to in economic policy was somewhat limited. Most members preferred to remain silent after the initial attacks on Yukos,[113] echoed Putin's vague stance on revisiting past privatization deals,[114] or even acted indirectly as facilitators in expanding the state's control over Yukos's assets.[115] In effect, with the old Kremlin elite removed from the executive branch, the passive approach taken by economic liberals gave the two remaining factions a free hand in the fight over the future of oil assets. Unlike the old Kremlin elite, however, economic liberals managed to keep their positions within the executive, continuing to shape Russia's economic policy-making in the aftermath of the Yukos Affair.

The *siloviki* constituted one of the two groups that were on the offensive to orchestrate a change in Russia's rent generation model. *Siloviki* has been

generally used to describe a rather broad group of people: current and former members of Russia's "force" structures, such as its intelligence services, the
police and the military. Here the focus is on a narrower group of individuals
who shared a particular role in the ongoing fight over Yukos and Sibneft. This
faction was relatively large. Its members were on the rise in different parts of the
Russian executive branch, the legislature, and regional governments following
Putin's ascent to power.[116] The leading members of this faction have been identified in a number of important studies on the Russian elite.[117] They include key
personalities such as the deputy heads of the Presidential Administration Igor
Sechin and Viktor Ivanov, Putin's immediate successor at the intelligence service
FSB Nikolay Patrushev, and Russia's Prosecutor General Vladislav Ustinov.[118]

Many members of the *siloviki* faction shared the view that the state needed
to expand its control over the economy, particularly in its strategic sectors such
as oil.[119] They were discontent with the outcome of asset distribution dating
back to the 1990s and were determined to restore "justice" through various
means, including nationalization. It was not difficult for them to present such
objectives under the guise of broader ideals for the Russian state and society,
such as expanding state power at home and regaining Russia's "great power"
status abroad. As these were ideals shared by President Putin, this helped to
strengthen this faction's position. The *siloviki* had another advantage in this
fight against rival members of the political elite: they could intercept communications, collect compromising material on selected businessmen, and use their
influence within coercive agencies for purposes of harassment. Russia had no
well-developed mechanism to deter the intelligence community from using its
informational and coercive capabilities against business competitors. The legislature had never established effective oversight over the intelligence community, which provided its members opportunities to abuse their power.[120] The
decline in power of the legislature under Putin further limited any opportunity
for reforming the intelligence agencies.

There was one additional group, which I refer to as "independent Putin loyalists," that was central to Russia's political contest over oil assets. Members of this
group were Putin loyalists in the sense that they derived their power mainly from
their individual associations with Putin rather than to each other as a group.
It is not entirely clear how cohesive they were as a group. Yet, they were evidently independent of any of the three elite factions described so far, while they
actively participated in the struggle for redistribution of assets. Some analysts
had provided early notice about their growing role following Putin's arrival in
the Kremlin, cautioning against overestimating the rising power of the *siloviki*.[121]
This group of loyalists rapidly emerged as a counterweight to the *siloviki* faction.

Many members of this faction had business backgrounds from the 1990s,
mainly in St. Petersburg, and Putin elevated them to important positions within
the executive branch during the early 2000s. Several individuals were at the

core of this group. Dmitry Medvedev has been frequently referred to as a leading personality from Putin's early days in the Kremlin; he did not belong to the *siloviki* faction and served as a potential counterweight. He had headed Putin's presidential election campaign in 2000 and served as the deputy head of the Presidential Administration until October 2003. Bremmer observes that, following the departure of Voloshin, many expected that his position would be filled by a leading member of the *siloviki*, such as the other deputy heads of the Presidential Administration Igor Sechin and Viktor Ivanov. Instead, Putin picked Medvedev. Moreover, he appointed Dmitry Kozak, a close associate of Medvedev, as first deputy head of the Presidential Administration.[122] Kozak was known for his ongoing work within the administration on several key projects such as judicial reform, administrative reform, and restructuring of local governments,[123] and had authored a controversial draft of the new Subsoil Law, which sparked concerns about the state's intensifying intervention in the oil sector in mid-2002.[124] There were other high-ranking officials who did not fit into any of the three factions but could be included in this group, and some played key roles in monitoring economic activities.[125]

This group gained a major advantage in the fight for the oil sector's assets through their control of Russia's gas behemoth Gazprom. Only weeks after his victory in the 2000 presidential elections, Putin appointed Medvedev as the new chairman of Gazprom.[126] A year later, Putin assigned another of his close fellows from St. Petersburg, Alexei Miller, as the president of Gazprom. These moves constituted some of the earliest signs that the state was intent to reassert itself in Russia's natural resource sectors. Putin's appointments in Gazprom set the stage for the emergence of a major player in the ongoing struggle for redistribution of assets, including in the oil sector. As Gazprom was Russia's largest company, it was likely that it would emerge as a formidable competitor for oil assets. There was no evidence of this at the outset but it remained a distinct possibility, as Gazprom frequently served as a vehicle for realizing state objectives.[127] Were Putin to decide in favor of expanding the role of the state in the predominantly privatized oil sector, Gazprom would be a natural candidate to accomplish such a task.[128]

Once the attack on Yukos was launched in the summer of 2003, the real fight over redefining ownership in the oil sector occurred between the *siloviki* and the independent Putin loyalists.[129] Sechin was reportedly among the instigators of the attack on Yukos. With the help of Prosecutor General Ustinov and Minister of Natural Resources Vitaly Artyukhov a series of accusations were made against the company and its main shareholder, Khodorkovsky.[130] According to Konstantin Simonov, director of the Russian Energy Security Fund, Dmitry Medvedev opposed the attack, but the process went on regardless.[131]

By mid-2004, the burning question was what would happen to Yukos assets and who precisely would acquire them at an impending auction. Rosneft and

Gazprom were widely cited as potential bidders. Before the auction of Yugan-skneftegaz, there were two important developments. First, Sechin made a major advance in the fight when he was appointed as the board chairman of Rosneft in June 2004, replacing Igor Yusufov, the minister of energy, who had alleg-edly been Kasyanov's protégé.[132] Second, in September 2004, the government announced its plan to merge Gazprom and Rosneft into a single state-owned company.[133] Medvedev, now the head of the Presidential Administration, was a major supporter of this merger plan.[134] Based on the plan, the "enlarged" Gaz-prom would take over Yuganskneftegaz. The proposed merger, reportedly con-cocted in September 2004 at a meeting between Putin, Prime Minister Fradkov, and the head of Gazprom, Alexei Miller, heightened the prospects of an all-out clan war between Sechin and the independent Putin loyalists, led by Medve-dev.[135] Would Putin, who had strived to maintain a balance among competing groups, allow such an outbreak?

By the middle of 2005, ownership in Russia's oil sector had been transformed in surprising ways. Rosneft proved too large and resilient to be taken over by Gazprom. Its management approached the merger reluctantly, which led to disputes on a variety of issues crucial to the merger.[136] In the end, the two companies failed to merge before the auction for Yuganskneftegaz in Decem-ber 2004. Also, it was Rosneft, rather than Gazprom, that managed to acquire Yuganskneftegaz.[137] Baikal Financial Group, a mysterious company set up by Rosneft a few weeks earlier, offered the winning bid. Shortly after the bid, Ros-neft announced its acquisition of Baikal without clarifying how it was able to secure 9.7 billion USD for the bid.[138] The government launched another effort to merge Gazprom and Rosneft in 2005, but this too failed as a result of resis-tance from Rosneft.[139] Finally, Gazprom's ambition to expand into the oil busi-ness was rewarded shortly after the merger talks collapsed. In July 2005, Putin confirmed that Gazprom was holding talks to acquire Sibneft. Two months later, Gazprom purchased 72.7 percent of the company for 13.1 billion USD.[140]

Putin's direct role and objectives in this process are less clear. The big winner was Sechin's group: it not only managed to acquire the biggest prize, Yugan-skneftegaz, it also avoided Rosneft's merger with Gazprom. There are some indi-cations that Rosneft's success had Putin's blessing. The funding it put together to acquire Yuganskneftegaz most likely necessitated the president's intervention behind the scenes.[141]

Had Putin insisted on the merger and secured Gazprom's dominance, the oil sector, and perhaps Russian politics in general, would have taken a different direction. According to Konstantin Simonov of Russia's Energy Security Fund, the outcome would have further constrained competition in the oil sector. It could have also simplified the process of finding a successor for Putin. This is because, as Rosneft and Gazprom continued to evolve as separate entities, they provided a substantial material base for competing political clans.[142] It is unclear whether Putin intentionally maintained this complexity but it did allow him to maintain a balance between competing factions.

It is fair to conclude that the entire process of nationalizing Yukos and Sibneft helped Putin generate rewards for loyal members of competing political elites. Both the *siloviki* and the independent Putin loyalists were able to acquire a sizable chunk of Russia's oil sector. These two groups had missed out on the big privatization wave that swept the oil industry during the 1990s. Now, they emerged as the beneficiaries of the newly transformed oil rent generation model. In the meantime, this transformative process could not but ensure loyalty among the remaining private oil companies. After the Yukos Affair, they had to cultivate good relations with the state, and demonstrate that they were ready to return their property if it was what the leadership demanded.[143]

Explaining the Elements of Continuity in the Rent Generation Model

Amid the profound changes in ownership, a few elements of Russia's rent generation model have endured. As noted earlier, several aspects of the oil industry's organizational setup have remained fairly stable. First, foreign players have never managed to make substantial inroads. They failed to do so during the 1990s. In 2008, the Russian government adopted a new law that set further limits on foreign investments in so-called strategic sectors, which included the oil industry.[144] Second, VICs have maintained primacy over smaller oil companies as the latter have failed to gain a substantial market share.[145] This is despite years of lobbying by owners of smaller companies and repeated advice from Russian experts about the potential advantages of such companies in surmounting Russia's geological and technological challenges.[146] Finally, a degree of competition in the oil industry has been maintained as multiple VICs have competed with each other.

It is striking that in these three areas, Russia has largely maintained the status quo it inherited at the end of the 1990s despite key developments that could have prompted a new direction in the government's approach. For instance, a possible policy choice in response to growing geological challenges after the mid-2000s would have been to allow a greater role for foreign companies as well as smaller and mid-size Russian oil players. Likewise, exogenous shocks, such as the rise of international sanctions targeting Russia's oil industry after 2014, could have also prompted some major changes in the sector's organizational setup.

One could draw several conclusions in explaining these continuities. In the case of foreign companies' involvement in Russia, the approach of the Russian leadership has been to maintain their role within certain limits. It has not allowed IOCs to pose a threat to Russian oil majors in the form of hostile takeovers, nor has it entirely closed the door to their engagement. There is no evidence to suggest that key members of the Russian executive have disagreed on this issue. As noted earlier, even leading liberal reformers such as Kudrin and Gref did not see the involvement of IOCs as essential for the future of the Russian oil industry.[147] When, in the early 2000s, there were growing signs that Russia's oil majors were looking for partnerships with IOCs, the process was interrupted by the Yukos Affair.[148]

In retrospect, a more intense involvement of IOCs in the Russian oil sector was doomed after the demise of Yukos. There are several additional reasons for this. It would have been difficult to align potential inroads of IOCs in Russia with the growing emphasis of the Russian leadership on building a state-owned oil champion (Rosneft) as well as with the broader tendency of state-led development in the economy. Furthermore, letting IOCs acquire Russian oil majors would have had no particular political value domestically for the Russian leadership. Each major change of hands in Russian oil assets has signified a key outcome in the fight over the oil windfalls. As the chief decision-maker, Putin has had more to gain by keeping these assets available for redistribution among competing members of the Russian political and business elite. Had IOCs gained control over key segments of the oil industry, Putin would have had far less flexibility in rearranging the winners and losers in the battle over Russia's oil assets.

In the meantime, the door for investing in Russia has never been completely closed to foreign players and they have been a continuous source of new capital and technology. Even with the onset of international sanctions targeting Russia's oil industry, the Russian leadership has abstained from reciprocating against foreign oil majors. Instead, it has fostered new partnerships in areas not affected by sanctions.[149] Yet, it is apparent that the Russian leadership has maintained its conviction that its home-grown oil industry can keep generating rents for the foreseeable future, thus not requiring a major turnaround in its approach to IOCs.

It is not entirely clear to what extent the limited role of smaller and independent oil companies, as an enduring feature of Russia's rent generation model, has been a deliberate choice of the Russian leadership. It is common for such companies, operating in a highly capital- and technology-intensive sector, to face disadvantages as compared to oil majors. Yet, governments can take action to compensate for their disadvantages. In reality, Russia's tax regime and licensing policy has perpetuated such disadvantages over time, remaining fixated on the needs of the oil majors.[150] From the standpoint of the Russian leadership, one could argue that the existing organizational setup, whereby a handful of VICs account for about 90 percent of the oil rents, has been simpler to manage.

While having fewer players might have brought some simplicity to the Russian oil industry, the coexistence of these players – private and state-owned – has been another enduring feature of the Putin era. Despite consolidation of oil assets around Rosneft, the Russian leadership has strived to maintain a degree of competition. It has not opted to emulate other oil-rich developing countries by building a national oil company that single-handedly dominates the entire oil sector. The existing model has had some proven benefits, which have arguably helped to perpetuate it. The presence of multiple companies with divergent corporate cultures and investment strategies has evidently proven to be a winning formula in the context of Russia's numerous and divergent oil fields. The Russian oil sector has managed to maintain its consistent growth, surmounting many geological and economic challenges since 1999. Furthermore, the organizational setup, based on multiple oil players, has made collective action more difficult, thus empowering the state. The government has ensured that state-owned oil majors thrive in this setting by securing for them exclusive access to select prospective fields.[151]

By the same token, the enduring role of this coexistence of private and state-owned oil majors may be explained by considering the potential risks of its alternatives. Re-privatization of the entire oil sector was understandably never an option under Putin, as this would be in conflict with his objectives for state-led development. By contrast, a full nationalization would have brought a fundamental problem, as exposed during the sale of Yuganskneftegaz: an intense fight within the Russian elite with uncertain consequences.

Overall, one can suggest that at the start of his tenure, Putin had no blueprint for Russia's rent generation model. The model went through numerous transformations while some elements which Putin inherited at the end of the 1990s were maintained. The continuities can well be explained by the fact that there is no evidence of significant disagreements among members of the executive on key aspects of the model, such as the limited role of foreign companies and smaller players. For Putin, maintaining the status quo has been preferable to unleashing additional changes in the rent generation model, changes with potentially unwelcome results.

Conclusion

In the Putin era, Russia has witnessed a monumental inflow of rents derived primarily from its oil industry. Export revenues from oil amounted to over 3 trillion dollars between 2000 and 2018. Before examining the many contests over how to allocate these rents, this chapter has described a different battle with distributional consequences – the battle over who would control Russia's oil assets. This has been a continuous battle, reshaping ownership in the oil sector.

The identity of those generating Russia's oil rents has changed substantially during the Putin era. President Putin inherited a rent generation model marked by the dominant role of several private companies. This model was profoundly altered over time. Some of the largest oil companies at the start of Putin's first presidency ceased to exist, while one of the smallest, the state-owned Rosneft, emerged as the national champion for the oil industry. The fate of private oil company owners has ranged from imprisonment with no compensation to a lucrative payment for their assets. In the meantime, several private companies have remained intact, continuing to expand.

The periodic shifts in ownership in the Russian oil sector indicate a continuous lack of stability in the rent generation model under Putin. Several factors help to explain this instability. First, the weakening of Russia's veto players turned the executive branch into a more decisive actor, capable of launching drastic policy shifts. Second, Putin inherited a weak rule of law, making it possible to enact sweeping changes in the rent generation model. At the same time, oil companies lacked significant safeguards to defend the status quo. This outcome was far from predetermined, however, and reflected Putin's own desire to substantially alter the rent generation model, even if this meant further compromising the property rights of the oil companies. Had Putin prioritized the rule of law, the rent generation model would have arguably been more stable, albeit not necessarily static. Russian companies would have almost certainly continued to engage in mergers and acquisitions. Yet, unlike in the current case, whereby oil company owners have faced widely different fates, one could expect they would have ended up with rewards consistently commensurate with the fair value of their assets.

Third, the extent of cohesion within the executive has been significant. Several distinct aspects of the rent generation model have warranted attention in this respect. For some aspects, there has been no evidence of major disagreements within the leadership. This has been the case with some enduring features of Russia's rent allocation model, such as the limited role of IOCs and independent smaller companies, along with the coexistence of multiple VICs, which has ensured a degree of competition. Yet, with respect to ownership in the oil sector, there has been an obvious lack of cohesion. Russia's executive and the ruling elite overall have remained engaged in competition over the country's oil assets. Unsurprisingly, ownership in Russia's rent generation model has been in flux.

Finally, Putin's position with respect to the rent generation model has been of critical importance. In some cases, it has proven beneficial to maintain the status quo. For instance, giving IOCs and independent smaller oil companies a more potent role within Russia, along with abandoning the competitive nature of the Russian oil industry, would have been of limited value and it could have brought unforeseeable consequences.

By contrast, the instability in ownership in the oil sector has served a significant political function at low economic cost. Putin's weak commitment to the rule of law has fostered the above-mentioned competition within Russia's ruling elite over the oil assets, which in turn has contributed to the instability of the rent generation model. This competition has placed Putin in the position of arbiter. As the chief executive, he has had multiple means at his disposal to guide this competition. Allowing one company to acquire another, imprisoning an owner of a private company who has demonstrated disloyalty, partially privatizing a state-owned company, and changing company management have all been tools available to Putin. He has responded to the competition by periodically rearranging the winners and losers. Arguably, this approach has advanced Putin's objective for political survival, helping to weaken potential political opponents while securing for the Russian leader leverage against members of the ruling elite. The lack of stability in ownership amid weak rule of law has made oil assets both a carrot and a stick at Putin's disposal, though there have been risks involved in utilizing them.

In a sense, the shifts in the rent generation model have mirrored broader tendencies in Russia's executive branch and the ruling elite overall, which have almost inevitably hampered the likelihood for cohesion. The initial rise of Rosneft as Russia's oil champion may be viewed as a reflection of the growing role of personalities with a *siloviki* background in Russian politics. Rosneft's continuing growth through further cases of nationalization between 2013 and 2016 could serve as evidence of the *siloviki's* enduring role over time. Igor Sechin has remained a key personality both for Rosneft and the executive branch throughout most of the Putin era.

Yet, it is possible to conclude that Putin has cautiously hedged against the potential risks of entrusting the entire sector to one particular part of the ruling elite. Thus, Rosneft has not devoured every remaining player in the oil sector. Instead, parts of the industry have remained in the hands of oligarchs whose control over these assets goes back to the 1990s. Furthermore, as an additional state-owned company, Gazprom Neft has maintained its grip on a segment of the oil industry, continuing to compete with Rosneft. The coexistence of these distinct players has ensured some diversity in terms of ownership and control over Russia's principal rent-generating sector. This diversity has not only helped to maintain a degree of competition within the oil industry itself, but it has also helped Putin to remain as a central figure in determining who should control the oil assets and who should be left out. For competing members of the ruling and business elites, the diversity in the industry and the instability in the rent generation model have signified ongoing opportunities to control oil assets, but also a potential threat to what the existing status quo has brought them. This has provided a good reason for them to compete with each other – to prove their loyalty to Putin.

Remarkably, the economic costs of this instability have remained limited. Amid changes in ownership, the Russian oil industry has managed to maintain consistent growth. One may ask whether Russian oil majors could have been more effective in surmounting longer-term geological challenges under a more stable model, thus securing even higher growth rates.[152] Yet, a crisis in Russia's fairly mature oil industry has been avoided, albeit through the use of a number of policy tools, such as tax breaks, that will be examined in the next chapter. In sum, the instability of the rent generation model has not done obvious damage to Russia's ability to generate rents.

Finally, Putin's approach to the rent generation model confirms a key underlying assumption of this book: the chosen approach has benefited the leadership by expanding the availability of resources to mitigate potential political risks. It has brought substantial flexibility to take action with major redistributive consequences. It is fair to suggest that having an oil sector operating under strict rule of law would have hampered the leadership's ability to wage major battles over redistribution of oil assets. Likewise, the rather exceptional features of Russia's rent generation model have been beneficial in many additional ways. Having a limited involvement of IOCs and a fairly competitive oil industry structured around multiple Russian-owned VICs has brought greater flexibility to the leadership to rearrange the winners and losers. A sector dominated by IOCs, or by Rosneft alone, would have provided fewer such possibilities; it would have brought more lawsuits with foreign players, fewer possibilities for acquisitions within the Russian oil industry, and fewer opportunities to make key appointments to state company's boards and management positions in the industry.

4 Collecting the Rents: The Contest between the State and the Oil Industry on Dividing the Windfalls

So far we have looked in detail at how the question of who should generate Russia's oil rents was resolved. Another fundamental contest was about how to divide the rents between the state and the oil sector. The stakes were high, and were about to get even higher as a major oil boom was on the horizon. For the government, its redistributive policies hinged on the amount of rent it could collect from the oil sector. Likewise, the oil sector's future investments as well as its own redistributive activities were a function of the rents it was allowed to keep.

This chapter looks at the evolution of taxation in the oil sector. Two facets of the oil tax regime are of particular interest: the ability of the state to capture the majority of the rents from the oil industry, and the stability of the oil tax over time. Having inherited an oil tax regime that essentially failed to capture a fair share of rents for the state, Putin's administration wasted no time laying the foundations for an entirely new tax model. This led the state to gradually displace the oil sector as the main beneficiary of Russia's oil windfalls. Successive governments have managed to maintain this outcome while refining the model. Yet, the tax rules remained far from stable from Putin's early days and have continued to undergo changes throughout his tenure. How can we explain these results: why have some aspects of taxation remained stable while others have fluctuated? What made it possible for Russia to overhaul the tax regime inherited from the Yeltsin era? Why was the oil sector incapable of keeping the lion's share of the rents? What guided the Russian government's evolving approach when refining the oil tax?

I argue that, with the upsurge in executive power under Putin, the state emerged as "decisive" in enacting oil tax reform; it effectively further refined its policies as the need arose. A more cohesive executive, along with a weakened legislature and weakened regional governors, helped to ensure that the state secured, and then maintained, its role as the principal beneficiary of Russia's oil rents. Meanwhile, several factors have contributed to the lack of stable tax rules. Ensuring the state's primacy in the flow of oil rents has often come at the cost of instability in the oil tax regime. The powerful role of the risk-averse Finance Ministry to guide the reform process has helped to perpetuate this instability. The lack of flexibility built into the tax regime itself, and a lack of collective action by the oil industry following Khodorkovsky's arrest, have also contributed.

I start by reviewing the key outcomes with respect to Russia's oil tax reforms from the late 1990s until Putin's fourth term as president. In the second part of the chapter, I look into how the political context helped to yield the major tax overhaul of the early 2000s. The final part provides explanations about the government's chosen path to refine the oil tax regime after 2005. I explain why the government, under pressure to reform, abstained from another major tax overhaul, and instead adopted piecemeal tax solutions, which remained distinctly unstable.

Transforming "Rent Collection": The State as the Winner in the Oil Boom

Russia's tax policy in the oil sector represents a continuous struggle between the state and the oil companies over the sector's colossal rents. I examine the major outcomes in the evolution of the tax policy in three phases. First, I briefly analyze some of the key aspects of the tax regime Putin inherited at the end of the 1990s. Next, I describe the measures that allowed the Russian government to completely overhaul the tax regime, and emerge as the chief beneficiary of Russia's oil windfalls. Finally, I look into how the government revised its approach to the oil tax in response to new challenges emerging in the oil sector after 2005.

The Tax Regime Putin Inherited

Throughout the 1990s, taxation of the oil sector was a major disappointment for the Russian government. Even coercive efforts failed to significantly improve tax collection from the oil companies.[1] As an oil executive recalls, "At the end of the 1990s, oil companies were paying taxes nearly as much as they deemed necessary."[2] The pressure to pay more was constantly there, but companies found ways to lower their tax burden.

The government's failure to tax the oil sector was partly a product of Russia's broader economic predicament. Amid economic decline, the amount of uncollected tax revenues across the economy had skyrocketed from about 3.3 billion USD in 1993 to 31.3 billion USD in 1997.[3] Furthermore, the Russian government had granted far-reaching tax exemptions to prop up companies. Such tax privileges, part of them acquired by the oil industry, accounted for nearly 30 billion USD of lost potential revenues in 1996.[4]

Yet, the design of the oil tax regime was also responsible for the government's lost revenues. There were three specific problems. First, the tax model presented extensive loopholes for oil companies. Second, its successful enforcement necessitated an administrative capacity that Russia had never developed. Finally, the tax model granted multiple parts of the federal executive branch and regional governments the authority to provide various forms of tax relief. This presented ample opportunities for oil companies to minimize their tax bill through lobbying.[5]

The tax regime built during the 1990s was composed of three oil industry-specific taxes and several additional economy-wide taxes, such as corporate profit tax and value added tax (VAT). The three industry-specific taxes – royalty, excise, and mineral resource replacement tax – represented Russia's efforts to align its tax regime with international trends. The government opted for a rather sophisticated tax model that took into account the varying costs and profitability across Russia's oil fields. The royalty tax, for instance, was set as a range, from 6 to 16 percent of the sales value of the oil, depending on the attributes of the oil deposits. Likewise, the excise tax on crude oil was also set to vary depending on the economic and geographic conditions of the oil fields.[6] The mineral resource replacement tax, also known as the "geological tax," was set as a fixed percentage, but oil companies were granted tax refunds if they operated within more costly fields.[7]

In practice, these taxes did not function as intended. The amount of tax paid by companies generally reflected their lobbying power and their ability to benefit from various tax optimization schemes rather than from the attributes of their oil deposits. Lacking the necessary administrative capacity, the government was unable to monitor actual costs in the sector, compounding its tax predicament. The Finance Ministry recognized this problem, voicing concerns that it was common for an oil company operating a costly field to pay a higher tax rate than its peers extracting cheaper oil.[8] This was the opposite of what the tax regime had intended. It caused revenue losses for the government, while discouraging new investments in the oil industry.

There were additional flaws in the tax design. For instance, both the royalty tax and the geological tax were indexed to domestic oil price. With no truly functioning market at home, Russia's oil majors were able to present their accounts based on artificially low oil prices. Also, they could cut their corporate profit tax bill by selling their low-priced oil to affiliated trading companies registered in international or domestic "tax havens." The corporate tax bill could be further minimized by lobbying regional governments, which had the discretion to grant a series of deductions to businesses operating within their jurisdiction. Thus, while this tax was set at 35 percent, oil companies paid significantly less.

Laying the Foundations of a New Tax Model

As the oil tax regime of the 1990s failed to deliver the revenues the government expected, tax reform remained a constant item on the political agenda. The August 1998 crash brought additional urgency for change. Indeed, the tax regime soon went through a complete overhaul. This did not happen overnight, however. Numerous incremental steps laid the foundations of a new tax regime.

The tax overhaul consisted of three major initiatives: reintroduction of an export duty on oil, elimination of the three oil sector-specific taxes (royalty, excise, and geological) and their replacement with a new mineral resource extraction tax (Nalog na Dobychu Poleznykh Iskopaemykh, known as NDPI in the Russian acronym), and reform of the corporate profit tax. Export duty on oil was reintroduced by Prime Minister Primakov at the beginning of 1999 as a means to cover the budget deficit.[9] Initially, it was set fairly low.[10] Hardly anyone expected that this tax instrument would become the government's most significant source of oil revenues within a few years. Several consecutive steps led to this outcome. In September 1999, one of Putin's first acts as prime minister was to raise the export duty,[11] followed by another raise shortly after.[12] In April 2000, the government revised the rules to allow the export duty to adjust automatically to rising international oil prices. However, prices rose faster than expected, leading the government to recalibrate the rules a few more times to allow the state to collect more revenues. By 2004, the government had set steep tax intervals, subject to periodic revisions, ensuring it got the lion's share of rents when oil prices rose.

In another step towards building a new tax regime, the Russian government introduced the NDPI in 2001, replacing all three taxes specific to the oil sector. Similar to the export duty, it was calibrated in a few consecutive steps throughout 2004, leading the government to benefit proportionately more than the oil companies from rising oil prices.[13]

Additionally, the Russian government launched a series of reforms related to the corporate profit tax. As of 2002, it agreed to a significant rate cut (from 35 percent to 24 percent) in exchange for abolishing a number of investment incentives and allowances that had been used quite arbitrarily. Oil companies were among those hit the hardest, as they had been major beneficiaries of such allowances.[14]

Despite this measure, according to the Institute for Financial Research in Moscow, Russian oil companies continued to benefit from other remaining schemes that minimized their profit tax payments.[15] They were able to pay less by conducting part of their business in free economic zones and "closed administrative-territorial formations."[16] Such regions had emerged as domestic tax havens where companies could reduce their profit tax payments through a practice known as transfer pricing, and benefit from additional tax privileges related to other taxes such as VAT and excises on petroleum products.[17]

The year 2003 was a turning point for oil companies' ability to take advantage of tax minimization schemes. Suddenly, Mikhail Khodorkovsky, the owner of Russia's largest oil company, Yukos, found himself behind bars. Accusations of his deliberate underpayment of taxes sent shockwaves through the oil sector and the economy. This development led many other oil companies to voluntarily renounce the use of internal tax havens. According to Igor Nikolaev, partner at a company involved in auditing some of Russia's major oil companies, "Following the confrontation of Yukos with the state authorities, oil companies became increasingly careful about their tax payments. They noticed that using schemes that minimize tax payments could be punishable. As a result they shifted away from such policies."[18] Even the reason oil companies were hiring auditors was changing. Instead of benefiting from their advice on how to optimize their tax payments, the priority had shifted to ensuring that their records were in line with existing tax laws.[19]

At the end of 2003, shortly before the Duma elections, Putin's administration took one more decisive step against tax minimization. An amendment to the Tax Code established the legal basis to eliminate the domestic tax havens. The new legislation also nearly abolished all tax privileges granted under regional and municipal laws.[20] Oil companies did not fight against the government's moves.

All these measures laid the foundations for a new tax model that addressed the flaws of the previous tax regime head on. The introduction of export duties and the NDPI brought simplicity in taxation that helped to tackle two important challenges at once. First, both tax instruments left no room for manipulation by oil companies or arbitrary enforcement by tax authorities. The precise rate for export duties and the NDPI was determined through straightforward formulas. The only criteria used to set the rate were the quantity of oil produced (in the case of the NDPI) or exported (in the case of export duties), and the international price of oil. As the reference price was the world price, oil companies could no longer manipulate the value of their revenues.

Second, the new tax regime no longer necessitated a complex administrative capacity to monitor costs and profitability. The government could effectively collect export duties and NDPI without having such a capacity. All it needed was the ability to monitor only oil production/export volumes and international oil prices – a relatively easy task. Profit tax remained an exception and necessitated more advanced administrative capabilities. Yet, the fallout from the Yukos Affair made it less challenging to collect it. Furthermore, the profit tax was no longer as significant as a tax instrument. Its share in the tax bill of the oil sector dropped from 41 percent in 2000 to merely 7.4 percent in 2005. By contrast, export duties and the NDPI cumulatively accounted for 83.5 percent of the sector's tax bill in 2005 (see table 4.1). This was a highly peculiar

Table 4.1. Typology of Taxes in Russia's Oil Sector* before and after the New Tax Regime (2000–5)

	2000		2001		2002		2003		2004		2005	
	$(bn)	%	$(bn)	%	$(bn)	%	$(bn)	%	$(bn)	%	$(bn)	%
Profit tax	6.17	41.0	4.63	25.9	4.05	18.9	5.42	18.6	7.24	14.8	6.51	7.4
NDPI**	2.51	16.7	3.21	18.0	7.92	37.0	10.51	36.2	16.24	33.3	29.58	33.5
Export Duty	3.92	26.1	5.6	31.3	5.45	25.5	8.65	29.8	19.15	39.2	44.17	50.0
VAT (paid to government)	0.53	3.5	0.59	3.3	0.07	0.3	0.33	1.1	0.98	2.0	2.15	2.4
Excises (on petroleum products)	0.45	3.0	2.19	12.3	2.11	9.9	2.22	7.6	3.51	7.2	4.22	4.8
Other taxes	1.46	9.7	1.65	9.2	1.81	8.5	1.94	6.7	1.68	3.4	1.78	2.0
TOTAL taxes	15.04	100	17.87	100	21.41	100	29.07	100	48.8	100	88.41	100

* Oil sector refers to upstream oil production, refining, and trade.

** On 1 January 2002, NDPI replaced three oil-sector specific taxes. The figures for 2000 and 2001 refer to the revenues from these three taxes.

Source: *Rossiiskaia Ekonomika v 2005 godu – Tendencii i Pespektivy*, No. 27, Institute for the Economy in Transition, Moscow, March 2006, pp. 210–25

development, one that defied international trends: while many oil-rich countries had gradually shifted towards taxes focused on profits, Russia had moved in the opposite direction.[21]

Export duties represented a major step towards institutionalizing the state's relations with oil companies, providing mutual benefits. Prior to their introduction, the Russian government tended to rely on ad hoc policy measures to ensure that there were no shortages of petroleum products in the domestic market. Such measures came in the form of compulsory delivery requirements and administrative restrictions on companies' exports.[22] For both the government and the oil companies, the introduction of export duties as a policy tool helped to remove the ad hoc nature of bargaining over administrative export restrictions.

The redesign of the tax regime helped to tackle another flaw: the previous tax regime had been fairly decentralized, granting numerous access points for oil companies seeking tax relief. Thus, introducing the NDPI, in place of the royalty tax and the geological tax, led the Finance Ministry to sideline the Ministry of Natural Resources. The latter had maintained the authority to negotiate these taxes during the 1990s. Similarly, measures to curb profit tax minimization severely constrained the oil sector's ability to get tax relief through lobbying of various government branches and in Russia's regions.

Yet, a true victory over oil companies' use of lobbying to pay less tax necessitated more than an overhaul of the tax regime. None of the new tax rules were set in stone. For instance, in 2002, the Duma approved a new piece of legislation known as the "Yukos Amendment," which provided a new form of tax relief benefiting select oil companies.[23] It was the centralization of power that ultimately ensured the state would get its due share in oil rents.

Overall, the new tax regime helped the Putin administration fundamentally transform rent collection. The government drastically increased its oil revenues at the expense of the oil sector. Table 4.2 illustrates the astounding shift in the distribution of oil rents between the state and the oil sector during the first few years of the new tax regime. In nominal terms, the state was able to increase its oil tax revenues fifteen-fold – from 5.6 billion USD in 1999 to 83.2 billion USD in 2005. The oil sector's revenues also rose, but by much less – about fivefold. Equally striking was the rise in the government's share in the total profits generated by the sector, defined here as the size of total oil rents. In 1999, the oil industry retained more after-tax profits than the amount of taxes it paid to the state. By 2005, the government was already taxing 83.8 percent of the sector's profits.[24] For every one-dollar rise in the oil price (when it was above 25 dollars/barrel), the government effectively captured 65 cents through export duties, and an additional 21 cents through the NDPI tax.[25] The new tax regime, through several calibrations, assured that the state was the main beneficiary of any future increase in the price of oil.

Table 4.2. The Allocation of Oil Revenues and Profits between the Oil Companies and the Government before and after the New Tax Regime (1999–2005)

	1999	2000	2001	2002	2003	2004	2005
Oil companies (includes both crude oil production and refining sectors)							
Gross revenues (bn USD)	26.9	47.9	48.5	54.8	69.2	98	143.6
Production and commercial costs (bn USD)	14.5	19.7	24.1	26.9	32.6	39	44.3
Share of production and commercial costs in gross revenues (%)	*53.9*	*41.1*	*49.7*	*49.1*	*47.1*	*39.8*	*30.1*
Profits before taxes – oil rents (bn USD)	12.4	28.2	24.4	27.9	36.6	59	99.3
Rent allocation between state and oil companies							
Taxes collected from oil companies (bn USD)	5.6	12.1	16.1	19.5	24.7	44.6	83.2
After tax profits for oil companies (bn USD)	6.8	16.1	8.3	8.4	11.9	14.4	16.1
Share of government revenues in total oil sector profits (before taxes) (%)	*45.1*	*42.9*	*66.0*	*69.9*	*67.5*	*75.6*	*83.8*
The remaining share for oil sector in total profits (after tax payment) (%)	*54.8*	*57.1*	*34.0*	*30.1*	*32.5*	*24.4*	*16.2*
Share of government revenues in total oil sector revenues (%)	*20.8*	*25.2*	*33.2*	*35.6*	*35.7*	*45.5*	*57.9*

* Source: Development Center, Moscow. Table available at Berezinskaia and Mironov (2006), p. 143.

The Government's Dilemma: How to Reform the New Tax
Regime without Losing Rents

There was no question that the new tax regime delivered what the government wanted the most: a higher share in the oil rents. As oil prices kept rising, the government collected the bulk of the rents. Oil companies were also earning more. What was growing was not just the price of oil, but Russia's oil output as well. An unprecedented oil boom meant that the amount of rents available to share grew. On average, oil production increased annually by 8.7 percent between 1999 and 2004.[26] Oil sector insiders tended to describe this as a "miracle" in West Siberia, still the heartland of Russian oil.

How long could this last? Could the state keep collecting more without hurting the prospects for further growth in the oil sector? Could oil companies continue to prosper without a change in the rules of taxation? It quickly became obvious that rising oil prices would not suffice to keep both sides pleased. Quite abruptly, in 2005 the growth rate in the oil sector dropped to 2.5 percent despite rising oil prices.[27] It was getting clear that the "West Siberian miracle" had been a temporary phenomenon.[28]

The new tax regime was successful in collecting revenues, but its effectiveness came at a cost. It discouraged investments in hard to develop, highly depleted, and especially new fields where production and operating expenses were higher. As Vladimir Feigin, the president of the Institute of Energy and Finance, puts it aptly, the "West Siberian miracle" managed to mask how overly simplistic the tax rules had become. The tax regime did not take into account the economic fundamentals of oil fields, namely their relative costs and profitability. Everyone had to pay the same amount of export duties and NDPI for a given volume of oil.[29] The corporate profit tax was sensitive to the varying costs and profits across the oil industry, but it had become a rather small portion of the sector's tax bill.

Oil companies kept warning the government that the new tax regime spelled trouble for investments. The companies needed to move increasingly to new fields, where costs of production were expected to be higher. But the tax regime was not ready to respond to the impending geological shifts in Russia's oil industry.[30] The oil majors insisted the tax model had to be reformed or their industry would face an actual contraction as it did during the 1990s. The sharp decline in the sector's growth rate throughout 2005 gave some credibility to their warnings.

The Russian government faced a dilemma: it recognized the need to undertake reform but wanted to make sure it did not lose its dominant share of the oil rents. There was a range of options to reform the tax regime to make it more sensitive to the conditions of individual oil fields. The government could launch another overhaul of the tax regime, tailoring it to target costs and profits rather than the companies' gross revenues. It could also opt to introduce a new profit-based tax instrument alongside the NDPI and the export duties, while diluting the importance of the latter two. Or it could adopt a minimalist approach by simply providing tax incentives to a handful of carefully designated oil fields, while maintaining the same tax rules for the rest of the oil industry.

In 2006, after over a year of deliberations with the oil sector, the Russian government chose what was possibly the simplest option. It agreed to provide special exemptions for select projects and fields, namely "greenfield" projects that were yet to start production in East Siberia. Oil companies would be exempt from paying the NDPI for several years. Likewise, highly depleted fields were allowed to pay their NDPI at a reduced rate.[31] The new rules were set in force in 2007, following the legislature's approval.

These first tax relief measures were just the beginning. Oil companies continued to seek help while bringing proposals for more comprehensive tax reform. Surprisingly, at a time when international oil prices reached their historic peak in 2008, Russia's monthly oil output saw its first contraction in a decade.[32] The oil industry's pleas for new tax holidays multiplied. This time, their target was the export duty, which had effectively become the most burdensome part of oil companies' tax bill. They proposed various fields as candidates for a reduced rate or no export duty.[33] In February 2009, at a meeting with oil executives in Kirishi, Putin announced his support for such tax holidays. Only certain fields in East Siberia would gain this privilege. But oil companies were forewarned: they were expected to use the savings for investment and ensure growth in output.[34]

Over time, the Russian government continued to discuss additional tax relief measures. Oil majors succeeded in acquiring tax holidays for a few new categories of oil deposits. Several unconventional oil fields, including the largest one – the Bazhenov Formation – acquired tax breaks, as did producers of extra heavy oil.[35] A few small fields were also granted the right to pay the NDPI at a lower rate.[36] By 2014, the Ministry of Natural Resources reported that there were over 200 licensees in the oil sector that benefited from some form of tax relief.[37] The amount of oil benefiting from tax relief rose steadily over the following years. In 2007, just 5 percent of Russia's oil output benefited from incentives related to the NDPI and/or export duties. This figure rose to 20 percent by 2009.[38] After 2014, while facing geological challenges, the Russian government was under further pressure to incentivize oil sector investments in part as a response to lower oil prices, but also in response to international sanctions targeting the sector.[39] Thus, by 2018, 43 percent of Russia's oil output, and 51 percent of Russia's oil fields, emerged as beneficiaries of some form of tax relief.[40]

The proliferation of tax holidays epitomized the government's chosen approach. Rather than adopting a more comprehensive tax approach for the oil sector as a whole, it opted for piecemeal solutions, each time negotiating with oil companies the parameters of the tax break. In 2014, the government approved what it called a big "tax maneuver."[41] It aimed to remove some of the distortions created by the tax regime in the early 2000s.[42] Yet, even this effort represented the continuation of its piecemeal approach, as it merely involved establishing a new balance between the export duty and the NDPI tax. It wasn't until 2018 that the government agreed to experiment with a new tax instrument that would actually take into account project costs and profitability. Effective in 2019, it adopted the Tax on Supplementary Income. Remaining cautious, however, the Russian government introduced this new measure only on a limited scale through a handful of pilot projects.[43]

Overall, the government's piecemeal approach to reforming the oil tax largely met its principal objective: it averted a crisis in the oil sector and ensured its further growth, while preserving the state's dominant share of the rents. Indeed, after 2008, Russia's oil output continued to expand without interruption through 2016, though the growth rate remained modest – on average 1.5 percent a year between 2005 and 2016.[44] After a deal with OPEC to voluntarily cap production in 2017, oil output resumed growth in 2018. By 2018, when Putin was re-elected for president for the fourth time, Russia was producing 82 percent more oil than in 1999 (figure 3.2). Notably, thanks to tax holidays, oil companies continued to expand into new fields, reflecting the ongoing geological shift in the industry: over a third of oil produced in 2014 came from wells launched after 2008.[45] Output continued to grow even after 2014, when oil prices dropped sharply and Russia's oil sector was suddenly confronted with international sanctions.

The tax relief came at a cost for the state, but the high tax burden on the oil sector was carefully maintained. Forgone revenues for the federal budget kept rising in line with the proliferation of new tax incentives and higher oil prices. Thus, while the government sacrificed about 1.5 percent of its NDPI revenues in 2007, this amount rose to 11 percent by 2014.[46] However, the overall impact on the federal budget was insignificant. In fact, both in absolute and relative terms, the importance of oil revenues in the budget continued to rise through 2014 (see chapter 5). Furthermore, even with the tax relief, Russia's oil sector overall remained among the highest taxed in the world.[47] The Russian government remained resolute about avoiding any significant tax breaks for the relatively mature brownfields, which continued to account for most of the country's oil output.

How Did the Russian Government Win the Contest over the Oil Rents?

Within a few years of his ascent to power, President Putin was able to entirely transform taxation of the oil sector. This went far beyond a few revisions to existing tax rules. It began with the creation of a new tax regime and, from there, the state kept raising the tax burden on the oil companies, managing to capture an overwhelming share of the oil rents by 2004–5. Determined to hold to this approach, the Russian government became the biggest winner of the oil boom during the 2000s and beyond. What made such a victory for the state possible? Why was the oil sector unable to continue business as usual and keep the bulk of the rents it generated? As previous efforts to collect more rents from oil companies had failed, what was different this time for the Russian government?

Few studies have attempted to examine the underlying causes behind Russia's oil tax transformation.[48] In general, studies on taxation of Russia's oil sector have been rather technical in nature, dedicated primarily to the implications of oil tax reforms for the sector's investments and production.[49] Here I explore how the Russian government won the battle over the oil rents in several parts. I start by illustrating that the oil sector, the biggest beneficiary of Russia's oil wealth by the end of the 1990s, faced a largely untenable status quo. This led to widespread dissatisfaction not seen in any other sector of the economy – a point that has been widely overlooked. I examine how Putin enjoyed a growing "coalition of discontent" directed at the oil companies. Then, I illustrate in detail the upsurge in executive power and how it helped Russia transform its tax model for the oil sector. This process involved a cohesive executive determined to take action, along with the gradual weakening of other institutional veto players. Finally, I provide a summary assessment of the new tax model in terms of its overall effectiveness, and also in terms of the key potential problems it introduced.

The Oil Sector's Wealth Drawing Public Ire

The oil companies emerged as the main beneficiaries of the oil rents by the end of the 1990s, a situation that did not escape the attention of the public, the media, or politicians from across the political spectrum. Even in the aftermath of the major tax overhaul of 2001, there was a common perception that the oil sector should pay much more. A poll conducted by VTsIOM towards the end of 2003 revealed that the public was most inclined to associate the oil sector, among Russia's natural resource sectors, with the need to collect more rents.[50] Another poll from the start of 2004 indicated that collecting more taxes from natural resources sectors was one of the most urgent issues the government needed to address.[51]

Sensing public concern, the Russian media seized on the country's "missed opportunities" to collect more resource rents. A content analysis of Russian print media conducted by *Kommersant-Vlast* illustrates the rising popularity of this theme. Examining the frequency of articles mentioning the term "resource rents" between 1994 and 2004, the study revealed the rather muted interest in this matter during most of the 1990s. By 1999–2000, however, there was a spike in interest, due in large part to the media's growing attention to Russia's oligarchs as winners of resource rents. A further spike in interest was recorded in 2001, the year Russia took a major step in overhauling the oil tax regime. By 2003, discussions on resource rents in Russian print media reached unprecedented levels.[52]

Politicians also took an increased interest in natural resource rents. The shifting mood was epitomized by the stark contrast in their public rhetoric between the two election cycles for the Duma in 1999 and 2003. The topic of resource rents was largely absent in political debates in 1999.[53] By 2003, as one astute observer noted, candidates for the Duma felt obliged to declare their stance on the question of rents,[54] and to outdo one another in proclaiming ever-higher amounts of oil rents awaiting collection by the state. Andrey Illarionov, serving as Putin's economic advisor during this period, warned against this growing fascination with oil rents as a means for resolving Russia's economic woes. Amid heated debates in December 2003, he jokingly noted that the idea of oil rents had gradually emerged from obscurity to "capture the minds of the majority of politicians and people."[55]

Indeed, by the early 2000s, rising oil prices and output had changed the fortunes of Russia's oil industry. Nevertheless, a high level of profitability existed in some other sectors of the economy as well.[56] Moreover, nearly all discussions about resource rents were focused on the oil sector, even though the gas sector (as well as other mineral sectors) also generated a sizable amount of rents. In fact, the terms "oil rents" and "resource rents" were used interchangeably. Discussions of oil rents were generally accompanied by specific estimates of uncollected rents along with proposals on how to make oil companies pay more. This was rarely the case with respect to rents from natural gas or other mineral resources.

There was something different about the oil sector that kept it much more in the spotlight compared with other natural resources. It was not just that it was Russia's largest source of export revenues. The entire oil rent generation model was structured in a very peculiar way. A handful of private companies controlled the entire sector and somehow had managed to capture the majority of the oil rents, leaving the smaller pieces of the pie to the state to redistribute. This nurtured public dissatisfaction. Not only was the rent generation model the "wrong" one, the "wrong" parties benefited from it. The oil tax reforms of the 1999–2001 period had significantly reversed the distribution of rents between the state and the oil companies. But this was not enough. As oil prices kept increasing and the value of Russia's oil rents swelled in 2002–4, the oil sector was even more in the spotlight, prompting demands to collect even more taxes.

It is probably fair to say that Russia's oil companies did their part to stay in the public spotlight. The non-transparent privatization deals of the 1990s had not been forgotten, and the media was keen to provide coverage of how oil majors were still engaging in transfer pricing and other means of tax avoidance during the early years of the new decade. This tarnished the image of the oil companies. Additionally, the high degree of visibility of the oilmen's wealth did not work to their advantage. Unlike in the gas sector, where bureaucrats who acquired wealth through unreported deals hid their fortunes, most oilmen did not. Since the mid-1990s, many of Russia's leading oilmen were already well known to the public as oligarchs. Few of them were shy about their wealth. The purchase of the English soccer team Chelsea in 2003 by Roman Abramovich, the then owner of the oil company Sibneft, was one of many displays of excessive wealth by Russian oilmen.[57] Generous dividends paid by oil companies were also perceived as rents the state had failed to capture.[58]

What emerged as an additional problem, prompting pressures on the oil sector to pay more, was the fuzzy nature of the concept of resource rents. Russia's Tax Code lacked a definition of "rents."[59] The Finance Ministry made an attempt to define this concept, hoping this would assist with the process of estimation.[60] Its failure to come up with a practicable definition kept the door open for arbitrary interpretations about the actual size of the oil rents. Practical difficulties in measuring rents – particularly during the early 2000s when widespread transfer pricing put a veil on the oil industry's actual costs and revenues – also contributed to estimates that were more likely to be politically motivated than based on a thorough calculation. Prior to the 2003 Duma elections, estimates for uncollected oil rents, almost never backed by methodology,[61] ranged from about 3 billion USD to nearly 100 billion USD.[62] Often, it was not clear whether estimates referred to the oil industry alone or to Russia's entire resource sector. For many Duma candidates, aware of the public's growing dissatisfaction, it seemed advantageous to remain ambiguous on the issue of excessive gains in the oil sector.

Putin's stance in these debates was noteworthy. For many years, he criticized the oil companies for not paying sufficient taxes but resisted giving an estimate of how much more the state could collect. Shortly after the December 2003 Duma elections, Putin finally uttered a figure that was below what many expected – about 3 billion USD. The Russian president warned against "exaggerated" figures and cautioned against "killing the goose with the golden egg." Russia's tax policy needed to take into account the strategic role of the oil sector in the economy, as well as its investment needs. Yet, Putin insisted that a moderate increase in taxation was still desirable, as Russian oil companies were still paying less than their counterparts around the world.[63]

Putin and the Rising "Coalition of Discontent"

As the bulk of the oil rents were captured by a handful of private oil companies, Putin faced a major distributional problem. In addressing it, he built what could be described as a "coalition of discontent," demanding oil majors to yield a larger share of their rents to the state. This coalition grew stronger over time, benefiting from the support of the public and the wider political spectrum. By 2003, there was hardly any other distributional matter in which the government could enjoy such broad support to reform. Other areas pertaining to the oil rents, such as the management of the federal budget and Russia's oil fund turned out to be much more controversial.

In large part, the support to transform taxation of the oil sector came from a widespread sense of injustice about the flow of Russia's oil rents. Putin played a major role in drawing attention to this "ongoing injustice." As noted earlier, his academic writings had already given a hint about his dissatisfaction with the dominant role of the private companies in the oil sector. It soon became obvious that he was also displeased with the way the rents were shared between these companies and the state. At a meeting with oil executives in Surgut in March 2000, while promising the oil companies more stable tax rules, Putin criticized them for underpaying their tax dues by maintaining offshore accounts.[64] He drew attention to the companies' "superprofits," one of the recurring themes in his major speeches following this meeting.[65] He kept the issue alive after the December 2003 Duma elections as well, calling for further tax hikes for the oil sector.[66] Remarkably, Putin's attention was focused only on the rents of the oil industry, not on the other resource sectors. The main culprit was clearly defined.

What also helped to build an effective coalition to raise the tax burden on oil was how this objective fit the broader economic agenda of the president and key segments of the policy-making establishment. Evidently, Putin would not be satisfied even if oil companies avoided tax minimization schemes. They needed to bear a higher tax burden to facilitate a structural shift in the Russian economy. Addressing the Federal Assembly in April 2001, the president emphasized that Russia needed to diversify its economy to reduce its dependence on natural resources. For this, other sectors of the economy required tax cuts, financed by the natural resource sectors, oil in particular.[67] This idea was widely supported within the executive branch. The team put in charge of the economy. composed of mainly so-called economic liberals (also known as "liberal reformers"), believed more tax revenues from oil would help bring about fiscal stability.[68] Others in the political spectrum, namely so-called statists, who preferred to see a more interventionist state in the economy, were even more inclined to raise the tax burden on oil and redistribute the rents to support the economy.

President Putin had an additional incentive to transform the rent distribution between the state and the oil sector: curbing the financial power of the oil oligarchs, whom he perceived as potential political threats. Many of Russia's oligarchs, such as Boris Berezovsky, were involved in the oil industry and had proven to be important players in Russian politics during the second half of the 1990s. They had facilitated Yeltsin's re-election in 1996, and the possibility that they could still wield this kind of influence remained.[69] Their interference would hardly be compatible with the growing centralization of political power under the Putin administration. But unlike state bureaucrats and enterprise managers, oil oligarchs were not so easy to replace.[70] As an oil industry insider recalls, by means of an overhaul in the taxation of the oil companies, Putin hoped to weaken a "select" group of oligarchs, first financially and then politically.[71] There was a more radical option for dealing with the oligarchs: nationalizing their companies. While Putin did go this route eventually, his initial focus was on fundamentally changing the oil tax regime.

A "coalition of discontent" helped Putin's administration to transform its tax relations with the oil industry, but this coalition emerged only gradually. To pass major pieces of legislation overturning the existing tax regime for oil, the Russian government needed the backing of the legislature. Such support was still absent when Putin started confronting the oil sector as the new prime minister. Nor did the new Duma give Putin unconditional support after the 1999 elections. Thus, Putin's first measures to raise taxes from the oil sector were accomplished through government decrees altering the export duty rates on oil.[72] These were urgent measures that allowed the government to pay pensions and meet other pressing commitments.[73] They were not yet a product of broader political discourse. It was still far from obvious whether and how the government would proceed with respect to reforming the oil tax regime. By 2001, the year in which the NDPI was introduced, public attention had just started to turn on the oil sector's "excessive" gains. It was not until late 2003, however, and particularly after the new Duma elections, that Putin enjoyed the backing of a wide coalition determined to transform how the oil sector shared its rents with the state.

Widespread discontent with the oil companies' gains was a boon for Putin, but hardly sufficient to effectively transform rent collection. The oil sector continued to benefit from some support both within the executive and the legislature. It was determined to continue business as usual, engaging in political duels with the government to defend its rents. The discontent did help to build greater cohesion within the executive. Yet, it was Putin's further efforts to streamline the executive and the weakening of Russia's other veto players that ultimately helped turn discontent into action and fundamentally change the way Russia collected rents from the oil sector.

The Makeover of the Executive Branch in Charge of Oil Tax Reforms

Putin inherited a highly diffuse institutional structure in terms of decision-making on taxation of the oil sector. This diffusion had multiple dimensions. The constitution granted all four of Russia's institutional players some authority to affect tax policy, giving oil companies plenty of access points through which to channel their demands. The government had the power to issue decrees, while both chambers of the legislature could propose federal legislation on taxation that could override government decrees. Subnational governments and legislatures were also authorized to enact legislation pertaining to the regional component of various taxes in the oil sector.

The second dimension of diffusion in the decision-making process was located within the executive branch itself. Here there were multiple agencies in charge of collecting taxes and a number of institutions involved in tax policy and tax reforms for the oil sector. Along with the Finance Ministry, which was responsible for the revenue and the expenditure side of the federal budget, there were three additional bodies involved in tax collection: the Ministry of Taxes and Collections,[74] the State Customs Service,[75] and the Federal Service of the Tax Police as the coercive arm of the state. Decision-making on tax policy and reform was even more diffuse. The crucial role the oil sector played in the Russian economy invited institutional infighting. Throughout the 1990s, distinct ministries and the Presidential Administration came up with competing proposals for tax reform. Several other agencies were also capable of making decisions that affected the oil companies' revenue flows. For instance, the Interdepartmental Commission on Protective Measures in Trade and Tariff Policy was put in charge of determining export duties following its reinstatement in February 1999. Another interdepartmental commission, set up in 1995, regulated oil companies' quarterly access to pipelines and terminals, largely determining the size of their export revenues.

On paper, this institutional diffusion within the executive branch persisted throughout Putin's first presidency. In 2004, however, the number of ministries was cut from 23 to 17. This was a major administrative shake-up that helped to limit diffusion.[76] Accompanying this shakeup was further consolidation of decision-making on taxation within the Finance Ministry, which absorbed many of the tax functions of other ministries.[77]

And yet, Putin had already secured a more cohesive executive on taxation in his first year as president. The cohesion was reflected in the well-coordinated stance of key ministers on issues related to taxation of the oil sector. They were finally speaking with one voice, and those who opted to diverge had little to no impact. How did this turnaround transpire?

At the very start of his first presidential term, in May 2000, Putin reshuffled the cabinet and entrusted key portfolios related to the oil industry to a "trio" of ministers: Alexei Kudrin, German Gref, and Viktor Khristenko. Within this trio, Alexei Kudrin's role was critical. He became deputy prime minister in charge of the economy and finances as well as finance minister, which gave him a leading position on fiscal matters.[78] Based on the powers vested in him, Kudrin became the de facto first deputy prime minister, though this title had been officially eliminated.[79] He acquired one additional position that was crucial for the oil sector: as of June 2000 he became the chair of the influential Interdepart-mental Commission on Protective Measures in Trade and Tariff Policy.[80]

German Gref, who had been working on a new economic program for Rus-sia, was assigned to head the newly created Ministry of Economic Development and Trade (MEDT). He was assigned to chart and oversee Russia's new eco-nomic strategy. His ministry was delegated a leading role in developing reform proposals, including ones related to fiscal issues.

Viktor Khristenko, whom Putin appointed as deputy prime minister in charge of energy and natural resources was the other key personality in this trio. He had occupied critical positions in charge of Russia's fiscal policy in the past and now his role was substantially enhanced.[81] Khristenko acquired direct control over a major part of the portfolio of the Ministry of Energy. In Novem-ber 2000, he was authorized to head the commission regulating the access of oil companies to pipelines and terminals. Henceforth, this entity was known as the "Khristenko Commission."[82]

A major consequence of the government reorganization of 2000 was the weakened role of the Ministry of Energy.[83] This ministry had traditionally been allied with the oil companies, representing their interests in intra-government meetings. Under Minister Viktor Kalyuzhny, whom Putin replaced with Alex-ander Gavrin, the ministry had vigorously lobbied against a tax raise on the oil sector.[84] Now, the ministry was transformed into a "second-rank" entity on issues relevant to the oil sector. Some key duties it retained, such as managing potential fuel crises in the winter and mandating oil companies to supply the domestic market, were a source of recurring tensions with oil majors. Gavrin soon lost his job amid accusations that he had mismanaged these tasks. In evi-dence of the ministry's reduced significance, his position remained vacant for months.[85] His successor, Igor Yusufov, fought hard to regain the ministry's lost influence, requesting the president's help, but to no avail.[86] It was not until 2004 that the ministry regained part of its portfolio, including the authority to regu-late oil companies' access to pipelines.[87] Yet, Khristenko's leading role was pre-served, as he was appointed to head the revamped ministry.[88]

The trio reflected an important choice on Putin's behalf. Shortly before the cabinet reshuffle, Putin had formed an alliance within the KPRF in the Duma, when Unity, the party of power, and KPRF had split the most significant com-mittee leaderships. He did not opt for a similar "compromise" when appointing the new cabinet. Instead, he chose to empower personalities who were known as "liberal reformists," though their adherence to the reform agenda was far from strict. Kudrin, Gref, and Khristenko exhibited some differences with respect to economic policies and reform but shared the view that the oil sector received an excessive portion of rents and that this needed to change.

Another aspect of Putin's choice of ministers proved quite important. The trio was capable of appearing as a voice of reason and moderation amid growing discontent with the oil industry's "excessive" rents,[89] catching the oilmen off guard. In 1999 and 2000, when the first tax hikes occurred, oil companies could not have imagined how far this would go within only a few years.[90] After all, Putin had entrusted a few "liberal reformers" to oversee fiscal issues that could affect the oil sector. Indeed, Kudrin, Gref, and Khristenko did not subscribe to the so-called statist views favoring a large-scale direct redistribution of the government's oil revenues in order to support other sectors and social welfare programs. Such views were correlated with more "radical" estimates about the size of uncollected rents from the oil sector. The trio resisted more radical proposals for a tax hike on the oil majors, and Putin took their side.

Yet, the trio made it clear that they were intent on collecting more from the oil industry. Kudrin and Gref warned against the "Dutch Disease" if Russia failed to improve taxation on oil.[91] Khristenko also hoped for a higher tax burden on oil to compensate for broader tax cuts in the economy.[92] Amid rising oil prices, the trio did not indicate how far the government could increase the taxes without hurting the oil sector. By 2003, the public mood had overwhelmingly shifted against the oil companies, which made setting a particular ceiling politically difficult. The result was the further calibration of tax rates on oil in 2004, shifting the distribution of rents decidedly in the government's favor.

The trio's decisive role, especially Kudrin's lead, was evident in regard to two major facets of the oil tax reform: the growing importance of export duties and the emergence of the NDPI as a key tax instrument. In the case of export duties, Kudrin effectively used his authority as the head of the Interdepartmental Commission on Protective Measures in Trade and Tariff Policy. He and his deputy, Sergey Shatalov, prepared proposals to revise the oil export duties and led the commission's meetings. In a decisive manner, they raised the duties several times in 2000 and 2001. Gref and Khristenko, also members of the commission, lent their support.[93]

Yet, raising the export duty was not a smooth process, as oil companies decided to resist. They were alarmed by the ever-changing rules and rates. Having found no meaningful support within the executive branch, oil companies had a partial victory within the Duma. In February 2002, an amendment to the Law on Customs Tariffs granted the legislature the right to set a scale determining the maximum amount of duty to be charged at corresponding oil prices.[94] Oil companies had also managed to instill some pessimism regarding the future of oil prices.[95] Hence the new scale was not well suited to deal with the forthcoming price surge. This was doomed to change, however, with the growing "coalition of discontent" demanding more from the oil sector. In April 2004, the law was fundamentally revised, with the Duma's approval, allowing the commission to set much steeper rates for the export duty.[96]

The Finance Ministry took on a central role in the introduction of the NDPI as well. A working group was formed in 2001 to coordinate a number of proposals from different parts of the government. The Ministry of Natural Resources, in particular, fought vigorously to maintain the existing three taxes that the NDPI was set to replace.[97] In the end, it was Shatalov's draft that formed the basis for discussions. The Finance Ministry was determined to eliminate opportunities for the oil sector to cheat and underpay, especially through transfer pricing. Interestingly, its initial draft proposed taking into account the different geological and economic conditions of Russia's oil fields, and taxing them accordingly.[98] Ministry officials soon revised their approach, however, recognizing that administering such a tax would be difficult and could perpetuate the oil majors' ingenious ability to create new loopholes.[99] Its revised draft set the NDPI as essentially a simplified tax, treating all fields the same, irrespective of their costs, but also leaving no room for tax minimization. Gref strongly supported this version of the tax, emphasizing its benefits from an administrative standpoint.[100] Several oil majors led by Yukos also lobbied for this simpler approach to the NDPI, knowing that it would benefit their relatively newer and lower-cost fields.[101] Other oil majors, such as Surgutneftegaz and Tatneft, were clearly opposed to this proposal.[102] The Duma approved the draft, with only minor revisions, effective in 2002.[103] With rising oil prices in 2002 and 2003, the Finance Ministry pushed for steeper rates for the NDPI. It had agreed to cut several other taxes for the overall economy, and needed the oil sector to compensate for the loss.[104] Thus, the scale for the NDPI was further revised by 2004, with the Duma's approval.

The Finance Ministry had Khristenko as an important ally during these tax initiatives. Unlike past ministers with his portfolio, he did not defend the oil sector against the tax hikes. Additionally, he leveraged his role in the commission regulating access to oil pipelines and terminals by offering oil majors additional export quotas as a "sweetener" amid growing tax pressure.[105]

To improve the effectiveness of the tax measures, Kudrin also benefited from the state's coercive resources. He created a new entity within the ministry called the Committee on Financial Monitoring. Tasked to investigate money laundering mainly, it granted the ministry valuable information on the flow of oil money.[106] Along with these investigations came the tax raids by the Federal Tax Police on the offices of the oil majors. Such raids were not new for Russia. Now they happened in the context of major tax reform initiatives, granting the government additional leverage.

By 2004, tax collection in the oil sector fundamentally shifted in the government's favor. Putin confidently launched a new administrative reform and reshuffled the cabinet. Prime Minister Kasyanov, who had often come to the defense of the oil industry but avoided challenging Putin with respect to taxation in the oil sector, was replaced by Mikhail Fradkov, the head of the Federal Tax Police.[107] The trio was preserved. Gref, Kudrin, and Khristenko emerged with expanded portfolios in the new cabinet. For the oil sector, however, rising concerns about its future soon shifted the mood in favor of some tax relief. Kudrin faced a new conundrum: how to maintain the high tax burden while simultaneously encouraging the oil sector's growth.

The Duma's Fight for Influence and Its Waning Role as a Veto Player

During the first years of Putin's presidency, the Duma remained a significant player in shaping tax policy reform. The constitution had granted it the power to block a government-sponsored bill, to revise it, or propose its own version. This power could be exercised as long as deputies could align and form a majority (226 seats) when voting on a bill. Despite the relatively successful showing of pro-Kremlin parties at the 1999 Duma elections, they still fell short of the necessary 226 seats. To get the Duma's consent, the government needed to build coalitions around its policy agenda.

The Duma's challenge to the government's oil tax reform agenda came from two directions. A group of deputies, described by its critics in the Duma as "populists,"[108] found the government's tax approach insufficient, and demanded a harsher tax hike on the oil sector. These deputies belonged predominantly to left-wing factions (the KPRF and APR during the Third Duma, and the KPRF and Rodina during the Fourth Duma) and to the group of Independents.

Another group, which could be labeled as the "restrainers," worked to limit the scope of the tax increase on the oil sector. Their support for the government was conditional on granting certain concessions to the oil companies. Some members of this group were likely concerned by the potential impact of "excessive" taxation on the oil sector. Others, however, had more personal interests – they were associated with the oil industry as former employers, shareholders, or lobbyists. According to the Center for Current Politics in Russia, the oil sector enjoyed its peak in terms of the number of allied deputies during the Third Duma. These deputies were predominantly based in Yabloko, SPS, and to some extent in Unity. Yukos, Sibneft, TNK, and Lukoil, often referred to as the "Gang of Four," were the best-represented oil majors in the Duma.[109]

To help demonstrate how the Duma voted and to assess the extent of the influence exercised by the "populists" and "restrainers," table 4.3 outlines the voting results on five pieces of legislation on taxing the oil sector. Among the four legislative proposals examined under the Third Duma, the government proposed the first two, while the latter two came at the initiative of the opposition parties. The fifth legislative proposal examined here was brought forward by the government under the new Duma in 2004.

It seems the Russian government benefited from the constant presence of a majority congruent with its position: its proposals were approved while those coming from the opposition were rejected. Unity/United Russia, People's Deputies, and OVR provided nearly unanimous support. Depending on the bill in

Table 4.3. Votes by the Duma on Key Bills with Implications for the Oil Sector's Tax Burden*

	Law introducing the NDPI (2nd reading)	Law on the Revision of Part Two of Tax Code, which included the Yukos Amendment (final reading)	Ishtenko and Co.'s proposal for establishing state-owned trading companies in charge of oil exports (as a means to curb tax minimization)	Proposal for introducing differentiated NDPI across oil fields. (Proposed Amendment No. 56)	Proposal for an increase in the NDPI and export taxes (final reading)
Date	6 July 2001	24 May 2002	13 June 2002	20 June 2003	23 April 2004
Third Duma					
Unity	98	96	0	17	
People's Deputies	91	98	16	13	
Russia's Regions	47	79	23	87	
Fatherland All Russia (OVR)	86	100	6	17	
Union of Right Forces (SPS)	92	56	0	3	
Yabloko	94	94	0	65	
KPRF	1	76	98	84	
APR	0	65	98	86	
LDPR	100	92	17	0	
Independents	47	50	21	38	
Total votes (yes)	**266**	**369**	**154**	**198**	

Fourth Duma

United Russia	89
Rodina	70
LDPR	100
KPRF	94
Independents	80
Total votes (yes)	**395**

* Numbers indicate the percentage of each faction voting "yes."

Source: Accessed via www.duma-digest.ru (accessed January 2009).

question, the executive formed alliances with SPS, Yabloko, and LDPR. It also helped that the position of the "populists" and the "restrainers" were often diametrically opposed. Otherwise, in theory they held enough seats to oppose the executive. The low degree of cohesion among independents worked in the government's favor as well, as it secured a few additional votes each time. Often divided on issues with regional implications, deputies from Russia's Regions also let the government gain more votes.

The "populists" had limited power to affect the voting outcome on oil tax reform. Despite the fairly high degree of cohesion within KPRF and APR these two parties lacked the necessary majority. A few votes coming from independent deputies did not suffice. They came closest to victory when pushing for an amendment that would allow for the differentiation of the NDPI tax across Russia's oil fields. This proposal had secured some support from Russia's Regions and Yabloko (table 4.3).

Yet, the "populists" were not irrelevant. After all, the tax burden on the oil sector kept rising, just not as high as they hoped for. Other than voting, they had additional means to make their voices heard. They participated actively at key Duma committees, persistently bringing the issue of taxation to the floor. Sergey Glazev, a deputy from the KPRF, was particularly unyielding in his critique of Kudrin.[110] At the request of the "populists," Kudrin and Gref had to repeatedly appear at a "government hour" at the Duma to defend the government's position. Other parties in the Duma also felt the need to adjust their position, not least to prevent the monopolization of resource rents as a policy issue by the populists. By 2003, United Russia shifted its attention to the uncollected resource rents, debating this theme actively in the legislature, and even sponsoring a nationwide forum to discuss it prior to the 2003 Duma elections.[111] Even SPS and Yabloko, traditionally allied with the oil companies, came to the point of recognizing the presence of sizable uncollected oil rents.[112] Andrey Illarionov blamed them for abandoning "liberalism" and legitimizing the "populist" ideas of the left-wing opposition.[113]

Though Russia's oil tax was raised consistently during Putin's first term as president, there is considerable evidence that "restrainers" were also influential under the Third Duma. Deputies from this camp were actively involved in various Duma committees, fighting to shape oil tax reform. The Budget and Tax Committee in particular proactively discussed and revised government-sponsored bills or own drafts. Deputies with ties to the oil sector occupied key roles in these committees. For example, Vladimir Dubov, one of Yukos's main shareholders (and member of OVR) headed the Tax Subcommittee within this committee. The head of the committee itself was Alexander Zhukov (member of Russia's Regions), who was an outspoken defender of the oil companies against "excessive" taxation.[114] Additionally, the "restrainers" were part of the "Energy of Russia" faction established to defend the interests of the entire energy sector during the Third Duma. It was headed by former prime minister Viktor Chernomyrdin, and had over a hundred deputies. Yet, the faction's effectiveness remained somewhat constrained by its overly broad agenda and the dominant role of deputies from pro-government parties who abstained from opposing the Kremlin.[115]

The "restrainers" recorded a number of victories. When the draft legislation introducing the NDPI reached the Duma in May 2001, Dubov lobbied vigorously in Yukos's favor, arguing against proposed revisions that would have differentiated the tax across oil fields. The base rate of the tax was also eventually reduced in favor of the oil sector. Meanwhile, the Duma secured some authority in the determination of export duties in exchange for supporting the NDPI bill.[116] During the following year, the "restrainers" had two consecutive victories. First, they managed to set an upper limit for export duties levied on petroleum products.[117] Dubov's involvement was reportedly critical in passing this bill, dubbed as the "Yukos Amendment," through the Duma.[118] During the following months, the "restrainers," aligned with pro-Kremlin parties, successfully defeated a "populist" proposal led by independent Duma deputy Yevgeny Ishtenko. The proposal called for granting the exclusive right for exports to state-owned trade companies as a means to curb tax minimization efforts.[119] The interests of the oil sector and the government coincided once more in 2003, when the opposition made another attempt to amend the tax law and differentiate the NDPI according to the geology and the economics of the fields. Deputy Finance Minister Shatalov's warnings that the proposed measure would foster corruption resonated well with the leading oil majors defending the status quo.[120]

Yet, the "restrainers" experienced a major setback following the eruption of the Yukos Affair. After the arrest of Khodorkovsky, few deputies would choose to openly defend the oil companies' interests. Shortly before the Duma elections in December 2003, President Putin requested the Duma's support to raise the tax pressure on the oil sector. Deputies voted nearly unanimously to revoke the "Yukos Amendment" and approved new measures further restricting the oil sector's opportunities to engage in transfer pricing.[121] Another setback was Dubov's decision to flee Russia following Khodorkovsky's imprisonment. He was excluded from the list of Duma candidates and was soon charged with tax fraud and other crimes.[122]

An even bigger setback, however, came in the wake of the 2003 Duma elections. Yabloko and SPS were no longer in the Duma. Rodina, a new faction led by Sergey Glazev, appeared as the biggest political surprise of the election, managing to pass the 5 percent election threshold. Glazev's single most important campaign promise had been to raise more revenues from the oil sector. There were still a few deputies with ties to the oil sector – at least seventeen of them in United Russia.[123] But none of them were as forthcoming in continuing to defend the oil sector. When the Fourth Duma voted for a major tax hike on the oil sector in April 2004, the government finally enjoyed overwhelming support, with no need for lengthy bargaining with deputies. Henceforth, the Duma was no longer an effective veto player in further reforming taxation of the oil sector.

The Fading Role of the Federation Council and Regional Governments

Many of the fights on oil tax reform took place in the Duma, where deputies representing regions could defend their interest. Regions had additional options to affect oil tax policy and even exercise some veto power. At least until the resounding victory of United Russia in the 2007 Duma elections, the executive lacked the necessary (300) votes in the lower chamber to override a potential veto by the Federation Council. Regional governments also maintained some levers to frustrate the federal government's tax policies. Throughout the 1990s, they had colluded with oil companies and let them pay less tax, based on mutual agreements.[124] At the start of Putin's presidency, regions still had the option to grant various forms of tax relief to oil companies at the expense of the federal government. They still controlled many seats in regional legislatures and it was common for governors, their family members, and deputies in regions to sit on the boards of oil companies.[125]

Following Putin's arrival at the Kremlin, both the Federation Council and regional governments experienced a rapid decline in their ability to shape oil tax policy. The weakened role of the upper chamber was apparent in how it voted (table 4.4).[126] It supported the introduction of the NDPI even though this tax bill proposed to considerably reduce the amount of oil revenues directly flowing to regional coffers. Also, the upper chamber never came up with any significant alternative oil tax proposals during these years of fundamental tax reform.

The failure of the Federation Council to act as a veto player was in large part due to the centralization measures Putin launched early in his first term. Evidently, the president had gained significant leverage to affect their votes. However, additional factors were also in play. First, when tax bills related to the oil sector reached the upper chamber, they were already part of a larger reform package. If deputies representing regional or oil sector interests had major objections to any parts of the package, they would have already relayed them during deliberations within the Duma. Deputies from the upper chamber were not willing to appear as opponents to a comprehensive reform package that had already been approved by the Duma.

Second, some of the tax proposals were designed in a way that left little incentive for collective action among regional representatives. This affected deputies in both chambers as well as regional governors. In theory, Russia's many mineral resource-rich regions could join forces on key legislative acts.[127] However,

Table 4.4. Voting Results in the Federation Council

	Date	Yes	No	Abstain
Law on the Revision of Part Two of Tax Code (1)	7/20/01	135	10	6
Law on the Revision of Part Two of Tax Code (2)	5/29/02	143	0	7
Law on the Revision of Law on Customs and Part Two of Tax Code (3)	4/28/04	132	0	1

(1) This package of laws included the introduction of the NDPI, which replaced royalty, geological tax, and excise tax on crude.
(2) This package included the "Yukos amendment."
(3) This package included an increase in the rate of export duties on crude oil and in the base rate of NDPI.

Source: Compiled from Russia's Federation Council (www.council.gov.ru)

the NDPI bill set different rates for distinct types of mineral resources. Oil was hit particularly hard by this tax, while gas and metals continued to enjoy lower rates.[128] Regions rich in mineral resources other than hydrocarbons were also happy that they were allowed to keep a much higher share of the NDPI revenues collected from such resources.[129] Even oil-rich regions were not treated uniformly and this disparity weakened the prospects for an effective alliance based on regional interests.

Two additional developments helped to sideline regional governors with respect to taxation of the oil sector. If they had the ability to frustrate or block the successful implementation of a new tax initiative in the past, they lost this ability in the aftermath of the tax overhaul that took place between 1999 and 2001. The Russian government embarked on a successful process of fiscal centralization for oil revenues. Thus, export duties on oil were designed to accrue exclusively to the federal budget. Likewise, the NDPI replaced three oil-sector specific taxes that had previously accrued heavily to regional budgets.[130] Both of these new tax instruments left regional authorities with no room to play by different rules. Regions were left with some limited discretion on the profit tax,[131] but this tax instrument became increasingly trivial in the overall flow of oil rents. Henceforth, if there was to be any substantial preferential tax relief for oil companies, the decision would have to be made within the federal executive.

Russia's regional governments received another blow when the Putin administration launched a reform of the Subsoil Law. This law, dating back to the early 1990s, had introduced the "two keys principle" which required the Ministry of Natural Resources to secure the consent of regional authorities when granting and suspending a license for developing mineral resources. This had become a source of leverage for regional governors, with respect to both the federal government and oil companies. In 2002, the deputy head of the Presidential Administration, Dmitry Kozak, prepared a bill that proposed eliminating the "two keys principle."[132] The bill was presented as part of a broader legislative package and was approved by both chambers in August 2004.[133] Its approval removed this crucial veto power at the disposal of regional governors.[134]

Assessing Putin's New Tax Regime

By the start of his second presidential term, Putin had finally managed to transform the way the state and the oil industry shared the rents. The government had succeeded in establishing a fundamentally new tax model. By 2004, the state was able to capture over three-quarters of the total rents in the oil sector (see table 4.2). Were oil prices to climb higher, the government was guaranteed to capture about 90 percent of the extra rents.[135] This was a resounding success for the state in asserting its control over the oil industry's windfalls.

Clearly, the upsurge in executive power helped to secure a successful outcome. The fading role of veto players (outside the executive) weakened the ability of oil companies to shape the evolving tax policy. The "coalition of discontent" helped to bring together the different veto players while enhancing cohesion within the executive with respect to oil tax reform. It is notable that the process of reforming the oil tax was accomplished largely through formal channels, namely through legislative approval.[136] The reform also benefited from the rather technical nature of taxation. Unlike practices related to the state's budgetary policies, the oil tax reform remained within the domain of only a few players within the executive branch. Putin's determined efforts to streamline the executive between 2000 and 2004 further helped to enhance cohesion.

Arguably, the lack of extensive foreign involvement in Russia's oil industry also facilitated the tax overhaul. The limited extent of special tax arrangements with foreign players, such as PSAs, ensured that tax reform could progress without reneging on agreements binding the state's hands.

There are a few additional aspects to consider with respect to this new oil tax regime. Typically, tax regimes for the oil industry vary in three dimensions: simplicity, flexibility, and stability.[137] Russia's new tax regime undoubtedly brought simplicity. It was based on a few clearly accountable criteria to levy taxes on the oil companies, necessitating a minimal administrative capacity in ensuring that companies complied. Oil majors could also worry less about an arbitrary approach by the state in collecting their tax dues.

Simplicity, however, typically comes at the expense of flexibility. Flexibility refers to the tax regime's ability to capture additional resource rents that are a product of improvements in the economics of a project, without making some fields unprofitable.[138] Putin's new tax model was too rigid to account for costs and profitability in the oil industry as it made no distinction across fields. It left little incentive for the oil companies to invest in relatively costly fields, raising questions about Russia's ability to invest in new oil fields and generate rents.

In terms of stability, there are two ways to look at Russia's oil tax regime. One is to examine stability in terms of how often tax rules were altered. In this respect, the new tax model was a fairly unstable one. Rules about export duties after 1999, and the NDPI after 2001, were subject to numerous revisions, each time making the tax burden on the oil companies higher at a given oil price. Yet, there was a high degree of stability in terms of the government's policy objectives and the actual winner of the evolving tax model. From the very start, the government was determined to acquire the majority of the oil windfalls. Each tax revision moved the government into this direction. The oil industry had only partial success in resisting – the Yukos Amendment was one of its few victories. Overall, there was no backtracking by the Russian government in its fundamental objective to become and remain the main beneficiary of Russia's booming oil windfalls.

Reforming the New Oil Tax Regime: A Piecemeal Approach and an Unsettled Policy

Despite its success in capturing rents, further reform of the tax regime was imminent. The model was too rigid to function well for long. Parts of the oil industry remained dissatisfied with the tax regime and were calling for change. While Yukos, one of the chief proponents and beneficiaries of the current tax regime, was no longer in a position to shape tax policy after Khodorkovsky's arrest, the oil sector's complaints were getting louder. Soon, rounds of discussions were resumed between the Russian government and oil sector representatives on how to further reform the tax regime. The Russian leadership had to make some major choices.

The government's subsequent approach had several key features. First, Russia was fairly quick in finding a solution: by 2006 the government had developed its policy response, which in retrospect has helped the oil sector maintain growth. Second, the Russian leadership adopted a highly cautious approach, one that, while helping the oil sector, would not risk jeopardizing state revenues. It abstained from a new tax overhaul, instead favoring ad hoc tax relief measures. Third, this approach remained intact throughout the following decade. Finally, the government soon demonstrated that it was not strictly bound by the new rules it set. Tax relief measures could be rolled back as easily as they had been brought in. What could explain the government's approach? Why did it prefer ad hoc solutions, and for so long? And why did it not remain committed to the rules it set?

The Victory of the Piecemeal approach over Another Tax Overhaul

Renewed discussions around reform of the oil tax regime began in 2004 in a political context that was quite distinct from the one that had brought the major overhaul between 1999 and 2001. After Putin's first term as president, Russia's executive branch no longer faced veto players capable of shaping the reform process. The discourse moved almost exclusively within the executive branch and remained there henceforth.

Yet, while the executive branch was more powerful than ever, its cohesion on the oil tax regime started to break down. The government's success in gaining an overwhelming share of the oil rents created growing differences within the Kudrin–Gref–Khristenko trio once the oil industry's pleas for help grew louder. Some of the earliest signs of disagreement emerged in 2004 and concerned whether and how the government should take into account the variable economic attributes of Russia's fields. For Kudrin, maintaining the high tax burden on oil remained a priority. Gref, however, soon started warning that an excessive level of taxation would harm the performance of the oil sector.[139] The revamped Ministry of Energy and Industry, led by Khristenko, joined such calls, increasingly willing to voice the oil industry's pleas. Amid mounting signs of difficulties in the oil sector in 2005, the awareness that the state needed to experiment with new tax initiatives was spreading within the government.[140] Proposals abounded, including from Gref's ministry, whose officials called for a more comprehensive approach to reforming the oil tax in a way that would strengthen the connection between what companies paid and their costs and profitability.[141] Recent changes in the rent generation model were also significant. Soon after its acquisition of Yukos, state-owned Rosneft became active in calling for tax relief for the oil sector. The company's chief, Igor Sechin, continued to occupy the position of deputy head of the Presidential Administration through 2008. This gave him a key role in the discourse within the executive branch. Reportedly Sechin emerged as a major advocate for finding a solution to the oil industry's difficulties with a highly rigid tax regime.[142]

In the end, the Russian executive proved it could act decisively and initiate a much-needed reform. What helped the state once again was the broad support within the executive to continue with oil tax reform. No government agency opposed the need for reform. Instead, members of the executive diverged on the proposed path.

Ultimately, it was the Finance Ministry that won this new battle in guiding the reform process. Minister Kudrin had come to recognize that some reform was indeed necessary, so revisiting the tax model was not out of the question. However, the ministry agreed to experiment with new measures only under its strict scrutiny. There would not be a new overhaul of the oil tax regime: export duties and the NDPI would continue to be the sector's two most critical taxes.

Instead, effective in 2007, a handful of carefully designated fields would be allowed to enjoy limited tax relief dubbed as "tax holidays." The cabinet upheld the ministry's position.[143]

This was not a one-time victory. After this initial step for reform, the Finance Ministry maintained its position as the central player on oil tax policy, while the role of other key agencies, such as the MEDT and the Ministry of Energy, faded over time.[144] Kudrin and his successor after 2011 continued to guide and set the limits of oil tax reform. The Finance Ministry remained consistent in its approach. It responded to further demands for reform by granting new forms of tax holidays for a growing number of oil fields, presumed to be operating at higher costs. However, it abstained from experimenting with more fundamental reform measures that would abandon the existing setup of the tax regime.[145] While the ministry agreed to expand the scope of fields benefiting from tax relief, it remained opposed to spreading them to most of Russia's so-called brownfields. According to an industry report, most of them developed in the 1970s and 1980s were "famously cheap" to develop and maintain, serving as "cash cows" for Russian oil majors.[146] The Finance Ministry remained focused on getting as much revenue for the state as it could from these fields, prompting oil majors to put serious effort into improving their efficiency.[147]

The Finance Ministry's conservative stance was driven largely by its mission within the Russian government. For a government agency in charge of fiscal discipline, experimenting with a more comprehensive set of tax reforms bore some heavy risks. As the Russian federal budget became even more dependent on oil revenues over time, the potential cost of a failed experiment grew.[148] By adopting ad hoc tax relief measures, Russia preserved the tax regime that had proven exceptionally successful in capturing rents, while it retained its ability to help the oil sector. Putin characteristically kept his distance from the discourse on the technocratic details of the evolving tax reform. Yet, in line with the position of the Finance Ministry, he consistently warned against tinkering with the tax model in a way that could reopen opportunities for the oil companies to underpay taxes.[149]

Opting for ad hoc solutions instead of a major tax overhaul offered the Finance Ministry additional advantages. The ministry occupied the central position in managing the tax holidays. Ministry officials, in direct negotiations with oil companies, were key to determining the parameters and the duration of the tax relief. They could conduct periodic reviews and propose whether to renew or terminate a particular tax holiday. Even a complete rollback of a particular form of tax relief was not out of the question if the ministry deemed it to be excessive.[150] By contrast, a potentially more comprehensive tax reform bore some risks for the Finance Ministry. Its central position in oil tax policy could be challenged, as could the flexibility accompanying its ad hoc approach.[151]

The primacy of the Finance Ministry in charting the path of further oil tax reform, and the preference for ad hoc solutions, could be interpreted as going along with the broader tendencies in the management of the Russian economy. The outcome empowered the state in its interactions with the oil sector, reflecting the creeping rise of an interventionist state in the economy after the middle of the decade (2000s). The victory of ad hoc tax relief as a solution, versus another tax overhaul that could have introduced a built-in flexibility in dealing with oil companies, perpetuated the state's ability to make further changes at will.

The Finance Ministry's unwavering defense of the existing tax model also reflected its limitations in administrative capacity. In more sophisticated tax regimes that target costs and profitability of oil companies, government agencies need the capacity to monitor such parameters. Russia never developed such capabilities. It failed to do so during the 1990s when the tax model was more inclined to take into account the cost and profitability of oil fields. It faced no necessity to develop such capacity under the tax regime brought in in the early 2000s. The ministry remained overwhelmingly reliant on data provided by oil companies to monitor their key parameters.[152] Owing to the convenience derived from the tax model's simplicity, according to one oil industry insider, "the Finance Ministry had been intent to continue with the current tax regime as long as it could."[153] In the meantime, beneath the surface, the ministry's position exposed its continuous lack of trust in the oil industry's willingness to pay its dues.[154] Ministry officials have worried that if oil companies were allowed to pay in accordance with their costs and profits, they could still find ways to artificially inflate these costs and underreport profits, as they did in the 1990s.

The weak administrative capacity of the Finance Ministry has also been arguably the product of the powerful role the ministry has occupied in the collection of Russia's oil tax revenues. Following the tax overhaul of the early 2000s, other ministries and agencies were sidelined from this process. In many oil-rich countries it has been common to entrust the authority of tax collection to multiple agencies. Ministries in charge of energy and mineral resources have typically been able to leverage their technical expertise in regulating and auditing resource-developing companies. In some cases, a ministry of economic development has also been assigned tax duties. Such a division of labor has helped to complement but also counterbalance an overly powerful finance ministry.[155]

A Tax Policy in Flux

Russia's oil companies were pleased to receive the tax breaks, but this help only went part of the way in meeting their expectations. Oil producers were hoping not just for lower tax rates for costlier fields but for more stability in the tax rules. Instead, they got a policy that appeared to be largely unsettled. As the share of oil fields qualifying for tax relief grew, so did the uncertainty about these rules. Tax relief measures could easily be rolled back. What could explain this outcome?

Since the introduction of the tax holidays in 2007, Russia's oil sector has faced frequent changes in tax legislation, including the rollback of some of its hard-earned tax breaks. In 2009 and 2011 alone, legislation governing export duties and the NDPI was revised 12 times and 16 times, respectively.[156] The Russian government was open to giving the oil companies some tax breaks. Yet, it was determined to keep its share of the oil rents, and would not hesitate to reverse tax relief measures when it thought they had become too generous. Changing market conditions, such as the spike in oil prices in late 2009[157] and the devaluation of the ruble in 2015,[158] prompted the government to backtrack on some of the tax holidays. The Finance Ministry made it clear that it did not wish to create a "tax paradise," even on a limited regional scale.[159] Tax relief, once acquired, could not be taken for granted.

This instability in the rules could be traced to several factors. First the dominant role of the Finance Ministry in guiding tax reform has yielded a lack of stability in the tax regime. The characteristically fiscally conservative ministry has not hesitated to alter the tax rules in order to maximize state revenues. Its desire to maintain the tax regime adopted in the early 2000s, and its opposition to a new tax overhaul, have reflected its risk-averse approach. This approach has helped to extend the life of the tax regime through ad hoc solutions, which, under the direction of the ministry, have been relatively easy to revisit and amend.

Second, the lack of stability has also been caused by the growing and rather unintended complexity of the tax model. When in 2006 the Finance Ministry first opted in favor of tax holidays as an ad hoc solution, it could have hardly conceived the extent to which they would proliferate over time. The mushrooming tax relief measures made it more difficult for the government to administer these tax holidays. Within a few years, the simplicity brought about by the tax regime laid out at the turn of the century was no longer there. Resolving the dilemma of promoting growth in the sector while not losing rents for the budget would not be an easy task in a context of a vast number of fields requiring different levels of taxation. The Finance Ministry maintained manual control by overseeing the ever-growing number of projects benefiting from tax relief. Unable to monitor each oil field, however, it became a highly cumbersome task to determine when the tax relief was too generous or too scanty. Tax rules were frequently changed to ensure the oil sector did not underpay.

In theory, oil companies could balance this weakness through collective action when dealing with the executive branch. They failed to do so, however. The rise of an autonomous and effective group of oil industrialists would have hardly been compatible with the growing concentration of power within the executive under Putin. The political and commercial atmosphere following the nationalization of Yukos, characterized by weak property rights, was not conducive to defiance of the government through independent action. Instead, what emerged was a corporatist structure of interaction between the oil sector and the government. The Ministry of Energy and the Finance Ministry regularly brought together oil company representatives to discuss reforming the oil tax regime. Oil companies provided data and feedback, but never a jointly elaborated alternative tax proposal.[160]

There were additional causes for the oil industry's failure to act collectively. Despite some major changes in ownership, Russia's rent generation model continued to be based on multiple players. As Rosneft never emerged as a typical NOC in charge of the entire oil industry, the Russian oil sector continued to enjoy a degree of competition among multiple large oil players. They remained divided on how to reform the oil tax. There was no consensus on whether to address the industry's investment concerns with a more radical and comprehensive tax overhaul or with piecemeal solutions through tax holidays for select fields. Each path to reform had its own appeal, but also brought its own risks. A major tax overhaul could finally help Russia establish a clear correspondence between an oil field's costs and its tax liability. Such a step would bring the country's tax regime in line with those of many advanced economies, such as the United Kingdom and Norway. However, oil companies also worried they could easily be accused of tax underpayment if the government found their costs too high.[161] Ad hoc tax holidays, on the other hand, seemed like a convenient solution. They lowered the tax rate for fields with high costs of production and operation. But the government had proven that such relief could be taken away.

The government's piecemeal approach to reform also weakened potential unity within the oil industry. Tax holidays enticed oil companies and distracted them from seeking an alternative and more comprehensive path to reform. Rather than choosing to lobby for tax holidays collectively, oil majors promoted their cases individually.[162] In part this had to do with differences in their resource base, particularly in terms of geology and geographic location. The resource base determined what companies considered their most urgent investment challenge.[163] Also, the government had a phased approach to tax holidays. It gradually added new types of fields to the list deserving special treatment, each time benefiting only parts of the oil industry.

The rise of Rosneft also affected the oil sector's ability to collectively shape oil tax reform, while also weakening cohesion within the executive itself. During the initial discourse on reforming the tax regime between 2005 and 2006, Rosneft emerged as a strong voice for the industry in its demand for tax relief. Over time, however, Rosneft's privileged access to the government only fostered growing division within the oil industry. Its management had little incentive to lead the sector in joint initiatives. Though regularly attending government-led meetings along with other oil companies, Rosneft maintained a direct line of communication with the Kremlin through Sechin.[164] Rosneft received the most extensive tax relief within the oil sector. This has been attributed mainly to legislation that assigns exclusive rights to state-owned companies in a range of new fields, though Rosneft's lobbying has also been a factor.[165]

In sum, following the revisions after 2005, Russia's oil tax policy has brought greater complexity, some flexibility to account for differential costs across Russian fields, and also much instability. The state has demonstrated its decisiveness in terms of its ability to shift its policy in response to the industry's evolving geological challenges. Indeed, in retrospect, tax relief measures have been successful as they have ultimately helped the industry stay on a trajectory of growth.[166] The state has also managed to maintain its role as the chief beneficiary of the country's oil rents. Yet, the Russian government has clearly not remained committed to the new rules it sets.

Conclusion

Reforming taxation in the oil sector was one of President Putin's earliest political battlegrounds over Russia's oil rents. It was a major victory for the state: by 2005, over 80 percent of the oil rents were flowing into the state's coffers – a drastic change from the situation in Putin's first year in power. Putin's new tax model represented a key effort to institutionalize the relationship of the state with the oil sector. It was a fundamental step towards a mode of interaction governed by new, clearer rules. These rules ensured the state would get more rents, while the oil industry could enjoy the simplicity of a new model that left little room for arbitrariness by tax collectors. In the end, however, the real winner was the state: it managed to alter the allocation of rents in its favor, while the oil industry's desire for greater predictability was met only halfway.

This initial success in establishing a fundamentally new oil tax model can best be understood by viewing it in the context of Russia's broader political evolution. The emergence of a more cohesive executive, and the gradual demise of other veto players, helped to transform growing discontent within the public and Russia's ruling elite about the oil sector's "excessive" gains into a series of new tax measures, laying the foundations of a new tax model. The executive successfully enacted and implemented these measures, fundamentally transforming the way rents were collected.

The "decisiveness" of the state has been apparent as well during the subsequent efforts to reform the new tax model. By 2005, the "West Siberian Miracle" was over, and it became obvious that the new tax model was too rigid to respond to the industry's emerging geological challenges. Faced with a growing need to take action, the Russian government was able to swiftly enact new measures. It continued to refine taxation in the oil sector, ensuring its continued growth.

One particular area has exhibited a striking continuity throughout the Putin era. Once the government succeeded in changing the allocation of oil rents decidedly in its favor during Putin's first term as president, there were never any significant slip-ups despite recurring reform measures. Many factors explain this policy stability. As Russia's (non-executive) veto players have remained weak, they have provided no significant opportunities for oil companies to shape the oil tax reform in a way that would fundamentally shift the flow of rents back in their direction. The very high stakes involved in sustaining this policy point to another contributing factor. The government's redistributive policies have hinged largely on its success in collecting rents. Arguably, this success has been imperative for the Russian leadership to ensure its political longevity. Access to revenues from a sector under permanently high tax pressure has brought a degree of flexibility for redistributive policies, which would have been unthinkable had the state failed to collect its share, as had happened in the 1990s. Third, a cohesive executive – one intent on maintaining the state's privileged position as the main beneficiary of oil rents – has also been crucial. Members of the executive branch have disagreed on how to refine the oil tax. However, given the high stakes, there is no evidence to suggest that any of them supported backtracking on the state's privileged position. Furthermore, the technical nature of tax reform has helped to confine decisions to a narrow group of players within the executive branch, contributing to executive cohesion. Within the executive branch, the Finance Ministry has held the upper hand, allowing a fiscally cautious approach to prevail.

While the Russian leadership's approach to sustaining the state's role as the chief beneficiary of Russia's oil wealth has been notably stable, this rare example of policy stability should not to be confused with the stability of the tax rules per se. The rules of taxation faced by oil companies have remained in flux since Putin's early days in the Kremlin. The Russian government continually recalibrated the tax model in order to establish steeper tax scales during Putin's first term as president. Subsequently, when the government came up with tax relief measures after 2006, it repeatedly proved that it could take them back as easily as it brought them in.

This instability in the tax rules for the oil sector can be attributed to several factors. First, the Finance Ministry's powerful role in the tax policy process, and its pursuit in ensuring a fair share of oil rents for the state, have frequently compromised the stability of the tax rules. For the Russian leadership, safeguarding the state's primacy in the flow of oil rents has been a higher priority than the stability of the oil tax regime. In retrospect, the oil sector has managed to sustain its growth; this indicates that the lack of stability has not been detrimental, although the opportunity costs are difficult to estimate.

Second, the tax regime adopted at the start of the Putin era has had some inherent lack of flexibility. Oriented towards finding an administratively simpler means to collect taxes, it has largely ignored the oil companies diverging costs and profitability. Inevitably, the tax regime came under pressure for reform by the mid-2000s. The Finance Ministry, it seems with Putin's support, set the limits on what was permissible to change. Amid a range of reform possibilities and alternative proposals coming from within the executive, the Russian government resisted another tax overhaul. Instead, it opted for piecemeal solutions in the form of ad hoc tax holidays for carefully selected oil fields. By avoiding the riskier path, Russia postponed the opportunity to align its tax regime with international trends. With limited measurement tools to judge the effectiveness and generosity of the tax holidays, the Finance Ministry has responded with periodic rollbacks when it deems the relief measures an unnecessary sacrifice for the state.

Finally, this lack of stability in the tax regime is not surprising in a political setting marked by a high concentration of power within the executive branch. Oil companies have had no capability to resist – no veto players could help them establish greater stability in the rules of taxation. Their inability for collective action, in part a product of the political setting but also the result of diverging interests among oil players, has also weakened their ability to ensure more stable rules.

5 The State as a Redistributor of Oil Rents: The Contest over Russia's Budget and Economic Priorities

If rearranging who generates Russia's oil rents and how to collect them brought political struggles, redistributing these rents brought even more intense contests. Redistribution, by nature, is expected to invite competition. How the leadership manages the process can be critical for its political future. It can choose to appeal to the wider public, meet the demands of select members of the elite, or disappoint them. Its redistributive choices can have broad economic ramifications. As oil prices tend to fluctuate, there is a continuous risk of trade shocks, which leaders can either prepare for or ignore.

This chapter focuses on the Russian state as the chief redistributor of oil rents. I examine two principal means for redistribution: the federal budget and government tax policy. Most of the redistribution has been implemented through the federal budget, though tax cuts for the non-oil sectors have also constituted a significant means to indirectly redistribute oil windfalls throughout the economy. In the next chapter, I examine two additional policy instruments: oil savings funds and sovereign debt payments. How the Russian leadership has managed the latter two instruments has determined the amount of oil windfalls available to be redistributed *within* the Russian economy.

These two chapters examining Russia's redistributive policies since the late 1990s reveal several interesting puzzles. The Russian leadership has oscillated between strictly fiscally conservative to highly expansionary approaches to redistribution. There have been some notable contrasts in Russia's fiscal balances during Putin's long tenure. Russia has seen the rise of a vast financial cushion against imminent crises. But the country has also gone through a period when even oil prices hovering above 100 USD/barrel have been insufficient to balance the budget. Since 1999, Russia has had two major oil booms and two relatively short oil busts, and each has elicited a different response from the government. Furthermore, some of the government's redistributive policies have fluctuated widely, while others have remained stable. Namely, the Russian government's approach to redistribution through the federal budget and the oil funds has varied substantially over time. By contrast, its approach to tax cuts for the non-oil economy has generally remained intact following key changes during Putin's first presidency. Likewise, Russia has maintained a highly resolute stance with respect to maintaining outstandingly low sovereign debt.

The analysis illustrates several key points. The fading role of Russia's veto players explains Putin's ability to maintain a highly fiscally conservative course during his early tenure. The subsequent shifts in Russia's approach to redistribution are the product of a lack of cohesion within the executive branch. They also reflect Putin's choice to balance competing visions on the economy, in line with his evolving perceptions on political risks relative to the available resources to mitigate such risks.

Budgetary Spending and Tax Cuts as a Means for Rent Redistribution

Depending on the oil price cycle – boom or bust – an oil-rich country's redistributive policies may be procyclical or countercyclical. Procyclical policies during an oil boom entail an increase in budgetary spending and tax cuts, which ultimately enhance the dependence of the economy on revenues from oil. Such fiscal policies (also known as expansionary policies) are generally known to exacerbate a country's vulnerability to a negative oil price shock. It has been common for oil-rich countries to adopt procyclical policies during oil booms, policies that become unsustainable over time.[1] By contrast, a countercyclical fiscal approach calls for conservative fiscal policy during booms and an expansionary policy during only bust periods. Such an approach has been more helpful in ensuring stable economic growth in the long term.[2]

I examine the redistributive policies of the Russian government over three periods. First, I look at Putin's early years, from 1999 to 2005. During this period, the Russian government largely avoided procyclical expenditure polices, defying a trend often seen in oil-rich countries. In the meantime, Russia's tax system, both for the oil sector and for the rest of the economy, went through a fundamental overhaul. The tax burden on oil was raised, while the rest of the economy benefited from modest cuts. Next, I analyze the period between 2005 and late 2008. During this time frame one can identify the first signs of relaxation in Russia's budgetary spending amid a continuing boom in oil prices. Finally, I look at the period after the onset of the global recession in 2008. This period has been marked by significant oil price disparities – Russia went from boom to bust twice within six years.

The initial objective here is to examine the main fiscal policy outcomes in terms of their cyclicality, while the rest of the chapter explains how the political context affected these fiscal policies. Most of my focus is on public spending as the government's primary means for redistribution. I rely on multiple measures to trace the evolution of Russia's expenditure policies and to assess their cyclicality over time.[3] I examine tax breaks as an additional tool for redistribution, focusing primarily on Putin's early years in the presidency when Russia adopted fundamental changes in the tax system. These tax measures remained largely intact in subsequent periods. Avoiding strictly technical details, I illustrate that the Russian leadership opted to lower the tax burden on the economy at a time when it took the opposite course of action with respect to the oil sector.

Regaining Russia's Financial Health: From a Deficit-Ridden Budget to a Steady Surplus

Putin's ascent to power was preceded by a financial crash. In August 1998, the Russian government declared a default on its domestic debt and a moratorium on repaying its external debt. The ruble's value sharply plummeted. The crisis was partly the result of low oil prices that exposed the dependence of the Russian economy on oil rents. But essentially it was a debt crisis driven by Russia's fiscal policies.[4]

There were two big flaws in Russia's fiscal approach under the Yeltsin administration. On the one hand, despite numerous efforts, consecutive governments largely failed to move away from an expansionary spending policy. The leadership was often compelled to spend more in response to enterprise managers asking for subsidies, regional leaders requesting additional transfers from the federal center, and employees in the public sector demanding increased wages. On the other hand, the Russian state had a revenue problem. Tax compliance, both in the oil sector and the rest of the economy, remained low. The combined result was a chronic budget deficit. That prompted the government to resort to high-risk financing, ultimately contributing to the financial crash in 1998.

Table 5.1 shows the evolution of Russia's financial health during the Yeltsin era and the first five years of Putin's presidency. Looking at Russia's general budget, comprising both the federal and regional budgets along with extra-budgetary funds, allows one to control for periodic shifts in interbudgetary transfers occurring between levels of budgets.[5] It is noteworthy that during the early 1990s, the Russian government opted to drastically cut public spending – it was reduced by about 17 percent of GDP between 1992 and 1995.[6] Yet, this approach did not last long. Public spending rose consistently between 1996 and 1998, bringing the average size of the budget deficit to 7.8 percent of the GDP.

Following the 1998 crisis, Russia's expenditure policies entered a new stage. The general government budget deficit shrunk to 3.1 percent of the GDP in 1999, reflecting the emphasis on fiscal discipline by the Primakov government in its efforts to pull Russia out of the crisis. It is notable that Putin maintained this conservative approach on public spending. Thus, in 2000, for the first time in Russia's post-Soviet history, the general budget recorded an overall surplus.

Table 5.1. Russia's General Government Budget (as % of GDP)

	1992	1993	1994	1995	1996	1997	1998	1999	2000	2001	2002	2003	2004	2005
Expenditure	57.7	43.6	45.1	40.2	42.4	44.4	41.4	39.4	33.7	34.6	37.0	35.5	33.6	31.9
Overall Budget Balance	−18.4	−7.4	−10.4	−6.1	−8.9	−7.7	−6.0	−4.2	0.8	2.7	1.3	1.4	4.4	8.1
Non-Oil Balance*	–	–	–	–	−12.2	−10.0	−7.5	−6.4	−3.9	−2.9	−4.4	−4.7	−3.9	−4.6

* "Non-oil" refers to sectors outside crude oil, petroleum products, and natural gas. Figures for 2005 exclude one-time revenues from the sale of Yukos.

Source: IMF

The surplus kept rising in the following years, reaching the record-high level of 8.1 percent of Russia's GDP in 2005.

Undoubtedly, Russia's fiscal balance benefited from favorable oil prices. It also benefited from the tax overhaul in the oil sector, as discussed in the previous chapter. The rapid economic growth rate achieved in the aftermath of the 1998 financial crash also facilitated the government's task in collecting revenues from other sectors. So did the devaluation of the ruble following the crash, which encouraged economic growth while securing additional tax revenues from exporters.

At the same time, there was a deliberate effort to slash public spending, which also contributed to the surging budgetary surplus. Public spending dropped consistently between 2002 and 2005, reaching the record low of 31.9 percent of the GDP (in 2005). By contrast, average public spending between 1992 and 1997 had stood at 46.1 percent of GDP.

The Russian leadership had clearly decided to adopt and sustain a prudent fiscal approach. Booming oil revenues could well have been translated into expansionary spending policy. Given the mounting pressures from various political circles and the public, Russia could have easily afforded to spend more. A budget surplus that kept growing was not a predetermined outcome – it was a choice.

The turnaround in Russia's public spending caught many observers by surprise. Many officials from the IMF and the World Bank were bewildered by the abrupt shift in Russia's fiscal approach.[7] They strongly praised Russia's disciplined fiscal management following the 1998 crisis. The success of fiscal stabilization efforts during Putin's first presidential term was outstanding not only in comparison to Russia's earlier attempts. A joint study by the IMF and the Bank of Italy comparing the fiscal balances of a large set of oil-exporting countries reveals that Russia was one of the main overachievers. Controlling for the relative size of oil and gas revenues in the budget and a country's starting point shows that Russia recorded some of the most notable improvements in fiscal balances between the low-oil price period of the 1990s and the years between 2000 and 2004, when prices recovered.[8]

The government's unexpected approach prompted many in Russia's policy circles to question its rationale.[9] Had Putin gone "too far" at a time when Russia could afford to spend more, at least in some priority areas such as education and health? Russian economists were divided, too. For some, the country's ailing infrastructure and health sector became victims of this policy.[10] For others, namely liberal economists who had hoped to see a fiscally conservative policy throughout the 1990s, their wishes had finally come true. For them, high oil prices could never be taken for granted, necessitating caution in spending Russia's oil windfalls to avoid another financial crash.[11] Oil company representatives also found the government's approach praiseworthy.[12] A shift away from fiscal prudence yielded risks for the sector in the form of ever-increasing taxes to cover more spending.

In theory, Russian officials could have adopted an even more conservative approach. The IMF has typically evaluated oil-rich countries through additional measures, most notably the so-called non-oil fiscal balance.[13] The "non-oil balance" excludes oil-related government revenues and expenditures. Unlike the overall budgetary balance, the non-oil balance is under government control– it does not depend directly on fluctuations in world oil prices. As a result, this measure could reveal some tendencies that might remain disguised in more traditional budget indicators. Accordingly, Russia's "non-oil deficit" dropped drastically between 1999 and 2001, reaching its lowest level (see table 5.1). This was indicative of the government's fiscal discipline at a time when oil prices and revenues began to rise. However, this trend was reversed in 2002. The "non-fiscal deficit" started to expand, though it did not rise much further during the following few years.[14]

While the Russian government exercised restraint on spending, it was able to redistribute part of the increased surplus indirectly through comprehensive tax reform. The process exhibited two contrasting trends. On the one hand, the tax burden on the oil sector was raised quite dramatically after 1999, as shown in the previous chapter. By 2005, oil and gas revenues accruing to the government (in percent of GDP) were more than five times higher than they had been in 1998[15] (table 5.2). Their share in the total general government revenues jumped from 8.1 percent in 1998 to 36.7 percent in 2005. In the case of the federal budget, oil and gas accounted for about half of the revenues by 2005.[16] Undoubtedly, rising oil prices contributed to this outcome, though the new oil tax regime also had a defining effect.

On the other hand, the tax burden on the rest of the economy moved in the opposite direction. "Non-oil" tax revenues went through a steady decline after 1997, dropping from 34.8 percent of GDP to 27.4 percent of GDP by 2005. The decline was particularly notable after 2002, as the Russian economy started to witness the impact of recent tax reform measures.

The drop in the tax burden on the rest of the economy was not coincidental. The government's effort to enact comprehensive tax reform ultimately contributed to this outcome. The Russian leadership took the first major step by adopting Part I of the new Tax Code in July 1998.[17] The groundbreaking tax reforms, however, came after Putin became president.[18]

Putin's comprehensive tax reform involved several key strategies. First, many existing taxes were nominally reduced (table 5.3). This aimed to improve compliance, which could ultimately expand the country's tax base. Second, Russia's tax system was fundamentally simplified, which facilitated tax collection. From over 200 types of taxes affecting businesses in the late 1990s,[19] the number was cut to 40 by the end of 2001, then to 15 by 2005.[20] Some turnover taxes that

Table 5.2. Revenues of the General Government from "Oil" and "Non-Oil" Sectors*

	1997	1998	1999	2000	2001	2002	2003	2004	2005
Oil related revenues (% of GDP)	4.5	2.8	3.9	7.5	7.5	7.5	8.7	11.1	15.9
Non-oil revenues(% of GDP)	34.8	31.5	29.6	29.4	29.8	30.1	28.0	27.5	27.4
Share of oil revenues in total revenues (%)	11.3	8.1	11.7	20.2	20.1	20.0	23.6	28.7	36.7
Total revenues	**39.3**	**34.3**	**33.5**	**36.9**	**37.3**	**37.6**	**36.7**	**38.6**	**43.3**

* Oil revenues refer to revenues from the following: excises and export taxes on oil, petroleum products and natural gas, mineral resource taxes (NDPI as of 2002), parts of the profit and income taxes pertaining to the oil and gas sectors, and Road Fund taxes (collected until 2003).

Source: IMF

Table 5.3. Major Tax Reform Measures Reducing the Tax Burden on the Economy, 1999–2005

Effective as of 2001	
Personal income tax	The progressive personal income tax with a maximum rate of 35 percent was transformed into a flat tax of 13 percent for all residents.
Unified Social Tax	Introduced in order to unify contributions to pension, social, and medical funds. The total rate for these funds was reduced from 39.5 percent to a regressive tax ranging from 35.6 percent to 2 percent. Also the 3 percent contribution to the Unemployment Fund was abolished.
Housing Fund Tax	Turnover tax of 1.5 percent of gross sales was abolished.
Road Tax	Turnover tax reduced from 2.5 percent to 1 percent of gross sales.

Effective as of 2002	
Profit Tax	Reduced from 35 percent to 24 percent. However, most of previous tax allowances were abolished.

Effective as of 2003	
Road Tax	Following a reduction of its rate in 2001, it was eventually abolished.

Effective as of 2004	
Sales Tax	The 5 percent tax was abolished.
Value Added Tax	The standard rate of 20 percent was reduced to 18 percent.

Effective as of 2005	
Unified Social Tax	The maximum rate was further reduced from 35.6 percent to 26 percent.

had been imposed on companies' gross revenues, and that proved to be highly burdensome, were entirely abolished. Third, the tax reform brought some uniformity in taxation. According to Russian economist Vladimir Popov, the government opted in favor of tax cuts that would benefit the economy as a whole, while curbing particularistic tax measures enjoyed by distinct sectors or companies.[21] Existing exemptions and special tax deals that had been the product of negotiations with larger taxpayers were mostly abolished or further limited. They had fueled corruption throughout the 1990s and resulted in significant loss of revenue for the government.

In sum, Russia went through a successful phase of comprehensive tax reform, which was nearly complete by the middle of the decade. There were not many new changes enacted during the following years. The path undertaken was straightforward. The tax burden on the economy overall was lowered with a notable exception: the oil sector had to singlehandedly bear a rapidly rising tax burden.

The Early Signs of Fiscal Relaxation

On the surface, Russia's budget continued to register a surplus between 2005 and 2008 (see table 5.4). It also rapidly accumulated international reserves while further cutting the foreign debt. Moreover, Russia's fiscal record remained impressive when compared to many other oil-rich countries such Azerbaijan and oil exporters in the Persian Gulf.[22] Evidently, Russia did not abandon the fiscally conservative approach it had adopted in the aftermath of the 1998 crisis.

And yet there were some major signs of fiscal relaxation during this period. The IMF has traced the first of these to 2005, though the impact became increasingly obvious in subsequent years as the evidence for expansionary fiscal policies multiplied.[23] At least two measures are highly indicative. First, both the overall balance and the non-oil balance of the general government budget clearly weakened by 2007 (see table 5.4). Second, there was a notable upturn in the so-called breakeven price for oil – the minimum price of Urals blend crude oil needed to prevent the Russian budget from falling into deficit. In 2004, the breakeven price for Russia's general government budget stood at 20 USD/barrel. By 2005, this figure had risen to 25 USD/barrel and reached 52 USD/barrel by 2008.[24] Some of this increase can be justified by longer-term changes in international oil markets.[25] Yet, by 2008, it was increasingly obvious that the Russian budget had become more dependent on higher oil prices, and more vulnerable in the event of a price crash. Indeed, the Russian Federal Treasury has estimated that the share of oil and gas revenues in the federal budget jumped from 17.9 percent in 2002 to 47.3 percent in 2008.[26]

It appears the growth in public spending targeted rather broad segments of the Russian economy during the period between 2005 and 2008. One could see the early signs of a shift towards expansionary spending in the social sphere,

Table 5.4. Russia's General Government Budget (as % of GDP)

	2005	2006	2007	2008	2009	2010	2011	2012	2013	2014	2015	2016	2017	2018
Expenditure	31.9	31.2	33.1	34.3	41.4	39.0	35.7	37.2	37.3	34.9	35.1	36.4	34.7	32.6
Overall budget balance	8.1	8.3	6.8	4.9	−6.3	−3.4	1.5	0.4	−1.3	−1.1	−3.4	−3.7	−1.5	2.9
Non-oil balance	−4.6	−4.5	−6.2*	−7.7	−15.6	−13.0	−10.0	−11.3	−12.2	−11.4	−11.3	−8.9	−7.7	−6.6

* Excludes one-time government revenues from Yukos tax penalties.
Source: IMF

infrastructure, development, and the military. Russia was clearly leaning towards spending more on guns, butter, and development.[27]

In 2005, the government introduced an amendment to the federal budget, securing a significant raise to public sector wages and pensions, along with increased transfers to regions. The IMF warned that this additional spending was ill-targeted as it entailed recurring fiscal commitments that would be hard to reverse in future.[28] During 2005, the Russian government undertook further budgetary commitments by announcing the launch of four National Priority Projects. This initiative designated health, education, housing, and agriculture as priority areas.[29] Meanwhile, special funds were allocated outside these priority projects to finance large wage increases in the military and the judiciary in 2006 and 2007.[30]

The extent of fiscal relaxation in 2007 was striking. This coincided with the rise of several institutions dedicated to promoting economic development, as well as the establishment of a number of state-led corporations to act as vehicles for economic growth and innovation. These new entities were set up to absorb substantial funds that were made available through tapping into Russia's oil windfall savings (see chapter 6). As spending commitments piled up, record growth in public spending was recorded in 2007: federal spending grew by 15 percent in real terms and 40 percent in nominal terms, widening Russia's non-oil deficit.[31] In 2008, prior to the Great Recession, Russia was on track to further expand its spending.[32] As a clear indicator of Russia's expansionary fiscal policies, the inflation rate more than doubled within a year, reaching 15 percent by the middle of 2008.[33]

Two Oil Busts and a Boom: Russia's Fiscal Response after 2008

In a twist of fate, the oil boom that coincided with Putin's first presidency came to an end almost right after Dmitry Medvedev replaced Putin in the Kremlin. During the next few years Russia witnessed several sharp reversals in the price of oil. By the end of 2008, oil markets were in the midst of a full-scale bust.[34] This did not last long, however.[35] Oil prices recovered by the end of 2009. Between 2011 and 2014 average annual oil prices remained even higher than at the historic annual peak reached in 2008. Then came another downturn in the price of oil, coinciding with the launch of international economic sanctions against Russia in 2014.

The fiscal response of the Russian leadership to the swings in the price of oil sheds light on its key redistributive policies. A fiscally conservative approach, in theory, would necessitate a continuous countercyclical policy: providing a fiscal stimulus to the economy during an oil bust, but reverting to cuts in public spending when the bust is over. How did the Russian government react to the first "oil bust" of the Putin era? Could it return to a more fiscally conservative approach once the bust was over, in preparation for another in the future? How different was its reaction to the next oil bust that set in after 2014? Finally, how did Russia balance its redistributive policies between guns, butter, and development during this period?

By late 2008, the effects of the global financial crisis were heavily felt in Russia. In essence, this was another debt crisis, this time driven by the mounting foreign debt exposure of Russian banks and the private sector rather than the government. The drop in the value of the ruble, closely associated with plummeting oil prices, further exacerbated the financial position of Russian banks and corporations. Amid the risk of defaults, the stock market crashed, losing two-thirds of its value between May and November.[36] The drastic drop in the price of oil once again exposed the economy's vulnerability to such price shocks.

The Russian government was quick to respond. In contrast to the response to the 1998 crisis, when Russian authorities announced a debt moratorium and devaluation, they instead came up with a massive anti-crisis stimulus package, one of the largest financial packages within the G-20 countries.[37] The government's first priority was preventing potential defaults in the banking and the real sector. No major bank was allowed to fail. Banks were quickly recapitalized through a series of rescue measures, financed in part by the federal budget but also through savings in Russia's "rainy day" oil funds (see chapter 6).[38] Subsequently, in March 2009, as part of a new package of anti-crisis measures, the government announced an extensive list of strategically important companies eligible for direct financial support by the state.[39] Key industries, such as defense and security, were among the chief beneficiaries of discretionary extra spending. Furthermore, the real sector also benefited from tax cuts, such as a modest reduction in the rate of corporate income tax.[40] The Russian leadership shifted its focus to social expenditure in the second half of 2009. It approved a raise in public sector salaries and benefits, especially for those employed in health and education. Pensioners also enjoyed several big raises through the end of 2010.[41]

Unlike in the 1998 crisis, when most of the costs were borne by the public, the banks, and companies, this time the Russian government bore most of the burden. The public was nearly unscathed by the global recession: by the end of the crisis Russia's real wages dropped by merely 3.5 percent, whereas pensions rose by more than 10 percent in real terms.[42] Banks and firms were also spared from defaults. Clearly, the government was now much better prepared to face a crisis. Years of fiscally prudent policies paid off, securing for the state substantial buffers to aid in the event of a crisis. Furthermore, the government was able to finance its massive new commitments in 2008 and 2009 entirely from its own resources, pulled from the budget and the oil funds, without resorting to new debt.

Russia's effort to counter the crisis with these countercyclical measures had a major effect on budgetary performance. Once again Russia was back to a budget deficit – a problem that had disappeared under Putin (see table 5.4). The rapid changes in Russia's non-oil budget balance, and the oil price needed for the budget to break even, indicated the magnitude of the government's countercyclical measures.[43] The general government's non-oil deficit rose sharply from about 7.7 percent of GDP in 2008 to 15.7 percent of GDP the following year. Both increased spending and declining non-oil revenues due to a contraction of economic activity contributed to this outcome.[44] In the meantime, the oil price balancing the general budget jumped drastically to 94 USD/barrel in 2009.[45] For the first time since the early 2000s, the actual price of oil in global markets stood below what was needed to balance the Russian budget.

By the beginning of 2010 it was getting increasingly clear that Russia had overcome the crisis. Economic growth had resumed and oil prices rebounded, reaching above 75 USD/barrel.[46] It was not immediately obvious to the Russian leadership, but the country was about to enter a massive new oil boom. In 2011 oil windfalls reached a new post-Soviet record.

The key question at this point was whether and how the Russian government would shift to a new countercyclical policy, phasing out anti-crisis stimulus measures and reverting to a more conservative fiscal approach. Indeed, the government anticipated a post-crisis fiscal consolidation, and announced key steps towards that objective as early as the start of 2010. It elaborated measures to cut overall public spending while raising the rates for some non-oil taxes such as the tax on payroll. By 2011, the headline (nominal) budget was back to a surplus (see table 5.4).

And yet Russia's approach during this new oil boom can hardly be described as a return to fiscal conservatism. From the start, it was apparent that the Russian leadership was not in a rush to adjust its fiscal policies, and was not entirely committed to adopting a new countercyclical approach. First, the midterm budget plan for the 2011–13 period envisaged a return to a balanced budget no earlier than 2015.[47] Russia's return to a balanced budget in 2011 was the unexpected consequence of oil prices remaining above the government's forecasts. Second, it did not take long for the budgetary balance to start deteriorating again. By 2012, the surplus in the nominal budget was much smaller. The deficit was back in 2013 and 2014 despite continuing high oil prices (see table 5.4). More importantly, after a mild improvement in 2010 and 2011, the non-oil deficit grew during the following years. It remained in excess of 10 percent of GDP – far from the 4.7 percent long-term fiscal target set by the Russian government prior to the crisis.[48] Furthermore, the break-even oil price for the federal budget reached the record-high 110 USD/barrel in 2012.[49] Russia was increasingly exposed to a potential oil price shock. Finally, at the very start of his third term as president in 2012, Putin issued a series of decrees – the May Decrees – instructing the government to devote significantly more resources in social policy areas including education, healthcare, demographic development, and housing.[50]

Overall, Russia's fiscal response to the new boom entailed a partial attempt to phase out the anti-crisis measures adopted during the Great Recession, followed by further growth in public spending. One may conclude that the government's challenge in shifting to a more conservative fiscal approach was in part predetermined by its policies during the preceding crisis. According to IMF estimates, some of the measures adopted during the Great Recession, such as increased pensions, brought commitments that were difficult to reverse once the crisis was over.[51]

Yet, there was nothing predetermined about running a nominal budget deficit in the midst of record high oil prices. As examined below, it reflected policy choices favoring more state-led development and increased public spending in new select areas. In 2010, the Russian government announced a vast military rearmament program that raised the demand on public funds.[52] Additionally, in the midst of booming oil windfalls, Russia started to dedicate more funding to ambitious infrastructure projects.[53] Investment in infrastructure had been generally neglected during the first oil boom of the 2000s and had not emerged as a priority area in the government's anti-crisis measures during the Great Recession.[54]

By the last quarter of 2014, Russia was experiencing the beginning of a new oil bust. It came in a rather different economic context than the previous bust, which had interrupted nearly ten years of rapid growth. This time the bust hit Russia when its economy had already started to stagnate – even oil prices above 100 USD/barrel had not sufficed to prevent a major economic slowdown, highlighting deeper structural problems in the Russian economy.[55] Furthermore, Russia was confronted with intensifying economic sanctions as a response to its annexation of Crimea in 2014. And, having failed to adopt a truly countercyclical policy during the oil boom of 2011–14, this time around Russia's financial buffers were much weaker. The government had opted to redistribute the majority of the oil rents during the boom, saving only a modest portion (see chapter 6).

Compared with its response to the previous bust, Russia's fiscal response to the new bust appeared to be much more complicated in terms of its cyclicality. As expected, the Russian government did adopt some countercyclical measures to stimulate the economy. It announced a new major anti-crisis stimulus package in early 2015.[56] Once again the government rushed to recapitalize banks to ensure the flow of credit to the real sector. In addition, it designated 199 large companies, many of them state-owned and overall accounting for about 70 percent of Russia's GDP, to be of systemic importance. They were made eligible for support in the form of state guarantees. Meanwhile, amid ongoing military tensions with Ukraine and a decision to get militarily involved in Syria in 2015, the Russian leadership continued to increase military spending.[57] Another anti-crisis package, announced in March 2016, redistributed funds mainly to regional governments and to select industrial sectors such as car production and railways.[58]

Still, there were signs of restraint in the government's new fiscal approach. Russian economist Vladimir Mau has described the fiscal response to the new crisis as prudent, though not entirely conservative.[59] The leadership undertook a series of unpopular measures. Unlike during the 2008–9 crisis, pensions actually declined in real terms in 2015 and 2016, while civil servant salaries were frozen.[60]

Despite some worsening in the headline budget figures, the non-oil deficit essentially improved in 2016 (table 5.4). This was in part thanks to revenues from the sale of major stakes in state-owned corporations such as Bashneft and Alrosa.[61] Yet, even these sales were indicative of the government's newfound commitment to improve the health of the budget: its leadership was once again considering raising revenues through privatizing select state-owned assets. Further signs of fiscal prudence were recorded in 2017, when overall spending was cut and the budgetary balance figures improved significantly. By 2018, Russia was back to a balanced budget. While an increase in oil prices helped to bring about this outcome, there was a notable improvement in the non-oil budget balance, indicating the leadership's re-appreciation of fiscal discipline. Furthermore, the Russian government adopted a new approach in its budget-making process. In the aftermath of the 2008–9 crisis, the Russian government had adhered to overly optimistic forecasts for the price of oil to guide the budget.[62] At long last, it reverted to a practice prevalent during the first half of the 2000s: keeping oil price assumptions deliberately conservative to facilitate a more prudent fiscal approach.[63]

Putin's First Years: Explaining the Victory of Fiscal Prudence

So far I have outlined the main outcomes of Russia's policies to redistribute its oil wealth, leaving aside the causes behind them. Some puzzles have emerged in the process. Putin's ascent to the Kremlin coincided with the beginning of a major oil boom that lasted until the Great Recession. Until the middle of the decade, the Russian leadership adopted a highly conservative fiscal approach. What explains this initial victory of fiscal prudence? How can one explain the gradual rise of expansionary fiscal policies after the middle of the decade? What accounts for Russia's different reactions to the two oil busts after 2008? And why was the Russian government not able to effectively adhere to countercyclical policies during the new oil boom between 2010 and 2014? In other words, why did the appeal of rapidly redistributing the oil wealth triumph over longer-term fiscal considerations?

In searching for answers, I examine in detail how changes in executive power shaped Russia's rent redistribution policies, focusing on three critical aspects of executive power. First, I look at the waning role of Russia's veto players (outside the executive branch) under Putin. This factor alone is significant in accounting for the fiscal prudence of Putin's first few years. Yet, it provides no satisfactory explanation about policy shifts and continuities subsequently, when weak veto players can be assumed as constant.

Second, I focus on the presence or lack of cohesion within the executive branch itself. My underlying assumption is that recurring policy shifts are more likely if the executive is divided rather than cohesive. This calls for clarification on how I define cohesion within the executive with respect to rent redistribution. Policies on redistribution are inherently prone to disagreements within the ruling elite.[64] Not every case of intra-executive squabbling is relevant to this chapter. Instead, I examine executive cohesion specifically with respect to "fiscal prudence," which I define as a preference for fiscally conservative policies (such as adopting a countercyclical approach to an oil boom and a return to restraint by the end of an oil bust), calling for a favorable budget balance.[65] In this respect, the divisions within the executive that are the most relevant to this chapter are those between the proponents of a fiscally conservative approach versus those advocating expansionary fiscal policies. I refer to the former group as "fiscal conservatives," a designation that overlaps with "economic liberals" and "liberal reformers." For the proponents of expansionary fiscal policies, I use the term "statists." I recognize that the latter group is highly extensive and diverse. Thus, I use the label mainly for those favoring state-led development. In order to analyze the extent of intra-executive disagreements, I devote most of my attention to the position of the Finance Ministry relative to others within the executive branch. The ministry's default position has been to support countercyclical fiscal policies.

Third, I examine how perceptions of political risks, and of the available resources to mitigate them, have evolved within the Russian executive, and with Putin in particular. My underlying assumption is that a change in the balance between political risks and available resources can shape policies on redistribution. Political risks are defined as a possible loss of elections and rising public protests, whereas the availability of resources, in this particular case, refers to the overall fiscal health of the Russian government.

What links executive power to rent redistribution outcomes is a complex *policy process*. I examine this process in detail by focusing on two policy areas directly related to rent redistribution. Russia's budget-making process constitutes the core of this analysis. The preparation and execution of a federal budget is a fairly institutionalized process, one the public can observe. Admittedly, the analysis has some limitations as it focuses on the formal process only. As Fortescue notes, it would be naïve to ignore that there is a parallel informal process whereby members of the ruling elite discuss, behind closed doors, policies that can substantially affect the budget. Yet, as he argues, one should expect that informal decisions and practices are generally reflected in the institutionalized budget-making process, not least because they need to go through a fairly technocratic process in order to be implemented. Thus, informal actors need to work with bureaucratic actors whose task is to pursue their positions.[66] I observe the formal budget process through an extensive overview of Russian government open sources, official statements from key members of the executive, daily news reports, and personal interviews. This allows me to assess the degree of cohesion within the executive branch with respect to fiscal prudence.

I also look at the policy process of tax cuts as an alternative means to redistribute rents from the oil sector to the rest of the economy. While tax policies inevitably affect the budget, the policy discourse on the budget and various tax cut initiatives are not necessarily part of the same policy process. In fact, the discourse on tax cuts is formally distinct from the budget process, though it often involves many of the same players.

To help shed light on the process of these two redistributive policies, I start by examining two important contextual elements. First, the Putin era has ushered in multiple official economic programs that deserve closer attention. Many of these programs have shaped the evolution of budgetary and tax policies. Examining the discourse around them can help reveal the extent of executive cohesion on redistributive policies, while the ultimate fate of these programs sheds light on whose preferences emerged victorious over time. Changing priorities across programs can also highlight major shifts in policy preferences within the executive branch.

Second, I look at Putin's choices of cadres in charge of the economy since late 1990s. The focus of my analysis is on major continuities and changes with respect to key personalities that could be described as fiscally conservative versus those favoring a more expansionist fiscal policy and an interventionist state. If one assumes that Putin's choice of cadres reflects his policy preferences, major changes may potentially explain shifts in redistributive policies.

Competing Economic Approaches at the Start of Putin's Presidency

Since the very start of the Putin era, the Russian leadership has announced a series of major economic programs, though their implementation has varied widely.[67] Such programs have involved a wide array of experts, along with officials from within the Russian executive branch. Putin has held a direct role in the initiation of many of these programmatic proposals[68] and his involvement has been instrumental in determining their fate.[69] Julian Cooper has described Putin's adherence to strategic plans as a key part of his style of governance.[70]

The beginning of Putin's presidency was marked by competition between two alternative proposals for the economy: the Gref Program and the Ishayev Concept for Development. Named after their chief developers, the two programs reflected deep divides within the Russian expert and policy-making communities. Many of the ideas have remained contentious throughout the Putin era.

The Gref Program, officially titled "The Strategy of Social-Economic Development of the Russian Federation until 2010," was announced shortly after Putin's first presidential victory in March 2000.[71] It was prepared by the newly established Center for Strategic Research, headed by the then First Deputy Prime Minister German Gref. The center brought together some of Russia's leading economists, many known for their adherence to market reforms. The government endorsed the document in July 2000.[72] According to Aslund, this was, thus far, the most comprehensive and detailed reform program in post-communist Russia.[73]

Nevertheless, policy debates on Russia's economic future continued at the highest level throughout the rest of the year.[74] It was during this period that an alternative economic program emerged under the leadership of Viktor Ishayev, the governor of Khabarovsk Krai. Reportedly, Putin asked Ishayev to lead a working group to prepare an alternative draft strategy, one that would put more emphasis on the development of Russia's regions.[75] In November, Ishayev and his team officially presented their draft, entitled "Strategy for the Development of the State until 2010."

The two programs reflected the distinct ideological bases of their proponents, providing two alternative paths for the Russian economy. There were some common objectives, such as "modernizing" the Russian economy, diversifying the economy away from natural resources, and establishing a new "social contract" between the state and the people. The two programs also converged in terms of their stance on tax cuts as a means to foster economic growth, especially in the non-resource sectors.[76] Yet, there were enormous differences in their overall approach to the economy, mainly with respect to the role of the state in fostering growth and building a new "social contract." The Gref Program put clear emphasis on market-led development. It called for further restricting the state's involvement in the economy through deregulation and reduced administrative barriers. The government's focus had to be on launching series of reforms, creating an environment conducive to investment, and improving property rights. The program called for strictly adhering to a balanced budget, which would necessitate further cuts in public spending. Social welfare programs had to be scaled back in favor of better-targeted assistance programs.[77]

Ishayev's draft proposed a fundamentally different role for the state, even though, at least in principle, it envisaged Russia as a market economy. The government needed to expand investments in selected sectors, including machine building, infrastructure development, the military-industrial complex, and agriculture. Russia's Central Bank would need to allocate a portion of its reserves to commercial banks, which in turn would provide these amounts as loans to the real sector. Welfare spending needed to expand on a large scale, while the government could go as far as mandating wages paid by businesses.

The two alternative programs could be expected to yield fundamentally different policies. The Gref Program clearly adhered to a fiscally conservative approach. By contrast, Ishayev's plan called for wider-scale redistributive policies. These would necessitate a drastic increase in state funding of economic activities. Ishayev's plan said little about the source of such funding or about the macroeconomic implications of a spending boost.[78]

Despite the emergence of Ishayev's plan as an alternative to the Gref Program, there was no backtracking on behalf of Putin and his government. The Gref Program remained in force without incorporating any elements from Ishayev's plan. Given their fundamental differences, it would have been hardly possible to reconcile the two proposals into a single program. As Ishayev's plan gradually vanished from the government's economic agenda, this was a major victory for Gref and his team.

Yet, the mere presence of two fundamentally distinct programmatic proposals for the Russian economy was an early indication of the impending difficulty in building cohesion within the executive on key redistributive matters.[79] While the Gref team won, the fight between fiscal conservatives and proponents of greater state intervention in the economy was far from over. Debates on the proper role of the state returned in full force as oil prices kept rising in the following years. Many ideas in Ishayev's proposal reappeared periodically in policy discourse, including in President Putin's speeches. Soon, the fiscal conservative camp splintered as more members started calling for a more active state role in development. This presented Putin with a critical challenge on how to find a balance in Russia's economic policies between the proponents of fiscal discipline and those calling for more state intervention.

Putin's Choice of Key Officials in Charge of Economic Policy

The way in which Putin filled key positions within the executive branch provides further indication of his endorsement of the liberal reformist camp rather than the proponents of state-led development. At first, as Russia's new prime minister, Putin opted to keep the key individuals in economic policy-making that had been appointed by his predecessor Prime Minister Stepashin. His first major cabinet reshuffle came shortly after his presidential victory in March 2000. Putin clearly favored those known as liberal reformists.[80] He appointed Mikhail Kasyanov as the new prime minister.[81] As a chief negotiator with the IMF and the World Bank, Kasyanov had been an active proponent of prudent fiscal policies in the aftermath of the 1998 economic crisis. His appointment was met with jubilation by Russia's business community, as it reinforced the belief that Russia was on a path of continued market reform.[82] Alexei Kudrin, known for his close ties to Anatoly Chubais and his liberal reforms in the 1990s, was chosen as deputy prime minister in charge of finance and economy, as well as finance minister.

The fate of those who had participated in the preparation of the two alternative economic programs was particularly revealing. Many involved in the Gref Program acquired key government positions and maintained them for many years. Putin instantly elevated Gref to head the newly created Ministry of Economic Development and Trade (MEDT), which subsequently emerged as one of the chief establishments within the executive in charge of elaborating and implementing economic reforms. Other participants, such as Elvira Nabiullina, Arkadii Dvorkovich, and Mikhail Dmitriev, were enlisted as deputy ministers within his ministry. Alexei Ulyukaev was elevated to the post of first deputy minister of finance. Andrey Illarionov became Putin's chief economic advisor.[83]

By contrast, none of the contributors of the Ishayev Program acquired a comparable position within the federal executive. Ishayev maintained his position as a governor of the Khabarovsk Krai, but his career did not progress any further for the rest of the decade. Most of his associates, already with advanced academic careers, remained within universities and Russian think tanks. Some of them acquired minor advisory positions in government commissions, working groups, or nonprofit entities with government connections. Sergey Glazev, a vocal player in Ishayev's team and a strong proponent of state-led development, went on to serve as a key member of the opposition in the Russian Duma until 2007.

In the following years, Putin maintained his preference for liberal reformists. In a major cabinet reshuffle in 2004, he opted to keep Gref and Kudrin in their ministerial posts, though he discharged Kasyanov. Putin moved Dvorkovich from the MEDT to head the Expert Department within the Presidential Administration – a unit with the task of preparing many drafts dealing with economic policy along with many of Putin's speeches on economic matters.

This analysis of competing elites in economic policy making would be incomplete without a reference to the role of the *siloviki*. As indicated earlier, the *siloviki* secured for themselves a key place in the battles over Russia's oil rents. Yet, their role remained limited mainly to issues regarding ownership and management in the oil sector. In economic policy-making, namely fiscal policy, the *siloviki* did not become a distinctly powerful group. According to economist Mikhail Deliagin, this was in part owing to their background – they lacked a strong grasp of economics and never devised an alternative economic strategy.[84] There were other reasons as well. Russian political scientist Alexei Zudin notes that understandings of the term "*siloviki* remained very fluid – it was hard to identify a common stance among its members on most economic policy matters.[85] Stanislav Belkovski, a close observer of Kremlin politics, suggests that the *siloviki* did share some common objectives, such as expanding state control over natural resources. However, they hardly had a common ideology or vision about most macroeconomic policies.[86] This weakened their ability to act together and propose a major alternative. Furthermore, the *siloviki* could hardly be regarded as a group opposed to the economic path undertaken by the liberal team at the beginning of Putin's presidency. Despite their diverging stance on property rights, they preferred to abstain from populist proposals and supported market reforms overall.[87] It is revealing that no prominent *siloviki* publicly endorsed the Ishayev Program.

The profile of Russia's expert community advising the leadership on economic policies provides further evidence about the influential role of liberal reformists. According to Evsey Gurvich, who worked closely with the Finance Ministry during Putin's presidency, the government conducted regular meetings with experts. Predominantly these were individuals who were supportive of the government's fiscally conservative policies.[88] It was primarily liberal reformists who had access to government officials and were able to advise them on economic policy. By contrast, expert economists known for their preference for state-led development and expansionary welfare programs had a different experience. Their policy proposals had wide appeal within the opposition parties in the Duma, and had some currency in parts of the executive branch overseeing areas such as social policy, industry, transportation, and agriculture. Yet, they were rarely invited to meetings with the Finance Ministry or the MEDT; when they were part of the discussion, their proposals were generally ignored.[89]

How does Putin compare to Yeltsin with respect to his choice of officials to run the economy following his ascent to the Kremlin? There was a major continuity in terms of the dominant role of economic liberals in key executive positions since the early 1990s. Moreover, it was mostly the same group of liberal-leaning economists who continued to advise the government after Yeltsin's departure.[90]

Unlike Yeltsin, however, Putin emerged as more determined to build a team in charge of the economy that was not a product of compromise with the opposition. Yeltsin had often bowed to pressure from the Duma, appointing some opponents to market reform to influential positions within the cabinet. On several occasions, he fired leading market reformers as well.[91] Putin made no similar concessions during his first two major cabinet reshuffles in 2000 and 2004. Additionally, Putin clearly opted in favor of stability in the team he selected to run the economy, a pattern he has continued throughout his tenure. The less than nine-years-long Yeltsin era witnessed ten ministers of finance and eight ministers of the economy. During the following eighteen years, Putin had only three finance ministers and six economy ministers. Finance Minister Kudrin maintained his position for eleven years, transcending even the 2008 presidential reshuffle.

In sum, while the presence of fundamentally different economic programs did not bode well for executive cohesion, Putin was determined to ensure a greater degree of cohesion through his choice of cadres in charge of key decisions on the Russian economy. Thus, during the first years in his presidency, he opted to fill key positions on the executive with "fiscal conservatives" instead of appointing individuals with competing economic agendas.

Yet, there were several factors that inevitably led to difficulties in maintaining cohesion in Russia's executive branch on budgetary matters, eventually setting the stage for major shifts in policy. First, except in the case of the oil tax, the scope of involvement of executive agencies in budget-making has been fairly wide. Nearly every executive agency has had a role to play in budget preparation. Kudrin and Gref acquired the decisive positions, but were far from being the sole members of the executive charting policies on the budget. This wider scope of agencies engaged in policy-making is one key area that distinguishes the budget process from many other key areas of economic reform, ranging from the oil tax examined earlier to land and social reforms that touch a narrower constituency.

Second, the fiscal conservatives won the key positions in the management of the economy at the start of Putin's presidency, but they remained politically weak, making their ability to sustain a policy, if not their positions within the executive, tenuous. As most of them were handpicked by Putin, they lacked their own political base. There was no political party behind them and they lacked an extensive network of the sort enjoyed by the *siloviki*.

Finally, how the fiscal conservatives translated their ideas into policy would largely hinge on Putin's policy preferences. Their political survival depended on the president's whim, and so did the possibility to maintain even a semblance of cohesion on critical policy matters. Thus, I turn to examining Putin's position on redistributive policies.

Putin's Challenge: Balancing Fiscal Prudence and State-Led Development

Putin entrusted the Russian economy to a team of liberal reformists, but did that make the president himself an economic liberal? Did he agree with the objective of fiscal prudence and the need for further market reforms advocated by the economic liberals? What was his view on the role of the state in promoting development and welfare? And what was his strategy when seemingly contradictory policy alternatives appeared on the agenda?

Many of the answers to these questions can be found in Putin's early years in power. A review of his major speeches during his first term offers many insights into his policy preferences.[92] It sheds light on the key policy challenges he faced as well as his style of governance. Many of these policy challenges reappeared

over time, prompting Putin to balance policies that were difficult, and sometimes impossible, to reconcile.

Putin's remarks during his first term as president indicate strong support
for the liberal reformists. In each of his annual budgetary addresses, the president emphasized the importance of avoiding a budget deficit and the need
for further market reforms. In one of his first speeches as president in 2000,
Putin clearly rejected the idea of adopting a paternalistic approach to government, noting that it is "economically impossible and politically inappropriate."
He advocated for fiscal discipline to ensure the ongoing economic upturn was
maintained.[93] According to Tompson, his annual address to the Federal Assembly in the following year was a major endorsement of the Gref Program.[94] Putin
urged the government to continue with market reforms. His calls for cuts to
government spending were reflected in the medium-term economic program
adopted by the cabinet for the 2002–4 period.[95] Putin maintained his support
for a prudent fiscal approach in the following years. In 2003, in the midst of
heightened debates over how to utilize the nation's oil windfalls, Putin warned
against populist proposals that could "ruin the budget."[96]

And yet, President Putin did not unequivocally support the liberal reformists. His public statements often included a mixture of liberal and "statist" ideas.
As an astute Russian journalist aptly described, this mixture often meant "more
trouble for the government, torn apart by irreconcilable contradictions."[97] The
mixed signals compromised cohesion within the executive as well. Proponents
of a more active role for the state in the economy were emboldened to come
up with new proposals. Under pressure to respond, the liberal reformist camp
often ended up arguing with each other.

Putin's amalgam of liberal and statist approaches to the economy was con-
ceivably a reflection of his own ideals. He viewed Russia's competing economic
approaches as neither fully contradictory nor fully complementary. As leading Russian economist Yevgeny Yasin has noted, even if Putin subscribed to
some liberal ideas, such as the need for lower taxes and strict control over budgetary spending, he never became a disciple of Milton Friedman or Margaret
Thatcher.[98] Putin clearly believed that the state should have a "powerful role
to play in promoting growth and revitalizing core industries."[99] In his *kandidat* dissertation Putin had prescribed a more active role for the state in the
economy. In addition, even though he abstained from using the "language of
egalitarianism,"[100] Putin's speeches consistently emphasized the need to reduce
poverty and increase state support for education, health, and military personnel. This emphasis became particularly pronounced during his second presidential term.[101]

Putin's views were naturally influenced by political considerations. For the
president, economic reform or fiscal discipline could hardly be more significant than his concerns about loss of popularity and the emergence of a viable

opposition. According to Fish, Putin would only selectively subscribe to laissez-faire economic policies, as they threatened to strengthen non-state actors and loosen state control: "Whenever the requirements for political liberalization clashed with the imperatives of political control," the latter would win.[102] By the same token, Deliagin describes the Russian president as a "hostage" of his concern for popularity ratings.[103] Thus, Putin endorsed policies requiring fiscal prudence, as long as they did not fundamentally threaten his public support. Subsequent shifts in Putin's approach to fiscal policy need to be regarded in this light.

Finally, another important factor was his heavy emphasis on high economic growth rates, which became a recurring theme in his public speeches. During his first address to the Federal Assembly in July 2000, Putin issued a stark warning: the growing developmental gap with advanced economies was transforming Russia into a "Third World country."[104] Amid signs of an economic slowdown in early 2002, he publicly criticized the cabinet for its lack of ambitious economic targets.[105] In 2003, Putin set the target himself: the size of the Russian economy had to double by the end of the decade.[106] Soon, he went a step further and claimed sustaining rapid economic growth for Russia was a matter of "national honor," one that would determine its future role in the world.[107]

Putin's calls for a more ambitious growth agenda were vague about the means to achieve this objective. It was not clear whether he advocated infusing more state money into different sectors or accelerating market reforms. This left much room for interpretation for the liberal reformists, while encouraging "statists" to come up with alternative proposals to meet Putin's targets.

The president's ambiguity, as well as his wavering between liberal and statist ideas could be in part tactical.[108] Being vague gave Putin more room to maneuver. Meanwhile, he strived to proceed with major decisions after at least creating an image of himself as a "compromise" builder by involving a large number of stakeholders on key economic matters.[109] This was the case with his decision to authorize Ishayev to prepare an alternative economic program while maintaining open discussions on the future of the Gref Program. His decision to involve "statists" in the national discourse was also an early indication of what was to come later.

There was a major dilemma that may at least partly explain Putin's ambivalent approach. On the one hand, adhering to fiscal prudence was crucial to prevent another financial crisis. After all, Putin came to power following a financial crash that shook the country. Another crisis would bear risks for his political survival.[110] On the other hand, he also hoped to rapidly close the developmental gap between Russia and the advanced economies, while keeping a close eye on his public support. Such priorities called for some relaxation of public spending. Putin's dilemma was softened by rapidly rising oil prices, which contributed to fast economic growth, his high popularity, and a healthy budget surplus.[111] The time to make hard choices had not yet arrived.

The Executive Branch and Redistribution: The Triumph of Fiscally Conservative Budgets

Putin inherited a very different budgetary status quo. The 1990s were characterized by constant fiscal deficits and unrealistic budgeting. The financial crash in 1998 brought a major turnaround. The government under Primakov had rhetorically subscribed to "statist" policies.[112] In reality, however, Primakov adhered to strict fiscal discipline through drastic cuts in public spending to balance the federal budget. His policies were dictated by the urgent necessity to overcome the crisis. In his brief time as Prime Minister, Stepashin maintained this approach. Thus, when Putin succeeded him in 1999, the key question was whether he would maintain this new fiscally conservative approach to the budget, and for how long.

Preserving the status quo would not be easy. The urgency created by the financial crash was already in the past when Putin moved to the Kremlin. Many tasks and reforms lay ahead, but it was no longer a period of "extraordinary politics," as had been the case right after the financial crash under Primakov. Putin had filled key positions with liberal reformists favoring a prudent fiscal approach. However, the public appeal of their approach was limited.[113] The veto players outside of the executive were still able to demonstrate some resistance during Putin's early years, though their power was in decline. The executive branch itself was also not unified on a conservative fiscal path, even though liberal reformists were clearly given the reins of the economy. The discourse on the Gref Program and its alternative, the Ishayev plan, illustrated the deep ideological divisions in Russian politics that would be difficult to reconcile. Furthermore, the differences among members of the executive were not limited to ideology, as would become more apparent over time.

There were at least three main groups within the executive who demanded increased funding for their jurisdictions, thus presenting a challenge to the status quo. One group was associated with the "power" branches of the executive – namely defense and law enforcement. Stretching across a large number of ministries and the Presidential Administration, they demanded increased funding for personnel, retired servicemen, equipment, and the military industrial complex overall. Another group belonged to ministries in the so-called social branch of the cabinet. These were mainly officials within the executive in charge of education, health, pensions, housing, and other community services. They demanded a boost in spending.[114] Finally, part of the cabinet, namely those associated with various branches of industry, aspired to a state-led "industrial policy" in the form of subsidies to various sectors of the economy.[115] This group was joined by some powerful nongovernmental organizations, such as the Chamber of Commerce and Industry (CCI), headed by former prime minister Primakov, and by some members of Russia's Union for Industrialists and Entrepreneurs (RUIE).[116] As oil prices increased after 2002, their demands increased as well. Neither of these groups appeared to be dedicated to maintaining the government's countercyclical approach to fiscal policy.

Given the pressure to relax budgetary discipline, why did Russia continue to adhere to fiscal prudence over the next few years? In large part the explanation lies in Putin's choice of cadres, along with his own policy preference. People in key positions clearly favored the austere expenditure policy Putin inherited in 1999. Among them, Kudrin and his ministry had the chief role in thwarting policy proposals that could have significantly jeopardized Russia's fiscal course.[117] According to Deliagin, the Finance Ministry functioned as a highly "unified" institution, as its leading staff members strongly favored fiscal prudence. This further enhanced Kudrin's authority.[118] Moreover, Kudrin had direct access to Putin and could generally rely on his support in case of conflicts with other cabinet members, including the prime minister.[119]

Gref's ministry was also influential in defending the fiscally prudent course adopted under Putin.[120] Gref's biggest critics reproached him for his reluctance to adopt an "industrial policy" supporting select sectors of the Russian economy.[121] Dvorkovich, who worked for several years as Gref's deputy before moving to the Presidential Administration in 2004, confirms the initial reluctance to support such a policy. He noted, "We believed that the objective should be to create favorable conditions for investors in the economy overall, rather than focusing on particular industries. Had we chosen a particular sector and supported it via government funds, there would be a high likelihood of making a mistake." For many years, it was not clear where Russia's comparative advantage lay. Hence, the government abstained from the risky decision of supporting state-led "industrial policy" or major investment programs.[122] Putin still did not appear convinced about state-led industrial policy. Amid rising calls for industrial policy, his address to the Federal Assembly in May 2004 still lacked a reference to such a new approach.[123]

What also helped Kudrin and Gref in defending fiscal discipline was the uniquely favorable circumstances they faced, though rising oil prices made their task harder. According to Lev Freinkman, a Russian economist, "Many people in the Russian government think that the 1998 crisis was the best thing that could have happened to Russia. It illustrated the importance of having a stringent fiscal policy as a means for avoiding a similar crisis."[124] Thus, despite rising oil prices, Dvorkovich recalls, there was widespread consensus within the Russian government that preserving macroeconomic stability was of utmost priority:[125] "Even though various ministries tried to protect their own interests and negotiated for more funding, everyone understood that macroeconomic stability had to be maintained."[126] The executive branch was particularly united on the idea that repeating the periodic hyperinflationary shocks of the 1990s had to be avoided.[127] Putin also made low inflation a priority.[128] This strengthened the hand of fiscal conservatives, though it also prompted a new discourse on the sources of inflation in Russia (see chapter 6). The high level of foreign debt inherited by Putin in the early 2000s served as another reason to avoid expansionary spending. Finally, though oil prices were rising during Putin's first term as president, the leadership remained highly pessimistic about a potential downturn in the oil markets, necessitating caution.[129]

Yet, the success in maintaining a fiscally conservative approach could also be credited to the Finance Ministry's skillful maneuvers during budget planning. The ministry tended to propose indicators that justified less spending during the budget implementation stage. For instance, it insisted on preparing budgets on the basis of highly pessimistic assumptions about oil prices and the GDP growth rate. At the same time, it tended to project highly "aggressive" drops in the inflation rate. In each case, these indicators allowed the ministry to project relatively low amounts of "federal revenues."[130] This justified its resistance to excessive increases in public spending, and provided some room to maneuver when negotiating budget parameters.[131]

Amid the victory of the proponents of a fiscally conservative path, there were also some "setbacks," though Russia still managed to maintain its highly conservative fiscal approach for several years. Some distinct budgetary areas such as defense and law enforcement managed to obtain notably larger increases in annual budgetary outlays.[132] Similarly, wages in the state sector, as well as pensions, were repeatedly increased above the inflation rate.

Such setbacks were the product of protracted negotiations within the executive and with the legislature. Less is known about the process that led to them. Yet, they did reflect Putin's occasional ambivalence on economic policy. Noticeably, the setbacks occurred specifically in areas where the president pushed for increased public spending during his annual budgetary speeches and his address to the Federal Assembly. For example, in almost every annual budgetary address, Putin boasted about the government's success in raising pensions and urged further improvements. Similarly, his speeches reflected concern about the economic needs of veterans and personnel associated with the military and law enforcement.[133]

Putin's ambivalent stance posed additional challenges for fiscal conservatives, contributing to a growing lack of cohesion within the executive over time. Thus, the president's heavy emphasis on rapid economic growth and his calls for more ambitious targets were not compatible with the Finance Ministry's preference for more "pessimistic" indicators. Putin's emphasis on economic growth sparked a growing divide between Gref and Kudrin. Gref became more willing to accept expansionary policies in certain areas such as social spending and development as a means of securing faster growth rates. By the same token, Gref became more tolerant towards an increase in the inflation rate. By 2005, Kudrin increasingly came to be the lone voice defending the continuation of the conservative budgetary policy.[134]

The Executive Branch and Redistribution: The Broad Consensus on Comprehensive Tax Reform

One of Putin's earliest tasks was reinvigorating a comprehensive package of tax reforms. Reforming taxation had been on the agenda for most of the 1990s, but little had been accomplished in that respect. Work on formulating the package had already started in 1999; it gained momentum during the following year when Putin's administration set tax reform as one of its top priorities.[135]

Tax reform turned out to be far less controversial than budgetary policy. Certainly, cutting taxes is generally expected to be a simpler task than reaching consent on key budgetary parameters. During this period Russia was able to bring about a broad comprehensive tax reform package with lower taxation at its foundations. Despite some minor disagreements, the Russian executive was highly cohesive on the need for comprehensive reform and lower taxation. As discussed earlier, there was a broad "coalition of discontent" demanding a higher tax burden on the oil sector. Likewise, it was far from challenging to build a case for a series of tax reforms that would lower the tax burden on the rest of the economy. The Finance Ministry, the MEDT, Prime Minister Kasyanov,[136] and major officials from the Presidential Administration, such as Illarionov, as well as President Putin, consistently reiterated their belief that a reduction in tax rates was a crucial means to spur economic growth.[137] A tax policy that raised the burden on the oil sector while reducing it for the rest of the economy was also perceived as a potentially effective means for economic diversification. Even staunch opponents of the liberal reformists supported this approach.[138] This broad consensus within the executive, along with the weakening of the other veto players, played an instrumental role in accomplishing a highly elaborate tax reform initiative during Putin's first term.

It is important to acknowledge key exogenous factors that aided Russia's efforts for comprehensive tax reform. Undoubtedly, the turnaround in the Russian economy was an opportune moment to enact major tax reforms while making it easier for taxpayers to pay their dues. The abrupt end of the economic decline in the late 1990s, the positive impact of devaluation following the August 1998 crisis on the export-oriented sectors overall, the rise in real wages, the rapid remonetization of the Russian economy, and the increase in profitability in a growing number of sectors after 1999 all served to create a larger tax base, making consensus on tax reform more likely. In the meantime, these factors helped to reduce incentives for hiding revenues and prompted various taxpayers to move out of the shadow economy. Also, nominal tax rates had been set excessively high during the 1990s, but few paid at these rates. In the words of one of Putin's economic advisors, "It was like an unwritten agreement between the state and taxpayers": the nominal rate did not mean much.[139] Thus, the government could afford to cut the nominal rates as long as it improved tax collection. Indeed, efforts to improve tax enforcement steadily continued, while the lower nominal rates reduced the incentives for taxpayers to hide their revenues.

Nevertheless, amid the high degree of executive cohesion on the need to cut taxes, there were some disagreements about the pace and the extent of the proposed tax reform measures. Differences between the Finance Ministry and the MEDT – the two key agencies in the process of tax reform – became increasingly apparent over time. The MEDT in particular acquired a highly active, if not the dominant, role during 2000 and 2001 – two key years in the tax reform process.[140] Unlike those of the Finance Ministry, the MEDT's reform efforts were driven by broad concerns about the economy.[141] Thus, citing data indicating economic slowdown in early 2002, Deputy Minister Dvorkovich openly criticized Kudrin's resistance to more ambitious reductions in the tax rates.[142] The Finance Ministry was accused of being overly oriented towards balancing the budget to the detriment of Russia's economic performance.[143]

The Finance Ministry remained as an effective proponent of a cautious approach to tax reform.[144] Pointing to pessimistic projections about oil revenues, the need to service substantial foreign debt, and impending risks to balancing the budget, Kudrin's ministry managed to slow down the pace and extent of the proposed tax cuts.[145] For instance, the VAT, the largest source of revenues for the federal government,[146] was reduced as late as 2004 by only 2 percentage points (from 20 to 18 percent).[147] Kudrin's conservative stance got an occasional boost by President Putin, who recurrently called for caution in the tax reform process.[148] Evidently, by 2002, the Finance Ministry regained the upper hand and steered the discourse on tax reform in line with its comparatively cautious approach.[149]

Overall, the government's tax policy was a significant alternative means to redistribute oil rents during Putin's early years in the presidency. The government maintained its highly conservative approach to public spending, but the overhaul of the tax regime for the oil sector made it possible to lower taxes for other segments of the economy. In effect, tax reform in the oil sector helped to fund a broad tax overhaul for the Russian economy as a whole.

The Duma's Declining Role in Shaping Russia's Redistributive Policies

Putin's economic team, compared with that of his predecessors, gradually emerged much less constrained by the Duma and better able to implement its policies. It was during the Third Duma, between 1999 and 2003, that the lower chamber steadily lost its ability to act as an effective veto player. Subsequently, it became increasingly common for the Duma to be described as the executive's rubber stamp. According to Russian political scientist Oleg Ignatov, the fading role of the legislature in fiscal policies was not coincidental. Putin and his key bureaucrats were well aware that many of Russia's fiscal difficulties during the 1990s were due to compromises made to the legislature. They knew that securing a comfortable pro-Kremlin majority in the Duma would facilitate the executive's primacy in fiscal policies.[150]

Formally, the Duma has a critical role in charting redistributive policies, particularly owing to its authority to approve the federal budget. According to the Russian constitution, the budget bill cannot be decreed by the executive; thus the Duma's cooperation is essential. Not only can Duma deputies reject the government's budget, they can introduce numerous amendments at various stages of the budgetary preparation process. Additionally, the budget bill needs to pass through several Duma readings, increasing the chances that it could be rejected.[151]

There is a glaring contrast in how the Duma voted on budget bills during the 1990s and how it voted under Putin. Roll call voting data provide unambiguous evidence of the Duma's role as veto player under Yeltsin, and its fading influence under Putin.[152] During the 1990s, the Duma's role in the budget process was apparent in many ways. First, the executive branch repeatedly faced difficulty securing the required majority (226 votes) to pass the budget bill. Second, budget bills were rarely approved on time, as negotiations between the executive branch and the Duma dragged on well into the following fiscal year. Third, lacking a pro-government majority during the First and Second Duma, the cabinet could secure the approval of a budget bill only after convincing key opposition parties to support it. For instance, every year from 1994 to 1999, the Agrarians eventually voted to support the budget bills, while KPRF deputies helped the government to pass the budget four times.[153] Fourth, it was common to witness factions switching their votes from "no" to "yes" across Duma readings. According to Troxel, such a switch signified concessions by the executive in the form of increased spending.[154] With such concessions to various Duma factions, the budget often became difficult to implement, as committed expenditures did not match the accruing revenues.[155]

The 1999 Duma elections signified a major turnaround for executive-legislative relations.[156] Roll call voting data illustrate the executive's enhanced ability to secure approval for its budget bills. Cabinets never failed to command the required majority among deputies for any of the readings of the budget bills during the Third and Fourth Duma. The budgets were consistently approved before the end of the year. In another contrast to the 1990s, the majority of the KPRF and the Agrarian faction regularly voted against the proposed budget bills in every reading between 2000 and 2003. This voting pattern persisted during the Fourth Duma with respect to the two key opposition parties, KPRF and Rodina. Furthermore, members of these factions almost never switched their votes across Duma readings. Apparently, the government was not as forthcoming as it had been in conceding to their requests.

Much of this change can be attributed to the rise of a relatively "friendlier" Duma following the 1999 elections. The surprisingly successful results for Unity provided the executive with a sizable loyal bloc, which formed the basis of a winning coalition during budget negotiations. It was also important that Unity members not only identified themselves as pro-Kremlin, but also many of them shared the economic ideals of the liberal reformists, including their preference for fiscal discipline.[157] This helped to alleviate pressure on the government to expand spending. In addition, Unity members in the Duma were predominantly affiliated with party lists rather than "single member districts" (SMDs).[158] According to Remington, party list-based factions tended to vote more cohesively.[159] Also, such factions were reportedly less likely to ask for "side payments" in the form of increased public spending to benefit their constituencies. Being less exposed to constituency pressures, they were more willing to support measures promoting fiscal discipline.[160]

Nonetheless, securing a winning coalition for the federal budget was not a simple task during the Third Duma. Despite their remarkably cohesive voting pattern, deputies from Unity could provide only about a third of the required 226 votes needed to pass the budget.[161] Three other pro-government factions, OVR, People's Deputies, and Russia's Regions, could barely secure the needed majority.[162] SMD-based Russia's Regions did not exhibit a cohesive stance during voting, complicating the cabinet's efforts to command a majority.[163]

Thus, during the Third Duma period, the cabinet had to actively work to convince deputies to support its budget bills. Negotiations on the 2001 budget proposal were particularly demanding – this was the first budget in post-Soviet Russia to propose a zero deficit.[164] The government had to step back and yield to some of the deputies' demands for increased public spending.[165] Likewise, during negotiations on the 2002 budget, the four pro-government factions negotiated jointly to secure more funds in electorally beneficial areas, such as defense, pensions, regional aid, road construction, and support for industry.[166] Members of Unity were particularly interested in securing more public funding for defense and law enforcement.[167] Yet, according to Remington, the improved coordination between the government and the four factions allowed the government to concentrate its bargaining efforts on the smallest number of factions that could deliver the required majority vote.[168] Additionally, the government could get some support from LDPR, SPS, Yabloko, and independents, which strengthened its bargaining power against Duma factions.

During the Fourth Duma, the executive branch finally enjoyed a comfortable majority – as of December 2003, the Duma de facto lost its capability to influence fiscal policy. United Russia, "the party of power," dominated the budgetary process to such an extent that all amendments to the 2005 budget proposed by the opposition were rejected. Glazev, one of the leaders of the opposition Rodina faction, noted that the budget-drafting process had become a partisan affair and sarcastically proposed to move it from the Duma's platform to the party congress of United Russia.[169] United Russia continued to negotiate with the executive on key budgetary matters. However, these negotiations took place primarily through direct communication with the executive branch rather than at the Duma's platform. The informal nature of these communications clouds the precise extent of compromises accepted by the Russian government. Yet, the latter maintained the upper hand and never faced difficulty in getting the party's consent to budget bills. Only a handful of United Russia members preferred to abstain from voting rather than vote against the executive's budget bills.[170]

Getting the Duma's support in lowering the tax burden on the economy was far less demanding for the executive than getting its support for budget bills. This was one of the few areas on the reformers' agenda that had a broad base of support within the lower chamber, even from KPRF members.[171] The other veto players, the Federation Council and regional governors, were also generally aligned with the government's goal to lower the tax burden on the economy through comprehensive tax reform.[172]

Inevitably, there were difficulties. Disagreements about the pace and the extent of tax reform plagued the government's attempts to build a winning coalition in the legislature. While the difficulty in building support varied across proposed tax bills and over time,[173] the government was often required to step back and cajole the deputies of both chambers, as well as regional authorities, by granting them various concessions. One source of discord was the distributional implications of the tax cuts and the effect on regional budgets. The government had to occasionally step back and slow down the implementation of the reform measures, while also compensating the regions for their potential losses.[174] Also, the Finance Ministry fought against proposals coming from Duma factions requesting more drastic tax cuts.[175]

Despite some compromises, the government was still able to shape tax reform as it envisioned. The pace of the reform and the extent of the tax cuts predominantly reflected the preferences of the Finance Ministry.[176] Kudrin's ministry had several advantages when negotiating with the legislature. First, it could bargain from a position of strength by openly threatening to suspend further plans for a rate cut if the government's demands were not met. The Duma deputies often yielded to the ministry's pressure or risked a delay in securing tax cuts altogether.[177]

Second, regional interests, represented in both chambers, were highly divided, failing to present a common approach on the proposed tax measures. The division was primarily between donor and recipient regions, as proposed tax measures affected them differently. During the negotiation of Part II of the Tax Code in 2000, Vladimir Yakovlev, governor of the Leningrad Region, bluntly accused the government of deliberately setting the regions against each other on the basis of this distinction.[178]

Finally, at critical moments, the government benefited from Putin's personal efforts to convince deputies and governors to accept the proposed tax reform measures. Thus, in the midst of heated debates on reforming the corporate profit tax in 2001, Putin intervened on behalf of the government. As the Duma's Budget Committee had come up with an alternative proposal to revise the profit tax, the president made it clear that he favored the government's version.[179] In June 2003, when the Duma and the government sparred over the details of reforming two other taxes, the Value Added Tax and the Unified Social Tax (ESN), Putin supported the government's more cautious approach to rate cuts. He actively worked to bring key opponents, such as Moscow's mayor Luzhkov and the deputy speaker of the Duma, Georgii Boos (a member of OVR), in line.[180]

The Demise of the Federation Council and Regional Governments in Shaping Redistributive Policies

The Federation Council and regional governors shared the same fate as the Duma during Putin's first term as president. Their role in shaping Russia's redistributive policies waned during this period, and did not recover afterwards. With these veto players weakened, the executive branch was even less restrained in charting its redistributive policies.

The ability of the Federation Council and regional governments to act as potential veto players in key redistributive policies is manifested in several areas.[181] Constitutionally, the Federation Council's approval is required for key bills, such as the one on the budget, which cannot be decreed by the president.[182] Also, *implementing* fiscal discipline is very much conditional on the cooperation of regional governments. To meet fiscally conservative targets, the federal government needs the cooperation of regions. For instance, the latter can run fiscal deficits, which have repercussions for the consolidated budget, as well as the federal budget, if the deficit is covered through a federal transfer. The regions' burden for the federal budget can arise due to both overspending and a lax approach to revenue collection.

The ability of regions to act as effective veto players under the Yeltsin administration had significant budgetary implications. Over half of Russia's autonomous regions signed special "bilateral agreements" with the federal executive, thereby gaining a degree of autonomy in their finances.[183] While limiting the size of revenues sent to the federal budget, these special deals hampered the federal executive's attempts to ensure fiscal prudence. Treisman notes that

Yeltsin often engaged in "fiscal appeasement" through additional federal transfers in order to secure allies among regional leaders. Ironically, the biggest winners were regions with the most "hostile" electorate and regional governors.[184] Also, during this period, Russia's regions were increasingly successful in capturing a growing share of revenues previously accruing to the federal budget. Their share in Russia's total government revenues expanded markedly during the 1995–7 period and remained at near 60 percent in 1998.[185] This further exacerbated the deficit in the federal budget.

Putin's presidency was marked by a major centralization of government revenues. While the beginning of this development goes back to the anti-crisis measures of 1998, the new president upheld this strategy. The regions' share in total revenues was reduced sharply from 54.2 percent in 1999 to 38.2 percent in 2005.[186] Unsurprisingly, this contributed to regional fiscal deficits amid the objections of regional authorities.[187] The federal government tried to alleviate the problem by increasing the size of federal transfers. Following the economic collapse in 1998, they had been cut sharply and stood at 1.9 percent of Russia's GDP in 1999. By 2005, they rose to 4.2 percent of GDP.[188] Federal transfers during the 1990s had often been the product of lobbying efforts by regional interests. Regions continued to lobby for federal transfers under Putin. What was different this time was that they were fighting to get a portion of the revenues they had lost to federal authorities owing to the centralization of revenues.

Fiscal centralization under Putin involved additional measures. Thus, the special bilateral agreements between the federal executive and regional governments were abolished, expanding the federal executive's ability to streamline regional budgets in accordance with its objectives. Other measures included new rules clarifying what regional governments were allowed to fund,[189] as well as legislative changes aimed at expanding Federal Treasury branches across Russia's regions.[190] Putin was actively involved in this process through his annual budgetary addresses outlining fiscal centralization measures as a major objective.[191]

The demise of the Federation Council as a veto player was far less dramatic, and in fact, its role in budgetary policy represented major continuities with the Yeltsin era. The Federation Council had never rejected the federal budget for the 1994–9 period. After 1999, a markedly higher share of deputies from the upper chamber voted to approve the annual budget bills.[192] The Federation Council's propensity to approve budget bills can be linked to the chronic difficulty among its members for collective action. This difficulty, in turn, may be associated with their independence from political factions. Federation Council deputies have represented highly diverse regions, whose interests have clashed during the preparation of the federal budget. Donor regions and recipient regions have had conflicting interests with regard to revenue collection and assignment of federal spending to regions. Meanwhile, the higher approval rates for the budget under Putin may be associated with federal reforms that significantly curtailed the authority of the upper chamber members.[193] Budget bills under Putin started to pass with a considerably higher majority in the Duma as well, which often made it possible to override a potential veto by the Federation Council.[194]

The Waning of the Fiscally Conservative Approach during the 2005–8 Period

As Putin moved into his second term as president, Russia's finances still looked sound. Rising oil prices made it possible to both expand budgetary spending and accumulate reserves in the newly established stabilization fund. Likewise, Russia took a further step to institutionalize public spending by introducing three-year budgeting in 2007. This allowed for the incorporation of longer-term planning into the budgetary process. According to Chaisty, this was a further blow to the legislature in the process of budget planning.[195] It predetermined some of the parameters for future fiscal years.

And yet, key policy outcomes – the rapidly declining foreign debt, the booming financial reserves, and growing nominal budget surpluses – were not the product of a policy consensus within the ruling elite. Instead, the executive branch was far from cohesive from the start, despite Putin's efforts to fill key positions with liberal reformists.[196] As we have seen, the Ishayev plan was an early counterproposal to the approach adopted by the Russian government. While it was quickly set aside, many of the ideas remained in circulation. Fiscal conservatives continuously confronted demands to alter their cautious approach to redistribution. They enjoyed Putin's support, but that support was not without limits. The president was torn between multiple objectives for the economy. He would also need to take into account the potential political impact of the chosen redistributive policies.

The fiscally conservative approach gradually faded, as its proponents started to face one setback after another. The first came at the beginning of 2005, when widespread public protests prompted the government to reappraise its approach to economic reforms. A few months later, President Putin, amid much fanfare, announced four "national projects" that would emerge as a major redistributive policy in the following years. In 2007 Russia witnessed a proliferation of institutions created specifically to promote economic development, along with the establishment of several state-led corporations, through additional spending.[197] In Kudrin's view, these institutions were generally ineffective and served as a substitute to a good investment climate, which was still lacking.[198]

How can we explain this turnaround? As the veto players outside the executive branch had already faded in importance, the answers must lie within the executive branch itself. The waning role of the legislature and regional governors facilitated the task of the executive to shift its policies in new directions.[199] In effect, as the veto players theory would suggest, the enhanced ability of the state to enact new policies came at the cost of its ability to commit to the status quo.

I suggest two explanations as to why the conservative fiscal approach proved untenable. Both focus on the executive branch. First, intra-executive disagreements intensified over time, further weakening and, in fact, isolating the few fiscal conservatives left in the decision-making process. Second, the hitherto fiscally conservative approach became increasingly associated with political risks for the leadership. In effect, the status quo policy approach could hardly be maintained without political costs for President Putin. By contrast, changing the policy course would minimize such risks by broadening the support for Putin among both the ruling elite and the public. Added to which, Russia had ample resources for such a shift.

Kudrin's Increasingly Isolated Role as Fiscal Conservative

Rising intra-executive disagreements were, at least in part, a result of Putin's own choices. Ministers Kudrin and Gref advocated redistributive policies that were widely disliked by different branches of the government. Yet, with the president's backing, they could chart policies without the need to build a broad consensus. Over time, Kudrin and his ministry became increasingly isolated in their defense of the policy status quo. There are several reasons for this.

As Russia's economy boomed and oil prices kept rising, there was a steady shift in the national discourse on the future of the economy. Memories of the 1998 crisis started to fade.[200] By the second half of 2004, Russia's foreign exchange reserves surpassed the government's rapidly dwindling foreign debt for the first time.[201] Boris Gryzlov, the head of United Russia, aptly summed up the shifting mood: "[Russia] has made a full transition from its policy of stabilization to a policy of development." Gryzlov urged the authorities to set new economic priorities, echoing common proposals that the state needed to spend more on infrastructure and priority sectors.[202] Gryzlov's call echoed a growing emphasis within the ruling elite on the need for more active state intervention and a paternalist approach to the economy. Ironically, while Russia had recently set up a special savings (stabilization) fund to accumulate the bulk of the oil rents for the future, the fund emerged as a major target for advocates of such a shift in economic policy. By the middle of the decade, Russia's economic discourse on budget policy and on what to do with its oil savings became almost indistinguishable (see chapter 6). Furthermore, growing pleas for state-led development were not limited to proposals to spend more public funds. What was lurking in the background was a steady rise in the state's share in the economy in the aftermath of Rosneft's acquisition of Yukos in 2004. By

2007, the share of state-owned companies in the total capitalization of Russian companies rose from 24 percent to 40 percent.[203]

As calls for a more active redistribution policy grew louder, Putin's response was critical. As the ultimate decision-maker,[204] he did not mount a strong defense of fiscal prudence; nor did he join the chorus of voices calling for a drastic increase in redistribution. Putin continued to recognize Russia's vulnerability as a resource-dependent economy and warned against excessive spending. He also urged for more spending for social needs, the military, and infrastructure, and set more ambitious targets for the economy. The state could now afford to spend more for guns, bread, and development.[205] His approach was to balance two very distinct visions for the Russian economy. In fact, as Kudrin recalls in an interview, Putin assigned him a key role to "moderate" the pace of relaxation in the government's fiscal approach.[206] It seems Putin found appointing "statists" to key economic positions risky: they could not perform the "moderation" role a financial conservative such as Kudrin could. Yet, Putin's stance came at a cost: it further weakened the fiscally conservative wing of the executive branch and contributed to a gradual split within this wing.

A case in point was the evolving stance of the Ministry of Economic Development and Trade. Putin's repeated emphasis on rapid economic growth served as a stern warning within the executive, and particularly for this ministry. Minister Gref, one of the chief advocates of reform and post-crisis stabilization, emerged as a vocal proponent of a more relaxed approach to redistribution.[207] The Gref and Kudrin ministries could no longer be described as working in tandem after 2005. Not only was Gref repeatedly coming up with new proposals that would necessitate tapping into Russia's oil windfalls, his ministry started to diverge from the Finance Ministry on key parameters of the federal budget. For instance, during the preparation of the 2007 budget, Gref's ministry insisted on shifting towards a more optimistic scenario for oil prices, which would warrant more public spending.[208]

Gref's ministry emerged at the center of a new economic program, one that manifested the shifting mood on the role of the state in the Russian economy. The ministry set to work on a program in 2006.[209] The draft was approved by the government in the fall of 2008 – about a year after Gref's departure from the ministry. Known as the Concept for the Long Term Social Economic Development of Russia by 2020 (*Kontseptsia Dolgosrochnogo Razvitia 2020*, KDR 2020 in the Russian acronym), many aspects of this new program represented a clear contrast with the Gref Program adopted in 2000.[210] While the Gref Program had prioritized market reforms, deregulation, and privatization, KDR 2020 emphasized the need for the state to take a more active role in development. It deemed state-owned corporations, development banks, and recently established "development" institutions as crucial for the future of the economy.

Changes in the composition of the executive branch point to additional set-backs for fiscal conservatives.[211] Many of the liberal reformists of the early 2000s did keep their positions throughout Putin's first two terms as president.[212] Yet, there were important exceptions. A key example was the replacement of Prime Minister Mikhail Kasyanov with Mikhail Fradkov in March 2004. Kasyanov belonged to the liberal reformist camp generally advocating fiscal prudence.[213] Fradkov, heading the Tax Police until 2003, could hardly be defined as a liberal reformist.[214] He became a vocal proponent of state-led development, actively advocating state-led industrial policy and a more relaxed approach to expenditure until his departure from the cabinet in 2007.

Another setback that directly affected the Finance Ministry was the arrest of Sergey Storchak, one of Kudrin's deputies, in November 2007. A close associate of Storchak interpreted this arrest as a rebellion instigated by members of the *siloviki* against the fiscal conservative camp and its policies.[215] Hanson and Teague share a similar interpretation: allegedly *siloviki* aimed to put pressure on Kudrin through arresting his deputy to weaken the ministry's resistance to a more active role of the state in the economy.[216] Caught by surprise, Kudrin continued to defend his colleague's innocence until he was acquitted in 2011.[217]

Rising Political Risks Associated with Maintaining the Fiscally Conservative Approach

Another reason for the policy shift towards more redistribution was the political risks associated with maintaining the status quo. In effect, the policy shift was a product of President Putin's need to balance various political risks. On the one hand, continuing with the fiscally conservative approach could have unpredictable political costs for Putin and his leadership. Rapidly growing oil windfalls made it more difficult to justify a conservative approach to redistribution.[218] On the other hand, a policy shift towards more redistribution was not devoid of financial risks either, risks that could have wider political implications. A sudden drop in the price of oil could never be discounted, as the economy remained highly vulnerable to an oil price shock.[219]

The gradual shift towards an expansionary spending policy suggests that Putin considered risks associated with maintaining the fiscally conservative approach worth more attention. The many setbacks for the fiscal conservatives during the 2005–8 period were evidently linked to concerns about public support and the approaching presidential elections. Several of these setbacks deserve closer review.

First, in a historic twist of events, on the centennial of Bloody Sunday, commemorating a peaceful protest in 1905 by Russian peasants that turned into a massacre by tsarist forces, President Putin faced Moscow's largest demonstration of social unrest since the early 1990s. Public protests spread rapidly across

Russia during the following weeks. What the protestors wanted was a rollback of a recent law that aimed to abolish in-kind social benefits and replace them with targeted cash payments.[220] This legislation on the "monetization" of social benefits, effective as of 1 January 2005, had been part of the government's effort to establish stricter control over social spending. Many of these in-kind benefits, affecting over 40 million Russian citizens, were a Soviet legacy, and had further mushroomed during the 1990s in the midst of rapidly declining living standards.[221] Those with the most to lose were primarily pensioners. Military staff were also strongly opposed to this legislation.[222]

The Putin administration was caught by surprise.[223] The unrest was spreading at a time when neighboring Ukraine was undergoing the "Orange Revolution."[224] The public blamed the government for the monetization crisis, but according to a public poll by the Levada Center, some of the anger was directed at Putin as well.[225] The monetization reform negatively affected the performance of United Russia in local elections in the spring of 2005.[226] Faced with few constraints within the legislature, the government had ignored calls by opposition parties to reconsider its approach to the reform. With United Russia's backing, it had no difficulty in passing the legislation in the summer of 2004. The government had not deemed it necessary to prepare a social impact assessment for the proposed reform.[227]

This first instance of public outcry had far-reaching implications for Russia's economic policy. The government was forced to take a few steps back. The monetization process was not entirely abandoned, but was considerably diluted in terms of its scope and impact. The government's main response was a commitment to raise public funding, amplifying its shifting approach to redistributive policies. President Putin rapidly tried to take control of the crisis. He agreed to raise pensions ahead of schedule and beyond what was budgeted for the year. Salaries for military staff were also increased. Also, the government committed additional funds to regions to compensate for their residents' lost benefits.[228]

Beyond these immediate actions, there were long-term implications of this monetization debacle. The government soon opted to delay other socially important reforms.[229] In fact, during the following few years, government officials were careful to avoid using the term "reform." As some observers noted, the term "projects" replaced "reforms" as policy-makers rushed to propose initiatives on how best to redistribute Russia's growing wealth.[230] Implementing some of the reforms already under way became more difficult. Pensions reform was particularly affected. The rapid increase in pensions beyond what was put forward in the approved budget not only set a precedent, it contributed to a growing deficit for the pensions system in the following years.[231]

Only a few months after the monetization debacle, Putin announced a major project to redistribute the state's growing oil windfalls. In September 2005, the president declared four priority areas that would receive special funding:

education, public health, housing, and agriculture. The effectiveness of these projects is debatable. Kudrin, never fond of this initiative, clearly noted his uneasiness about how these projects unfolded a decade later: "[T]here is no one accountable. That is, we do not know the results of the implementation of these key national projects."[232] He described the projects as an example of pre-election populism. Their launch represented a victory for the proponents of a more centralized approach to redistributing government funds for development. Dmitry Medvedev, then head of the Presidential Administration, was among the leading proponents of this approach, while Kudrin argued against the federal government undertaking such projects.[233]

The four national projects once again represented a political calculation by President Putin. They became a showcase for the government's shift towards a more generous approach to redistribution, rallying extensive support within both the executive and the legislature. In the meantime, Putin, driven by concerns about the next presidential election cycle, prompted a significant reshuffle within the executive branch. First, he put Medvedev in charge of the national projects in a newly created council. According to Sakwa, this council worked parallel to the government and undermined the authority of the prime minister.[234] Only a few days later, in November 2005, Putin appointed Medvedev as the first deputy prime minister, maintaining his key task of overseeing these projects.[235] Stanislav Belkovski, a renowned commentator on Kremlin politics, rightly predicted that Medvedev was being groomed to succeed Putin in the 2008 presidential elections. Putting Medvedev in charge of these highly popular national projects enhanced his political capital as Putin's designated successor.[236] Kudrin's disagreement with Medvedev on the national projects turned out to be an early sign of what became an intense competition between these two political figures. This was not an example of a split within the executive branch between liberal reformists and "statists." Instead, it was an indication of the growing isolation of Russia's fiscal conservatives among liberal reformers.

With rapidly rising pensions, delayed monetization of in-kind benefits, and newly designated funds for priority projects, a shift in Russia's redistribution policies was in full swing by 2006.[237] In 2007, Russia created several development institutions to promote economic diversification. Additionally, a growing number of state corporations got access to public funding in the name of accelerated development and diversification. Russia witnessed record growth in budgetary spending in 2007, even though its savings in the oil fund kept growing as well (see chapter 6). According to Russian economist Sergey Alexashenko, there was a clear link between this move towards redistribution and Russia's new election cycle. For years, the Russian leadership had insisted on a prudent approach to spending. But "the dam burst during the 2007–8 period," when Putin needed to resolve two political tasks simultaneously – securing an absolute majority in the Duma and a successor during the presidential elections – while also appealing to mounting demands to make use of Russia's booming oil windfalls.[238] Opposition leader Boris Nemtsov was more critical, suggesting that state-led development and building state corporations was merely a pretext for Kremlin affiliates to get their hands on a massive flow of rents.[239] In this context, the record growth in public spending in 2007 was not surprising: Putin was not willing to pay a possible political cost by maintaining the fiscal prudence that had defined the presidency to that point.

Managing Two Oil Busts and a Boom after 2008

Soon after President Putin stepped out of the Kremlin in 2008, the Russian economy went through an astounding boom and bust cycle. During the following ten years, Russia witnessed two oil busts and another oil boom in between. As noted earlier, Russia responded to the first fairly short-lived bust with massive countercyclical fiscal expansion. There was nothing particularly surprising about this response – it was in line with the approach adopted by many other countries to confront the Great Recession. However, Russia's subsequent fiscal choices raise some interesting questions. First, the government was noticeably slow in phasing out its expansionary fiscal policy during the new oil boom. In fact, it never truly returned to a fiscally conservative approach, as spending commitments swelled. This was the second big oil boom of the Putin era, yet the government's reaction was drastically different from its response to the first boom, when fiscal prudence was the dominant approach, at least till 2005. What explains this difference? Second, once Russia was confronted with another oil bust at the end of 2014, the government's reaction was more complex than it had been in the 2008–10 period; this time it blended elements of countercyclical policies and fiscal conservatism. There were clear indications of a preference for fiscal restraint, including the adoption of some unpopular measures. What explains this subsequent return of fiscally conservative elements in the government's policies?

Once again, the explanations proposed here center on Russia's executive branch and its evolving stance on fiscal and economic policies. I examine the extent of intra-executive disagreements by looking at the position of the Finance Ministry relative to other key players within the executive branch. I also look at how the executive's perceptions of political risks, relative to the available resources to mitigate them, shifted over time. The analysis reviews the period after 2008 in three stages: the first oil bust after the onset of the Great Recession, the 2011–14 oil boom, and the second bust in the aftermath of Russia's annexation of Crimea.

I devote much less attention to the other institutional veto players during this period as there is no evidence to suggest that they were capable of significantly shaping policy choices. Neither regional governors nor the legislature reversed their fading role in shaping key decisions of the government after 2008. They were not irrelevant: for instance, the executive still needed the legislature's approval of a budget bill, leading to passionate debates on where to allocate public funding. Yet, as Ben Noble notes, such debates can be broadly regarded as the spillover of intra-executive disagreements into the legislative branch. They have not been indicative of the Duma's capability to determine policy outcomes.[240] The Duma's dominant party, United Russia, maintained a direct line of communication with the Presidential Administration to relay its policy preferences.[241] Nonetheless, it continued to serve as a reliable voting bloc. The Russian executive experienced no difficulty in securing approval for any budget bill during any of the readings in this period.[242] If it were to decide to shift its policies from one direction to another, the executive faced no effective veto players. This could be considered as a major source of flexibility, but it also made policy instability more likely.

Responding to Putin's First "Oil Bust": The Newfound Executive Cohesion That Couldn't Last

Russia's policy response to the short-lived oil bust after late 2008 involved a robust injection of state funds to counter the effects of the crisis. This represented a major policy shift. Even the relaxation of the expenditure policy in the previous years had not amounted to an outright reversal of the government's fiscally prudent approach. Russia had still put aside nearly half of the oil revenues in special oil funds.

Remarkably, faced with a crisis, the executive branch emerged firmly united in the need for a massive countercyclical measure. The Finance Ministry itself led the anti-crisis efforts to fight the Great Recession, which started to engulf one country after another. Years of fiscal prudence were now paying off: Russia could afford a massive anti-crisis stimulus package without resorting to borrowing.

The anti-crisis stimulus had broad appeal and a large set of beneficiaries. For the Finance Ministry, it represented a continuation of its approach favoring countercyclical fiscal policies: Russia was faced with a different oil price cycle, hence more spending was the answer to avert a deeper crisis. The proponents and beneficiaries of spending were unsurprisingly numerous. Many Russian regions faced default and were bailed out with federal funds or loans given by the regional branches of state banks. A new generation of oligarchs also benefited from public funds. Unlike those who had risen to fame during the privatization of the 1990s, many members of this new generation had expanded their business during the 2000s by engaging in state-funded projects. The crisis, and the massive stimulus package, brought them new opportunities. Growing pressure came from Russia's military-industrial complex as well, especially in the form of requests for funds to modernize the military.[243] Putin acted as the chief redistributor, thus enhancing his appeal among the Russian elite and the public. It is unclear whether electoral concerns had any role in his policy choices. Incidentally, the Great Recession and the ensuing oil bust occurred shortly after Russia's presidential elections, leaving many years to prepare for the next election. And, despite the temporary crisis brought by the Great Recession, there were no public protests.

Nonetheless, within about a year after the crisis hit Russia, executive cohesion broke down. Disagreements flared up in the midst of the ongoing oil bust and Russia's first economic contraction since Putin succeeded Yeltsin. In an interview conducted shortly after his resignation at the end of 2011, Kudrin provided insights into two principal areas of disagreements between his ministry and the rest of the executive, including Prime Minister Putin.[244] First, injecting state funds into the economy had to be rationalized. Kudrin preferred to spend more on infrastructure projects, as they could promote long-term growth, while gradually curbing other expenses. Second, Kudrin emphasized the need for structural reforms. In his view, the crisis gave the government an opening to make unpopular decisions. Vulnerable to oil price shocks, Russia needed to improve its investment climate while maintaining sound macroeconomic management.[245]

In reality, the Russian government's approach evolved in a direction that was at odds with what Kudrin had hoped for. Kudrin notes his growing disagreements with Putin on key budgetary areas. Instead of promoting infrastructure development, the Russian government prioritized defense spending and approved drastic increases in pensions in 2009.[246] Likewise, Russia did not take the opportunity to undertake a new series of reforms. This outcome was particularly striking given the fact that President Medvedev emerged as a key proponent of economic reforms in the middle of the crisis. In September 2009, the president published an article titled "Go Russia," which served as a rallying call for modernizing Russia's economy. Medvedev rhetorically asked: "Should a primitive economy based on raw materials and endemic corruption accompany us into the future?" Russia did not need temporary solutions. According to Medvedev, it was the way the Russian economy was structured and functioned that needed to change.[247]

The Finance Ministry's calls for fiscal restraint and reform did not convince the rest of the executive, Putin in particular. Structural reforms stalled during the crisis. The crisis further increased the dominance of the state in the Russian economy. Reducing the dependence of inefficient enterprises on state support remained a challenge.[248] Russia opted to engage in a massive redistribution of the oil wealth it had diligently accumulated during most of the previous decade. Once the caps on public spending were removed, it was hard to go back: there was simply no political will to cut spending.[249] Kudrin's warnings rang hollow. The financial cushion built between 2004 and 2008 made it more difficult for fiscal conservatives to convince others to restrain spending. Having accumulated resources to fight an imminent crisis, the Finance Ministry found itself the lone voice calling for a return to fiscal prudence.

Riding the New Oil Boom

When the crisis was over and Russia began to experience another oil boom, the government did not change its approach to reform and public spending in any significant way. The Finance Ministry kept urging for a return to fiscal restraint in the name of maintaining a countercyclical approach.

The ministry's calls were not entirely ignored, as it was able to secure the approval of a few of its proposed policies. For instance, in 2010, the Russian government approved a comprehensive program to improve the implementation of the budget. It included measures that aimed to limit waste in public spending and to make the budget better targeted as well as subject to stricter monitoring.[250] Also, Russia returned to three-year budgeting rule by 2011. The rule had been suspended in the midst of the crisis. The reinstatement of the rule created opportunities to draw up plans that would curb spending in the medium term.

Yet, overall, the Finance Ministry remained isolated in terms of its fiscal position, as Russia steered away from a post-crisis fiscal adjustment. There were several major setbacks. First, it lost an intense fight on defense spending. At the end of 2010, the Russian government adopted a 10-year state rearmament program, allocating 21 trillion rubles (~620 billion USD) by the end of the decade. Spending on national defense rose from 2.8 percent of GDP in 2010 to 4.5 percent of GDP in 2015.[251] According to Julian Cooper, key decisions on military spending in Russia do not take place in formal meetings, making it hard to analyze intra-executive disagreements. However, vast disagreements were reported between the Finance Ministry and the Ministry of Defense prior to the approval of the 10-year state armament program. Eventually, Putin and Medvedev approved a commitment that far exceeded what Kudrin was willing to accept.[252]

The immense increase in military spending emerged as one key area that distinguished Russia's expenditure policy during this new boom from the one witnessed during the 2000s. Following the economically turbulent 1990s, military expenditure was also on the rise. The boost in spending was much more pronounced this time and set to last through the end of the decade. This turnaround highlighted Putin's growing emphasis on Russia's revival as a military power. After a decade of growth and an economic crisis that Russia managed to weather for the most part, the leadership was ready to drastically increase military spending. In 2008, a crisis in Georgia triggered Russia's first significant military intervention following the collapse of the USSR. With its ongoing military build-up, Russia seemed poised to reassert itself militarily in future crises.

Second, there was a further weakening of the fiscal conservative bloc within the Russian government during this new oil boom. In an interview with *Vedomosti* in 2011, Kudrin expressed his dissatisfaction with the weakening of this bloc, while offering an incisive description of the two main camps competing for influence in economic policy. In his opinion, his ministry was left with only a few allies, such as Igor Artemyev, the head of the Federal Anti-Monopoly Service, and Elvira Nabiullina, the economy minister. He described Nabiullina as economically "liberal," while recognizing their significant disagreements on spending priorities. The other camp, according to Kudrin, brought together a large part of Russia's political spectrum around the idea that the economy needed a much more interventionist state. It included some key political figures such as Deputy Prime Minister Igor Sechin and Deputy Prime Minister Viktor Zubkov. Apparently, the minister for industry, Khristenko, was also in this camp, pushing for more state involvement in the economy. Finally, in Kudrin's view, President Medvedev, despite some of his liberal credentials, was also in this bloc favoring more state-led development.[253] The president had emerged as an active advocate for "economic modernization." This concept of "modernization" never evolved beyond a catchword – no clear criteria were ever defined that would distinguish state spending for "modernization" versus other objectives. As a result, in the midst of a new oil boom, "modernization" became largely equivalent to a more active redistribution of the booming oil revenues. Kudrin's main disagreement with Medvedev, however, was on military spending. In the meantime, Kudrin notes, the fiscal conservatives were alone within the legislature as well. United Russia had acted largely as a center-right party until 2007, generally supportive of the government's overall fiscally conservative approach. But it shifted to an increasingly populist approach, and was joined by other key parties in the legislature after 2007.[254] Its changing mood mirrored the shift within the executive branch.

It was a major blow to the fiscally conservative camp when tensions between President Medvedev and Kudrin erupted, resulting in the latter's ouster from the government in September 2011. Medvedev swiftly discharged Kudrin after he made a rare public statement that openly questioned the president's competence in economic policy. Kudrin's eleven years' tenure at the Finance Ministry ended.[255] Putin did not rush to defend his finance minister. According to Kudrin, Putin had consistently maintained balance between the competing camps, but on critical issues such as military spending, he sided with President Medvedev.[256] Putin's political choice was likely a reflection of his own priority on military spending, though it is possible to argue that siding with the increasingly isolated Finance Ministry would have been unpopular. Once Kudrin was out of the ministry, it did not take long for him to return as an effective advisor, continuing to provide input to Russia's economic discourse. Also, his successor, Anton Siluanov, maintained the ministry's fiscally conservative approach, though unsurprisingly he lacked the clout Kudrin had enjoyed within the executive branch.

Third, as Medvedev's presidential term approached its end in 2012, much political attention was focused on the question of who would be his successor. Under the circumstances, a return to fiscal prudence posed political risks. A recent constitutional amendment had lengthened the duration of a presidential term from four to six years.[257] Just when Russia was about to go through another election season, multiple polls conducted during 2011 indicated a substantial drop in public support for Putin, Medvedev, and United Russia. Slow economic growth and fatigue with the existing leadership no doubt factored into this.[258] In September 2011, the Putin-Medvedev tandem announced their plans to swap their positions after the presidential elections: Putin would return to the presidency while Medvedev would lead United Russia through the Duma elections and, if successful, succeed Putin as the new prime minister. The ruling tandem was stunned to learn that there was no widespread public support for this maneuver. The main shock, however, came in December, when, nearly seven years after the last big protests, a new wave of public protest flowed into Russia's streets.[259] Allegations of fraud in recent Duma elections, amid largely disappointing results for United Russia, added fuel to the fire.[260] Nonetheless, by the time presidential elections took place in March 2012, Putin managed to regain much of his lost popularity, though he got fewer votes than Medvedev had in 2008.[261] His success was due to a combination of a carefully crafted public relations campaign, a few liberalizing political reforms to weaken the momentum of the opposition movement, and a newfound emphasis on conservative values.[262]

In the context of looming elections and a succession, the Russian leadership remained averse to the risks associated with a post-crisis fiscal adjustment. Thus, in September 2011, the government approved a three-year budget for the 2012–14 period, the parameters of which indicated that fiscal adjustment was being postponed.[263] The oil price assumption for 2012 had suddenly been raised from 75 USD/barrel to 100 USD/barrel.[264] It is not that Putin was no longer aware of the financial risks associated with increased spending. Shortly after the Duma elections in December 2011, he authored an article in the *Vedomosti* arguing that macroeconomic stability was one of Russia's greatest achievements in the recent past, and a prerequisite for building a modern economy. He noted "We have come to value macroeconomic stability and use tools for maintaining it even amid extremely adverse conditions."[265] Nonetheless, political calculations in the new election cycle led Putin to be more open to spending. It is also possible that the leadership genuinely believed that oil prices were likely to stay high in the foreseeable future; hence restraint was not an urgent necessity.[266]

After his inauguration as president in May 2012, Putin issued a series of decrees that indicate his caution against a return to fiscal tightening. Widely publicized as the "May Decrees," they outlined many of the campaign promises Putin wrote about in newspaper articles at the beginning of the year.[267] Now, these promises became legally binding targets for the government, most of them to be reached before the end of his presidential term. The decrees did not formally constitute a new economic program, though they offered a highly comprehensive plan for Russia's near-term economic development. Furthermore, they incorporated many of the ideas of an extensive proposal for reforms developed by a group of Russian economists during 2011. This proposal, known as Strategy 2020, had been commissioned by the government but was never adopted.[268] Putin's May Decrees promised generous increases in public pay, improved social benefits, and new funding for regional development programs, affordable housing, and health services.[269] Right after Putin issued these decrees, the Russian government adopted an amendment to the 2012 budget. It further raised the already optimistic assumption for the price of oil to 115 USD/barrel. This staggering assumption facilitated more spending.[270] The Finance Ministry estimated that Putin's decrees would raise public spending by about 2 percent of GDP annually.[271] The amendment showed that, despite some progress, the institutionalization process of the Russian budget remained weak. It was still easy to put aside already approved budgetary parameters to meet political campaign promises. A new oil boom made fiscal restraint less of a priority.

Putin's May Decrees exemplified his continuing emphasis on social policy. According to Kudrin, Putin was driven by concerns about his own popularity and public support for United Russia.[272] According to Marina Khmelnitskaya, there were additional reasons for the leadership to prioritize social spending: a desire to address Russia's poor demographic prospects to ensure the country a greater role on the world stage in the future, a perception that the liberal reforms of the early 2000s had ignored social policy, and a recognition that social policy could help promote developmental goals.[273] Social policy had also been prioritized in earlier strategic documents such as KDR 2020 and Strategy 2020.[274] In a context of weakened veto players and a lack of a well-structured system of interest representation, Putin's welfare policies were inevitably based on top-down economic programs or targets.[275]

And yet, the renewed emphasis on social policy could hardly be understood without taking into account its distributional implications and its place in the country's broader fiscal context. A study by the World Bank examining Russia's social spending from the Great Recession till 2014 offers some insights. Because Russia introduced a flat income tax during the early 2000s, the government lacked sufficient means to reduce inequalities through taxation. Instead, generous indexation of pensions and public sector wages emerged as the most effective means to reduce inequality. Households, particularly those in the bottom deciles, appeared to be very sensitive to such income flows.[276] Because of these critical distributional implications, Putin could ignore social policy only at his own risk.

What also nurtured Russia's growing emphasis on redistributive policies was the growing role of state ownership in the economy. By 2015, the share of state-owned enterprises had risen to about 30 percent of GDP, while the contribution of the public sector as a whole had jumped to 70 percent of GDP, up from 35 percent in 2005.[277] Since the previous oil boom, state involvement in the economy had fundamentally grown: there were more state employees, more large infrastructure projects funded by the state, and more oligarchs who depend on state contracts.[278] All this made it more difficult for the state to adopt restraint, particularly when oil prices were still high.

It is astounding that, despite record high oil prices, Russia's budget was back to a deficit in 2013.[279] While expansionary spending contributed to the deficit, two additional factors also played a role. First, high oil prices were no longer enough to deliver rapid economic growth, indicating deep structural problems in the Russian economy. The growth rate was down to just 1.3 percent in 2013. Slower growth reduced the government's tax revenues, negatively impacting the budget balance.[280]

Second, the Russian leadership chose not to address the revenue side of this problem. The tax regime set in place by the middle of the 2000s remained largely intact. There was a general consensus on not altering the existing setup. During his budget address after his electoral victory in 2012, Putin made a promise not to raise taxes on the non-raw material sectors of the economy till 2018.[281] Even the Finance Ministry was reluctant to usher significant changes in the tax code. Finance Minister Siluanov opposed calls from within the expert community to launch a new phase of tax reforms, fearing that this could further complicate Russia's growth prospects.[282]

Russia's slowing growth rate during the second oil boom of the Putin era left the policy-makers and expert community divided on the merits of state-led development and increased public spending. Fiscal conservatives like Kudrin have argued against more state involvement and public spending as a means to spur growth. Russia had already experimented with this path and ended up with slowing growth rates and eventually stagnation in the midst of an oil boom, despite increased public spending.[283] By contrast, staunch proponents of state-led development have argued for furthering the role of the state in the economy and channeling even more funds to support growth.[284]

The fact that Russia was back to a budget deficit in the midst of record-high oil prices exemplified the ultimate failure of fiscal conservatives to gain Putin's backing. The fiscal conservatives maintained their key position within the Finance Ministry. But this time, the lack of executive cohesion clearly weakened

Russia's "decisiveness" to adopt a precautionary fiscal approach to avert another crisis, if oil prices were to fall again.

A New Oil Bust – A Different Response

When the oil boom ended in 2014, the Russian government had not yet fully shifted to a post-crisis fiscal adjustment. Suddenly, it was faced with another crisis and an oil bust. As mentioned above, Russia's response to this new oil bust was rather different from the previous one. It involved a series of anti-crisis fiscal stimulus measures. Yet, the government's fiscal approach clearly leaned in favor of restraint. Its approach was decidedly more fiscally conservative than during the 2008–9 crisis.

Here again it is possible to shed light on the actions of the Russian government by looking at how much support the Finance Ministry's position enjoyed within the executive, the risks associated with maintaining the inherited status quo policy, and the extent of available resources to mitigate these risks. Khmelnitskaya has aptly described the contrasts in Russia's response to the two successive crises with respect to its social spending policy.[285] During the 2008–9 oil bust, social spending increased drastically. The Finance Ministry had supported the use of a massive stimulus package for the economy but disagreed with the rest of the executive on the extent of social spending. This time around, the Finance Ministry put greater emphasis on fiscal restraint from the very start. Moreover, it was not alone in its fiscally conservative stance as it enjoyed the support of the Economy Ministry under Ulyukaev. During the summer of 2015, amid heated discourse within the cabinet, both ministries suggested freezing growth in public sector salaries and cutting some social benefits. The cabinet eventually approved many of their proposals calling for fiscal restraint.[286]

Meanwhile, the executive branch was still engaged in major disagreements on economic and fiscal policy. By 2017, in the midst of a struggling economy, the fight for influencing policy was best exemplified by the emergence of three competing economic programs with widely different proposals. Some observers described it as a "beauty contest" arranged by Putin, who asked competing groups to prepare a strategy to revive the economy.[287]

Yet, not only were the two key ministers, Siluanov and Ulyukaev, able to present a unified position on fiscal restraint, they could mount convincing arguments about the risks involved in maintaining the existing expansionary fiscal policy. During discussions on adopting Russia's three-year budget for the 2016–18 period, the Finance Ministry provided a realistic account of Russia's alternative paths forward: the government could maintain the existing expansionary fiscal approach and deplete all of its savings in the oil funds within the span of a year, it could adopt a budget sequestration except on social policy, or it could focus on budget cuts for select social policy areas and government programs. The ministry leaned towards the last option as the most likely to contribute to Russia's growth. It highlighted that during the 2006–15 period real wages had gone up much more rapidly than productivity, thus inhibiting economic growth.[288] The Finance Ministry's warning about depleting the "rainy day" funds was also critical. Russia had just gone through another oil boom but managed to save only a modest amount, as the post-crisis fiscal adjustment kept being postponed (see chapter 6). Unlike the previous crisis, which caught Russia well-prepared with a vast financial cushion, the new crisis came too soon. It also more closely resembled the 1998 crisis rather than the Great Recession. The latter affected many countries around the world, and the Russian government, like many others, responded with a stimulus package. This time, however, the crisis was largely confined to Russia.

The Economy Ministry also called for fiscal restraint for the sake of ensuring a return to positive growth. In 2016, the ministry presented its forecasts for Russia's macroeconomic development through 2019. Its proposal underlined the need for a shift in Russia's growth model from one spurred by rising consumption to one driven by a growth in investments. Its forecast emphasized that such a shift would come at the expense of public sector salaries and pensions.[289]

As debates on the need for fiscal restraint raged on, President Putin faced a dilemma. He could let oil savings diminish and start accumulating debt, but this could bring serious risks for Russia's financial stability in the future. Alternatively, he could support a policy of fiscal restraint that would come at a cost for the public –social and military spending would need to be cut and rationalized.

In the end, Putin opted for fiscal restraint. Arguably, the record-high popularity attained in the aftermath of the crisis with Ukraine and rising tensions with the West facilitated his choice.[290] In other words, the Russian leadership could afford to enact less popular measures amid record-high public support for Putin, galvanized largely through its approach to foreign policy. The government approved many of the Finance Ministry's proposed cuts in social spending, and adopted the Economy Ministry's main parameters set for the 2017–19 period.[291] Nonetheless, key decisions on social policy spending were delayed until after the September 2016 Duma elections.[292] In effect, the government took a step back from implementing some of the items proposed in the May Decrees, such as raising public sector salaries substantially above inflation. Regional governments, hitherto carefully monitored for their implementation of these decrees, were permitted to forgo some key targets because of financial constraints.[293]

Fiscal conservatives had additional victories. One key development was the government's announcement of an ambitious privatization campaign starting in 2016. While the process aimed to bring in additional state revenues, it was a significant departure from approaches of previous years, which saw the state assume a greater role in the economy. Indeed, privatization proceeds, particularly those coming from the sale of a stake in Rosneft, helped to cut the budget deficit in 2016.[294] Another victory was recorded with respect to military spending, as Putin recognized the need for restraint. He justified the restraint by arguing that the process of modernization in the armed forces had largely come to fruition. In a speech addressing the military industry at the Kalashnikov factory in Izhevsk in September 2016, Putin bluntly noted that strained public finances prompted his choice: Russia needed to find the "golden mean" between spending for the military and meeting other vital needs for society.[295]

In a sense, Putin's reference to a "golden mean" could be used to describe his overall stance on economic policy during his entire tenure. A "golden mean" has remained an elusive concept, with no clear targets on either end of the range from fiscal conservatism to state-led development that relies on expanding the budget. This lack of clarity on what ultimately constitutes the "golden mean" has secured Putin a degree of flexibility, allowing him to balance these two divergent paths for economic policy. The approach has not delivered the economic growth the Russian leadership aspired to after Putin's first two-term presidency. But arguably, it has been effective in extending Putin's tenure at the helm of Russian politics.

Conclusion

Russia went through two major oil boom and bust cycles during the Putin era. The leadership's approach to redistribution has oscillated from fiscally conservative to highly expansionary. Also, facing two oil booms and oil busts, its response has been different each time. By contrast, Russia's approach to taxation outside the oil sector has exhibited a high degree of stability over time.

In this chapter, I have tried to explain Russia's redistributive policy choices by relating them to several aspects of executive power. First, the fading role of veto players during Putin's first presidency appears to be crucial in explaining key redistributive policy outcomes. In the case of budgetary policies, the Russian leadership was able to maintain a fiscally conservative approach. The origins of this approach go back to the aftermath of the crash of August 1998. While Primakov's efforts for financial stabilization could be viewed primarily as emergency measures, Putin was able to maintain strictly fiscally conservative budgetary policy in the midst of rising oil prices. In effect, thanks to weakened veto players, the executive branch gained "decisiveness" to enact and implement conservative fiscal policies, instead of redistributing the bulk of the booming oil windfalls. Likewise, after years of trial and error during the 1990s, the new administration under Putin undertook a series of tax reforms that simplified taxation across the board while lowering the tax burden on the economy (at the expense of rising taxes on the oil sector).

Another key factor shaping policy over the long-term has been the cohesiveness of the executive branch. The presence of cohesion has made it more likely that the government will maintain its approach on the policy status quo over time. By contrast, it is possible to refer to an in-built propensity for policy instability in areas that do not enjoy executive cohesion. Accordingly, there was major continuity with respect to one of the key tools for redistribution: tax cuts for the non-oil sectors. The tax reforms leading to lower taxes legislated during the early years of Putin's presidency had enjoyed a wide consensus within the executive branch and beyond. The cohesive stance of the executive branch was largely maintained thereafter. Tax rates were neither reduced nor increased significantly at times of crisis when the Russian budget needed more revenues. By contrast, the Russian executive had never enjoyed cohesion with respect to the conservative approach to public spending adopted during Putin's first presidential term. This eventually contributed to a policy shift favoring expansionary budgetary policies after 2005. This lack of cohesion also explains the long delay in the government's ability to return to fiscal restraint. It failed to do so after the 2008–9 crisis was over. Proponents of fiscal prudence were able to once again gain the upper hand only after the next big crisis in 2014. In effect, a lack of cohesion detracted from executive power, weakening the "decisiveness" of the state to respond to an emerging economic risk– even 100 dollars per barrel became insufficient to balance Russia's budget during the period between the two crises.

What also complicated building cohesion in the case of budgetary policies was the inevitably extensive scope of involvement of executive agencies in the policy process. Nearly every executive agency played a part in the preparation of the federal budget. By contrast, taxation in the oil sector has remained within the domain of only a few ministries, the Finance Ministry in particular. This helped maintain executive cohesion and policy stability with respect to securing a continuous high tax burden on the oil industry. One could expect that other areas of reform that were similarly narrow within the scope of executive engagement would face fewer difficulties in maintaining executive cohesion, contributing to higher policy stability.

Finally, policy shifts can also be linked to the leadership's evolving perceptions on political risks relative to the available resources to mitigate them. The 1998 crisis appears to have taught the Russian leaders a key lesson: failing to maintain a balanced budget and being unprepared for a slump in the price of oil could trigger a financial crash, with fall-out for political stability and public support. The government remained remarkably conservative in its expenditure policies through the first half of the 2000s. Then, this approach eventually lost favor because of the rising political risks the Putin administration faced. Public protests in the winter of 2004–5, and the increasingly important question of finding a successor before the end of Putin's second term, prompted a shift towards a more expansionary budgetary approach. Subsequently, during the next oil boom that started in late 2010, similar concerns about impending political risks empowered the voice of proponents of state-led development and more public spending. Such considerations drove the Russian executive's response to the two oil busts as well. During the first oil bust, starting in late 2008, Russia responded with one of the world's largest stimulus packages. For a brief period, the Russian executive was cohesively behind this countercyclical policy. The cohesion broke when the traditional proponents of a fiscally conservative approach, namely the Finance Ministry, called for a return to fiscal restraint. During the next oil bust, beginning in 2014, Russia's resources were much more limited, while sanctions imposed by the US and the EU added further unpredictability. Amid record-high public support for Putin, in large part energized by tensions with the West, the proponents of fiscal restraint could gain more influence in guiding the budgetary policy.

Overall, since 1999, Putin has strived to balance widely different approaches on the Russian economy. He has not committed to either side of the discourse on how to redistribute Russia's oil windfalls. Such a lack of commitment has brought him a high degree of flexibility. Sometimes Putin has aligned himself with the strictly conservative Finance Ministry and sometimes he has chosen to ignore the ministry's warnings and support policies that appeal to proponents of greater public spending and state-led development.

Putin has clearly not sought to build a cohesive executive aligned with a particular approach to redistribution. Instead, he has kept a high profile for fiscally conservative figures, particularly in the Finance Ministry, letting them play their part in balancing the proponents of more spending. He has carefully extended his personal support to this group of personalities at key junctures, while ensuring that his blessing remains their principal, if not sole, source of power. His desire to maintain a flexible approach in this permanent battle has produced policy instability.

6 The State as a Redistributor of Oil Rents: The Battle to Save the Windfalls

Many oil-rich countries have been experimenting with special oil funds in the past two decades. International financial institutions have led the way by encouraging a more prudent fiscal and monetary approach through the adoption of such funds.[1] In theory, oil funds allow countries to save part of their windfalls for the future. They offer a way to institutionalize the management of oil windfalls, which are unpredictable in size. Yet, in reality, oil funds come with monumental challenges if they are to function as intended by their founders. It is common for them to become the principal targets of competing economic policies, and ultimately fall victim to political battles. In effect, the mere presence of an oil fund does not ensure effective management of the oil windfalls.

Soon after Putin's rise to power, Russia joined the club of countries with oil funds, albeit as a relative latecomer. Its first fund, operational in 2004, started to save the growing proceeds that came along with the oil boom of the 2000s. Remarkably, more than half of the oil rents collected by the state were accumulated in its oil funds between 2004 and 2008. Pressures to spend the bounty were overwhelmingly rebuffed. Thanks to this approach, Russia enjoyed a powerful financial cushion when heading into the Great Recession at the end of 2008. Soon, however, it became increasingly obvious that Russia had not necessarily created robust institutions for saving the oil windfalls. Instead, the Russian leadership frequently altered the rules governing the oil funds, and even suspended them on several occasions after 2008. The windfalls started to flow in many directions, eventually depleting a significant portion of Russia's savings.

The Russian government's approach to its oil funds represents yet another case where a decisive state was able to launch a rather unpopular undertaking – a reform that set formal restrictions on how oil windfalls could flow. This case also illustrates a high degree of policy instability in the Russian leadership's approach to managing the oil windfalls. This chapter argues that this instability was largely a product of a lack of cohesion within the executive branch from the very start. It also demonstrates that the oil funds' formal rules, and the entire process of building these new institutions, inevitably fell prey to Putin's shifting economic and political priorities.

The chapter also focuses on the repayment of Russia's sovereign debt as a key economic priority during Putin's first presidency. This particular tool for redistribution constitutes one of the rare cases where a lack of executive cohesion from the very start did not yield instability in the government's approach over time. I argue that repaying the debt was largely accomplished during the early years of Putin's tenure, when countercyclical policies still remained dominant. It was neither politically feasible nor financially expedient to reverse the government's approach afterwards.

I start the chapter by examining how Russia's oil funds have operated since their launch. Next, I turn to the question that remains central throughout the book: what explains the key policy outcomes?

Going through an Oil Boom and a Bust with an "Oil Fund"

Russia's experience with an oil fund is relatively recent. In the footsteps of many other oil-exporting countries, the Russian government launched its first oil fund in 2004. The structure of the fund evolved over time along with its financial capabilities. I examine its evolution in two stages – before and after the Great Recession. The first stage corresponds to a period when Russia witnessed a continuous boom in oil prices. The second stage is more diverse, as Russia went through both booms and busts. For both periods, my initial focus is on how the Russian government managed the oil funds: How successful has Russia been in meeting the missions typically prescribed for oil funds?

Saving the Windfalls during the Oil Boom of the 2000s

Oil funds are set up to perform several distinct functions – sometimes simultaneously – tackling a range of anomalies commonly associated with economies dependent on oil. First, oil funds can help with "stabilization." As international oil prices fluctuate, so do the budget revenues. Oil funds save part of the rents during an oil boom and make them available to be spent during an oil bust. The "stabilization" here refers to the reduced vulnerability of the government budget to drastic changes in oil prices. "Sterilization" constitutes another goal. Namely, inflowing oil export revenues can cause an appreciation of the national currency, weakening the country's international economic competitiveness and causing inflation rate to rise.[2] An oil fund makes it possible to "sterilize" part of these export revenues by temporarily removing them from the domestic economy, alleviating the pressure for currency appreciation and inflation. Finally, oil funds can be part of a much longer-term objective, through the establishment of rules about how to save today's windfalls for future generations. An oil fund can be designed specifically to address this question, by restricting the amount that can be withdrawn from the fund in the near term.

Given the multiple functions served by oil funds and Russia's decades-long history of dependence on oil revenues, it is surprising that its leaders took so long to experiment with this policy tool. Many mineral resource-exporting countries set up special funds as early as the 1970s.[3] Soviet leaders never took this path. By the mid-1980s, the USSR had become ever more dependent on oil export revenues, but it had not saved the windfalls to deal with an imminent oil bust. According to Yegor Gaidar, this historic mistake came at a steep price. The economic crisis that ensued and the collapse of the USSR were ultimately linked to this lack of preparedness.[4] The 1990s were hardly the time to experiment with an oil fund. Amid low oil prices, economic turmoil, chronic budget deficits, and a bulging sovereign debt, saving oil rents for the future was not a viable option. At last, the Putin administration opted to set up an oil fund, known as the Stabilization Fund, as late as 2003 – several years behind two other oil-rich post-Soviet nations, Kazakhstan and Azerbaijan.

Accustomed to spending as much oil revenues as it could acquire, the Russian government faced an unfamiliar problem at the start of 2000s: the federal budget was running a surplus for the first time.[5] The surplus kept getting larger with rising oil prices, prompting intense debates about what constituted the best use of it. Broadly speaking, there were three options: redistribute the surplus through the budget, use this extra money to pay Russia's sovereign foreign debt, or save it in an oil fund. Adopting the latter two options was equivalent to removing part of the oil windfalls from the Russian economy, permanently (in the case of foreign debt payments) or temporarily (in the case of saving the windfalls in an oil fund).[6]

It was in this context that the idea of establishing Russia's first oil fund was born. Approved in 2003 and formally launched in 2004, the fund was a major step towards institutionalizing the management of the federal budget surplus. The oil fund's mere presence, however, was not sufficient: to perform its functions it needed to accumulate Russia's growing oil rents and not be subject to indiscreet government raids to meet various commitments. Could this new institution work in Russia?

In the first few years of its operation, Russia's Stabilization Fund expanded beyond anyone's expectations. Its initial rules had set the target to accumulate up to 500 billion rubles before the fund's savings would be available for spending. The threshold was reached by the end of the fund's first year, but it continued to accumulate oil windfalls.

In 2007, the rules were revisited when the fund was split into two new entities: the Reserve Fund and the National Wealth Fund.[7] The amendment to the Budget Code authorizing the split made it clear that the Reserve Fund was inheriting the functions of the Stabilization Fund – minimizing the risks for the Russian economy in case of low oil prices. The main task of the National Wealth Fund was to support Russia's pension system.[8] Along with this reorganization, revenues from the gas sector were also added to the funds' portfolio, while the 500 billion rubles limit was scrapped. As the two funds continued to accumulate windfalls, their savings reached the record amount of 225 billion USD at the end of 2008, equivalent to 16 percent of the GDP.[9] Russia had successfully built a financial cushion for potential crises (see table 6.1).

Beyond the remarkable rise in the oil funds' savings, there were several noteworthy developments. First, the establishment of the Stabilization Fund marked a clear break with the past: a massive amount of oil rents was excluded from annual budgetary commitments. During 2000–3, surging oil revenues had contributed to budget surpluses. Most of the surplus revenues were spent on servicing the foreign debt. With the Stabilization Fund, the amount removed from the Russian economy grew drastically. Between 2004 and 2007, the fund captured nearly two-thirds of the oil rents collected by the government.[10] With the onset of the new rules in 2008, this share dropped, though slightly less than half of its oil and gas revenues still went into the savings funds.

Second, the emergence of the Stabilization Fund facilitated servicing Russia's sovereign foreign debt. A special "financial reserve" had been set up to service the debt in 2002 and 2003.[11] Among its other functions, the Stabilization Fund took over this task. Throughout its existence, such payments constituted its single most important outlays.[12]

Russia recorded remarkable progress in paying its foreign debt during Putin's first two-term presidency. Foreign debt peaked at 158.7 billion USD in 1998, standing at 144 percent of Russia's GDP. By 2005, nearly half of the debt was paid, and its size now represented barely 10 percent of the Russian economy.[13] Also, in 2005, Russia made a series of agreements to make early debt payment. It paid all of its remaining dues to the IMF (3.3 billion USD), along with a major advance payment (15 billion USD) to the Paris Club.[14]

Prioritizing foreign debt payments helped to significantly reduce the Russian government's financial burden over time. By late 2008, when the Great Recession started to affect the Russian economy, sovereign debt was down to only 32.7 billion USD – a mere 2 percent of GDP.[15] Along with the sizable oil windfall savings, this low level of debt provided another financial cushion. Russia's approach to debt remains outstanding in comparison to the historic record of oil-exporting countries. A study examining the world's 25 largest oil exporters between 1979 and 2010 reveals that these countries were particularly prone to take foreign loans and incur high levels of debt. Seventeen of these countries defaulted on their debts, including Russia in 1998.[16]

Third, the oil funds contributed to the government's efforts to fight inflation and the ruble's appreciation. Their savings were deposited in foreign currency

Table 6.1. Accumulation of Rents in Russia's Oil Fund(s) (in billion USD)*

	2000	2001	2002	2003	2004	2005	2006	2007	2008
Total oil and gas revenues to the federal budget	7.7	11.2	15.9	21.2	35.9	76.4	108.3	113.3	176.9
Oil and gas revenues kept outside the budget (bn USD)	1.5	1.2	2.2	0.7	23.3	51.7	74.1	70.3	82.2
(as percentage of oil and gas revenues to the federal budget)	19.5	10.7	13.8	3.3	64.9	67.7	68.4	62.0	46.5
Size of savings in oil fund(s) at the end of the year (bn USD)	–	–	–	–	18.8	43.1	89.1	156.8	225.1
(as percentage of GDP)	–	–	–	–	3.1	5.7	8.8	11.6	16.0

* The 2004–7 period refers to the savings of the Stabilization Fund. Figures for 2008 provide the combined values for the Reserve Fund and the National Wealth Fund. Values at the end of the calendar year.

Source: Ministry of Finance of the Russian Federation; Kudrin (2013), p. 15.

accounts handled by the Russian Central Bank, helping to constrain the money supply of the national currency. Had these savings been converted to rubles and put back into the Russian economy, according to estimates by the Institute for the Economy in Transition, the average rate of inflation could have been significantly higher during the 2004–8 period. Also, the ruble would have appreciated substantially more, hurting the competitiveness of a range of sectors abroad.[17]

However, as Russia's windfall savings grew and its foreign debt shrank, there were some setbacks. Rules governing the Stabilization Fund were periodically relaxed to divert more money into the economy. For instance, originally the cut-off price for crude oil had been set fairly low at 20 dollars per barrel. This ensured that a larger share of the oil rents would accumulate in the fund whenever oil prices exceeded this level. This cut-off price was raised to 27 dollars per barrel in 2006, making it possible to allocate more for budgetary purposes. Likewise, when the Stabilization Fund was split into two funds, the new fiscal rules let the government get an immediate hold of a growing share of the oil and gas revenues.

The Russian government also made several direct withdrawals from the Stabilization Fund and channeled the funds into the domestic economy. In 2005, a small portion of the savings of the Stabilization Fund was used to replenish the bulging deficit in Russia's Pension Fund.[18] In October 2007, the government decided to make further withdrawals in order to fund several projects by newly launched development agencies. About 10 percent of the oil fund's savings – 300 billion rubles or about 12 billion USD – were allocated for this purpose.[19] These transfers were not big enough to interrupt the further growth of Russia's oil funds, but they constituted early examples of Russia making use of its savings. The withdrawals were also indicative of the growing appeal of an expansionary fiscal policy.

Yet, Russia's overall experience with an oil fund, from its establishment until the Great Recession, could be described as fairly successful and in line with the preferences of the fiscal conservatives in government. Most of the oil rents collected by the state were saved for "rainy days" and the amounts withdrawn went overwhelmingly to service the foreign debt. As noted in the previous chapter, Russia had initiated an increasingly expansionary budgetary policy since the middle of the decade. Yet, the impact on the oil funds remained modest as its savings remained mostly untouched and kept growing rapidly.

Economic Crises and the Oil Funds

When the Great Recession reached Russia in the middle of 2008, the government was not caught off guard. It had two oil funds flush with foreign currency savings, in addition to record high reserves held by the Central Bank. Altogether its international reserves, standing at nearly 600 billion USD, were the third-largest in the world.[20] Furthermore, plunging stock markets around the world did not significantly affect Russia's oil funds. The Russian government had opted to invest in low-yield but reliable government securities denominated in major foreign currencies. This strategy brought minimal financial rewards but turned out to be the right choice. Also, as the value of the ruble plunged by the beginning of 2009, the savings in the two funds suddenly swelled to record heights in ruble terms.

The Russian government made use of both savings funds to fight the crisis, though it adopted a different approach for each fund. The Reserve Fund constituted the main tool to inject the windfalls back into the economy. Following the first major withdrawal in March 2009, more than half of the fund's savings were used by the end of the year. The last major withdrawal in relation to this crisis was in December 2010, when the size of the Reserve Fund reached a new low of 25.4 billion USD, down from 137.1 billion USD at the end of 2008 (see table 6.2). The fund's savings were used to provide a stimulus for the economy and to cover the rising budget deficit caused by the slump in oil prices and contraction in tax revenues. The Reserve Fund served a similar function when Russia faced international sanctions following the onset of the crisis in Crimea and east Ukraine in 2014. After several outlays, its savings dropped to 16 billion USD by the end of 2016. The Reserve Fund was eventually exhausted at the end of 2017, as the federal government used it to cover the budget deficit.

The Russian government took a different approach with respect to the savings in the National Wealth Fund. Formally, the fund remained intact through both crises. Its savings were not used to cover the budget deficit and no direct withdrawals were made. But through quasi-fiscal measures, the government was able to use the National Wealth Fund to generate off-budget stimulus for the economy. A portion of the fund's assets was used to support the Russian banking system. Another portion was invested in the domestic economy through a purchase of Russian company shares. The National Wealth Fund also supported a number of large-scale infrastructure projects.[21] The fund, while shielded from direct withdrawals, fluctuated in terms of overall value (in dollar terms), reflecting mainly losses and gains associated with the Russian stocks it held.

Overall, the performance of the two funds is best understood in light of the main functions they were assigned. The Reserve Fund had a key task: guard the federal budget against oil price fluctuations. Typically oil funds transfer part of the savings to the budget during oil busts and collect revenues during booms. The withdrawals from the Reserve Fund fit this pattern well. There were two periods of withdrawals: 2009–10 and 2015–16. Both periods coincided with a major slump in oil prices and ensuing economic crises.[22] Indeed, the savings of the Reserve Fund proved to be indispensable. Its contribution to economic policy was most evident during the Great Recession. The fund's savings let the Russian authorities develop anti-crisis measures without resorting to external

Table 6.2. The Value of Russia's Saving Funds (in billion USD)

	2008	2009	2010	2011	2012	2013	2014	2015	2016	2017	2018
Reserve Fund*	137.1	60.5	25.4	25.2	62.1	87.4	87.9	49.9	16.0	0	0
National Wealth Fund*	88.0	91.6	88.4	86.8	88.6	88.6	78.0	71.7	71.9	65.1	58.1
Urals-blend oil price – annual average	94.4	61.3	78.3	109.3	110.3	106.3	94.5	51.2	41.9	53.0	69.6

* Value at the end of the calendar year.

Sources: Ministry of Finance of the Russian Federation; IMF

or domestic borrowing. This gave Russia a significant advantage over other major economies going through a drastic rise in government debt. The Russian government was back to borrowing from international capital markets in April 2010,[23] but savings in the Reserve Fund helped to keep foreign borrowing at a limited level. There was no reversal in the government's approach to maintain very low sovereign debt. By 2018, Russia's sovereign external debt remained still as low as 3.8 percent of its GDP.[24]

However, Russia was noticeably slow in putting windfalls back into the Reserve Fund during periods of more favorable oil prices. The government made two big deposits into the fund – once in January 2012 and then again in January 2013. This reflected the new upturn in oil prices in 2011 and 2012. As oil prices remained high through 2014, an opportunity emerged to quickly replenish the Reserve Fund. The Russian government, however, opted to channel most of the booming oil and gas tax revenues into the budget.[25]

The National Wealth Fund was shielded from direct withdrawals as part of anti-crisis stimulus measures, despite growing pleas to use its savings. Overall, however, the fund did not perform as originally intended. First, the government found multiple means to circumvent the rules designed to restrict withdrawals from the fund, and used its savings to help Russian banks and state corporations. Second, the fund did not perform as an intergenerational oil savings fund that would help to replenish the growing deficit in Russia's pensions system. Supporting the pension system had been a major intention behind its creation, though the precise process to implement it was left unclear. In 2014, Russia's economy minister Alexei Ulyukaev continued to emphasize this gap in regulations – it was yet to be determined how the fund would support the pension system.[26] Finally, according to Gurvich, the government gave up on the idea of accumulating new savings in this fund.[27] It abstained from adding new savings to it during 2012 and 2013, when the Reserve Fund was partially replenished. No significant revenues went into the National Wealth Fund until 2018.

It was only after the Reserve Fund was dissolved at the end of 2017 that the National Wealth Fund absorbed the task of the Reserve Fund to collect additional oil revenues. The first major increase in its savings, worth nearly 14 billion USD, occurred in July 2018.[28]

The process of replenishing both funds reflects a significant failure on the part of the Russian government to enforce established rules. When Russian authorities decided to split the Stabilization Fund into two new entities in 2007, they had also set a formal fiscal rule governing the conditions under which savings would go to the federal budget, the Reserve Fund, and the National Wealth Fund. Following the onset of the Great Recession, however, the fiscal rule was suspended. Subsequently, a new fiscal rule was introduced in 2013. With the onset of another crisis, the new rule was also suspended in 2015. Without such rules, the two funds fell prey to the government's shifting fiscal and economic policies. This weakened the two funds as institutions in terms of their capability to enhance policy stability in managing oil windfalls.

Saving vs Spending the Oil Rents: The Political Battles over Russia's Oil Funds

Oil funds, once established, commonly emerge as targets for political battles. The battles revolve around one major policy question: should the oil rents be saved or should they be redistributed? The assets of an oil fund represent latent opportunities to redistribute the oil rents to meet present needs. But being caught in a crisis, sparked by low oil prices, with little or no savings, also poses a risk. In either case, the choice to spend or to save comes with wider economic and political implications.

The story of Russia's oil funds is also a story of relentless political battles between proponents of a fiscally prudent approach and those preferring more redistributive policies. The starkest differences have typically arisen during oil booms. These respective positions in the battle have tended to get closer to each other during periods of an oil bust and economic crisis, though differences have persisted.

Viewed from the standpoint of proponents of a fiscally conservative approach, the analysis so far has illustrated that Russia's experience with oil funds has been mixed. The Stabilization Fund and its two successors rapidly accumulated oil rents prior to the Great Recession. More than half of the oil rents collected by the government were saved in these funds between 2004 and 2008. In the aftermath of the Great Recession, some of the policy outcomes were also partly in line with a fiscally prudent approach. Thus, the National Wealth Fund was shielded from direct withdrawals. Furthermore, its savings could have well been exhausted through stimulus measures over the course of two consecutive economic crises.

There were a few setbacks. The operations of the Stabilization Fund exhibited some early signs of fiscal relaxation in the form of several ad hoc withdrawals, while its ability to constrain the growth in budgetary spending had already been somewhat weakened before the Great Recession. Subsequently, after 2010, the government was slow in replenishing the Reserve Fund, and no significant new amount of rents were put into the National Wealth Fund. Perhaps the biggest setback, however, was the persistent inclination to revise, suspend, or circumvent existing rules about these two institutions. Oil funds are typically built to provide stability and predictability about the management of oil windfalls. In Russia's case, their operations often symbolized shifting policy preferences and policy instability.

What explains Russia's partial success with the oil funds? Given persistent demands to redistribute the rents, how was Russia able to build substantial savings in its oil funds? Why have the rules governing the oil funds remained fairly unstable and to what extent was this instability due to faults in the design of these funds? Was instability the result of disagreements within the executive branch about economic priorities? To address these questions, I put Russia's experience with oil funds into broader political context. I examine the political battles over the oil funds in three stages: the initial period leading to the establishment of the Stabilization Fund, and the periods before and after the Great Recession.

Establishing the Stabilization Fund

At the beginning of 2001, the Institute for the Economy in Transition launched an extensive report proposing the establishment of a "stabilization fund."[29] The primary idea was to save oil windfalls during times of high oil prices, securing Russia a potential cushion against future crises. It also aimed to resolve an unexpected "problem": amid rising oil prices the budget finally showed a surplus, triggering intense debates on what to do with it and the extra oil revenues that kept coming. Setting up a stabilization fund was seen as a possible solution and a way to formalize some rules.

While discussions on how to set up a Stabilization Fund continued, its implementation was delayed by about two years.[30] There was a much more urgent task to accomplish: servicing Russia's foreign debt on time. The government still had sizable foreign debt in 2001 (standing at 127 billion USD). The amount required to service the debt was scheduled to peak in 2003 at about 17 billion USD.[31] Minor periodic slumps in the price of oil heightened these concerns. Negotiations to delay and restructure the debt payment to the Paris Club had failed at the start of 2001. Russia had to find the needed funds.

Servicing the debt was central to discussions around how to manage the budget surplus, paving the way for the establishment of Russia's first oil fund in 2003. This was another key policy area that suffered from lack of cohesion within the executive. Kudrin and Illarionov emerged as the chief proponents of prioritizing foreign debt payments. For these fiscal conservatives, it was obvious where to spend the extra revenues if Russia were to run a budget surplus in 2001–3.[32] They faced stiff resistance within the cabinet, including from Prime Minister Kasyanov.[33] Many opponents believed the budget surplus could be better used. Cabinet members called for using the surplus to finance tax cuts, social spending, and even state-led industrial policy.[34]

Convincing the legislature was also a challenge. It had an important role to play in policy discussions on foreign debt payments. As an item in the annual federal budget, the amount to be spent on servicing the foreign debt necessitated legislative approval. Also, in case of a budget surplus, the legislature needed to authorize additional spending by approving a budgetary amendment. The legislature's impact was apparent during the approval process of the 2001 and 2002 budgets. There was strong resistance to prioritizing foreign debt payments.[35] After lengthy negotiations and compromises offered by the Finance Ministry, the Duma was convinced to let the bulk of the budget surplus go to debt servicing.[36]

Amid this lack of cohesion within the executive branch, Kudrin and Illarionov had one major advantage in their struggle to prioritize servicing Russia's foreign debt. President Putin was on their side.[37] His continuing support was evident in his annual budgetary statements at the Federal Assembly in the following few years. There he consistently pointed to the urgency of servicing the foreign debt and praised the government's determination to reduce Russia' debt burden.[38]

With Putin's support, it was possible for the Finance Ministry to take a further step with respect to foreign debt. The discourse had exposed the need for creating a more formal mechanism to handle the budget surplus. Instead of lengthy negotiations within the government and with the Duma on periodic budgetary amendments, there was a simpler solution. The surplus could go to a special fund and be spent in accordance with previously agreed-upon priorities. The impending peak for debt payments in 2003 strengthened Kudrin's hand to create such a fund.[39] Thus, a special financial "reserve fund" was established with the principal purpose of paying Russia's foreign debt in 2002 and 2003.[40] Decisions about withdrawals from the fund belonged fully to the Finance Ministry and were not subject to the legislature's approval.[41] The fund's revenue base was defined as the entire surplus in the federal budget rather than revenues from the oil sector alone.

With servicing the foreign debt on track, the Finance Ministry revived the idea of establishing a stabilization fund at the beginning of 2003. The ministry prepared its own proposal, which formed the basis for lively discussion among cabinet members, with input from external experts.[42] Determining the revenue sources of the fund turned out to be the least controversial task. Revenues would accrue from three sources: export duties on crude oil, mineral extraction tax from the oil sector, and the surplus of the budget of the preceding fiscal year.[43] On the fund's other key parameters, however, there was much pushback from within the executive. The Finance Ministry aimed to set an ambitious cut-off price for oil: revenues would accrue to the fund whenever oil prices stayed above 18.5 USD/barrel. Under pressure from Prime Minister Mikhail Kasyanov and Minister Gref, Kudrin agreed to raise the cut-off price for oil to 20 USD/barrel.[44] Also, Kudrin proposed to set a minimum threshold for the size of the fund: the government would not be allowed to tap into the fund until the size of its savings reached 8.5 percent of GDP.[45] Once again, a compromise was required, yielding a much lower threshold, set at 500 billion rubles.

The final draft was sent to the Duma for approval as an amendment to the Budget Code. Final voting occurred right before the new Duma elections and in the shadow of the Yukos Affair. The bill obtained the consent of 302 deputies during the final reading. Factions aligned with the Kremlin cohesively supported the bill, along with Yabloko and LDPR.[46] The legislature could claim some success in carving itself a role in the future of the Stabilization Fund. The government was required to provide annual projections of the revenues expected to be saved into and withdrawn from the fund. The amounts would be set in the annual budget bill, subject to legislative approval. Any intermittent government proposals for spending from the Stabilization Fund would also require both chambers' approval. However, the Duma became much less relevant as a veto player following the new elections in December 2003. Thus, subsequent changes in the rules of the fund, introduced by the executive branch, would face little resistance.

In all of this, timing turned out to be crucial. By 2004, the peak year for foreign debt payments was in the past. It was getting increasingly difficult to justify spending the budget surplus on the remaining foreign debt. Incidentally, oil prices continued to rise in the following years, causing a massive surge in Russia's federal government revenues. Without the Stabilization Fund, Russia would have needed to continue juggling competing demands on the surplus revenues through numerous budgetary amendments.

Once the Stabilization Fund was established to manage the budget surplus and the extra oil revenues, it would no doubt remain in the spotlight of policy discourse on economic and budgetary policies. The key question was how it would function. How well would its rules be enforced? How long would it take to revise them in response to shifts in the government's policy?

There were several issues with the way the Stabilization Fund was designed, inevitably complicating its ability to manage the oil wealth. To begin with, the fund's rules said nothing about how its revenues could be spent once the prescribed threshold (500 billion rubles) was surpassed. This ambiguity stemmed from the fairly pessimistic oil price assumptions at that time. Many thought it would take years to fill the fund, so they had time to rethink its rules and implications for the future. No one expected the savings in the fund to reach the threshold by the end of its first year of operation.[47]

The ambiguity regarding the Stabilization Fund's rules was actually an indication of a broader problem. The ultimate function of the fund was never fully elaborated. From the legislation it was clear that "stabilization" was a key goal.[48] A "sterilization" function was not explicitly stated in the legislation, but its presence was evident from Kudrin's repeated emphasis on it. The question of whether the fund would serve any long-term objectives was left undecided.[49] Thus, when confronted with the demand to spend the savings in the fund, the Finance Ministry found itself in a weak position. There was no legal basis to prioritize saving for future generations over spending the bounty on current needs.

There was an additional problem with respect to the fund's source of revenues. The legislation left substantial amounts of rents outside the control of the fund, directly accruing to the federal budget. The gas sector was entirely left out. Also missing were tax revenues related to petroleum products. These gaps contradicted the government's goals to make its budget less dependent on fluctuations in the international price of oil and gas.

Finally, the process through which the Stabilization Fund was established also made it more vulnerable to major policy reversals in the future. Establishing a savings fund was a rather technocratic move by a narrow group of executive officials and experts.[50] The fund was not a product of extensive bargaining across the political establishment. The few involved from the executive branch lacked cohesion from the start and never reached a consensus on how the fund would work.[51] In this setting, President Putin's support for establishing the Stabilization Fund was decisive.[52] Yet, it also brought a new question to the fore: would the Finance Ministry, the chief proponent of the fund, enjoy such support in the future?

Compared to the case of servicing Russia's foreign debt, fiscal conservatives faced a bigger problem. Repayment of debt was largely accomplished years before the Great Recession, and the question of foreign debt dropped off the political agenda. By contrast, the pressure on fiscal conservatives to revisit the status quo policy on the use of the savings of the oil funds was about to get more intense. With respect to both policies, Kudrin and his team lacked the support of a cohesive executive, but had Putin's blessing. His blessing was no longer essential with respect to foreign debt servicing, but was critical for the future of the oil funds.

Shielding the Stabilization Fund against the "Spending Party" before the Great Recession

As soon as the Stabilization Fund was established, it faced mounting challenges. Its design left it open to pressure to spend its revenues. The 500 billion ruble threshold was surpassed quickly, and there was no explicit rule that required the fund to continue adding to its savings. It was not modeled on Norway's oil fund, designed to keep accumulating for the benefit of future generations.

The bigger challenge for the fund, however, was the general lack of support for it as a tool to regulate the flow of oil rents into the Russian economy. Having savings in an oil fund was a new phenomenon for Russians.[53] Thus, the savings of the Stabilization Fund quickly became a visible political target. Suddenly, an intensifying discourse on economic policy centered on one theme: what was to be done with the windfalls of the Stabilization Fund?

There were two highly unequal sides to the debate. Gurvich describes them as the "saving party" versus the "spending party."[54] The "saving party" was represented by the Finance Ministry, led by Kudrin, and enjoyed the support of Russia's Central Bank and the presidential advisor Illarionov. It was a fairly small "party" dedicated to shielding the Stabilization Fund against withdrawals. The "spending party" was much more extensive.[55] It was not limited to Russia's traditional political forces favoring more state-led development. The "party" transcended the ideological divisions of the 1990s and included significant representation from the executive branch. As early as August 2004, the new prime minister, Fradkov, was quick to request that cabinet members present their proposals on how to spend the fund's savings.[56] Surprisingly, Gref emerged as one of Kudrin's chief opponents. Driven by concerns to meet Putin's target of doubling Russia's GDP by the end of the decade, he insisted that some of the savings could be used to finance large-scale infrastructure projects.[57] Gref suggested the creation of a distinct Investment Fund to support such infrastructure projects.[58] Cabinet members responsible for the social sphere also pleaded for portions of the oil fund to help with their respective areas, such as health and education.[59] According to Russian journalist Yulia Latynina, the *siloviki* within the executive constituted another source of pressure. Hoping to get access to the cash flows of the Stabilization Fund, they urged Kudrin to allocate money for infrastructure projects, the military, and technological innovation.[60]

The reach of the "spending party" went far beyond the executive branch. Following the weak performance of the "liberal" parties in the 2003 Duma elections, the Fourth Duma was also decidedly in this camp. United Russia, the faction that mattered the most in the Fourth Duma, emerged as a vocal proponent of tapping into the fund.[61] Additionally, prominent political figures joined the discourse. Moscow Mayor Luzhkov suggested the savings be used to enhance Russia's defense industry and road infrastructure.[62] Sergey Mironov, the chairman of the Federation Council, recommended the fund be used to provide financial incentives to raise the birth rate.[63] The rhetoric around spending the oil rent savings appealed to some segments of the business community as well. For instance, industrialist Oleg Deripaska suggested the oil money should be used to finance the automobile and aviation industries, in which he had shares.[64] Members of the Russian Union for Industrialists and Entrepreneurs (RUIE) and the Chamber of Commerce and Industry (CCI) also called for tapping into the Stabilization Fund for sponsoring investment projects.[65] Finally, the public was also clearly on the side of the "spending party." A 2005 poll reflected the public's unequivocal support for spending the fund's revenues.[66] According to another poll, taken two years later, the mood remained largely the same.[67]

The principal argument of the "saving party" was that Russia had to keep accumulating more into the "rainy day" fund in order to fight inflation and prevent the excessive appreciation of the national currency. For its adherents, rapidly servicing the foreign debt remained a high priority in 2004 and 2005. The Finance Ministry conceded that some of the savings in the fund could be spent, but only for the purpose of paying Russia's foreign debt. It argued this would also help to sterilize the rapid inflow of foreign currency.[68]

Looking back on his career as finance minister, Kudrin expressed one overarching concern that drove his resolve to shield the fund's savings. The economic crisis of 1998 had a profound effect on his way of thinking. By saving a chunk of the oil rents and prioritizing foreign debt payments, he hoped to prepare Russia for future crises.[69] This was a risk-averse approach that could only appeal to Putin: the 1998 default had brought down the Russian government and further weakened Yeltsin's popularity. Rapid debt payments minimized the chances of a similar default, while savings in the oil fund could serve as a buffer when Russia needed it the most.

According to Deliagin, Kudrin and his supporters had additional concerns when guarding the Stabilization Fund against withdrawals. They believed that unlocking the fund to support spending within the Russian economy would almost certainly result in the misuse of the resources. Possible bureaucratic turf wars also played a role. If the fund were to be tapped, other parts of the executive, namely Gref's ministry, could get significant authority over its operations. This was an area in which Kudrin's ministry was reluctant to cede its dominance.[70]

The "spending party" had many arguments to counter Kudrin's countercyclical approach to the fund. Many were not convinced that there was any viable link between the rapid flow of export revenues and inflation. They had other explanations for Russia's persistent inflation, such as the effects of local and natural monopolies.[71] Their hand grew stronger as foreign debt payments became less urgent over time. By contrast, foreign borrowing by Russian banks and the corporate sector was rising rapidly.[72] Many in the "spending party" found this situation inconceivable: Russia was sitting on cash that could have been used to finance domestic projects. Kudrin was in the spotlight. Some of his ardent supporters might have likened him to the statesman Sergey Witte,[73] widely credited for tsarist Russia's rapid economic resurgence at the end of the nineteenth century?[74] But those in the "spending party" had a rather different view. Some compared Finance Minister Kudrin to Plyushkin, the fictional character of Gogol's novel *Dead Souls*, who obsessively saved everything he could.[75] Others found a different reason to disparage Kudrin. The oil rents saved in the fund were not invested well.[76] For two years its money just sat in an account at Russia's Central Bank, bringing no returns.[77] When the Finance Ministry finally decided to invest them in foreign government securities in 2006, returns were dismal and the appreciation of the ruble further eroded the value of the savings.[78] Furthermore, Kudrin was accused of propping up foreign economies at Russia's expense by investing the oil money abroad.[79]

Limited in size, and with no independent political base behind it, the "saving party" had little chance against the much more extensive "spending party" unless President Putin tilted the balance in its favor. Indeed, Putin chose to support the "saving party," and this proved decisive in the way the Stabilization Fund and its successors funds evolved.[80] Nevertheless, the president's support shifted from one issue to another and evolved over time, resulting in numerous compromises between the two "parties."

Kudrin's first concession to the "spending party" came as early as 2004 when he agreed to transfer a limited amount (30 billion rubles) from the stabilization fund to cover the deficit of the Pension Fund during the following year.[81] As intended, this proved to be a one-time transfer for the duration of the Stabilization Fund.

The bigger victory for the "spending party" came in 2005 when it succeeded in securing a raise in the cut-off price for oil from 20 USD/barrel to 27/USD per barrel. The "spending party" hoped this move would allow more oil revenues to accrue to the federal budget rather than the Stabilization Fund. Kudrin's resistance proved unsuccessful in the context of the ongoing shifts in economic policy.[82] The four "National Projects" announced in the fall of 2005 clearly necessitated more spending. The cabinet's propensity to spend more was reflected in the 2006 budget proposal as well. Suddenly, the cabinet's projections about the price of oil became more ambitious: 40 USD/barrel was the new price used to calculate the budget.[83] In effect, Kudrin had succeeded in preventing the direct use of savings from the Stabilization Fund. But the raise in the cut-off price opened the path for more budgetary spending across the board as well as for dedicated areas, such as the national projects and Gref's Investment Fund.

Despite record growth in the size of the federal budget in 2007,[84] pressure to spend the savings of the Stabilization Fund remained. With the Duma and presidential elections on the horizon, proposals for using the assets of the fund multiplied. Some of the proposals outlined broader objectives, such as promoting Russia's economic diversification and its potential for innovation. Backed by a bulging federal budget in 2006 and 2007, Russia witnessed the rise of several so-called development agencies dedicated to reaching these broader goals.[85] These agencies were already getting funds from the federal budget,[86] but for the "spending party," the savings of the Stabilization Fund could be put to use to expand the reach of these new agencies.[87] It became obvious that this approach had the president's support. Addressing the Federal Assembly in April 2007, Putin announced a decision to split the Stabilization Fund into two parts: the Reserve Fund and the National Wealth Fund. He urged some of the assets in the latter to be invested in the Russian economy.[88] Kudrin complied, and completed the transfer of 300 billion rubles (about 10 percent of the value of the Stabilization Fund) to Vneshekonombank and to Rosnanotech, before the fund was split at the beginning of 2008.[89]

Despite these compromises, the "saving party" had its own victories, which turned out to be critical in ensuring the continued growth of savings until the Global Recession reached Russia in 2008. The new cut-off price for oil adopted in 2005 was maintained until the final days of the Stabilization Fund. Also, the transfer of funds to the development agencies in 2007 was a one-time phenomenon. No new cash inflows were prescribed for the following year. The lack of any other withdrawals from the Stabilization Fund was particularly noteworthy given the absence of formal restrictions to spending its windfalls after the 500 billion rubles threshold had been reached.

The influence of the "saving party" was evident in the discourse that led to the split of the Stabilization Fund. Kudrin was able to actively influence the process. The reform of the fund brought several improvements. First, tax revenues from the gas sector and petroleum products would finally be allowed to accrue to the newly created Reserve Fund. Second, the split of the fund brought more clarity about the overall purpose of saving Russia's oil and gas rents. The Stabilization Fund never had a clear mission to meet some long-term objectives such as saving for future generations or supporting Russia's pension system. The creation of the National Wealth Fund as a separate entity set the ground for accumulating funds for such objectives. However, some uncertainty remained. During his address to the Federal Assembly in April 2007, Putin urged that the fund be used to support Russia's pensions system, while also suggesting its assets be used to support the newly created development agencies.[90] Until a month earlier, this fund went under the name of Future Generations Fund.[91] The name change was indicative of its expanding scope.

Third, the Finance Ministry was able to convince the government to set the size of the Reserve Fund as a percentage of Russia's GDP. While its size was capped at 10 percent of the annual GDP, extra oil and gas revenues would fill the National Wealth Fund.[92] No upper limit was set for the latter fund. Moreover, proposed changes about the size of the Reserve Fund and rules for withdrawal were put into a much more comprehensive and clear-cut budgetary framework. Russia introduced a new fiscal rule that brought clarity about the conditions under which oil and gas tax revenues would flow to the federal budget.[93] In line with many other oil-rich economies, Russia finally introduced the concept of non-oil-and-gas deficit into its budgetary process. A ceiling was set for a deficit in the annual budget by hypothetically removing oil and gas revenues. By implication, this set a limit on the amount of oil and gas revenues that could supplement the budget.

Kudrin, however, conceded on a three-year transition period between the launch of the new funds and the end of 2010. During this period Russia would not have to comply with the fiscal rule and could have a non-oil budget deficit above the predetermined long-term target. In effect, Russia could keep spending more through the federal budget.[94] It was apparent that the Putin administration was reluctant to set major constraints on public spending in 2008 – a critical election year. The fact that the "transition" period was scheduled to last two years beyond the approaching presidential election was a troubling sign for Kudrin's fiscal conservatives. It is worth noting that the decision for such a "transition" period was taken in 2007 – still early for the Russian leadership to be alarmed by the impending global financial crisis that could justify a hike in public spending. This indicated the growing appeal of a more "statist" approach to the economy among members of the executive, including Putin.

Yet, overall, the "saving party" could be described as fairly successful in shielding Russia's oil funds from the pervasive pressure to invest their assets in the domestic economy. Even in 2008, nearly half of the oil windfalls were saved. Against all odds, Kudrin, the main target of the "spending party," remained a key figure in charge of the oil savings. Remarkably, he survived another cabinet reshuffle in the fall of 2007. While Gref was out of cabinet, Kudrin maintained his position in the Finance Ministry, along with his role as deputy prime minister.

The successes of the "saving party" could hardly be conceivable without Putin's support for prudence in managing the oil windfalls, despite his growing inclination to spend more of the rents to boost the economy. Kudrin recognized this point in an interview following his departure from the government in 2011, noting that the Stabilization Fund would not have existed without Putin's backing.[95]

However, these successes also need to be viewed in the broader context of rent allocation. Russian economist Yakovlev points to an alternative explanation, whereby the rapid growth in oil prices made it possible to accomplish many things at once. Russia could build sizable oil savings, pay off a massive amount of its foreign debt, and still significantly expand budgetary spending.[96] In effect, throughout Putin's first presidency, Russia's oil rents represented a progressively growing pie. Furthermore, there were alternative avenues to get hold of oil rents without tapping into the oil funds or the budget. Oil companies were sharing part of their rents, bypassing the state.

Without the oil funds, Russia's oil rents would have probably been spent differently. The fact that these funds still managed to remove more than half of the oil windfalls during the 2004–8 period was a major achievement. International development agencies have strongly praised this episode in Russia's handling of the oil funds.[97] But the real test was yet to come. A collapse in the price of oil would expose how Russia's oil funds would fare in a different economic setting.

Testing Russia's Oil Funds after the Great Recession

For nearly a decade during his tenure as finance minister, Alexei Kudrin kept warning that Russia faced great risks owing to its dependence on oil export revenues. Speaking in the midst of the Great Recession, he recalled:

> Certainly, I understood that there would be a crisis. Frankly, we were thinking of a crisis spurred by oil prices. I thought Russia could face a cyclical crisis. Remember what I was saying throughout all these years of high oil prices: we are already at the point where we got everything we could. Prepare for a fall. However, as long as oil prices went up, no one believed me.[98]

Kudrin was proven right. His warnings had helped build a sizable cushion for the Russian economy. Many started to appreciate the fiscal conservatism he had so ardently defended during the boom years of the 2000s.[99] But could he and his ministry finally convince the "spending party" to be more prudent in the future? The big question at this point was how the crisis would shape Russia's broader economic policies. Could the government take the opportunity created by the crisis to relaunch stalled reforms and return to the prudent fiscal policies of the early 2000s? Or would the crisis reinforce recent trends towards state-led development, whereby the solution to problems was to throw more money at them?

As the Great Recession reached Russia, the savings in the oil funds quickly became central to policy discussions. There was a widely shared understanding that it was time for Russia to enjoy the benefits of its "rainy day" savings. The Finance Ministry was open to supporting robust anti-crisis stimulus measures, though it called for moderation.[100]

The chosen path became increasingly clear. Reforms were being postponed while fiscal prudence was put on hold. Vladimir Milov, former Deputy Energy Minister, has argued that the accomplishments of the 2000s actually had some unintended effects during the crisis. Ironically, the savings in the oil funds and the strikingly low foreign debt made many officials overly confident about the path the country had taken. They saw no urgency in returning to the earlier fiscally conservative approach to the economy. Russia had the funds to further increase government spending and expand the role of the state in the economy.[101]

There were two troubling signs with respect to the oil funds. First, budgetary commitments were raised inordinately, with repercussions for Russia's oil savings long into the future. Some of the funds allotted to fight the Great Recession could be justified by pointing to the adoption of similar stimulus packages worldwide. However, as noted in the previous chapter, a big part of the fiscal expansion involved permanent spending commitments that would strain Russia's finances well after the crisis. Indeed, these commitments turned into a major constraint for replenishing the oil funds when the crisis was over. Russian economist Alexashenko argues that there was a structural change in the Russian budget during the Great Recession, as social expenditure surged to unprecedented levels.[102] Growth in social spending during the crisis was largely financed through the Reserve Fund, and subsequently constituted a significant burden on the budget. A further long-term commitment for budgetary spending was undertaken through a new program to modernize the military through 2020. According to Milov, even the one-time bailouts, channeled by the government through the Reserve Fund, were questionable. Many highly inefficient state companies, which could have been left to go bankrupt, were bailed out during the crisis. In effect, much of the savings accumulated during the boom years were spent for the "wrong" purposes.[103]

Second, it quickly became apparent that the fiscal rules meant to ensure the long-term growth of the Reserve Fund and the National Wealth Fund were easy to bend or ignore altogether. Already at the outset of the crisis, in the fall of 2008, an amendment to the Budget Code relaxed the restrictions on the Reserve Fund. Accordingly, when oil prices dropped below 70 USD/barrel, a level that was rapidly reached as early as October 2008, the government could decide to withdraw funds without consulting the legislature.[104] The government took a more radical step in 2009 when it suspended the fiscal rule governing the two oil funds since 2007, despite its fairly flexible directives set for the "transition" period through 2010. Hence, the government would no longer be required to propose additional budgetary amendments and seek legislative approval in order to use the savings of the Reserve Fund.[105] In the case of the National Wealth Fund, while avoiding direct withdrawals, the government adopted quasi-fiscal measures. A part of the fund's savings was invested in Russian blue chip companies, while extensive credits were provided to Russian banks to help them maintain their liquidity and meet their debt obligations because of a weaker ruble. Subsequently, when the crisis was over and the investments of the National Wealth Fund started to deliver positive returns, the bulk of its profits were randomly appropriated and incorporated into the annual federal budget.[106]

After Kudrin's departure from the Russian government in September 2011, the Finance Ministry continued to work on developing a new fiscal rule.[107] Its proposal was successfully adopted at the end of 2012. The new rule reflected another attempt to curb government expenditures, though it involved significant compromises on the ministry's behalf. On the one hand, it set a cap on government spending in the annual budget based on a benchmark oil price.[108]

On the other hand, the new fiscal rule lowered the Reserve Fund's ceiling (from 10 to 7 percent of GDP), and put further limits on the amount of savings that could accrue to the National Wealth Fund.[109] Furthermore, it granted the government substantial flexibility. Thus, only a few months into 2013, the government stopped depositing oil and gas revenues into the Reserve Fund in order to cover an expected shortfall in privatization receipts. Such a move was in line with the new fiscal rule. Subsequently, during 2013 and 2014, a period of continuing high oil prices, the Russian government simply opted to spend the additional revenues that were originally targeted for the Reserve Fund.[110]

The fiscal rule was more restrictive in the case of the National Wealth Fund, as its savings could not be used to cover the budget deficit. Arguably, this restriction saved the fund from sharing the fate of the Reserve Fund. Nevertheless, the new fiscal rule permitted the government to continue employing various off-budget mechanisms when deemed necessary. Thus, the National Wealth Fund went on acting as an investor in various infrastructure projects, which otherwise could have been funded through the annual budget. One of the original intentions of the fund – supporting the pensions system – lost its priority. The fund gradually evolved into an agency dedicated to investment in development projects.[111]

In 2015, the new fiscal rule, despite all the flexibility it offered, was suspended as well. As in the case of the preceding fiscal rule (from 2007), it did not survive the first economic crisis it faced, when Russia witnessed a double shock caused by low oil prices and international sanctions. The abandonment of the new fiscal rule was in part due to its design flaws, but it also reflected the government's preference for a free hand in handling the new crisis.[112] The Reserve Fund's savings proved essential to cover the budget deficit. As the oil bust turned out to be longer than the previous one, however, these were exhausted by the end of 2017, and the fund ceases to exist.

Overall, the Finance Ministry, officially in charge of the funds, was far less successful after 2008 than in the period before the Great Recession in shielding the funds' savings and ensuring their continuous growth. Little went to replenish the Reserve Fund during the new oil boom between 2011 and 2014. The two consecutive fiscal rules, even during the periods when they were not suspended, did not present a formidable constraint on the government in its use of the oil fund savings. The "spending party" could claim a victory: policies regarding the fund became largely subordinate to the executive's broader economic agenda, an agenda favoring an expansionist fiscal policy (see chapter 5). Putin's support for many of the aspects of this policy, such as greater social and military spending, made it difficult to enforce the agreed upon rules on the two oil funds.

Putin's overall approach to Russia's oil funds after 2008 was more favorable to the "spending party." The failure to significantly replenish the oil funds during the 2011–14 oil boom demonstrates that the "saving party" could no longer claim the same level of support of the chief executive as during the previous oil boom. Putin's support had tilted the balance in favor of the "savings party" prior to the Great Recession. Without such support, it became apparent that objectives set for the oil funds had little meaning, and the rules could easily be ignored or circumvented. The lack of effective legislative oversight ensured this outcome as well. The Russian legislature remained largely irrelevant when fiscal rules were abandoned during the crises.

And yet, Putin demonstrated some appreciation of the merits of fiscal restraint, once Russia faced another crisis and an oil bust after 2014. The Reserve Fund was exhausted more slowly than many had predicted.[113] This emphasis on restraint in public spending helped to prolong the life of the Reserve Fund, and ensured that Russia maintained at least one of the funds, the National Wealth Fund, as a financial cushion for future crises.

Conclusion

Russia's oil funds quickly emerged as another battleground over the country's vast oil rents. These battles were closely intertwined with the competing visions and priorities of the executive branch on economic policies examined in the previous chapter. The story of how these funds evolved says a lot about the "decisiveness" of the Russian state and the ability of the executive to commit to some of its policy achievements.

Turning the idea of an oil fund into a reality constituted a crucial piece of reform during Putin's early tenure. It was yet another indication of a "decisive" state, whereby an idea that greatly lacked popularity was quickly transformed into a formal institution that set new rules on how to handle Russia's oil windfalls. The entire episode of establishing and accumulating the majority of Russia's oil tax revenues into the Stabilization Fund would have been much harder to accomplish had the president faced a powerful legislature.

Yet, committing to this reform and maintaining a countercyclical approach in managing the oil funds was far from easy. There are several key aspects of this case that shed a light on reforms and economic policy in Putin's Russia. First, setting formal rules has been of little significance in guiding the allocation of rents. Russia never managed to establish the oil funds as robust institutions whose rules and principles would matter more than political battles within the executive branch. The Stabilization Fund accumulated substantial savings, not on account of stringent rules but despite a clear lack of them. The fund kept saving oil windfalls far above the legal threshold, which had been set fairly low and exposed it to potential raids. Subsequently, there were two separate attempts to establish new rules governing the amounts of withdrawal – once in 2007 and again in 2012. Each time, the new rules were quickly suspended at the early signs of economic crises. Despite historically high oil prices between

2011 and 2014, Russia failed to significantly replenish its oil funds. Any regulations that remained in force were easily amended or circumvented to allow for more spending. In the end, one of the oil funds, the Reserve Fund, was entirely exhausted by the end of 2017. The National Wealth Fund survived as an entity and preserved the bulk of its savings. Yet, its function was fundamentally transformed. Originally set with the principal goal to support Russia's pension system, this oil fund gradually turned into a de facto development agency, disbursing funds in areas selected by the Russian leadership.

Second, a lack of cohesion within the executive branch resulted in policy reversal and instability. The establishment of the first oil fund, the Stabilization Fund, was a rather technocratic decision, devoid of an extensive bargaining process. The executive branch itself lacked cohesion on the need for an oil fund and on its intended functions. Many within the executive branch remained displeased. For them, a dollar saved in an oil fund represented a missed opportunity for rent redistribution. In this context, the continuing battles within the executive branch proved far more significant than formal rules in deciding how the oil funds functioned. Putin's preferences largely determined the outcome of these battles. Putin initially extended support to the few voices within the executive branch demanding a fiscally conservative approach. His choice helped the Finance Ministry establish an oil fund and subsequently shield its savings against an extensive "spending party." Yet, Russia's fiscally conservative approach on the oil funds could last only as long as it enjoyed Putin's support. When his support shifted in a new direction, a policy reversal became inevitable, and any formal restrictions carried little weight.

Third, Putin's support for the status quo approach on the oil funds could last as long as it was not perceived as detrimental to broader economic and political objectives. Thus, concerns about elections and succession in 2008 could explain the first withdrawals from the Stabilization Fund. With Putin's support, however, such withdrawals remained modest in light of the ongoing shift in Russia's economic agenda towards state-led development and expansionary fiscal policy after 2005. The shift was sustained primarily through higher expenditures from the budget. The onset of the Great Recession reinforced the state's interventionist approach in the economy and its relaxed fiscal policy. The Finance Ministry's efforts to return to fiscal restraint during the 2011–14 oil boom were unsuccessful. Its proposed approach was increasingly in conflict with the government's economic priorities. Russia's "spending party" could rejoice: Putin was on their side, and redistribution of the oil windfalls now faced little resistance.

Overall, there has been a mutual connection between Russia's oil funds and the leadership's policy considerations. Their savings have provided an essential financial cushion – when plentiful they have secured critical resources to mitigate economic and political risks. Russia reaped the benefits of sizable oil funds during the Great Recession, and once again when the country faced economic sanctions in 2014. The economic crises Russia faced would have almost certainly been deeper without this cushion, and one can only speculate about their potential political implications for the leadership. The presence of such a cushion, however, has arguably helped to empower the proponents of expansionary fiscal policy, amplifying their voices, particularly during periods of increased political risks for the leadership. The prolonged expansionary budgetary policy, well after the 2008–9 oil bust was over, could be explained through the availability of sizable reserves in the oil funds. In this respect, the executive's subsequent return to fiscal restraint has become conditional on the lowering of political risks and the near-term prospects of exhausted oil savings.

How Russia serviced its foreign debt represents a rather rare case illustrating that the state could both act decisively and maintain its approach over time. The repayment of Russia's debt in the early 2000s was launched and accomplished without a cohesive executive to back this process. Putin's continuous support proved critical. Unlike policies in other areas, however, this policy necessitated no continuous adjustment. Once the debt was largely paid off, there was no field left on which to wage significant political battles. Admittedly, there was nothing predetermined that Russia would opt to avoid resorting to new debt and thus emerge as one of the countries with the lowest sovereign external debt in the world. In this respect, the availability of savings in Russia's oil funds ensured that members of the executive branch would prefer to make use of them first rather than see their government again resort to substantial foreign loans.

7 The Oil Sector as a Redistributor of Rents

Rents generated by Russian oil companies go through an intricate cycle of redistribution. Both the state and the oil companies act as agents for redistributing these rents. Clearly, the state has taken the leading role in redistribution. The fundamental overhaul of the oil tax regime at the start of Putin's first presidency ensured that the state would capture the bulk of the windfalls derived from oil. As most of the oil money has had to pass through state institutions – namely the federal budget and oil fund(s), controlled by Russia's executive branch – the state is effectively the chief redistributor of the oil wealth.

Yet, Russian oil companies have also acted as agents of rent redistribution. The story of the battles over Russian oil windfalls will be incomplete if this form of rent allocation by the oil companies is not taken into account. The oil producers' contribution to the Russian economy has been far greater than the taxes they pay to the government. They have shared their windfalls with a large set of actors, ranging from select individuals to Russian society as a whole. Operating within an extensive value chain, oil companies have had to share their wealth with numerous players.

The Russian leadership has not been a passive bystander in this process. Instead, it has strived to shape the process. This chapter illustrates that the upsurge in executive power under Putin helped the federal executive become more "decisive" in influencing how oil companies redistributed their windfalls.

The analysis yields several important questions. First, oil majors' redistributive activities have exhibited much instability in terms of their key beneficiaries over time. As the state under Putin has become more capable of guiding the flow of rents, what explains this instability? This chapter argues that the instability is associated with the primacy of informal rules in shaping outcomes in this segment of rent allocation. This brings us to another key point. The executive's preference for informal rules has a long history. In a way, the state's continual reliance on informal rules in handling oil companies' redistributive activities could be considered a form of "stability." This leads to the next key question:

why has this approach endured for so long? The chapter argues that persistently weak rule of law and the broader political value for the leadership to maintain control over rent flows have ensured the primacy of informal rules.

This chapter starts with a detailed review of the multiple avenues through which oil companies have shared their windfalls with a diverse set of beneficiaries. In developing the main arguments above, it addresses several additional questions. In what ways has Russia's broader political context, and more specifically the upsurge in executive power, affected the oil companies' engagement in redistribution? What has made it possible for the leadership to guide this engagement? Finally, what have been the broader political functions served by the leadership's control over oil companies' rent flows?

The Complex Cycle of Oil Rents: How Russia's Oil Sector Redistributes Rents

As oil rents can go through a long and complex cycle, analyzing how oil companies redistribute them is subject to some formidable methodological constraints. The oil sector can distribute its wealth through numerous means and in various directions, yet there are no precise ways to measure many of its interactions that involve payment. No study has quantified this process. The problem is further magnified if one tries to establish certain longer-term patterns within the oil sector's rent redistribution activities. Fluctuations in the amount of rents redistributed by oil companies may well be mirroring changes in oil prices. Such methodological constraints have been absent with respect to other aspects of rent allocation examined so far.

Nonetheless, there is sufficient evidence to illustrate how oil companies have been engaging in rent redistribution. This chapter reveals that the oil companies' involvement in rent redistribution is a significant part of the wider process of oil rent allocation in the Russian economy. Also, the political underpinnings of this type of rent redistribution need to be examined in order to fully understand the contests over Russia's oil wealth.

Looking at the oil companies as rent-redistributing entities requires a further elaboration of the concept of rents. Oil rents examined so far have been equivalent to industry profits – the difference between total revenues accruing to the oil companies and their overall costs. As illustrated earlier, the state has imposed a heavy level of taxation on these profits. Yet, the story of oil companies as rent redistributors is more complex. This is because they can engage in rent redistribution with respect to both their pre-tax revenues and after-tax profits. Examining these avenues for rent redistribution reveals the multifaceted role oil companies play in the Russian economy.

The analysis below describes the multiple paths – beyond paying taxes – through which Russia's oil producers share their wealth with a wide set of beneficiaries. Overall, I distinguish between three categories of such rent redistribution. First, oil companies can share their rents with other beneficiaries by forgoing a portion of the revenues. I examine two specific cases that fall into this category: the provision of price subsidies to consumers and the sale of oil to intermediary trading companies at below international market prices. Second, the oil sector can redistribute rents by incurring costs when paying for various goods and services. To illustrate this point I look at three distinct areas. A key one is the oil transportation sector, which has managed to capture a substantial part of the oil rents from Russian oil producers. Social responsibility projects funded by oil companies constitute another area of importance. Also, I recognize that oil companies may face additional costs, dubbed by Gaddy and Ickes as "informal" or "excess" costs.[1] Such costs would include overpayment for procurement of goods as well as bribes. I look at the evolution of transparency and corporate governance in the oil sector as a proxy measure for these additional costs. Finally, I look at the oil companies' dividend policy. This is one area that refers clearly to post-tax profits that are subject to redistribution.

Oil Subsidies

Russia's domestic oil prices were liberalized during the mid-1990s. The International Energy Agency (IEA), tracking fossil fuel subsidies around the world, has consistently noted that Russia's oil consumers have not received subsidies. This is in contrast to gas and electricity, where consumer subsidies have remained substantial.[2]

And yet, the oil price liberalization of the mid-1990s did not amount to the elimination of subsidies in practice. Prices for petroleum products in Russia, although tracking international prices, have remained significantly below them. This gap has tended to widen particularly during periods of high international prices for oil.[3] In effect, Russian consumers have managed to capture part of the oil rents by enjoying lower petroleum product prices, albeit clearly not to the extent experienced, for instance, in oil-rich Venezuela and countries in the Persian Gulf.

Since the mid-1990s, the setting of petroleum prices in the Russian market has been guided by a principle known as export price parity. Export parity is the price point where companies see no relative advantage between selling their products at home or selling them abroad. Russia's domestic crude oil and petroleum product prices have tended to track export parity, and deviations have proven to be temporary. At export parity, Russia's domestic product prices have been significantly lower than international prices. Two factors account for this gap. Transportation expenses and export duties have added to the cost of exporting, ensuring that the domestic market clears at prices lower than those abroad. Russian oil producers have forgone significant revenues, particularly at higher oil prices when export duties have also gone up.

Export duties, a product of government policy, have been the main source of the price wedge between Russian and international prices. These duties have not only been crucial to collect oil rents, but have also resulted in indirect subsidies to the Russian economy, thus contributing to their resilience as a policy instrument since their reintroduction in 1998.

A distinguishing feature of "price subsidies" is that they have had the widest set of beneficiaries compared with any other aspects of rent redistribution involving the oil sector. Other redistributive activities by oil companies have typically benefited a narrow group of winners, some of them hard to identify. In the case of "price subsidies" the benefits have been spread universally. Some market players, oil-intensive sectors such as transportation and freight, have benefited more than others. Also, Russian refineries, mostly owned by oil-producing companies, have managed to capture much of the forgone rents, thanks to market distortions created by export duties.[4] Regions with significant refining activity have been well positioned to take advantage.

Rents Diverted to Oil-Trading Companies

Oil trading is another area in which Russian oil companies have forgone revenues, effectively letting other players capture a share of their rents.[5] It has been common for Russia's oil producers to engage intermediary companies, buying their crude oil and petroleum products at a significant discount in exchange for their trading services. The mere presence of an intermediary, however, does not constitute evidence of any wrongdoing, as it is a common practice worldwide.[6]

To understand how oil trading evolved during the Putin era it is worth examining the mercurial rise and subsequent decline of Gunvor, an oil-trading company. Established in 1997, this company emerged from obscurity to become Russia's largest oil trader by the mid-2000s. The extent of Gunvor's involvement in handling Russian oil reached its peak in 2011, when it accounted for 40 percent of oil shipments abroad, and its annual turnover reached 80 billion USD.[7] By 2012 the tides had turned. Gunvor started losing some of the big tenders from Russia's oil majors such as Rosneft, Surgutneftegaz, and TNK-BP. Its market share in Russian oil trading dropped rapidly.[8] Other international oil traders and affiliates of Russian oil majors quickly overtook Gunvor in handling Russian oil exports.[9]

Gunvor's rise and fall is revealing in many respects. It underscores how the flow of rents through oil traders has been closely intertwined with broader changes in the oil industry and the ongoing competition within the Russian elite. The company, founded by long-time Putin associate Gennady Timchenko, owed much of its initial success to profitable deals concluded in the late 1990s with the Russian oil producer Surgutneftegaz.[10] Yet, it was after the "national-ization" of Yuganskneftegaz and Sibneft that Gunvor's turnover surged. Gunvor positioned itself as a major trading intermediary for Russian oil.[11] Report-edly, Rosneft's deal with "exclusive" traders involved marked-down prices for oil.[12] Gunvor's competitors blamed it for using the administrative support of the Kremlin to cut favorable deals with oil producers.[13] Russian political activ-ist and minority shareholder Alexei Navalny brought an unsuccessful lawsuit against Rosneft, Gazprom Neft, and Surgutneftegaz, demanding that they dis-close more information on the terms of their contracts with Gunvor, alleging the latter to be at the core of widespread corruption.[14] Russian political expert Stanislav Belkovski alleged that Putin was the real owner of Gunvor, while the oil trader's management rejected the accusation.[15] Amid allegations of crony-ism, the Russian leader publicly denied that he had aided the rise of Gunvor.[16]

The subsequent decline of Gunvor in handling Russian oil sheds additional light on the contests over the oil wealth. First, by the end of the 2000s, a growing number of Russian oil producers shifted towards more transparent commer-cial tenders with traders. However, this did not apply to everyone.[17] Russian oil majors have continued to use offshore trading outfits, some of them possibly linked to high-ranking officials.[18] Second, the rise of Rosneft as a national oil champion did not bode well for the status quo in oil trading. In 2011, Ros-neft established its own offshore oil-trading outfit in Switzerland.[19] The fol-lowing year, Gunvor repeatedly lost many of Rosneft's tenders. Russian media outlets linked this outcome to an intensifying conflict between Sechin and Timchenko – the two formidable personae of the Russian oil industry.[20] Third, Timchenko managed to compensate for Gunvor's relative decline in the Rus-sian market by making gains elsewhere. Gunvor shifted towards a new strategy of diversifying its role in international oil trade while reducing its exposure to Russian oil.[21] In the meantime, Timchenko's business empire expanded into new sectors, such as infrastructure development and rail freight. Reportedly, his fortune rose from 4.15 billion USD to 14.1 billion USD between 2010 and 2013.[22] Finally, in 2014, the US government included Timchenko in a list of individuals subject to sanctions for allegedly engaging in corrupt deals through the US financial system. This proved to be a further setback for Gunvor, as Tim-chenko sold his entire stake to his foreign partner (44 percent).[23] Ironically, the sanctions further boosted the diversification of Timchenko's business in Russia, as his companies continued to win big tenders.[24]

Rents Diverted through Russia's Oil Transportation Sector

Oil companies are part of an extensive value chain, spanning exploration and production of reserves to the delivery of petroleum products to consumers. It is the oil producers that generate the rents, but they need the services of a whole range of market players in order to convert reserves into cash. Each segment of the value chain presents numerous possibilities for other players to acquire a portion of the oil windfalls.

Here I present the case of the oil transportation sector, which has managed to capture a substantial portion of the oil producers' rents. Oil companies' transportation expenses can be surprisingly large. For instance, in 2008, when oil prices reached a historic high, Rosneft paid over 5.5 billion USD for transportation, equivalent to nearly half of its entire cash costs (excluding taxes).[25] About 37 percent of its transportation expenses went to the national oil pipeline operator Transneft. Railway and maritime shipment costs accounted for the rest.[26]

Transneft's case is particularly revealing. Serving as Russia's de facto oil pipeline monopolist since 1993, the company has played a critical role in the flow of oil rents. Its ability to capture oil rents was drastically enhanced during Putin's first two terms as president. In 2002, Transneft was known to charge some of the lowest tariffs among its international peers.[27] By 2008, following several consecutive tariff hikes, its tariffs were among the world's highest, potentially indicating "excess costs" incurred by oil producers.[28] Transneft enjoyed exceptional profitability relative to the rest of the oil industry, and tariff increases clearly secured this distinction.[29]

While Transneft gained an increasingly pronounced role in capturing oil windfalls, it has been subjected to much lower taxation than oil producers.[30] In exchange, it has served multiple functions. Transneft has been actively engaged in rent redistribution. In Putin's first presidential term, Minister Gref noted an anomaly with respect to Transneft: it tended to pay low taxes and fairly low dividends, while making exceptionally high charitable contributions. Gref insisted that Transneft could deliver more to the federal budget.[31] Not much changed despite his plea. For most of the 2000s, Transneft remained Russia's largest charity contributor, eclipsed by Gazprom in 2010.[32] While disclosing the amounts paid annually to charity, Transneft has shied away from identifying the specific beneficiaries. This lack of transparency, typical for charitable contributions in the oil sector (see below), prompted Navalny to request the relevant information from Transneft. The request was ignored.[33]

Transneft has also been accused of overpaying its contractors. In 2013, a group of Duma deputies sent an inquiry to the Accounts Chamber to investigate the possible misuse of funds by Transneft.[34] The incident exposed the brewing tensions between Rosneft's head, Sechin, and Transneft's president, Nikolay Tokarev, as the latter accused Rosneft of orchestrating the attack.[35] The Accounts Chamber revealed irregularities in Transneft's tenders, considering them a potential indicator of overpayment for services and equipment.[36]

Transneft has performed geopolitical tasks predicated on the construction of new pipelines. Expensive pipeline projects have justified continuous hikes in tariffs. In retrospect, Transneft has built more pipelines than Russian oil producers may ever need.[37] Tokarev has boasted that having plenty of capacity is of strategic importance, reducing Russia's reliance on transit states while securing greater diversity in export routes.[38]

Rents from oil producers have benefited many other players in the oil transportation sector.[39] For instance, rapid growth in oil shipments on Russia's rail network during the first half of the 2000s was accompanied by a massive surge in the production of oil tanker cars, benefiting a handful of manufacturers.[40] Oil and petroleum products have been a key source of revenues for state-owned Russian Railways as well. As Russia's largest employer, Russian Railways has been repeatedly charged with operating at excessive costs, while investing little in its network. Incidentally, its operating costs tripled between 2004 and 2014, while the size of the rail network barely changed and freight train shipments actually got slower.[41] Some service providers, such as Stroytransgaz, a pipeline construction company owned by Timchenko, have thrived on account of the oil and the gas sectors.[42] Rents from the oil sector have been crucial for maritime ports as well as the steel industry.[43]

While prospering from oil rents, these industries have not been subject to the same punitive taxes as oil producers. This has resulted in stiff competition between key oligarchs for control over assets in such industries.[44] For Putin, this competition has presented an opportunity to intervene in the further redistribution of oil rents.

Redistributing Rents through "Social" Projects

Russian oil companies have been widely involved in supporting projects that, at least formally, aim to contribute to the welfare of society. Such projects, often considered part of companies' "corporate social responsibility" (CSR), have become increasingly common among oil companies not only in Russia but in many countries around the world. CSR encompasses a variety of activities companies undertake in order to maintain a "social contract" with stakeholders.[45] In reality, the meaning of CSR and the definition of a stakeholder have varied widely.[46]

The involvement of Russian oil companies in social projects has deep historic roots. Soviet oil production associations have been credited as the "founding fathers" of many Soviet oil towns.[47] When the Soviet Union collapsed, a new form of paternalism emerged as cash-constrained regional and municipal governments maintained expectations that companies would continue to provide welfare services.[48]

The engagement of Russian oil companies in social projects during the Putin era has involved some significant continuities with the past. Expectations that companies maintain this paternalist approach have been shared by Russian policy-makers as well as the public.[49] Regional and local governments have been particularly inclined to view companies as a source of "extrabudgetary" funding for social and cultural activities. Oil companies have gone as far as covering shortfalls in regional budgets by paying salaries to state employees.[50] A general lack of stakeholder involvement in CSR projects has been another historic continuity. Decisions to fund projects have been commonly made without community engagement. Oil companies have instead negotiated with political authorities over the scope of their contributions, with little input from local residents.[51]

Despite these continuities, the Putin era has seen major shifts in the way oil companies get involved in social projects. In the early 2000s, Russian oil companies started operating more like their international peers in many respects. More oil companies began adopting CSR programs in line with international practice, while voluntarily adhering to a code of social conduct.[52] The oil industry as a whole took a leading role in reporting CSR payments in Russia.[53] Yet, significant discrepancies in the quality of reporting persisted among these companies; legally such reporting has been voluntary.[54] Local communities have occasionally voiced their complaints about the lack of transparency and accountability of CSR projects funded by oil companies.[55]

In the aftermath of the Yukos Affair, there was a shift in the underlying motives for the oil sector's engagement in social projects. According to Russian political scientist Alexei Zudin, the fear created by the attack on Yukos gradually transformed the generally voluntary nature of "social responsibility" programs into an unofficially compulsory one. As social contributions started to feature more frequently in Putin's speeches, the oil sector got the message that being socially responsible was now a key condition to their operating in Russia.[56] In this new context, if an oil company refused to help the state, it faced, at a minimum, the risk of "excessive regulation."[57] State-owned oil companies were not exempt from pressure by government officials to contribute to designated "social projects."[58] Thus, unsurprisingly, during periods of economic downturn, oil companies came under pressure to share the state's financial burden.[59] During the Great Recession, and in the aftermath of the crisis in Crimea, the oil companies' general response was to avoid cutting CSR programs, while some even expanded their social project payments.[60]

Following the Yukos Affair, the oil industry became increasingly constrained in the areas it could fund through CSR payments. Yukos had emerged as a leading player in CSR payments, while also embracing autonomy in selecting its beneficiaries.[61] It had actively funded nongovernmental organizations (NGOs) and did not shy away from payments for political lobbying and support to opposition parties.[62] Following the attack on Yukos, oil companies felt pressure to limit the scope of what they could support financially and it became typical to bypass collaborative opportunities with local NGOs.[63]

Finally, the Putin era witnessed a growing centralization with respect to the oil sector's engagement in social responsibility projects. Regional authorities remained significant players and it has been reported that most CSR funding by oil companies remained at a regional level.[64] However, negotiations on key CSR projects moved increasingly within the domain of the federal executive, namely the Presidential Administration.[65] Industry insiders note that legislative changes during Putin's early years in the presidency ensured this outcome. Centralization in taxation curbed the regions' powers to grant tax breaks to oil companies, while the abolition of the "two keys principle" on license approvals further empowered the federal authorities.[66] According to Latynina, it became common for oil companies to receive requests from the Kremlin to provide funding under various pretexts, such as supporting a designated political party or a military project.[67] Some of these payments have been public. For instance, Surgutneftegaz helped with the repair of a nuclear submarine base, gaining Putin's personal appreciation in a 2012 news article on Russia's defense policy.[68] A former government official and industry veteran has described Surgutneftegaz as a de facto "stabilization fund," holding tens of billions of dollars in cash, and a regular source of funding for projects prioritized by the Kremlin.[69]

Corporate Governance and Diversion of Rents

There are other ways in which oil companies redistribute rents. Any purchase of goods and services by an oil company amounts to sharing wealth with others. A key question is to what extent these transactions have involved "informal costs" such as bribes and overpayments for goods and services needed to produce oil. Such costs would be indicative of an additional set of beneficiaries that have managed to divert a portion of the oil rents to themselves.

Quantifying informal costs is a fraught and forbidding task. I explore such costs in two steps. First, I look at the state of corporate governance in the oil industry as a possible proxy measure on how open the management of an oil company might be to informal practices.[70] Next, I look at how the Russian oil industry has confronted two countervailing forces with respect to its reported (actual) costs. Such costs could also provide clues on "informal costs," albeit to a limited extent.

The Russian oil sector in general has made notable progress in corporate governance since Putin's rise to power. In the 1990s, the oil industry had a bad reputation due to massive violations of shareholder rights, unclear ownership, and shady financial information.[71] The 1998 financial crises prompted a growing number of Russian oil majors to alter their approach to corporate governance.[72] Yukos and Sibneft were credited with making the most progress in improving corporate governance, soon to be taken over by much less transparent state-owned companies.[73] However, the oil industry as a whole continued to improve governance.[74] The Russian government also took incremental steps to encourage better governance by limiting transfer pricing, adopting a Code of Corporate Governance, and taking measures to constrain the use of offshore tax havens.[75] The latter measure was adopted as late as 2014 in response to extensive capital flight following Western sanctions on Russia.[76]

Yet, this progress in corporate governance in Russia's oil sector is far from total as there remain opportunities to divert rents through informal channels. A key problem plaguing parts of the oil industry has been the lack of precise information on ownership. For instance, former deputy energy minister Vladimir Milov has described Surgutneftegaz's ownership as the "number one top secret of the Russian oil industry," alleging that its secrecy must be for the purpose of masking politically exposed shareholders, some of them possibly in the Kremlin.[77] Even the mayor of Surgut, where the company is based, once remarked that he had no information on who owned Surgutneftegaz.[78] A lack of transparency is also common among non-oil companies that have thrived on doing business with oil producers.[79]

Additional problems have arisen with respect to disclosure of information following the sale of major stakes in Russian oil companies. Major acquisitions, as in the case of the sale of Yuganskneftegaz and Bashneft, have been shrouded in secrecy, raising questions about who actually benefits from such sales.[80] A persistent lack of transparency with respect to the management boards of state-owned oil companies has been another trouble spot for corporate governance. Appointment of state officials to company boards has been dominated by informal rules.[81] In 2011, President Medvedev launched an initiative to remove highest-ranking state officials from company boards.[82] This policy was soon reversed, however, as many officials were back on their boards.[83] Also the financial benefits attached to representing the state at a company board have remained hidden, at least to the public.[84] Finally, the Russian government has been particularly slow in taking action against offshore tax havens, passing a bill as late as 2014. Reportedly, a government audit in 2011 revealed the extensive use of offshore organizations, including by the management of state-owned energy companies.[85]

Can changes in reported costs offer a clue to the oil sector's involvement in "informal" transactions? The situation is highly complex, as oil companies have operated under two countervailing forces. On the one hand, reported costs have been driven up since the early 2000s by the declining quality of Russia's oil fields.[86] At the same time, oil money has steadily migrated from oil producers to companies providing oil services for increasingly complex fields.[87] This migration has enhanced opportunities for capturing rents from oil producers, though it is impossible to say how much of this process has taken place through informal channels.[88]

On the other hand, rising costs and the government's determination to keep a high tax burden on oil have kept the oil industry under pressure to minimize costs. Cutting costs has become a key determinant for market capitalization for Russian oil majors. The relatively competitive nature of the Russian oil industry, especially as compared to the gas sector, has also helped the oil producers exert some control over the costs.[89] In this context, it is not surprising that Russian oil companies have managed to maintain their international edge as low-cost producers.[90]

Nonetheless, cost minimization efforts cannot preclude the Russian oil sector's engagement in informal transactions. As oil companies have tended to report average costs provided by their regional subsidiaries, there have been opportunities for inflated costs on the basis of individual fields and localities.[91] Additionally, as Milov notes, insider ownership in the Russian oil industry has rendered shareholder pressure less effective than in other contexts.[92]

Dividend Payments

A growing number of Russian oil majors have paid dividends since the beginning of the 2000s. The amount has varied substantially across companies and fluctuated widely over time. Such payments have also played a key role in redistributing Russia's oil windfalls.

Dividend payments to a diverse set of beneficiaries have performed several functions in the context of Russia's oil sector. They have allowed oil company owners to periodically cash out their earnings. The true beneficiaries have not been obvious in the case of oil companies that limit disclosure of information on their shareholders. It is noteworthy that private oil companies have traditionally paid higher dividends than state-owned oil majors. This could well be related to continuing concerns about weak property rights in Russia. In such contexts, opportunities for cashing out may not be there for long.[93]

In the case of oil companies whose shares have been partially owned by regional governments – Bashneft and Tatneft in particular – dividend payments have ensured that a portion of the rents is retained within the respective region. Dividends from such companies have been used to cover gaps in the regional budget.[94]

Lastly, dividends from state-owned companies have played a highly peculiar role in the flow of oil rents. Such payments from state-owned Rosneft, and to a lesser extent Gazprom Neft, have contributed to the formation of a de facto extrabudgetary fund for the state. At the core of this arrangement is the 100 percent state-owned holding company Rosneftegaz. Created in 2004, Rosneftegaz has held the majority of shares in Rosneft and about 10 percent in Gazprom – the owner of Gazprom Neft. Since its establishment, Rosneftegaz has acted as an intermediary, accumulating dividend payments from Rosneft and Gazprom, and passing a portion of them to the federal budget.

Throughout the 2000s, Rosneftegaz's finances remained fairly modest. It wasn't until 2012 that it emerged as an increasingly important source of extra-budgetary funding. During the 2000s, both Rosneft and Gazprom continued to allocate only a small portion of their profits to dividends, despite pressure from the Finance Ministry and the Ministry of Economic Development.[95] In 2012, the two ministries, supported by Deputy Prime Minister Dvorkovich, finally reached their goal, though benefits to the federal budget were limited. Hoping to plug expected funding gaps in the aftermath of Putin's pre-election promises, the government approved a decree that obliged state-owned companies to pay at least a quarter of their profits as dividends.[96] Rosneft and Gazprom lobbied heavily to pay less than the prescribed amount, while the government kept pressing for a higher share.[97] There was a discernible increase in Rosneft-egaz's receipts in the following years, indicating that the two companies started passing more dividends to the state holding company. Its cash holdings jumped from 78 billion rubles to 544 billion rubles between 2011 and 2016.[98] Rosneft-gaz's holdings in 2016 were equivalent to what the federal budget allotted to education and substantially more than what was earmarked for healthcare.[99]

While higher dividend receipts from Rosneft and Gazprom helped, Rosneft-egaz's rapidly rising fortunes were also due to its ability to shield a large part of its cash from the federal budget. Behind the scenes, there was an intense political battle. Igor Sechin, the chair of Rosneftegaz's board, fought against transferring funds to the federal budget.[100] Finally in 2012, despite Sechin's resistance, Putin instructed the holding company to move nearly all of its receipts to the budget.[101] Nonetheless, in the following years, President Putin came to support Sechin again. As a result, Rosneftegaz successfully resisted the government's pressure to cede its fortunes, transferring only a minor share of its earnings. By contrast, dividend payments from other (non-oil) state holdings to the federal budget were rapidly on the rise, putting Rosneftegaz in a unique position.[102]

As Rosneftegaz's fortunes attracted increasing levels of public attention, Putin felt it necessary to justify his concessions to the state-owned holding company. Speaking at a press conference in late 2016, Putin said, "We fund some items from this [cash], when the government forgets that there are priorities that need attention."[103] Scattered information about Rosneftegaz's investments reveals a highly diverse portfolio, including the construction of power plants in Kaliningrad and a shipyard in the Far East, the development of a new airplane engine, and funding for the Skolkovo Center and the Agency for Strategic Initiatives.[104]

In effect, Rosneftegaz has emerged as an extrabudgetary fund at the disposal of the Russian leadership. Unlike funds disbursed through the budget, Rosneftegaz's payments have not been subject to legislative approval. Furthermore, the holding company is not required to report accounting details about its investments.[105] In the meantime, the entity has continued to perform mainly as a distributor of funds without building an administrative capacity or a staff force to manage projects. It has relied on its subsidiaries to manage the bulk of the funds. Rosneft, for instance, undertook the task of building a shipyard in the Far East using primarily Rosneftegaz's funds. Large-scale projects, such as the power plants under construction in Kaliningrad, managed by Inter Rao, have been implemented through subcontractors, letting them seize a chunk of Rosneftegaz's growing fortunes.[106] As most of Rosneftegaz's cash has come from the oil sector via Rosneft, this has been yet another means through which to redistribute oil windfalls throughout the economy.

Understanding the Oil Sector's Role as a Redistributor of Rents

So far I have highlighted the numerous pathways through which Russian oil companies have channeled part of their rents to other recipients. In effect, the oil sector has not only paid taxes, but also acted as an agent of rent redistribution, though with some guidance from the political leadership. This practice has had a long history and has persisted throughout the Putin era. This calls for further explanation.

Centralization of Rent Redistribution amid Weakened Veto Players

The oil sector's participation in rent redistribution preceded Putin's ascent to power. In the 1990s, it was already common practice for oil majors to share their wealth through subsidies, social projects, and murky contracts with suppliers and traders. In fact, elements of this practice can be traced back to the Soviet era.

Unique to the Putin era, however, is the growing centralization of this practice. As the legislature and regional authorities weakened as institutional veto players, so did their ability to shape the process of rent redistribution by the oil companies. The federal executive branch grew in importance in determining how and where oil companies' rents could flow. Yet, within the executive itself, informal networks largely determined where rents would go, while, with a few exceptions, formal rules were of secondary importance.

Among the institutional veto players, regional governors witnessed the most observable decline in their ability to shape the flow of rents from oil companies. During the 1990s, regional authorities could be quite effective in this process. More power was devolved to regional levels of government, which granted them considerable leverage in dealing with oil companies. Governors could help an oil company cut its tax burden significantly. Also, they could reward or punish oil companies thanks to the "two keys principle" enshrined in the Subsoil Law, which granted them joint authority (with the federal executive) to approve licenses. As a result, throughout the Yeltsin era, regional governments actively negotiated with oil and other energy majors for energy subsidies and various social contributions for the regional economies.[107] Their leverage opened additional opportunities to extract rents through bribes or overpriced contracts.

Bills curbing the regions' powers in Russian politics, along with additional pieces of legislation clearly put new limits on the governors' leverage against oil companies. The tax reform of the early 2000s was particularly instrumental. It ensured that regions had only limited authority in negotiating tax deals with oil companies. Export duties and the NDPI were designed as federal taxes. Regions were left with limited autonomy in levying the corporate profit tax, which gradually faded in terms of its relative significance in the oil companies' tax bill. The growing importance of export duties as a fiscal instrument had further repercussions. Negotiations between governors and oil companies on oil subsidies became much less meaningful as export duties assured consumers throughout Russia a substantial price cut. Regional differences in fuel prices, usually an outcome of negotiations between governors and oil companies in the past, were now within the domain of the Federal Anti-Monopoly Service (FAS).[108] Another setback for the regions came through revisions in Russia's Subsoil Law in 2004 when the "two keys principle" was ended. With the federal executive now the only authority that could approve licenses, oil companies had less to worry about with respect to regional leaders' expectations.

The growing role of the federal executive is evident in Putin's interventions in decisions about how oil companies share their rents in select regions. For example, in 2016, when Bashneft's state-owned shares were offered up for sale to the private sector, the president of the Republic of Bashkortostan asked Putin to find an arrangement that would allow the company to keep contributing to the region's economy through dividends as well as payments for social projects.[109]

Ironically, the regional authorities' leverage over the oil companies declined at a time when they had an even greater incentive to negotiate for extra rents. The fiscal centralization, launched at the start of Putin's first term as president, reduced the regions' share of oil revenues at the expense of the federal budget. Regional authorities sought to compensate for this loss through lobbying for federal transfers. They also continued to put pressure on oil companies, asking for their contribution to the regional economy through various means, such as payments for social projects, contracts with local suppliers, and dividend payments in the case of subsidiaries with regional ownership. Negotiations between regional governors and oil companies continued. Oil companies continued to contribute to regions, which helped to keep a portion of the rents within those regions. However, with weakened leverage against the oil companies, regional authorities became more dependent on the federal executive in their pursuit of rents from these companies.

When considering the oil sector's engagement in rent redistribution, it is clear that the role of the Russian legislature, another institutional veto player, has remained peripheral as well. The declining role of the legislature represents primarily a continuity with, rather than a break from, the Yeltsin era. In theory, the legislature can have a significant role in institutionalizing the process of rent redistribution by oil companies. It can enact laws that provide greater transparency and accountability about the flow of rents, publicize murky transactions, and call for investigations.

In this respect, the Putin era has seen mixed results. On the one hand, there is continuity with the 1990s. During the Yeltsin period, the legislature failed to act as a force to institutionalize the interaction of oil companies with beneficiaries outside the tax system. The oil sector continued to share its rents with a wide range of recipients, predominantly through informal means. This included ad hoc negotiations with regional governments on social projects and subsidies, an uninhibited proliferation of oil trading licenses granted by the federal government, and bribes. Informal means to take away and distribute the oil sector's rents have survived through the Putin era, and the legislature has remained largely ineffective in bringing greater accountability to the rent flows. The Duma's failure to prevent the emergence of Rosneftegaz's cash as a de facto alternative budget, for example, is indicative of its ineffectiveness.

On the other hand, there have been some limited successes in the process of institutionalization, though the legislature's contribution to this is largely confined to the early years of Putin's presidency. One early example is the legislation on export duties. The Duma was able to secure an amendment to the Law on Customs Tariffs in 2002, thus acquiring a significant role in setting certain guidelines for export duties, administered by a specially designated government commission. Export duties remained a key instrument, indirectly institutionalizing the provision of a universal subsidy for Russian consumers. This instrument was primarily a product of Russia's fiscal circumstances rather than a wish to regulate domestic oil prices (see chapter 4).

When it comes to more recent progress in institutionalization, the Duma's contribution has been more tenuous. While there has been increased institutionalization, this has been due to other players and has little to do with the autonomous actions of Russian legislators. For example, the two chambers passed important pieces of legislation on corporate governance and offshore revenues. Yet, it was the executive that initiated and prepared these bills; they went to the legislature merely for formal approval. Also, any improvements in corporate governance are more likely to have resulted from the oil majors' growth strategies than from pressure from state institutions. In 2013, the surprising move by a group of Duma deputies to request an investigation into Transneft's alleged misuse of funds was far from being a sign of a legislature taking autonomous action to demand transparency. Instead, it was the spillover of an intensifying fight between Tokarev and Sechin.[110] Why the incident was not resolved within the executive branch (where Sechin played a key role) remains unclear. Following the 2012 elections, Putin created a new commission in charge of strategic development for the energy sector, appointing Sechin general secretary.

While the importance of the federal executive grew, its decision-making appears to have been plagued by weak institutionalization. The executive branch under Putin has emerged as the main stage for competition. Yet, contests have been resolved predominantly through informal networks instead of formal rules. There are only a few activities, besides tax payments, in which formal rules have determined the outcome of how oil companies share their wealth. For instance, the government established a clear decision-making process with respect to regulating Transneft's shipping tariffs on oil companies, while an interdepartmental commission was tasked with periodically setting export duties in line with existing legislation, indirectly determining the size of the oil subsidies. Both cases correspond to the leadership's ambition to extract further rents from oil producers for the federal budget or state-owned Transneft. In other words, the key area of progress in setting some formal rules has been principally linked to the state's enhanced capacity to collect more rents, whether directly through taxes (as in the case of export duties) or an intermediary state entity (as in the case of Transneft).

By contrast, most other contests have been resolved through informal networks. To describe how this process functions, it is useful to refer to Alena Ledeneva's concept of *sistema*, which she defines as a "system of governance with its peculiar formal rules and informal norms, combined in a way that is nontransparent to outsiders but recognized by insiders of the public administration in Russia." It is an implicit social contract between rent-seeking elites and the masses, who also benefit from the "trickle-down income" of the rent-saturated economy.[111] *Sistema* combines members of the executive branch and the business elite. There are formal rules, but informal practices are often decisive in determining how oil companies share their rents after paying their tax dues. Oil companies' forgone revenues through offshore trading intermediaries, ad hoc contributions to social projects, Transneft's practice of disbursing rents through social payments rather than dividends, and the futile attempts of the economy and finance ministries to rein in Rosneftegaz's cash, represent a long list of areas where contests over the oil rents have been resolved behind closed doors.

This "centralization" in rent redistribution, and the tendency to seek resolution to contests by informal means, have yielded some important outcomes. The centralization process itself has made Putin's Russia more "decisive" in its ability to alter the way in which oil companies redistribute their rents. It is this "decisiveness" that has let the leadership curb oil majors' ability to autonomously fund what they choose, help companies reportedly affiliated with the Kremlin to amass fortunes through trading and contracts with oil majors, and use the oil majors' cash to fund priority projects.

Yet, along with this decisiveness, there has been an inherent inability among the leadership to "commit" to the status quo. In effect, "stability" – defined as the winners of rents maintaining their hold over time – has been compromised over and over again. Notably, areas of redistribution where formal rules have held sway have exhibited greater stability. For instance, both consumers and Transneft have maintained their wins over time. Export duties have endured as a convenient fiscal tool for achieving multiple goals for the Russian government. Both the state and consumers have remained as winners. Similarly, Transneft, subject to formally defined rules for interacting with oil producers, has been positioned from the early years of the Putin era as a key agent for capturing oil companies' rents. Its tariffs consistently rose throughout the 2000s, helping to expand its network while advancing the government's broader geopolitical goals.

Yet, while formal rules have helped promote stability, the stability itself has not necessarily been the product of formal rules. As illustrated in earlier chapters, the Russian leadership has ignored, abandoned, or circumvented such rules when it has been expedient to do so. Instead, stability can be attributed to the lack of significant disagreements within the executive on the principal objectives served by the particular act of redistribution. Ultimately, export duties and Transneft's fees have been used to secure more rents from oil companies for the state or state entities – an objective widely shared within the Russian executive.

By contrast, areas where rent redistribution has occurred through informal channels have seen less stability. In the case of oil trading, the sudden rise and subsequent decline of Gunvor is indicative of intense contests over the oil rents and the emergence of different winners over time. Oil companies' contributions to "social projects" have been subject to major variations over the years as well. The amount they pay and the areas they fund have largely reflected annual, behind-closed-door negotiations with authorities rather than long-term plans.[112] Major fluctuations in how Rosneftegaz handled its cash between 2005 and 2018 are another indication of policy instability. On some occasions, Sechin won the battle over the holding company's cash. On others, the Finance Ministry won out.

To what extent stability in rent redistribution can be linked to cohesion within the executive branch is not always possible to assess. The informal aspects of rent sharing make the positions of key members of the ruling elite less clear. It is reasonable to suggest that the predominance of informal rent sharing, and the opportunity to gain through being part of it, promote contests within the executive, making cohesion much more difficult to achieve. The intense fight over Rosneftegaz's dividends between Sechin and key members of the executive represents a case of weak cohesion. The possibility of benefiting through the informal support of Putin, even if it meant not complying with a government decree that required Rosneftegaz to release a portion of its dividends to the state budget, could have only encouraged weaker cohesion. Such a possibility weakens formal rules, if they exist, and does not bode well for a clear-cut government policy on the redistributive activities of oil companies.

Weak Rule of Law and the Tenacity of Informal Rent Sharing

Amid variations in how the oil companies share their wealth, informal rent sharing has remained an entrenched feature in the allocation of oil rents in post-Soviet Russia. How can we explain the persistent recourse to informal channels? This book suggests two reasons: a chronic weakness in Russia's rule of law, and the functional political utility of maintaining an informal aspect in Russia's rent allocation process.

Gaddy and Ickes have suggested that informal rent sharing has been driven mainly by Russia's weak property rights. Simply put, Russian oil and gas companies have been compelled to engage in various transactions, sharing their rents with a distinct set of beneficiaries for the sake of building "relational capital" that buys them some protection. The authors argue that owners with secure property rights would have little reason to undertake such behavior.[113] Indeed, weak property rights have remained a key feature of the Russian economy since the early 1990s, with no significant improvement during the Putin era.[114]

Yet, oil companies' engagement in rent redistribution is prompted by something more than weak property rights. After all, Russia's state-owned oil companies, facing no threat of expropriation, have been actively engaged in rent redistribution. Contracts with Rosneft reportedly helped Gunvor's rise as a global oil trader. Subsequently, Rosneft's parent company, Rosneftegaz, became a key channel for the Russian leadership to redistribute rents, bypassing the formal budgetary framework. Similarly, along with Rosneft, Gazprom Neft and the pipeline operator Transneft have all been actively involved in sponsoring various social projects, often withholding details on specific beneficiaries. Transneft may have emerged as an effective collector of extra rents from the oil producers, but as a redistributor, its activities have remained opaque.

A more accurate and comprehensive explanation for the problem is Russia's chronic weakness with regard to the rule of law.[115] Apart from weak property rights, Russia has been plagued by rampant nontransparency and corruption, providing fertile ground for the diversion of rents from the oil producers.[116] According to Transparency International, corruption in Russia has been perceived as notoriously high, putting the country consistently in the ranks of the least transparent and most corrupt.[117] Additionally, Russia's judiciary has notably lacked independence – a problem that has consistently intensified in the Putin era.[118]

To what extent is Russia's persistently weak rule of law the product of its institutional setting – characterized by increasingly weakened veto players – and what role can be ascribed to the role of agency? As noted earlier, well-functioning veto players make it more likely that the rule of law will be stronger, while fewer or weak veto players can be beneficial for launching new undertakings that may ultimately improve the rule of law.[119] The outcome is not predetermined and depends, in large part, on the preferences of the executive.

Putin inherited a weak rule of law, and the weakening of the veto players during his tenure suggests he was not committed to reversing this. Improvement in the rule of law would have clashed with one of his key objectives: transforming Russia's oil rents generation model (see chapter 3). Realized through episodes of nationalization, the transformation in the model left a large part of the oil industry in a state of uncertainty: the question of who would be the next target of nationalization remained unsettled. In the meantime, changing patterns of ownership in the oil sector invited predatory behavior and intense battles within the ruling elite, which effectively precluded the possibility of building a cohesive executive dedicated to enforcing the rule of law. Oil companies had strong incentives to stay engaged in informal transactions that would align with the interests of the ruling elite.

Yet, the fact that informal transactions have involved state-owned companies suggests that other factors have been in play, contributing to the persistently weak rule of law. The broader functional utility of redistributing a portion of the oil company rents through informal channels demands attention.

The Broader Functions of Rent Redistribution by the Oil Sector

Rents redistributed by the oil companies almost entirely bypass the state coffers, and instead end up in the hands of various sets of beneficiaries.[120] The "winners" of this prize can be quite diverse. In the case of energy subsidies, as the indirect product of export duties, society as a whole enjoys lower prices. In other instances, such as Transneft's pipeline purchase orders or the oil companies' use of costly rail transportation, the winners are select industries and some of their stakeholders. Winners can also be the population of a region, as when oil companies fund an infrastructure project and make contributions to schooling and healthcare. At the other extreme, the winners may be individuals. For instance, a public official may facilitate an oil transaction in exchange for some form of compensation. Likewise, an oligarch can get hold of oil rents by charging an oil company for its goods and services. Not all of these transactions are necessarily shady. Rents can legitimately flow through a formal and genuinely competitive process.

As there are multiple paths to divert rents away from the oil sector, there are also plenty of opportunities for a political leader to reward beneficiaries and create winners. By the same token, the leadership can determine not only the winners, but also who is excluded from accessing the flow of rents.

Opportunities to become a beneficiary invite political battles. With weak veto players, the executive branch becomes the center of such battles. As Ledeneva notes, the prevalence of informal networks to disburse rents undermines the fundamental principles of the rule of law and the security of property rights.[121] And with weak rule of law, oil companies have limited discretion to resolve such battles; their resolution then falls to the executive branch.

One can think of the functional value of rent redistribution in Russia through Hale's notion of "patronal presidentialism."[122] Rent redistribution helps Putin as the leader of the executive to create and sustain an elite network dependent on himself. The prize is large enough to build and maintain a sizable group of oligarchs over time.[123] Putin intervenes as an arbiter in key battles among members of the political elite. He exercises his authority by selectively deciding who benefits.[124] Informal connections appear to matter more than formal institutions – even existing legislation can be occasionally circumvented with Putin's support.[125] Winners are then indebted to Putin and are expected to remain loyal.

In the context of informal rent sharing, there is another possible cause for elite members to stay loyal and dependent on Putin. If the process of rent capture has involved an activity that could be labeled as a crime, a government official facilitating this transaction and the winner of the rents will have to live in a state of "suspended punishment."[126] Such participants in the diversion of oil rents remain vulnerable to accusations, and a lawsuit against them can be brought up at any time, most particularly if there is a fundamental change in leadership.[127] Thus, maintaining the political status quo is critical.

There is a further functional value to redistributing rents from the oil sector, as it offers the leadership an additional source of flexibility. Funds diverted to beneficiaries with the help of oil companies are not subject to the same level of scrutiny as the federal budget. They can function as an alternative budget, albeit an informal one. Surgutneftegaz's financing of a nuclear submarine, the use of Rosneftegaz's cash to fund public projects, and the common practice of funding social projects through oil companies can be viewed as a part of this scheme. Limitations in state funding, whether due to a policy choice of fiscal prudence or a shortfall in revenues, could partially be alleviated through resorting to the oil companies' contributions.

Moreover, this mechanism of rent redistribution can be employed *continuously* in a variety of forms. Oil companies undertake acts of redistribution on a recurring basis: renewing trade and service contracts is a common practice, and so is developing a new portfolio for social projects. For the executive in charge, this provides the opportunity to rearrange winners periodically. Thus, an oil trader can rise and fall, and with its decline, its owner can be granted alternative means to capture sizable rents. To an extent, rearranging the beneficiaries of rent redistribution is similar to transformations in the rent generation model described in chapter 3. Nationalization of an oil company, a privatization initiative, and a major reshuffle in the top management allow for a rearrange-ment in who wins in a rent generation model. However, such transformative events happen only rarely, not least because they entail risks with respect to the capacity of the sector to generate rents. By contrast, altering the flow of rents from the oil companies is a process that is open to more frequent interventions.

Transformative changes in who generates the rents and who benefits from their flow are often interrelated. Rosneft, for instance, following the national-ization of Yuganskneftegaz, terminated contracts with existing traders in favor of new ones. The weak rule of law links the two aspects of rent allocation: it makes it possible to get rewards through engaging in informal networks. The incumbent chief of the executive may not need a change in the ownership of a company to rearrange winners in rent redistribution. Taking such a drastic measure, however, may present a rare, and larger, prize for those competing over the rents.

The leadership's ability to control the flow of rents from oil producers, accom-plished largely through informal means, can be viewed as another factor that enhances the incumbent chief executive's political survival over time. Control over these rents provides an additional tool to maintain patronage networks dependent on the executive.[128] It also helps to ensure that oil companies' funds do not flow in a direction that might empower groups likely to challenge the incumbent.[129]

However, the weak institutionalization represented by the primacy of infor-mal networks comes at a cost. The chief executive depends on these networks to mobilize elites and allocate resources. In effect, he becomes a "hostage" of this setup.[130] He can still rearrange the winners, especially if this is done in modera-tion, so as not to provoke a revolt within the informal networks. Yet, entirely removing this informal setup altogether poses greater risks. Reforming this aspect of rent redistribution, particularly through a newfound emphasis on the rule of law, remains a formidable challenge, one the leadership tends to avoid. The persistence of weak rule of law, which in turn perpetuates the informal flow of rents, is the most likely outcome.

Conclusion

Russia's oil rents have flowed through numerous channels, not all involving the state's existing institutions for redistribution. Granted, most oil rents have con-tinued to be handled through the state institutions, namely the federal budget and the oil saving funds. However, oil companies, in addition to paying taxes, have also performed the role of redistributor of rents. This chapter has described the multiple means through which Russian oil majors have gone about sharing their windfalls with a diverse set of players, ranging from consumers as a whole to select individuals within the business elite.

During the Putin era, the Russian government became more capable of influencing how oil producers redistributed their rents. The weakening of various institutional veto players during the early years of Putin's presidency turned the executive branch into the main arena for resolving contests over these rents. Legislative changes made regional governors weaker in terms of their leverage to extract rents from the oil companies. The legislative branch, in the meantime, failed to push for measures that could have helped to institutionalize the way oil majors shared their windfalls with other beneficiaries. In effect, oil companies have been agents of rent redistribution, though they have not always been the ultimate decision-makers as to where the rents should flow.

The executive branch itself has operated mainly through informal rules that direct how oil companies share their rents. There are exceptions, such as the indirect subsidization of Russian consumers through export duties and Transneft's shipping tariffs imposed on oil producing companies, which have been principally associated with the state's objective and capacity to collect more rents for the budget or state-owned entities. In other areas of rent redistribution, contests have been determined through informal networks, with key decisions taken behind closed doors. It has been possible to circumvent even formal rules, when they exist, as in the case of Rosneftegaz, whose dividend payments have been required to go to the budget but have occasionally been diverted to directly fund different projects. Putin has intervened periodically, backing different sides on different occasions, proposing informal solutions on the flow of rents.

The primacy of informal rules results from the confluence of Russia's weak rule of law and the broader functional value rent diversion serves in Russian politics. The multiple paths to divert rents away from the oil sector have each presented opportunities for the political leadership, namely its chief executive, to create winners and reward beneficiaries. The continuous process of rent diversion has made it possible for the leadership to periodically rearrange the winners and losers in the flow of oil company rents. The persistently weak rule of law has enhanced the leadership's ability to determine where rents flow, adding further flexibility to managing these rents. It has helped the leadership to create and maintain patronage networks ultimately dependent on the chief executive. The executive has also managed to dictate where rents should not go – no Russian oil company has ever tried to finance opposition parties after the nationalization of Yukos. In turn, the prevalence of informal means to resolve contests with respect to the oil sector's rent redistribution can be viewed as a valuable tool for the incumbent leadership in Russia. It has weakened the incumbent leadership's need for accountability and enhanced its capability for survival. While reliance on informal rules goes back to the Yeltsin era, Putin has strengthened the executive's ability to guide the entire process of oil windfall distribution.

Relying on informal rules has brought an inherent instability in oil companies' redistribution activities. Two areas have constituted an exception, meaning that the government's approach has consistently benefited the same beneficiaries over time: the indirect subsidization of consumers via the export tax and the transfer of rents to Transneft. This stability has not been necessarily due to the presence of formal rules. Instead, it could be traced to the widely shared objective within the executive to extract more rents for the state and its entities. It is possible to conclude that formal rules have not remained resilient over time, unless backed by the executive branch, whose members overall agree on the ultimate purpose they serve.

One can discern a broader pattern in the interaction of the state with the oil industry in Putin's Russia. It is possible to refer to a low degree of "autonomy" in Russia's oil sector in terms of its ability to independently decide its future. The organizational setup of the oil industry (the rent generation model) has been directed primarily from above rather than by market forces. Oil producers have paid taxes that are largely guided by the state's priority to collect rents, rather than by costs and the size of profits in respective oil fields. And finally, the state has managed to acquire an active role in guiding where oil companies further redistribute their windfalls after paying taxes. This low degree of autonomy for the oil sector corresponds to a greater ability of the Russian leadership to expand resources at its disposal.

Conclusion

One can hardly overstate the importance of oil for the Russian economy and its political establishment. It is worth reiterating several fundamental facts about oil during the Putin era. First, no other sector has been as vital as oil to the economy – it has been the single most important source of revenue. Russia's oil export windfalls amounted to nearly 3 trillion USD between Putin's arrival to the Kremlin in 2000 and the start of his fourth term as president in 2018.

Second, Russia's reliance on oil represents a unique case in modern history. With the exception of Spain in the sixteenth century, there is no other country in which mineral resources have had such a central place. For decades, oil has been a vital commodity for the leaders in the Kremlin, and that has been clearly so for Putin. The price of oil and the state of the oil sector in Russia are likely to continue to be of fundamental importance for Russian leaders.

Third, Putin has presided during a period of relative economic prosperity. Unlike his two predecessors, Yeltsin and Gorbachev, whose economic predicament was magnified by low oil prices, Putin has enjoyed a growing oil industry and oil prices that have remained high on average. The last leader in the Kremlin to enjoy similar economic tailwinds was Leonid Brezhnev, and it is worth emphasizing again that these two have been the longest-serving Russian leaders since Stalin.

This book has provided an in-depth review of the key policy areas related to the flow of oil windfalls in Putin's Russia. Its starting point is that oil rents inevitably invite contests over how windfalls should flow. Governments of oil-rich states respond to and attempt to guide these contests. To study such contests, and to understand governments' evolving approach to them, I presented a framework that accounts for several distinctly contested policy areas, and developed theories about what determines their main outcomes. Before analyzing its broader applicability, I offer a summary of this analytical framework and its implications for Putin's Russia.

Russia's historic oil windfalls have occasioned a series of political battles. As part of an innovative approach to examining the contested nature of this wealth, I introduced the term "rent allocation." I have focused on four sets of battles over Russia's oil rents. These battles have aimed to settle the following four questions. Who should (and should not) generate the rents? How should these rents be divided between the state and the oil producers? How should the state redistribute the oil revenues it collects; and how should the oil producers share their wealth over and above paying their taxes?

In examining these contests, one of my key objectives has been to explain what determines their outcomes. As the book has surveyed nearly two decades of Putin's leadership, I have found significant divergences in the government's approach to rent allocation over time. This has pointed towards one central puzzle: why some policies have endured while others have been liable to reversals.

In addressing these questions, I have developed an analytical approach that I hope will be useful to understanding other resource-rich countries. Aiming to avoid the determinism of many dominant paradigms on resource-rich countries, this approach has taken into account both structural constraints and the role of agency in explaining policy outcomes. Its central concept can be defined as "executive power." Through its many attributes, "executive power" allows one to explain when the executive branch is capable of adopting a new policy and when it is more likely to commit to them. I referred to the executive's ability to launch a policy as the "decisiveness" of the state, whereas its ability to commit to that policy corresponds to the state's "resoluteness."

I examined the link between executive power and each of the four sets of battles on rent allocation in several steps. First, I evaluated the significance of the upsurge in executive power under Putin, which has made the state more "decisive," but also less likely to stay "resolute" on key rent allocation policies. I have examined both the transition towards weakened veto players, during Putin's first few years in the Kremlin, and its aftermath, when their weakness can be regarded as constant.

As the chief executive and the main decision-maker in the contests over Russia's oil rents, Putin has played the key role in determining how they are settled. Thus, I have analyzed Putin's response to the status quo he inherited with respect to the distinct aspects of rent allocation, followed by a narrative tracing how his policy preferences have evolved over time.

I looked at the presence or lack of cohesion within the executive branch as a critical attribute of executive power, potentially determining whether a rent allocation policy will endure over time. Some areas of rent allocation have clearly benefited from greater executive cohesion than others from the very start.

Finally, I have illustrated how key policy choices with respect to the distinct aspect of rent allocation have also reflected the incumbent's ambitions for political survival. In effect, when guided in a particular direction by the incumbent, rent allocation has served broader political purposes.

Among the many battles over Russia's oil wealth, the first one I examined was the contest over who should and should not generate this wealth. This has been a battle about control over Russia's rent-generating oil assets. To promote greater clarity with respect to this battle, I have studied several distinct aspects of Russia's rent generation model. One particular aspect – ownership – has remained in constant flux. Other aspects, such as the roles of foreign oil majors and smaller independent Russian players, along with the presence of some degree of competition in the oil industry, have remained steady over time.

Overall, the continuous lack of stability in terms of ownership in Russia's rent generation model is related to several factors. Changes in ownership have been facilitated by a lack of robust institutional veto players. The upsurge in executive power under Putin yielded a state that had become more "decisive" in order to undertake fundamental changes in relation to the oil industry. Thus, by the end of Putin's first term as president, the owner of Russia's largest oil company was in prison and his assets were soon taken over by one of the industry's smallest players – state-owned Rosneft. The industry continued to witness additional shake-ups under Putin, including the partial privatization of national oil champion Rosneft.

Also contributing to the instability in ownership has been the weak rule of law and Putin's lack of commitment to strengthening it. Putin could have used his newly resurgent executive power to defend the rule of law, but that would have meant accepting the existing setup in the rent generation model. From the very start, Putin remained dissatisfied with this model he inherited.

Weak rule of law, in turn, has fostered competition over Russia's oil assets. Thus, Russia's executive branch and the broader ruling elite have emerged as key players in intense battles over the Russian oil industry. To an extent, this lack of cohesion has mirrored broader changes in the Russian ruling elite. With the rise of the *siloviki*, who had missed their chances during the privatization of the 1990s, asset redistribution has appeared as a means to accommodate them. Thus, the rise of Rosneft as the single most important player has mirrored the broader trends within Russia's executive branch, reflecting the growing and enduring role of the *siloviki* in Russian politics.

Yet, Putin has clearly contributed to this lack of executive cohesion as well. He has had multiple means to guide this competition. Each change of ownership or management could be regarded as an opportunity to rearrange the winners, and potentially sideline select members of the ruling and business elites. Takeovers of Yukos or Bashneft did not just result in transferring their assets to a state-owned company. These changes also determined who should be excluded from Russia's process of rent generation. In this regard, the instability in ownership has brought significant political dividends for Putin. It has given him leverage over key members of the ruling elite, helped to weaken political opponents, and ultimately advanced his objective for political survival. And as the oil industry has continued to grow and generate rents, this instability has come at a relatively low cost economically.

By contrast, other aspects of Russia's rent generation model have endured over time. The "decisive" state could have taken action in these areas as well, but it chose not to. The stability could be associated with the lack of significant disagreements within the executive in terms of the status quo. Evidently, maintaining the status quo in such cases has been Putin's preferred choice owing to its fewer unintended consequences and the additional flexibility it brings in managing the oil sector.

Another set of battles examined in this book are those between the state and the oil industry on how to divide the rents. This was one of Putin's earliest battlegrounds. I analyzed two particular aspects of the government's approach to taxation in the oil sector. One is the state's ability to collect the majority of the oil rents. The other one is the stability of the tax rules.

Overall, under Putin, Russia has appeared remarkably "decisive" with respect to taxation of oil. Determined to alter the distribution of rents between the oil companies and the state, the government was quick to enact a fundamental tax overhaul at the start of Putin's first presidency. It was also quick to respond to the oil industry's rising pleas for reform in the second half of the 2000s. In retrospect, the government's numerous tax reform measures have helped the Russian oil industry maintain continuous growth. For over a decade oil experts have expected Russia's oil output to reach its peak. Their forecasts have proved to be wrong; the peak is yet to be seen, albeit concerns about the geology of Russia's oil fields remain.

In the meantime, maintaining a high tax burden on the oil industry has represented a major area of policy stability. Since the overhaul of the tax regime in the early 2000s, the state has consistently secured the majority of the oil rents. Several factors account for this stability. The fading role of Russia's institutional veto players during Putin's first presidential term ensured that oil companies could not shift back the distribution of rents in their favor. A cohesive executive has also been critical to this outcome. Despite disagreements on the best way to tax the oil sector, there has been no evidence that any key members of the executive favored policies jeopardizing the state's privileged position in the flow of rents. The high stakes involved in this distributional matter have also been critical: the government's redistributive activities, and arguably the longevity of the leadership, have hinged on its ability to maintain a high tax burden on oil. Finally, the technocratic nature of oil tax reform has helped to limit the scope of those involved in the process, thus contributing to the cohesiveness of the executive.

In comparison, tax rules have been far from stable. The overhaul of the tax regime in the early 2000s was followed by numerous attempts to calibrate it. Subsequently, the government introduced new rules after 2005, but frequently revised them if they were found to be too generous. In part, this instability has been due to a lack of inbuilt flexibility in the tax regime adopted in the early 2000s. The government has had to correct for this through periodic changes. Yet, the instability has also been a product of the risk-averse approach of the Finance Ministry, which has remained the dominant player in oil tax reform. Its continuous efforts to reform the tax regime have been subordinated to the financial needs of the state. Rather than undertake comprehensive tax reform that would align Russia's oil tax regime with international trends, the leadership has opted for ad hoc solutions; however unstable, these solutions have maintained the essence of the existing tax model. This approach has also made collective action among oil companies more difficult, further empowering the state.

A third set of battles examined in this book is related to the state's redistribution of the oil windfalls. I examined four distinct policy instruments employed by the state. Russia's record on two of these instruments shows a major lack of stability. The approach of the government on the federal budget and its oil funds has oscillated between fiscally conservative and highly expansionary. This variation has been partly tied to changes in the oil price cycle. However, while Russia went through two oil booms and oil busts under Putin, its fiscal response has been widely different each time.

In comparison, the government's approach on the other two policy instruments – tax cuts and servicing foreign debt – has remained fairly stable. During Putin's early tenure, the Russian government undertook a series of tax reforms that reduced the burden on the economy at the expense of the oil sector. The government's approach to taxation outside the oil industry has remained largely intact. Similarly, after inheriting sovereign debt that exceeded the size of the economy, Putin undertook major efforts to eliminate the debt. Since lowering the debt to a negligible level in the mid-2000s, the government has upheld its policy of keeping sovereign foreign debt to a minimum.

Russia's rent redistribution policies, I argue, clearly reflect the state's decisiveness following the weakening of institutional veto players. Putin was able to accomplish what Yeltsin repeatedly failed to do during the 1990s. Putin's administration was able to deliver years of surpluses in the federal budget, to undertake a series of tax reforms, and to speedily pay back Russia's sovereign debt. Some of Putin's policies reflected newfound attempts at institution-building; these policies involved rule-based mechanisms that would guide how oil rents were redistributed throughout the economy. Setting up a special fund to handle sovereign debt payments, and subsequently an oil fund to help manage Russia's budgetary surplus, were key steps in this direction. Subsequently, when faced with economic crises, Russia was able to rapidly launch anti-crisis redistributive policies.

A key factor that has shaped the state's redistributive policies in the long run is the cohesiveness of the executive branch. Policy areas that have not been backed by a cohesive executive have suffered instability. In such cases, even formal rules and institutions have mattered less than political battles within the executive. Thus, for instance, the fiscally conservative approach of Putin's early years was destined to end, as it had little support within the executive. Many within the ruling elite perceived a budget surplus and swelling revenues in an oil fund as a missed opportunity to realize their vision for a better economy or to protect their vested interests. Eventually, rules governing the budgetary process and Russia's oil funds were easy to suspend or circumvent when the government determined it needed to spend more.

By contrast, the reforms resulting in tax cuts at the turn of Putin's presidency had essentially enjoyed consensus within the executive branch, amid some compromises. Russia's policy on paying its sovereign debt has represented a rare case where a lack of executive cohesion from the start has not produced instability in the government's approach. This may be explained by the relatively short existence of the policy – once the debt was nearly paid off in the mid-2000s, there was no room left for significant political battles.

Policy stability has also been closely associated with the leadership's evolving perceptions on political risks relative to the available resources to mitigate them. Thus, rising political risks in the form of public protests, an approaching election, or a pending presidential succession have empowered the proponents of state-led development and more spending. Ironically, some of Russia's achievements have made it more difficult for the government to maintain a fiscally conservative approach. They have shaped perceptions about the resources available to the leadership to deal with economic and political crises. In this respect, the return to fiscal restraint after 2014 has been in large part due to concerns about the depletion of the country's oil savings. Putin's record-high popularity, gained in the aftermath of rising tensions with the United States, has arguably also played a role.

Putin's own approach to policy-making has contributed to instability in policy areas prone to major disagreements within the ruling elite. Rather than build a cohesive executive around critical redistributive policies, Putin has maintained balance between proponents of fiscal conservatism and advocates of state-led development and expansionary policies. To achieve this balance, he has deliberately retained fiscal conservatives in key positions, most particularly within the Finance Ministry. He has not committed to either side, and has kept shifting his position over time. While this approach has brought him flexibility in his role as the chief executive, it has encouraged policy instability.

There is one other set of battles over Russia's oil windfalls: those concerning the rents redistributed by the oil companies themselves. Although the state has been primarily responsible for redistribution of oil rents, Russia's oil producers have also acted as agents of redistribution. I have analyzed six distinct practices with respect to rent redistribution.

The Russian leadership has been able to influence this process of redistribution, often determining where the rents should flow. Following the centralization of power under Putin, the battles over these rents have been settled primarily at the level of the federal executive.

Among the many channels through which Russian oil companies have redistributed their wealth, only a few can be considered to be formally backed by state institutions. These have been in areas directly related to the state's ability to collect additional revenues or regulating a segment of the market through state-owned entities, such as the pipeline operator Transneft. Instead, the contests over these rents have been resolved primarily through informal means, behind closed doors. The employment of informal rules by the government in this area extends back to the Yeltsin era, and has been perpetuated under Putin.

The prevalence of informal means can be attributed to the weak rule of law as well as their role in empowering the leadership to steer the flow of rents. The weak rule of law has been in part due to the fading influence of Russia's institutional veto players, but it is also due to Putin's own choices. Weak rule of law has enhanced the leadership's ability to steer the flow of rents from the oil sector. It has given the leadership and its chief executive additional flexibility. Control over these rents has provided additional opportunities to support patronage networks. The rents have invited competition among the ruling and business elites while promoting loyalty to the leadership and particularly to its chief executive. In effect, the state has been able to guide not only the windfalls that have been officially under its control, but also those at the disposal of the oil sector.

The primacy of informal rules in the redistribution of oil companies' rents has yielded instability in the sense that the beneficiaries of this approach have varied widely over time. There has been a partial exception in areas where formal rules have prevailed. But even then, what has helped with stability has not been so much the presence of formal rules. Instead, a lack of significant disagreements within the executive on the principal objectives served by the particular act of redistribution has proven to be the decisive factor.

What do these findings say about policy-making, reforms, and institution-building in Russia? What are the possible takeaways for a better understanding of authoritarianism in rent-rich settings? How can this book advance understandings of other oil-rich states? And what further theoretical implications could this study have?

Understanding Policy-Making in Russia

Throughout this book, I have examined an extensive set of policy areas as presented through four sets of battles. Some are highly specific to managing Russia's oil wealth (e.g., oil taxes, oil funds, the organization of the oil industry), while others touch on broader policy challenges in the Russian economy (e.g., taxation outside the oil sector, the budget, servicing the sovereign debt, the role of the state, and the rule of law). Each of the four sets of battles has elicited a policy response from the leadership. Furthermore, successive governments have had to constantly re-evaluate their response as Russia has gone from boom to bust twice within two decades. These dynamics have further helped to enrich the pool of information available for study. Also, some of the policies examined here have represented broader efforts towards institution-building. Developing a new tax regime for oil and the rest of the economy, charting new rules for the federal budget, establishing oil funds, and introducing legislation with broader implications on the rule of law have all constituted steps in Russia's institution-building process.

There are some significant conclusions to be drawn in regard to how policy is made in Russia, what has made its leadership more capable of enacting reforms and build new institutions, and what conditions have made it prone to stay committed to the undertaken path. The central subject of this study – executive power – has potentially broader applicability to the policy process in Russia and beyond. Looking at executive power with respect to Russia's political contests on rent allocation has yielded important insights. The upsurge in executive power during Putin's first term has had far-reaching repercussions on Russian policy-making. Institutional veto players outside the executive branch have remained weak thereafter. This has led to a more "decisive" state and major shifts in policy, many of which Russia had failed to achieve during the 1990s. Reforming taxation in the oil sector and the rest of the economy, securing a solid surplus in the federal budget year after year, setting an oil-savings fund, repaying Russia's sovereign debt earlier than required, and launching a fundamental redesign of the oil industry all represent sweeping policy achievements that embody the newly gained decisiveness of the state.

In utilizing the veto players approach, with its implications for executive power, I have referred to an expected trade-off between a state's ability to launch a new policy and to commit to this policy. Indeed, in a context with weak institutional veto players, one can expect that the executive will have a relatively free hand to launch new policies and face few constraints should it decide to revisit its approach. The analysis has demonstrated that the assumed trade-off is in reality much more complicated. The factual record on Russia's rent allocation policies indicates a substantial divergence. In some policy areas, the "decisive" state under Putin has maintained its approach, while in others, it has demonstrated a clear lack of commitment to the new policy status quo.

A key factor is the presence (or absence) of cohesion within the executive branch. As a critical attribute of executive power, this cohesion has largely determined whether a government's adherence to the status quo, or its pursuit of reform, will last. With a cohesive executive, it is more likely a government will maintain its approach to a new policy or reform over time. By contrast, there has been a propensity for policy instability in areas that do not enjoy such cohesion. In effect, in a setting with weak institutional veto players, the lack of executive cohesion over a given policy is a significant constraint on executive power.

But executive cohesion alone does not suffice in explaining how each of the examined policies on rent allocation evolved. This book has shown that the Russian leadership has been more likely to stay committed to the policy status quo if it advances or does not threaten the leadership's political survival. By implication, lessons drawn from this study may apply to other polices or reforms that have likely repercussions for a leadership's ability to stay in power.

A few additional factors have also proven significant in how Russia conducts its policies in the long term. Some policy areas have seen extensive involvement of executive agencies. This involvement has hampered the chances of a cohesive executive, which in turn, has affected policy stability in the long run.

The quality of reforms is another significant factor. A lack of inbuilt flexibility in the oil tax regime and in the rules governing Russia's first oil fund eventually necessitated revisiting earlier reforms in light of changing circumstances. Typically, reforms include an element of trial and error in adapting existing knowledge to a specific setting, thus presenting the possibility for policy reversals in the future.

The timeframe of policies offers an additional explanation of their durability. Thus, for instance, there was never executive cohesion around the decision to pay Russia's sovereign debt. However, the relatively short duration of the challenge helped to maintain the policy until the debt was nearly repaid and it was no longer high on the agenda. Policies and reforms for which the objective can be accomplished in a relatively shorter time span are less prone to reversals. In such cases, a political leader can ignore the lack of executive cohesion for the duration of the policy.

Further research could test the applicability of this book's findings on a wider set of policies and reforms in Russia. Identifying the policy status quo in a given area may indicate the potential direction of policy change. Examining the extent of cohesion within the executive may offer clues about the durability of the selected policies. If they bear broader economic and political risks for the country, a discourse analysis on these risks would also reveal whether these policies are likely to last.

The Russian leadership has proved again and again that it can alter the policy status quo with respect to the flow of oil rents. Yet, in the long run, the leadership has demonstrated a lack of commitment to some of its policies. Depending on one's standpoint on Russia's discourse on the economy, one could argue that the state has been liable to reverse some of its major policy achievements: some of them, such as the fiscally prudent policies of the first half of the 2000s, were widely praised by the international financial community. Alternatively, one may argue that policy reversals embody the ability of the political system to reflect the lack of cohesion within the executive branch – the only institutional veto player that matters.

One can expect that the Russian leadership will continue to oscillate between fiscally prudent policies and overspending. Its rent generation model is also likely to remain in flux, as long as major changes in the model continue to present opportunities to rearrange the beneficiaries of Russia's colossal oil wealth, and the constraints on executive power remain limited. Only policies backed by widespread consensus within the ruling elite and the public – such as the high tax burden on the oil sector – are likely to remain stable. Even then, in order to maintain the status quo, they should not bear risks for the political survival of the incumbent leadership.

Towards a Better Understanding of Authoritarianism in Rent-Rich Settings

This book confirms some of the key conclusions of existing studies on the link between wealth in natural resources and longevity of a political leadership. Bjorvaten and Farzanegan's finding that resource rents promote political stability and the survival of an incumbent in a setting where power is "sufficiently concentrated" around the executive is reflected in Putin's Russia.[1] Robinson, Torvik, and Verdier argue that strong institutions, ones that limit an incumbent leader's ability to engage in patronage and clientelism, render resource wealth less useful in extending the leadership's stay in power.[2] The absence of strong institutions might explain in part Putin's long tenure.

While I have not set out to analyze the multiple reasons for Putin's long tenure, this book does shed light on the longevity of an incumbent political leadership in rent-rich settings. There are two aspects of Putin's approach to rent allocation that have enhanced his political survival.

First, rent allocation policies under Putin have effectively expanded the resources at his disposal to mitigate political risks. Putin was quick to establish an oil tax regime that prioritized and ensured that the majority of the rents went to the state. Numerous measures to refine the tax regime have ensured that the oil sector continued to grow, while the state never abandoned its status as the chief beneficiary of windfalls. The rent allocation model inherited at the end of the 1990s was transformed in such a way that the state gained additional flexibility in guiding the entire oil industry. Maintaining multiple players in the industry while limiting foreign oil majors' involvement helped to sustain opportunities to rearrange winners and losers in the battle over Russia's oil assets. Weak rule of law ensured a large degree of flexibility in guiding the battle, while also helping the state to maintain its decisive position in determining where oil companies redistributed their rents. Meanwhile, building oil saving funds, whose formal rules appeared to be easy to bend, further added to the resources at the leadership's disposal. Rapidly repaying Russia's sovereign debt ensured that, in the event of a crisis, the leadership would not have to make difficult choices that could endanger its political survival.

Second, as resources have widened Putin's policy choices, he has maintained a decidedly flexible approach on the key battles, shifting his support from one side to the other. In redistributive policies, he has sought to strike a balance between fiscal conservatives and proponents of state-led development and more spending. Putin supported fiscal conservatives to build Russia's financial cushion during the first oil boom in the 2000s; he then supported a relaxation of fiscal prudence when political risks emerged. Even then, fiscal conservatives retained key posts, ready to redirect Russia towards fiscal restraint when conditions were ripe to give them the upper hand.

Putin's approach to rent allocation policies remained notably stable in areas where the status quo helped expand the state's resources without raising political risks. His polices remained in flux where a policy shift would help address such risks, especially when plenty of resources were available to draw from. Putin's preference for flexibility over a permanent alliance with one side or the other has helped him to avoid antagonizing key political factions.

Putin's main policy choices – the fiscal prudence of his early years, the shift towards more spending in response to mounting political risks, the massive bailouts and surge in public spending during the Great Recession and in its aftermath, and the partial return to fiscal restraint after 2014 – have continuously enhanced his ability to remain in power. Political crises that could bring him down have been avoided or managed.

This case study on Putin's Russia can help to promote understanding of political longevity, and by implication, authoritarianism in other countries where rent-seeking opportunities are abundant. Looking at how leaders in such countries have managed the flow of rents, one may consider the extent to which policies have advanced or jeopardized their access to rent-driven resources. What areas related to the flow of rents have seen policy stability or major shifts over time? To what extent has a leader maintained a flexible approach? If the leadership has been brought down, what aspects of rent allocation have been managed differently and in what ways? Case studies and comparative research may unearth important results about how executive power affects the ability of leaders to gain the necessary resources that provide new opportunities for redistribution and political survival. Further research may also explore how differences in the rent generation model matter for the leadership's ability to guide the flow of rents.

Studying Policy-Making in Mineral Resource-Rich Countries

The analytical framework and some of the key arguments in this book can be tested in a comparative context that includes a wider set of resource-rich countries. The "rent allocation" concept of this study provides a helpful tool for analyzing the contested nature of resource rents in countries besides Russia. While such countries may differ in many respects, they face many of the same battles over the flow of rents that we have examined in detail here.

Employing the concept of "executive power" can also yield answers about key outcomes in these policy battles. As the concept takes into account the constitutional framework of a country, its politics, and the role of agency, it has an applicability to a diverse set of countries, including non-democracies. Comparative research could determine how differences in executive power yield distinct policy results across countries and over time. There is much scope for research on how governments address the potential trade-off between the state's decisiveness and its resoluteness. Many oil-rich countries from the Gulf region to Latin America have weak institutional veto players as well. Future research could focus on other countries with strong executive power and examine how executive cohesion matters in explaining their key policy achievements and the durability of these policies over time.

This study has also examined how the weakened "autonomy" of oil companies in guiding the flow of their windfalls helped to expand the resources at the disposal of the state leadership. Resource-rich countries exhibit significant variation in this respect. In some countries, the organizational setup of the resource sector is directed from above while in others it is determined by market forces. Some countries tax the resource sector primarily on the basis of its revenues while others have developed and perfected the tax system to account for costs and profits. Countries also diverge in terms of whether the resource sector remains free to decide how to share its wealth after paying its taxes. Comparative studies could explore how this variation in the degree of "autonomy" of the mineral resource industries around the world impact policy performance and the durability of key achievements over time, as well as the ability of the political leadership to mitigate political risks and ensure its survival.

There is a need for comparative research into the link between key areas constituting political risks and policy performance in resource-rich countries. I have looked in detail at the relationship between emerging political risks and fiscal prudence with respect to Russia's budgetary policies and oil funds. Comparative studies could explore how key indicators for political risks, such as the extent of public protests, electoral cycles, and emerging questions on leadership succession, relate to their redistributive policy choices. Studying how fiscal prudence, its launch, and its duration relate to such indicators could yield invaluable information for policy-makers and international financial institutions engaged in advising governments of resource-rich states.

Further Theoretical Implications

This case study of Putin's Russia is centered on, and benefits from, the veto players theory, and it can contribute to expanding the applicability of this theory. Adherents have applied it widely to shed light on key policy areas with distributional consequences. They have examined distinct attributes of the veto players theory to study their association with policy outcomes. The theoretical approach presented here has brought together the multiple attributes of the theory, deriving the concept of executive power. By establishing key measures for executive power, the approach undertaken in this book offers a tool that I hope may be employed in a wide range of comparative studies on policy performance.

There is further scope for studying the trade-off between the "decisiveness" and "resoluteness" of states as laid out in the veto players theory. In democracies, many attributes of the institutional setting can affect this trade-off. My study offers an approach that helps to analyze such trade-offs within non-democracies as well, where the executive has emerged as the de facto single veto player. The case of Russia shows that, even in a non-democracy, a lack of cohesion within the executive can influence and ultimately be responsible for policy reversals. As a growing number of studies have started applying the veto players approach to non-democracies, the proposed focus on executive cohesion can contribute to our understanding of the effect of bargaining and negotiations on policies in such settings. There is also considerable scope for comparative research on executive cohesion and its impact on the stability of policies. In exploring the dynamics of executive power and the contests over Russia's oil wealth, this book can set the groundwork for further studies that will benefit from its analysis.

Notes

Introduction

1 Depending on the price of oil, it has not been unusual for this commodity to account for over half of Russia's entire export revenues and over 40 percent of the federal budget. Dittrick (2014).

2 Export revenues refer to the 2000–18 period. Sales in the domestic market, accounting for over a quarter of Russia's oil output, are not part of this estimate. (Source: Central Bank of Russia.)

3 Balzer (2005a), p. 222.

4 Lockman (1976), p. 297.

5 The definition of "rents" has been the source of some controversy. Some major sources examining the classical and neoclassical contribution to the theory of rent include Kurtz and Salvadori (2001), pp. 282–96; Schumpeter (1954); Worcester (1946), pp. 258–77; Dobb (1973). For a major contribution from the Marxist school of thought see Steedman (1982).

6 This is particularly true in the case of crude oil, the price of which is typically set in the world market, and has tended to go through boom and bust cycles for decades.

7 On the impact of ownership in the resource sector, see Luong and Weinthal (2006), pp. 241–63.

8 On how such funds function, see David, Ossowski, Daniel, and Barnett (2001), pp. 56–9.

9 Gaddy and Ickes (2005), pp. 560–1.

10 Clover (2013).

11 The exception would be if a government collects dividends from a state-owned company.

12 Based on data collected from annual IMF reports on Russia.

13 Cox and McCubbins (2001), pp. 26–8.

1. Understanding Policy-Making in Resource-Rich Countries

1 Some of the most groundbreaking sources within the "resource curse" literature are the following: Ascher (1999), Auty (1990), Auty ed. (2001), Beblawi and Luciani (eds) (1987), Sachs and Warner (1995), Karl (1997).

2 The term was introduced by Mahdavy, who defined a state as rentier if it received a substantial amount of external rents on a regular basis. See Mahdavy (1970), p. 428.

3 Luciani sets this threshold as 40 percent to qualify a state as "rentier." Luciani (1987), pp. 63–82.

4 Beblawi and Luciani (1987), pp. 49–62.

5 Ibid., pp. 63–82.

6 See, for instance, Ambrosio (2006), p. 35.

7 Tompson (2005a), p. 344.

8 Yates observes that the lack of an independent bourgeoisie is a common phenomenon for "rentier states." Typically, a small business class, heavily dependent on various contracts with the state, benefits from the status quo and favors its continuation. Yates (1996), pp. 30–4.

9 Introduction of new taxes for the non-resource economy, lowering of energy subsidies, and heavier emphasis on economic diversification could be viewed in this context.

10 Ross (1999), pp. 297–322.

11 Some authors have disagreed with each of these approaches, arguing that the link between mineral resource wealth and long-term economic growth may in fact be a positive one. See Alexeev and Conrad (2009a), pp. 586–98.

12 Personal interview with Alan Gelb, World Bank, Washington, DC, 12 April 2007.

13 Gaidar (2007a).

14 Ross (1999), p. 311.

15 Shafer (1994), pp. 39–42.

16 Dauderstadt (2006), p. 21.

17 Gaddy and Ickes (2002).

18 Migdal et al. (1994), p. 11.

19 Michael McFaul provides a partial solution to this conceptual confusion by claiming that state power could be treated as the broader concept that sums up the other two. He defines state autonomy as the ability of the state to determine independent preferences, while state capacity is a measure of the state's ability to implement its preferences. McFaul (1995), p. 214.

20 Almond (1988), p. 869. Fukuyama has emphasized the large number of attributes associated with "state power." He has distinguished between scope and strength of state power. See Fukuyama (2004), pp. 17–31.

21 Kohli and Shue have presented a skeptical view on state autonomy, arguing that its presence is at best an illusion. Even in highly authoritarian regimes, there are some limits to the reach of the state within the society. In Migdal et al. (1994), p. 309.

22 Ibid., p. 3.

23 Ruschemeyer and Evans (1985), pp. 61–2.

24 Nordlinger (1981), pp. 27–31.

25 Krasner (1978), p. 58.

26 Skocpol (1985), p. 17.

27 Here "regime" refers to the dichotomy between democracy and authoritarianism, instead of the form of government (such as presidential vs parliamentary).

28 Karl (1997), pp. 189–221.

29 Ibid., pp. 222–42.

30 See Wick and Bulte (2006), pp. 457–76.

31 Such concerns have led to global initiatives such as Publish What You Pay and Extractive Industries Transparency Initiatives.

32 This point is examined widely in the "rentier state" literature.

33 See Yates (1996), pp. 34–5.

34 Karl (1997), pp. 222–42.

35 Thus, for instance, in 2000, Russia appeared in the lower 10th–25th percentile in terms of regulatory quality, rule of law, and control of corruption. It ranked in the 25th–50th percentile in terms of voice and accountability. See Kauffman, Kraay, and Mastruzzi (2007).

36 The cognitive approach assigns some role for agency in policy outcomes. Yet, it does not explain why leaders who are aware of the pitfalls of the "resource curse" often end up with distinct policies.

37 I recognize that resource-rich countries may face peculiar economic challenges. Yet, there is something to be learned from the wider experience as long as these countries depend on taxing their citizens and businesses, have a formal budget to redistribute revenues, and the budget is compiled following some input from different institutions including the legislature. Russia's economic policy-making, in this respect, is more similar to the process in most OECD countries, rather than the classical cases of "rentier states" defined by Luciani.

38 Tsebelis (1995), pp. 289.

39 Stepan (2004), p. 326.

40 Tsebelis (2002), p. 2.

41 Tsebelis has added that courts and referendums could also be considered institutional veto players, though he and many subscribers to the veto players theory have focused mainly on the executive and the legislature. See Tsebelis (1995), p. 307.

42 The consent of institutional veto players is constitutionally necessary and it is sufficient condition for policy change, whereas the consent of partisan veto players is neither necessary nor sufficient.

43 Stoiber (2006).

44 Tsebelis (2002), p. 2.

45 Ibid., p. 6.

46 Ibid., p. 8.

47 Tsebelis (1995), p. 298.
48 Tsebelis (2002), pp. 61–3.
49 Ibid., p. 6.
50 Ibid., p. 7.
51 Tsebelis notes, "Institutions are like shells, and the specific outcomes they produce depend upon the actors that occupy them." Ibid., p. 8.
52 Putting party politics in the picture allows one to determine the number of *effective* veto players. Tsebelis developed the so-called absorption rule: if the same political party controls more than one institutional veto player, then it is possible to reduce the number of effective veto players. Some scholars have questioned the utility of this "absorption rule," arguing that it understates the potential for conflict between the executive and the legislature. See Eaton (2000), pp. 355–76.
53 The study examined sixteen countries in Western Europe for the period 1981–1991. Tsebelis (2002).
54 Acosta, Araujo, Perez-Linan, and Saiegh (2006), pp. 23–6.
55 Hallerberg and Basinger (1998), pp. 321–52.
56 Cox and McCubbins (2001), pp. 47–51.
57 Samuels and Mainwaring (2004), pp. 85–130.
58 They defined rule of law as a set of stable political rules and rights applied impartially to all citizens. Andrews and Montinola (2004), p. 65.
59 Ibid., p. 64.
60 The study covered 157 countries for the period 1960–95. The author constructed an index for political constraints based primarily on the number of veto players. See Henisz (2000), pp. 1–31.
61 This is in line with the major proposition of the veto players theory that the greater the number of veto players, the harder it is to accomplish policy change. See Tsebelis (2002), p. 188.
62 Franzese (2002).
63 Ibid., p. 56.
64 Tsebelis and Chang (2004), pp. 449–76.
65 Ibid., pp. 449–50.
66 LeVan (2015), p. 37.
67 Hagen and Harden (1995), pp. 771–9.
68 Freedom House ranks countries based on the political rights and civil liberties of their citizens. It rates a country as "free" (score ranging from 1 to 2.5), "partly free" (score ranging from 3 to 5), and "not free" (score ranging from 5.5 to 7). Russia's score has dropped from 4.5 in 1999 to 5.5 in 2005 and to 6 in 2016. See Freedom in the World Reports.
69 Such studies include LeVan (2015); Cheeseman and Tendi (2010), pp. 203–29; Frantz and Ezrow (2011); MacIntyre (2001), pp. 81–122; Korppoo (2016), pp. 639–53.
70 Tsebelis (2002), p. 90.

71 Arendt (1969), p. 44.

72 Korppoo (2016), pp. 647–9.

73 Noble (2017), p. 514.

74 LeVan (2015), pp. 38–40.

75 For a thorough review of the challenges in estimating the number of veto players, see Ganghof (2003) pp. 1–25.

76 Referendums can also be considered electorally generated veto players, but they are generally rare. Furthermore, they are not relevant to Russia during the period examined.

77 These measures could be adapted to other countries as well, though, depending on the constitutional setup, some of the veto players may need to be discounted or have their role reassessed.

78 For example, this would occur if a chamber is dissolved permanently or if de jure regional governors lose their ability to block the executive's policy.

79 The legislative powers of the president include the following: package veto, decree, budgetary powers, partial veto, exclusive introduction of legislation, and proposal for referendum. (Part of these powers, such as decree and introduction of legislation, are referred to as "agenda setting powers" by Tsebelis.) The non-legislative powers are in the following areas: cabinet formation, cabinet dismissal, censure, and dissolution of the assembly. See Shugart and Carey (1992), p. 150.

80 It needs to be recognized that strong public support for a president may not necessarily be equated to strong support on his particular policy.

81 A high degree of party discipline refers to the situation when party members vote predominantly in the same direction as prescribed by their leadership.

82 While many scholars would not count the legislature as a separate veto player under this condition, this would understate the presence of any bargaining between the legislature and the executive. Only in cases where the legislature acts as a mere rubber stamp for the executive, can it be discounted rather than considered as a veto player.

83 This proposition is in line with Tsebelis, whose analysis indicates that when the the legislative chambers are more divided, more possibilities are available to the president to secure an agreement on its policy proposals. Tsebelis (2002), p. 50.

84 Remington (2003), p. 667.

85 According to Peter Soderlund, such factors include the administrative status of the region (e.g., a republic or lower degree of autonomy), the presence of a special power-sharing agreement with the central government, the region's status as a net donor versus a net recipient of federal funds, the size of the electorate which favors parties that are in opposition to the federal executive, and the size of the electorate which supports the regional governor. See Soderlund (2006), pp. 71–85.

86 A new policy refers to policy changes that may or may not require changes in legislation.

87 Cox and McCubbins (2001), pp. 26–7.

88 Ibid., p. 28.
89 It has been left unclear, however, how these attributes of veto players would work under different combinations. Tsebelis (1995), p. 317.
90 Tsebelis (2002), p. 207.
91 This is more likely to be common in non-democracies, but is possible in a democratic setting where the executive maintains strict control over other institutional veto players (such as the legislature).
92 Tsebelis (1995) touches on the causes of policy stability, but looks primarily at the composition of a government, distinguishing between those that are based on a single party or a coalition of parties. According to this approach, policy instability is a potential outcome of a breakdown in a coalition government. Yet the applicability of this approach is limited in terms of explaining policy stability in single-party governments or an administration that is not formed on the basis of a political party.
93 Truex (2016), p. 6.
94 Gandhi (2008), p. 140.
95 Reuter and Robertson (2009), pp. 235–48.
96 For example, it is not uncommon for legislatures in authoritarian states to defeat some bills sent by the executive branch. They do not necessarily represent a victory for the legislature, and instead may reflect the spillover of intra-executive disagreements into the legislature. See Noble (2017), pp. 505–2.
97 Martyn and Vanberg (2011), p. 21; Noble (2016).
98 One may assume that a state bureaucracy built on merit may be prone to more disagreements with the executive as compared to one built on loyalty.
99 For instance, Anna Korppoo (2016) examines a case on Russia's climate policy whereby decisions are assumed to be made collectively.
100 While distinguishing between collective versus unilateral decision-making is important, observing the precise mechanism of the political process is typically fraught with methodological challenges. By contrast, it is possible to observe and analyze the extent of cohesion through statements coming from key executive members.
101 Korppoo (2016), pp. 648.
102 The survival of leaders and political regimes may well be linked, though in the case of political regimes the focus is on the continuity of authoritarian or democratic regimes irrespective of changes in the leadership.
103 Andreson and Aslaksen (2013), pp. 89.
104 Ross identifies a number of mechanisms employed by incumbent leaders serving this ultimate function. Resource rents let the state tax the society less ("taxation effect"), engage in selective redistribution policies to dampen opposition ("spending effect"), and co-opt and weaken existing/potential opposition ("group formation effect"). See Ross (2001), pp. 325–61.

105 Bjorvaten and Farzanegan (2014).
106 Andreson and Aslaksen (2013), p. 90.
107 Robinson, Torvik, and Verdier (2006), pp. 447–68.
108 Caselli (2006).
109 Some pieces of legislation, such as annual budgets, need to go through several readings in the lower chamber. Changes in votes across readings are particularly important to track.
110 Tsebelis (1995) has noted this difficulty.
111 Not every member of the executive branch would matter on a given policy. Some areas, such as taxation, are restricted to only a handful of participants within the executive branch.
112 Policies can be distinguished between procyclical and countercyclical This is examined in detail in chapter 5.

2. The Upsurge in Executive Power under President Putin

1 Aslund (2017).
2 Troxel (2003), p. 11.
3 Holmes (1993), pp. 123–6.
4 Huskey (1999), p. 37.
5 In a presidential system the executive (the president) is typically not dependent on legislative confidence and is elected publicly. By contrast, in a parliamentary system the executive depends on the legislature's confidence and is selected by the legislature. See Lijphart (1992), pp. 2–3.
6 Shugart (1996), pp. 6–11.
7 Their study measures the power of the president in a sample of 42 countries (Russia excluded) on two dimensions: legislative and non-legislative powers. Shugart and Carey (1992), pp. 148–58.
8 These were the following cases: Chile in 1925, Chile in 1969, Chile in 1989, Colombia before 1991, Brazil in 1988, and Paraguay. Some countries appeared more than once owing to constitutional changes.
9 On the constitutional powers of the president relative to the legislature, see Troxel (2003) pp. 20–42; Remington (2000), pp. 505–14; Tsebelis and Rizova (2007), pp. 1155–82.
10 Remington and Smith (1996), p. 166.
11 McFaul (2000), p. 165.
12 For a record of Putin's rapidly rising popularity following his appointment as prime minister, see Rutland (2000), pp. 313–54; Reddaway (2001), pp. 23–44.
13 "Putin's Approval Rating," Yuri Levada Analytical Center.
14 On the eve of his resignation, Yeltsin's approval rating was only 2 percent. See Metke (2007).

15 Some of the conventional measures for the legitimacy of a regime noted by Fish are trust in public institutions, public respect for the law, and the size of the vote for parties that are (or are not) committed to public politics. See Fish (2005), p. 226.

16 For an account of state pressures with respect to the media, electoral fraud, election-related coercion, and arbitrary exclusion of oppositional figures from elections during Putin's early years, see ibid., pp. 30–67.

17 Multiple examples of Yeltsin-era decrees that were specially tailored to serve various narrow interests are provided in Remington (2006), p. 275.

18 Remington, Smith, and Haspel (1998), pp. 287–322.

19 Ibid.

20 Chaisty and Schleiter (2002), p. 717.

21 Ibid., pp. 704–6.

22 Remington (2001), p. 293.

23 For instance, a month after the 1993 Duma elections, Russia's Choice, the "party of power," held only 72 seats. Likewise, a month after the 1995 Duma elections, Our Home Is Russia, the new "party of power," held only 65 seats. For the distribution of seats across factions, see Remington (2005), p. 47.

24 See Remington (2002).

25 Colton and McFaul (2000), pp. 201–24.

26 According to Russian political scientist Boris Makarenko, Unity's association with the increasingly popular Putin was the decisive factor for its unexpected electoral success in December 1999. Cited in Rutland (2000), p. 326.

27 It was common for them to be described "market Bolsheviks." Smith (2002), pp. 561–3.

28 Ibid.

29 Within Russia's hybrid electoral system, combining plurality and proportional representation (PR), Unity's success was heavily based on the PR part of the elections. Ibid., pp. 565–8.

30 Huskey (2001), p. 93.

31 KPRF's Gennady Seleznev kept his position as speaker of the Duma. See Rutland (2000), p. 335.

32 The deal was ended in April 2001, when the Duma committee chairs were redistributed to other parties. See Smith (2002), p. 571.

33 These were the People's Deputy, Russia's Regions, and LDPR.

34 United Russia secured 222 seats, however many independent deputies winning a seat in the Duma through single-mandate districts decided to join United Russia, securing it a safe majority.

35 This observation was expressed by several experts on Russian politics interviewed in Moscow in June 2007. Personal interviews with Alexei Zudin, Center for Political Technologies, Moscow, 18 June 2007; Pavel Salin, Center for Current Politics, Moscow, 18 June 2007.

36 Haspel, Remington, and Smith (2006), pp. 249–75.

37 According to Varga, Putin did not bypass the Duma with his decrees as often as before because he achieved the power to control the legislative outcome. Varga (2004), p. 54.

38 By contrast, under Yeltsin, the number of presidential decrees rose from about 64 per quarter to 165 during the second quarter of 1996. Haspel et al. (2006), p. 257.
39 Ibid., p. 261.
40 Some reforms preceded the 1993 Constitution. See Desai (2006), p. 32; McFaul (1995), pp. 210–43.
41 The exceptions were cases when Yeltsin used his veto power to overrule legislation that aimed to invalidate his decree. See Parrish (1998), p. 63.
42 A detailed account of this process is provided in Orttung and Reddaway (2004), pp. 19–52.
43 The Federation Council has comparatively less constitutional power than the Duma. However, it still has an important role in the legislative process, as its approval is required in a large number of areas.
44 The bill was introduced in May 2000, but it took two months of negotiations between the two chambers to finalize the draft. Evidently, the Duma had the required majority to override a veto by the Federation Council, prompting its ultimate approval on 26 July 2000. See Hyde (2001), pp. 727–31.
45 Cited in Remington (2003), p. 674.
46 They did not officially head a particular regional apparatus. As they were "selected" by regional elites rather than elected by a particular constituency, this could potentially weaken their legitimacy.
47 Unsurprisingly, the Federation Council vetoed this bill, but its veto was overridden by the Duma on 19 July 2000.
48 McFaul and Petrov (2004), p. 26.
49 Ibid., pp. 20–31.
50 Yeltsin had also relied on presidential representatives dispatched to each of Russia's regions. However, they became easily manipulated by regional authorities. See Soderlund (2006), p. 46.
51 Indeed, by March 2002 more than 5,800 regional laws had been annulled or amended, while 28 of the special treaties signed with regions during the 1990s were annulled. See ibid., p. 100.
52 Regional legislatures could still exercise their right to approve the president's nominees, but faced the risk of being dissolved by the president. See Blakkisrud (2005).
53 Remington (2003), p. 673.
54 There was a small spike in the share of bills rejected by the Federation Council in 2001. Russia was still in the midst of replacing regional governors and speakers of regional legislatures with nominees. The process was complete by the end of the year. Rejected bills dropped significantly in 2002.
55 See McFaul (1999), p. 23.
56 Colton and Holmes (2006), p. 302.
57 Such disagreements were not entirely absent. Prime Minister Kasyanov was often associated with large businesses' interests, leading to his dismissal in early 2004.

58 Sokolowski (2003), p. 433.
59 Colton and Holmes (2006), p. 300.
60 Remington (2001), p. 292.
61 The number of ministries was reduced from 30 to 17. Vardul (2004).
62 On the causes of institutional redundancies in Russia see Huskey (1999), pp. 115–43.
63 Colton (1995), p. 147.
64 Tseblis posits that members of the state bureaucracy (as agents) are more likely to be independent if they report to more than one principal. See Tsebelis (1995), p. 324.
65 Zweynert (2007), pp. 47–69.
66 See Kryshtanovskaya and White (2003), pp. 289–306.
67 According to Huskey this "militarization of cadres" coincided with the financial crash of August 1998 and "the war clouds" gathering again in the Caucasus. It was during this period that Yeltsin's three successive prime ministers (Primakov, Stepashin, and Putin) were drawn from the *siloviki*. See Huskey (2001), p. 84.
68 Waller (1995), pp. 3–10.
69 Ledeneva (2006).
70 Here the term signifies a group whose members are united around certain general political and economic objectives.
71 Tompson (2005b).

3. Russia's Historic Oil Windfalls and the Contest over Who Will Generate the Rents

1 In 1898, Russia and the United States produced 8.77 million tons and 8.47 million tons of oil, respectively. Alekperov (2011), pp. 134–5.
2 For an extensive review of the Soviet oil industry at its peak, see Gustafson (1989).
3 Alekperov (2011), p. 300.
4 "Vladimir Putin Preodolel Vekhu," *Rambler.ru,* 2017.
5 Gaidar (2007a).
6 Oil export revenues dropped by 38 percent and 42 percent in 2009 and 2015, respectively. (Source: RF Central Bank.)
7 For instance, the average nominal price for oil in the 2009–10 period remained at 64.9 USD/barrel; it dropped to 53.1 USD/barrel for the 2015–18 period. (Source: RF Central Bank.)
8 RSFSR produced 570 million tons of crude oil in 1987. Oil output declined to 303 million tons by 1998. (Source: Rosstat.)
9 A small drop was recorded in 2017 as Russia adhered to voluntary production cuts according to OPEC guidelines.
10 Russian oil and petroleum product exports peaked in 2015. They rose from 207 million tons in 2000 to 416.2 million tons in 2015. Total oil and petroleum product exports amounted to 410.9 million tons in 2018. The slight drop after 2015

reflected changes in the tax regime that aimed to encourage crude oil exports at the expense of petroleum products. (Source: RF Central Bank.)

11 Crude oil exports rose by 69 percent between 2000 and 2015, whereas petroleum product exports increased by 174 percent. (Source: RF Central Bank.)

12 This process of reorientation was largely complete by the end of the 1990s. In 2000, the CIS's share in Russia's total crude oil and petroleum product exports revenues was down to merely 8.6 percent. This share dropped further to 6.5 percent by 2017. (Source: RF Central Bank.)

13 Calculations based on RF Central Bank.

14 Blokhina, Karpenko, and Gurnskiy (2016), pp. 721–6.

15 On the impact of the ruble depreciation on costs, see Mazalov and Bolshakova (2000), pp. 8–11.

16 The peak was reached in 2014 when the share of hydrocarbon revenues stood at 51.3 percent. In 2015, this share dropped to 44.4 percent as oil prices went down. (Source: Finance Ministry.)

17 Dittrick (2014).

18 By 2017, oil exports were down to 42.9 percent of total exports. (Source: RF Central Bank.)

19 On the further importance of hydrocarbons for the Russian economy, see Movchan (2015).

20 Aslund (2005), p. 612.

21 *Novaia Struktura Rossiiskogo Neftianogo Sektora …* (2004), pp. 3–4.

22 Lane (1999), p. 17.

23 Presidential Decree No. 1403, 17 November 1992.

24 On key privatization measures in the 1990s, see Sim (2008), pp. 16–48.

25 Lane (1999), p. 23.

26 According to the "loans for shares" auctions, successful bidders would have the right to hold the shares in trust for three years in return for providing loans to the government. Akerman (2004), p. 117.

27 The government retained majority ownership in Rosneft, Slavneft, and ONAKO. These were relatively small companies. Rosneft, the largest among them, produced 12.5 million tons of oil in 1999. In comparison, Sibneft's output, the smallest private company in the group, was 16.3 million tons. (Source: "Osnovnye pokazateli raboty neftepererabotyvayuschchei otrasli," *Infotek*, November 2000.)

28 On the history of Russian oil majors, and the emerging distinction between "oil generals" and *finansisty*, see Gustafson (2012), pp. 98–144.

29 Yergin (2011), pp. 21–42.

30 Akerman (2004), p. 114; *Petroleum Economist*, 1992, no. 10, p. 13.

31 For the divergent experience of IOCs, see Bayulgen (2010).

32 Their output stood at 20 million tons in 1999. In 1995, oil produced by joint ventures with foreign partners was 19.8 million tons, accounting for 6.5 percent of the total output. (Source: "Osnovnye pokazateli …," *Infotek*, November 2000.)

33 It must be noted that not all foreign joint ventures were actually foreign-owned. Some belonged to Russians registered abroad for tax purposes.

34 In early 1998, Lukoil acquired a majority stake at Romania's Petrotel refinery. This was followed by numerous further acquisitions by Russian oil majors, mainly in Eastern Europe. Sagers and Vatansever (2002).

35 In most OECD countries, oil transportation has been considered a natural monopoly. As a result, it has required state regulation, though not ownership.

36 For historical information on Transneft, see "Istoria," *Trasneft.ru.*

37 Sagers and Vatansever (2002).

38 Such delivery requirements served additional objectives, such as securing supplies for harvesters and ensuring fuel stocks for the winter – two politically sensitive issues.

39 For a detailed account of various policies related to the state's attempt to regulate domestic crude oil and fuel prices, see Sagers, Kryukov, and Shmat (1995), pp. 401–10.

40 This point appears in an interview with Minister of Natural Resources Viktor Nekrutenko. See "Nedra Dolzhny Prinosit' …," *Segodnia*, 1998.

41 "Nedra Razdora …," 2002.

42 Gustafson (2012), p. 68.

43 See Poussenkova (2006).

44 "Bez Gosodarstvo v Rossii Dolgo ne Zhivut …" *Kompaniia*, 1999.

45 "Natsional'naia Neftianaia Mozhet Stat' …" *Kommersant*, 1999.

46 Thus, Sidanko was sold to TNK in 1999, and shortly after the state auctioned its remaining shares in TNK. In 2000, TNK acquired state-owned ONAKO. Lukoil purchased Komi-TEK in 1999. Yukos purchased a controlling stake in East Siberian Oil and Gas Co. (VSNK) and obtained the remaining shares (36.8 percent) of Eastern Oil Co. (VNK) in January 2001 and May 2002, respectively.

47 It was acquired jointly by TNK and Sibneft.

48 "Giant Steps: BP and …," *Nefte Compass*, 2003.

49 In September 2004, ConocoPhillips acquired the government's remaining stake (7.59 percent) in Lukoil, paying 1.988 billion USD. But no comparable acquisitions by foreign oil majors were recorded afterwards.

50 For an interview with Mikhail Khodorkovsky, see Sivakov (2003).

51 Adopted in June 2003, the bill suspended the right to sign PSAs in relation to most of the onshore projects that were already under negotiation. The only projects that remained eligible for PSAs were those which had received licenses for deposits located on continental shelves, at the bottom of the Caspian Sea, in special economic zones, or for projects to be exploited under international treaties.

52 Hill and Fee (2002), p. 481.

53 Grozovskii (2003).

54 For instance, the three PSAs that had been signed before the first bill on PSAs dating back to the 1995 remained grandfathered. Their share in Russian oil production, however, remained as very minor.

55 Yukos's remaining assets were not designated for sale yet. Yuganskneftegaz was producing 1 million barrels per day of Yukos's output (which totaled 1.7 million barrels per day). Ritchie (2004).

56 There were nine vertically integrated oil companies in 2004. Bashneft was the smallest one.

57 In 2004, Rosneft's output accounted for merely 4.7 percent of Russia's total oil production. By contrast, Yukos and Sibneft produced 18.7 percent and 7.4 percent of Russia's oil, respectively. Data compiled from *2006 Oil and Gas Yearbook*, Renaissance Capital, 2006, p. 21.

58 Ibid.

59 Rosneft paid 55 billion USD. As a result of the deal, BP engaged in share swaps with Rosneft, raising its share in the Russian company to 19.75 percent. The deal helped BP maintain its status as the leading foreign investor in Russia's oil industry, though as a minority shareholder.

60 See "Istoria," *Trasneft.ru*.

61 This includes production by Tatneft. Calculation based on data compiled from multiple Interfax sources. For an alternative measure for state ownership see "Russian Oil and Gas: Too Big to Fail," 2014, p. 19.

62 Katasonov (2013).

63 The government sold 19.5 percent of its stake in Rosneft.

64 The Russian government received nearly 1.040 trillion rubles as a result of selling its key stakes in Rosneft and Bashneft. See Rosneft's website on the company's history: "Istoria," *Trasneft.ru*.

65 Other (non-veto player) institutions, such as the judiciary and the media, were also ineffective against the actions of the executive. Arguably, such institutions merely facilitated the task of the executive branch.

66 Henisz (2000), pp. 1–31.

67 The two authors, however, find that having more veto players improves the chances for establishing the rule of law against expropriations by government. Andrews and Montinola (2004), p. 56.

68 Hale (2005), pp. 133–65.

69 Some observers have questioned whether Putin actually wrote the dissertation, given his multiple responsibilities. See Balzer (2005b). Clifford Gaddy, Senior Fellow at Brookings, has claimed that the dissertation involves substantial plagiarism. See Sands (2006).

70 Balzer (2005b).

71 The English translation of the article is available in Balzer (2006), pp. 46–54. The translation is based on Putin (1999), pp. 3–9.

72 In the article, Putin claims that developed economies grow by 2–3 percent a year. Thus, Russia's GDP should grow by at least 4–6 percent a year. Balzer (2006), p. 49.

73 Ibid.

74 Ibid., p. 52.
75 For instance, in the spring of 2002, Putin criticized the MEDT's medium-term economic program through 2004 for lacking ambition. See Kuznetsova and Gurevich (2002). Subsequently, in May 2003, Putin set Russia's target as "doubling its GDP within ten years." See President Putin's speech: www.kremlin.ru/events /articles/2003/05/44646/44827.shtml.
76 President Putin's speech on 3 March 2000.
77 One of the earliest speeches reflecting his resentment was delivered in June 2000. Putin said: "In Russia there are many fishermen that caught lots of fish and would like to maintain this situation in the longer run. I do not think that this fits the interest of our people …" Cited in Orlov (2003).
78 At a presentation delivered at the State Council, Putin noted that only 54 percent of the licensees were abiding by the terms of their licenses. See Sanko (2002). Putin blamed oil companies for having "excessively" high amount of idle reserves. See "Nedra Razdora," *Infomaker – Russian* Focus, 2002.
79 A poll conducted by VTsIOM in April 2000 revealed that 72 percent of the respondents were in favor of the nationalization of "the key sectors of Russia's economy." See http:// wciom.ru/arkhiv/tematicheskii-arkhiv/item/single/486.html (19 January 2015).
80 In another VTsIOM poll from December 2004, 45 percent of the respondents said they favored complete nationalization of the oil sector, 30 percent preferred "strengthening the government's control over the oil sector" to its complete nationalization, 7 percent preferred to maintain the status quo, and 13 percent had no answer. See http://wciom.ru/arkhiv/tematicheskii-arkhiv/item/single/1046.html (accessed 19 January 2015).
81 "Sovladelets AFK Sistema Yevtushenkov Osvobozhden …," *Ria Novosti*, 2014.
82 The previous owners, Ural Invest, had sold the controlling stake to AFK Sistema in 2009. The court decision required them to pay 70.7 billion rubles (1.1 billion USD) in damages. "AFK Sistema Dogovorilas' o Kompensatsii …," *Interfax*, 2015.
83 Roman Abramovich, Sibneft's owner, received 13.1 billion USD for his stake from Gazprom. Ostrovsky (2005).
84 In the deal completed in March 2013, BP received cash (about 12.5 billion USD) and 18.5 percent stake in Rosneft for selling its 50 percent stake in TNK-BP. See "Partnership with Rosneft," British Petroleum website.
85 Hanson (2009), p. 19.
86 Ibid.
87 Desai (2006), pp. 164–5.
88 Luong and Weinthal (2006), pp. 241–63.
89 Personal interview with Andrey Yakovlev, Higher School of Economics, Moscow, 11 April 2017.
90 Personal interview with an advisor to Russian oil companies, April 2017.
91 Zubanov (2006).

92 For instance, in the aftermath of the Crimea crisis, which sparked new economic difficulties for Russia, appointments at state-owned companies appeared as a key means to reward loyalists. See Korostikov (2015).

93 Luong and Weinthal (2006), pp. 247–8.

94 For instance, some questions about the winners were raised during the partial privatization of Rosneft. See Golubkova, Zhannikov, and Jewkes (2017).

95 North, Wallis, Webb, and Weingast (2007).

96 Stegen (2011), pp. 6505–13. Goldman (2008) has further emphasized the crucial role of oil (and gas) in raising Russia's international status.

97 Oil benefits from a global market, which allows a greater degree of flexibility for oil importing nations.

98 Balzer (2006), pp. 49–51.

99 "Yukos Khochet Stat …," *Neft i Kapital*, 2002.

100 Another battle revolved around the fate of Bashneft, as Igor Sechin fought with parts of the executive branch, led by Minister Ulyukaev, who opposed its sale to Rosneft. Intense disagreements have also been recorded between Prime Minister Medvedev and Igor Sechin, as the former demanded a speedier privatization of Rosneft after 2012. For an overview of this particular contest, see Tovkaylo (2013); Murtazin (2016).

101 Various authors have drawn attention to competing political clans in Russian politics. See Lynch (2005), pp. 153–4; Aslund (2007), pp. 170–1, p. 198.

102 Some major criteria have included professional and educational background and past work experience in St. Petersburg. See Bremmer and Charap (2006), p. 85.

103 Aslund (2007), p. 200.

104 Voloshin served as the deputy head of the Presidential Administration in 1997–8. In March 1999, he became the head of the Presidential Administration. www .peoples.ru/state/statesmen/voloshin/ – accessed 29 April 2018.

105 Kasyanov's biography available at: www.peoples.ru/state/minister/russia/kasyanov /index.html – accessed 29 April 2018.

106 Thus, Berezovsky, known to be one of the leading members of the "Family" clan, was sidelined at the outset of Putin's presidency. So were his protégés in the government, such as Interior Minister Valdimir Rushailo and Minister of Railways Nilolai Aksanenko. Aslund (2007), p. 226.

107 Rosneft was sidelined from the auction in late 2002. Belton (2002).

108 Their isolation was partly due to the submissive response of Russia's business community to the Yukos Affair. Neither RSPP nor the Chamber of Commerce and Industry came to the defense of Yukos. On their reaction following the attacks on Yukos in 2003, see Fortescue (2007), pp. 124–6.

109 On Kasyanov's response see Zagorodnaia and Korop (2003); Ivanov (2003).

110 "Voloshina i Kasyanova Mogut Otpravit' v Otstavku," *Delovaia Pressa*, 2003.

111 Latynina (2003).

112 Some key example are German Gref (chairman of the board of Rosneft between 2001 and 2003, board member of Gazprom after 1999, government representative at Transneft after 1999, board member at Sovcomflot after 2000); Viktor Khristenko (chairman of the board of Transneft after 2002, board member of Gazprom after 2000); Deputy Minister of the Economy Arkady Drvokovich (board member of Transneft after 2004).

113 This was true mainly for Gref's initial reaction, though his deputies, such as Arkady Dvorkovich and Mikhail Dmitriev, were critical of the attack on Yukos, noting that this could endanger Russia's economic growth prospects. See Fortescue (2007), p. 126.

114 See "Gref Obeshchaet Ne Peresmatrivat' Privatizatsiu," *BBC Newsletter*, 2003.

115 For instance, Kudrin bluntly accused Yukos of being the "most aggressive" of Russia's oil majors in trying to reduce its tax burden after 2000. See Jack and Ostrovsky (2003). Later, Yukos shareholder Leonid Nevzlin accused Kudrin of being an active participant in the attacks against his company. He claimed Kudrin personally issued orders to the tax authorities to attack Yukos (for various unpaid tax bills). See "Leonid Nevzlin Obvinil …," *Lenta.ru*, 2005.

116 Kryshtanovskaya and White have provided one of the most detailed analyses on this subject. Kryshtanovskaya and White (2003), pp. 289–306.

117 Kryshtanovskaya and White (2005); Rivera and Rivera (2006), pp. 125–44; Bladel (2008); Bremmer and Charap (2006), pp. 83–92.

118 Bremmer and Charap (2006), p. 87.

119 Kryshtanovskaya and White (2005), p. 1073.

120 Knight (2000), pp. 6–7.

121 See such a cautionary note in Rivera and Rivera (2006), pp. 25–144; Bladel (2008), pp. 51–4.

122 Bremmer (2003), pp. 22–9.

123 See Demchenko (2005).

124 Based on the draft law, not only the subsoil itself, but also the *extracted resources* from the subsoil would be considered state property. See Stoliarov (2002). Reportedly, Medevedev expressed a similarly "alarming" view by suggesting that state ownership and management in the economy's key sectors had "far from exhausted their potential." See Kryshtanovskaya and White (2005), p. 1071.

125 Key examples include Mikhail Fradkov (appointed first as the head of the Federal Tax Police, and eventually succeeding Kasyanov as prime minister); Sergey Stepashin (brought in by Putin to head the Accounts Chamber); Viktor Zubkov (assigned by Putin to head the newly established Financial Monitoring Committee at the end of 2001).

126 Medvedev became the chairman of Gazprom in June 2000. Rem Vyakhirev was brought back and served in this position between June 2001 and June 2002. Subsequently, Medvedev was reappointed.

127 Its acquisition of media outlets critical to Putin's administration constituted just one example.

128 The initial focus of Gazprom's new top management was on the reacquisition of many of the gas assets that it had lost under the previous management. For details on this process, see "Oil and Gas Industries as a Field for Elite Groups' Fighting," *CCPR*, 2004; "Redistribution of Property in Oil and Gas Sector …," *CCPR*, 2005; Radygin (2004), p. 45.

129 For various explanations about why Yukos emerged as a target, see Goldman (2004), pp. 33–44; Sakwa (2014).

130 Babich (2006).

131 Bladel (2008), p. 54, pp. 93–4.

132 "The Mechanism of Lobbying …," *CCPR*, 2004.

133 Glazov (2004).

134 Fortescue (2007), p. 143.

135 For an extensive analysis on the proposed merger, see: Gustafson (2012), pp. 338–42.

136 Company valuation and board composition emerged as two of the main sticking points. For a detailed overview of the failed merger, see "The Clash …," *Nefte Compass*, 2004; Butrin (2004).

137 Gazprom's participation at the auction was suddenly complicated when Yukos acquired a US court order to halt the sale of Yuganskneftegaz until its application for bankruptcy was finalized. Possessing assets in the US made Gazprom, unlike Rosneft, vulnerable to the court's decision. Still, Gazprom participated in the auction through the newly created Neftegazprom, but failed to win.

138 "Yukos Seeks Damages from Yugansk Sale," *Nefte Compass*, 2005.

139 This time the merger was complicated by the debt Gazprom would inherit in case of a marger. The potential for complicated litigation over Yukos's assets further deterred Gazprom. Glazov (2005).

140 Sharushkina and Tellinghuisen (2005).

141 Baikal Finance Group subsequently revealed that part of the funds came from Chinese banks as a 6 billion USD prepayment deal for future crude oil deliveries. The deal was very likely sanctioned by President Putin as a means of bilateral energy cooperation. See Sharushkina (2005).

142 Vinogradova (2007).

143 For a thorough analysis of Russia's nationalization drive in select sectors, including the oil industry, see Lowry (2014), pp. 13–15.

144 Federal bill (no. 57), dating 28 April 2008.

145 A large number of independent Russian oil companies (namely those not associated with VICs and PSAs) produced barely 9.5 percent of Russian oil in 2013. This share has remained fairly stable since the late 1990s. "Shans dlia Malykh Neftianykh Kompanii," *TEK Rossii*, 2014.

146 The lobbying has been conducted primarily through Assoneft – an agency representing smaller and independent oil companies.

147 Hill and Fee (2002), p. 481.

148 This is the period when BP acquired half of TNK.

149 As an example of a new partnership after the launch of sanctions on Russia, BP purchased a stake in Rosneft's Taas-Yuryakh field in 2015.

150 Alexei Topalov, "Kak Pomoch Nezavisimym," *Neftegazovaya Vertikal,* 8 (2018), pp. 60–3.

151 This was prescribed in the 2008 law governing investments in strategic sectors.

152 Kryukov and Moe (2016) also note the scant discourse in Russia about the oil industry's organization setup, and considers part of its geological challenges to be associated with this.

4. Collecting the Rents: The Contest between the State and the Oil Industry on Dividing the Windfalls

1 In 2000, according to one estimate, the Russian government collected only 22 percent of the oil and gas windfalls. Luong and Weinthal (2004), p. 141.

2 Personal interview with a private oil company executive based in Russia, April 2017.

3 Easter (2006), p. 26.

4 This amount constituted about a third of Russia's consolidated budget. Ibid., p. 36.

5 Appel (2008), p. 304.

6 The range was between 0 and 85 rubles per ton of crude oil.

7 For more information, see Bosquet (2002).

8 Kimel'man (2001).

9 It had been introduced in January 1992, but was completely phased out in 1997 following IMF pressure to liberalize Russia's export regime.

10 The initial rate was set as 5 euros per ton of crude oil.

11 Duties on crude oil were raised from 5 to 7.5 euros/ton in September 1999. "Poshlina na Neft' Budet Uvelichena …," *Segodnia,* 1999.

12 The duty was raised to 15 euros/tonne. "Russia Raises Oil Export Duty …," *Interfax Petroleum* Report, 1999.

13 For more details about the revised formulas, see Skliarova (2004); Lapunova (2001b).

14 "German Gref: Politicheskaia Elita Ustala ot Stabil'nosti," *Vedomosti,* 2002.

15 Four Russian oil majors – Yukos, Sibneft, TNK, and Lukoil – were still able to underpay by about 1.3 billion USD in total in 2002. Yukos benefited the most. Study referred to in Vyhuloeva (2004).

16 Such regions had the authority to grant tax privileges to businesses registered in their territories.

17 Three internal "tax havens" – Chukotka, Mordovia, and Kalmykia – were particularly important. See Bazina (2003). According to Russia's Accounts Chamber, in 2002, oil companies were able to underpay nearly 100 billion rubles thanks to internal tax havens. See Sapsay (2004).

18 Personal interview with Igor Nikolaev, FBK, Moscow, 15 June 2007.

19 Personal interview with an accountant at KMPG, June 2007.

20 The amendment allowed only a partial exception, whereby regions could reduce the profit tax up to 4 percentage points. Also it terminated all special tax privileges granted under agreements between investors and regional governments. Samoylenko (2004) pp. 84–5.

21 Vygon, Rubtsov, and Ezhov (2017).

22 *Russia Energy Survey 2002*, pp. 106–7.

23 The tax amendment, benefiting large exporters like Yukos, set an upper limit on the export duty for petroleum products. Visloguzov (2003).

24 The government's share deteriorated in 2003 prior to a major recalibration of taxation, setting a steeper tax interval at higher oil prices.

25 Ahrend and Tompson (2006), p. 59.

26 *BP Statistical Review of World Energy 2017*.

27 Ibid.

28 Apart from favorable oil prices, the devaluation of the ruble in 1998 and an extensive unused production capacity caused by the oil slump in the 1990s had fostered growth.

29 Personal interview with Vladimir Feigin, Institite for Energy and Finance, Moscow, 13 April 2017.

30 For the growing geological challenges of Russia's oil industry, see Gustafson (2012), pp. 449–79.

31 Shokhina, Rudneva, Sterkin, Ivanova, and Kornia (2006).

32 The decline in the first four months of 2008 was 0.3 percent.

33 Zateychuk and Sterkin (2008).

34 "Nagruzka na Neftianuiu Otrasl' Snizhena ...," *Kommersant*, 2009.

35 "Putin Podpisal Zakon O L'gotakh ...," *Ria Novosti*, 2012.

36 "Vstupaiut v Silu L'goty po NDPI ...," *Ria Novosti*, 2012.

37 Petlevoi and Starinskaia (2014).

38 Vygon, Rubtsov, and Ezhov (2017), p. 19.

39 On sanctions targeting Russia's oil sector, see Connolly (2018); Coote (2018).

40 Bazanova and Petlevoy (2018).

41 The maneuver set a longer-term plan for encouraging investment in exploration and development by gradually reducing the export duty for the oil sector, and compensating for forgone revenues with an increased rate for the NDPI. Kalyukov (2014).

42 Export duties on petroleum products had been set lower than those for crude oil in order to incentivize refinery upgrades. Yet, few companies met government's expectations to upgrade their refineries during the following decade. For a detailed review, see Yermakov, Henderson, and Fattouh (2019).

43 "Minenergo Predlozhit Kabminu Vybor ...," *TASS*, 2018.

44 *BP Statistical Review of World Energy 2019*.

45 184 million tons out of Russia's total production of 527 million tons came from new wells. Vygon, Rubtsov, Klubkov, and Ezhov (2015), p. 21.

46 Ibid.

47 Zhavaronkova (2015).

48 There are several significant studies: Luong and Weinthal (2004) details some aspects of the oil tax reform during the early years of Putin's presidency. Appel (2011), pp. 117–42, also examines the early success in reforming taxation, including the oil tax, under Putin's presidency. Gustafson (2012) provides a more detailed narrative of the subsequent years.

49 Such major studies include Alexeev and Conrad (2009b), pp. 93–104; Goldsworthy and Zakharova (2010); Fjaertoft and Lunden (2015), pp. 553–61.

50 The poll by VTsIOM conducted in October 2003 asked "What type of sectors should pay more for the natural rents they acquire?" Of the respondents, 19 percent said the "oil sector" and 17 percent "gas sector." See http://wciom.ru/arkhiv/ tematicheskii-arkhiv/item/single/9.html (accessed 24 December 2006).

51 It was recorded as the third most urgent issue for the public. Cited in Vostretsova (2004).

52 The content analysis study examined Russian print media on Integrum. It recorded a nearly ninefold increase in the frequency of articles mentioning "resource rents" between 2001 and 2003. "Uglevodorody – Narodu!," *Kommersant- Vlast*, 2004.

53 Till the late 1990s, the theme of resource rents was largely confined to a handful of left-wing economists and politicians, such as Sergey Glazev and Dmitry Lvov.

54 Nenarokov (2003).

55 Logvinov (2003).

56 Goskomstat data for 2002 reveal even higher level of profitability in other sectors such as gas, maritime transportation, and telecommunications. Likewise, in 2003, finance sector companies ranked highest in terms of profitability. See "25 Samykh Rentabel'nykh Kompanii," *Finans*, 2004.

57 Maksimov (2003).

58 Rybal'chenko (2003).

59 Buzdalov (2004).

60 Already in 2000, Russian Minister of Finance A. Kudrin noted that Russia urgently needed to come up with a clear definition for "natural rent." (See "Opasenie Nestabil'nosti Ostaiotsia," *Ekonimika i Vremia*, 2000.)

61 The prevalence of this problem is noted in Orlov and Nemeriuk (2001), p. 34; Nikolaev (2003).

62 The 100 billion USD estimate came from Gennady Zyuganov. Borozdina and Litvinov (2003).

63 "Sobytiia i Komentarii – Prostye Pravila Prezidenta," *Trud*, 2003.

64 Speech by President Putin's: www.kremlin.ru/appears/2000/03/03/0000_type 63378_28480.shtml.

65 Speech by President Putin: www.kremlin.ru/appears/2002/12/19/2049_type63381 _29647.shtml.

66 For example, on 19 March 2004, at a government meeting President Putin described uncollected "resource rents" as a major injustice to be addressed through tax reforms. Speech by President Putin: www.kremlin.ru/text/appears/2004/03 /62091.shtml.

67 Putin's address to the Federation Assembly on 3 April 2001. In 2001, following an overhaul in the oil tax regime, Putin boasted that Russia had lowered the tax burden on the economy at the oil sector's expense. See: "Nalogovaia Reforma Prodolzhaetsia," *Rossiiskaia Biznes Gazeta*, 2002.

68 Butrin, Netreba, and Sapozhkov (2011).

69 During the fall of 1999, oil sector representatives led by Lukoil's head, Vagit Alekperov, met to discuss whether to jointly support Yuri Luzhkov as a candidate for the upcoming election season. The minister of energy, Viktor Kalyuzhny, also attended the meeting. Bagrov (1999).

70 It took Putin only a year after his presidential election in 2000 to put a loyalist in place of Rem Vyakhirev, the powerful chief of state-owned Gazprom since 1992.

71 Evidently, if this was indeed a motive, it did not extend to all oil oligarchs. Many of them continued to expand their wealth in the Putin era. Personal interview with the managing director and head of equity research of a Russian investment bank, June 2007.

72 Russia's legislation on custom duties allowed the government such flexibility by authorizing it to revise duties with no legislative approval. This lasted till 1 February 2002, when an amendment in the Law on Custom Tariffs allowed the legislature some authority in setting export duties for crude oil.

73 "Neft'! Novy Lozung Vladimira Putina," *Kommersant- Daily*, 1999.

74 Initially established as an autonomous tax-collecting entity, it became a ministry in 1998.

75 It was in charge of collecting import and export duties.

76 The reorganization was authorized by Presidential Decree No. 314 on 9 March 2004.

77 For instance, the Ministry of Taxes and Collections was downgraded and renamed the Federal Tax Service, and was subordinated to the Finance Ministry.

78 Though the Ministry of Taxes and Collections remained as a separate ministry, Kudrin acquired the authority to oversee it owing to his position as deputy prime minister.

79 Shevchenko (2004).

80 Kudrin was appointed to head the commission in June 2000, replacing Khristenko.

81 For Khristenko's prior government positions see www.lenta.ru/lib/14160425/.

82 It met once a month to review supplies for domestic and export markets. See "New Look – MVK Replaced by New Federal Commission," *Nefte Compass*, 2000.

83 Reflecting its weakened authority, the name of the ministry was changed from the Ministry of Fuel and Energy to the Ministry of Energy.

84 For instance, in late 1999 Kzlyuzhni actively opposed an increase in the export tariffs for crude oil. See "Neftianiki Protestuiut ...," *WPS – TV and Radio Monitoring*, 1999.

85 Allegedly, Gavrin had acquired his post through lobbying by Alekperov. Alexandrovich (2000).

86 For instance, he asked to regain control over the "Khristenko Commission," Bekker (2002a).

87 Petrova (2004).

88 The ministry was renamed the Ministry of Energy and Industry.

89 Makarkin (2004).

90 Gustafson (2012), p. 261.

91 The argument was that the oil sector enjoyed much higher profitability than other sectors, which could result in underinvestment in such sectors, a condition known as the "Dutch Disease." "Prognozy Dnia ...," *Vedomosti*, 2001.

92 Borozdina and Litvinov (2003).

93 Gref was a major proponent of turning export duties into a more important tax instrument as an alternative to less transparent administrative methods. "Neftegazovy Kompleks v Rossiiskoi Politike: Itogi 2000 ...," *CCPR*, 2001.

94 The commission was allowed to set any rate below the maximum determined in the scale. It had the power to periodically (six times a year) readjust the export duty on the basis of changing oil prices.

95 "Russia May Approve New Scale ...," *Interfax Petroleum Report*, 2001.

96 Visloguzov (2004).

97 "Nalogooblazhenie Ispol'zovania Prirodnykh Resursov," *ABCentre – Russian Economy State Regulation*, 2001.

98 Lapunova and Reznik (2001).

99 Guk (2001).

100 Ivanov (2001).

101 Lukoil, TNK, and Sibneft adhered to Yukos's position. Personal interviews with Vadim Visloguzov, Kommersant, Moscow, 19 June 2007; Mikhail Subbotin, former advisor to Ministry of Energy, Moscow, 27 June 2007; Peter O'Brien, Vice President of Rosneft, Moscow, 28 June 2007.

102 Lapunova and Reznik (2001).

103 "Budget Committee Recommends Passage of Tax Code ...," *Interfax Petroleum Report*, 2001.

104 For instance, the VAT and the ESN were reduced and the turnover tax was abolished. See "Interviu: Mikhail Motorin ...," *Vedomosti*, 2003.

105 "Sale Power – Crude Export Bonanza on the Cards," *Nefte Compass*, 2001.

106 Gustafson (2012), p. 260.

107 Kasyanov frequently pointed out the need for maintaining a favorable investment climate for the oil sector, but did not openly oppose Gref and Kudrin's drive for a tax hike. Aslund (2007), p. 215.

108 The term was used by Alexander Zhukov, the head of the Tax Committee in the Third Duma. Granik (2003).

109 The Moscow-based Center for Current Politics in Russia periodically compiled data on deputies with affiliations to the oil sector. See "State Regulation of the Oil ...," *CCPR*, 2002; "Peredel Sobstvennosti ...," *CCPR*, 2003; "Gossudarstvennoe Regulirovanie," CCPR, 2004.

110 He was chairman of the Committee on Economic Policy and Entrepreneurship in the Third Duma.

111 Glazev's absence at the forum was noteworthy. See Borozdina (2003).

112 See "Alaska ne Nauchit ...," *UralPolit.Ru – Economic and Political Reviews*, 2003.

113 "Andrey Illarionov: Politika – Eto Vsegda o Den'gakh," *Novaia Gazeta*, 2004.

114 Nenarokov (2003); Granik (2003).

115 The leadership of "Energy of Russia" in particular was composed primarily of deputies from Unity, OVR, Russia's Regions, and People's Deputies. See Khamraev (2001).

116 Personal interview with Visloguzov, 2007.

117 Kravchenko (2002).

118 Visloguzov (2003).

119 Reshul'skii (2002).

120 *Stenogramma Zasedanii Gosudarstvennoi Dumy*, 20 June 2003.

121 Visloguzov (2003).

122 "Warrants Issued for 10 Yukos Executives," *RFE/RL Newsline*, 2004.

123 "United Russia List," *Moscow Times*, 2003.

124 In exchange for paying less taxes, companies made direct contributions to regional budgets, paid bribes, or financed the election campaigns leaders from the region. Treisman (1999), p. 146.

125 Kusznir (2007), p. 170.

126 The vote on the "Yukos Amendment" was still a vote in favor of the executive, as the amendment was part of a comprehensive reform package.

127 Bradshow estimated that 35 regions were deriving over 40 percent of their GDP from extraction of natural resources or their processing in 2004. Bradshaw (2006), p. 730.

128 The lower tax on gas was justified by government officials, including Gref, on the grounds of preventing a spike in inflation. As gas was sold mostly in the domestic market at subsidized prices, this also favored Gazprom's position to keep the tax burden low. Shokhina, Reznik, and Grozovskii (2006).

129 The NDPI bill approved in 2001 let regions keep only 20 percent of the revenues from the NDPI tax on hydrocarbons. For other mineral resources, this rate was set at 60 percent.

130 Tabata (2002), p. 620.

131 Regions were authorized to reduce only their (regional) portion of the profit tax by up to 4 percent. But most exemptions related to this tax were eliminated. These measures were negotiated and approved in conjunction with the NDPI tax in 2001. Lavitskii (2001).

132 Nikol'skii and Shterbakova (2002).
133 "Governors Question Constitutionality of Resource Bill," *Petroleum Report*, 2004.
134 Personal interview with Shawn McCormick, Vice President of TNK-BP, Moscow, 13 June 2007.
135 Ahrend and Tompson (2006), p. 59.
136 The reintroduction of export duties was conducted by the government, yet the legislature eventually acquired a role by setting constraints on the government's room for maneuvering. NDPI was introduced through legislative approval.
137 Fjaertoft and Lunden (2015).
138 Ibid., p. 559.
139 "Gref Urges Oil Tax Changes," *Energy in East Europe*, 2005.
140 Personal interview with McCormick, 2007.
141 "All Inclusive: Comprehensive Tax …," *Nefte Compass*, 2005.
142 "Kto i Kak Delit Rossiiskii TEK?" *CCPR*, 2005.
143 Personal interview with Feigin, 2017.
144 Ibid.
145 Lunden (2014), p. 50.
146 "Russian Oil and Gas: Too Big to Fail," Sberbank, 2014, p. 11.
147 See "Russian Oil and Gas: Two Weddings and a Funeral," Sberbank, 2014, p. 4.
148 Personal interview with Nikolaev, FBK, Moscow, 14 April 2017.
149 Starinskaya and Papchenkova (2014).
150 Personal interview with Maria Belova, Vygon Consulting, 13 April 2017.
151 A truly profit-based tax regime would involve automatic mechanisms to adjust the tax rate, leaving little discretion to the Finance Ministry.
152 Vygon, Rubtsov, Klubkov, and Ezhov (2015), pp. 33–5.
153 Personal interviews with Feigin; Vladimir Drebentsov, BP, Moscow, 14 April 2017.
154 Personal interview with Vladimir Milov, Moscow, 12 April 2017.
155 Calder (2010), p. 356–7.
156 These figures include a rollback of tax benefits as well as other changes in the tax legislation. See Lunden (2014), pp. 30–55.
157 'Stavka na Neft," *Vedomosti,* 2010.
158 Papchenkova and Starinskaya (2015).
159 Malkova (2010).
160 Drebentsov describes Russia's oil companies under Putin as "neither divided nor united." Unlike during the 1990s, they were no longer embroiled in bitter fights for acquisitions, but they could also hardly develop a joint stance on key matters. Personal interview with Drebentsov, 2017.
161 Personal interview with Milov, April 2017.
162 Personal interview with Belova, April 2017.
163 For instance, few Russian oil majors were operating in East Siberia when tax breaks were announced in 2006. Likewise, few companies are engaged in investing in unconventional oil. Personal interview with Sergey Drobyshevsky, Gaidar Institute, Moscow, 14 April 2017.
164 Personal interview with head of Moscow-based research center (consultant for Russian oil companies), April 2017.

165 Personal interview with a private oil company executive based in Russia, 2017.

166 While other factors, such as the devaluation of the ruble after 2014, have also helped with growth in the oil industry, tax incentives have been crucial to achieve this outcome. Personal interview with Drebentsov, 2017.

5. The State as a Redistributor of Oil Rents: The Contest over Russia's Budget and Economic Priorities

1 On the fiscal response of oil-rich governments to oil booms, see Ascher (1999), Auty (1990).

2 Gurvich, Vakulenko, and Krivenko (2009), pp. 51–70.

3 Gurvich et al. (2009) note that the degree of cyclicality of a fiscal policy is hard to determine and measure in oil-rich countries. To address this problem, they distinguish between oil revenues and non-oil revenues, and consider a country's non-oil budget balance as a measure for cyclicality. The price of oil needed to balance the budget constitutes an alternative measure. Ibid., p. 25.

4 *Russian Economic Report – 18,* World Bank, p. 8.

5 The general government budget is also known as a consolidated budget. Extrabudgetary funds refer to entitlements for pensions, mandatory medical insurance, and social security.

6 The most drastic cut in spending occurred in 1993 – about 14.1 percentage points. The government's liberalization efforts and a collapse in revenues that necessitated stringent cuts in spending were the main causes.

7 Personal interviews conducted with over 20 officials from the World Bank and the IMF in Washington, DC, and Moscow in the first half of 2007 yielded a general consensus that Russia had adopted a highly conservative fiscal approach, beyond the expectations of many.

8 Balassone (2005).

9 Personal interview with John Litwack, World Bank, Moscow, 15 June 2007.

10 Personal interviews with Vladimir Popov, New Economic School, Moscow, 8 June 2007; Mikhail Deliagin, Moscow, 15 June 2007; Vladimir Voloshin, Institute for the Economy, Moscow, 22 June 2007.

11 Personal interview with Evsey Gurvich, Economic Experts Group, Moscow, 23 June 2007.

12 Personal interviews with O'Brien, McCormick, and Sergey Verezemski, Neft i Kapital, Moscow, 21 June 2007.

13 The significance of this indicator is examined thoroughly in Barnett and Ossowski (2003). Another alternative measure typically considered by the IMF is the "constant oil balance," which assumes a long-term average price for oil as the constant price.

14 Russia never achieved a non-oil fiscal surplus. Nonetheless, as Barnett and Ossowski (2003) suggest, the true goal of oil-rich governments should be to establish a certain range for the "non-oil deficit" consistent with fiscal sustainability in the longer run.

15 Both Russian government sources and the IMF have lumped together oil and gas revenues, complicating the task of determining the precise share of each sector. Yet, the oil sector, owing to a higher tax burden, has accounted for a disproportionately larger share.

16 Based on Finance Ministry estimates.
17 Part I of the new Tax Code became effective on 1 January 1999. It focused mainly on procedural issues such as dispute settlement, defining the rights and duties of taxpayers and tax authorities.
18 The first major step was the approval of several chapters of Part II of the Tax Code in the mid-2000s. This included Chapter 21 (on Value Added Tax), Chapter 22 (on excises), Chapter 23 (on personal income tax), and Chapter 24 (on unified social tax).
19 Popova and Tekoniemi (1998), pp. 13–30.
20 The latter reduction was accomplished in 2005 when the law entitled "On the Fundamentals of the Tax System in Russia" (Law No 2118-1 of 27 December 1991) was officially repealed.
21 Personal interview with Popov, 2007.
22 Gurvich et al. (2009).
23 IMF's periodic reviews of the Russian economy through "Article IV staff reports" provide a glimpse at its ongoing consultations with Russian government officials. Its report from October 2005 includes its earliest warning about signs of an expansionary fiscal policy. See "Russian Federation: 2006 Article IV Report," *IMF Country Report*, 2006, p. 12.
24 In the case of the federal budget, the price of Urals crude needed to balance the budget was 19.1 USD/barrel in 2003, dropped to 17.5 USD/barrel in 2004, and rose to 21.5 USD/barrel and 49 USD/barrel in 2005 and 2008 respectively. (Compiled from IMF data.)
25 According to Gurvich et al. (2009), periods of consistently higher oil prices can justify an upward revision in budgetary oil price estimates.
26 In line with oil price fluctuations, the highest level was reached in 2014, when oil and gas revenues accounted for 51.3 percent of the federal budget's revenues. (Source: RF Federal Treasury.)
27 Fortescue details Russia's budgetary approach using these three categories. Fortescue (2017a), p. 534.
28 The amendment raised public spending by 1.75 percentage points of the GDP, though the budget benefited from one-time back taxes received from the sale of Yukos. "Russia Federation – Selected Issues," *IMF Country Report*, 2005, pp. 49–61.
29 The plan allocated 382 billion rubles (about 14 billion USD) to be spent in 2006 and 2007. See *Russian Economic Report – 12*, World Bank, 2006, p. 11; Bekker and Petrachkova (2006).
30 "Russian Federation: 2006 Article IV Report," *IMF Country Report*, 2006, p. 19.
31 The non-oil deficit rose by 0.8 percent of GDP, though the budget benefited once again from substantial revenues from tax penalties on Yukos. See "Russia: Mission Concluding Statement on the 2008 Article IV Consultation," IMF, 2008. Zubov (2008).
32 A budgetary amendment in February 2008 increased spending by an additional 310 billion rubles. See *Russian Economic Report – 16*, The World Bank, 2008, p. 9.

33 It rose from 7.4 percent in March 2007 to 15.1 percent in May 2008. See "Russian Federation: 2008 Article IV Report," *IMF Country Report,* 2008, p. 14.

34 Prices fell below 40 USD/bbl by December 2008.

35 In fact, one can define this price cycle as a bust mainly because oil prices went significantly below the budget's breakeven price. Yet overall, prices (in real terms) were significantly above what the world had witnessed since the mid-1980s. Thus, the average price for Russia's oil exports (outside the CIS market) was down to 57.5 USD/barrel in 2009, but rose to 76.2 in 2010. (Source: Russian Central Bank.)

36 This loss of value refers to the period between the peak on 19 May 2008 and 7 November 2008. *Russian Economic Report – 17,* World Bank, 2008, pp. 24–5.

37 Its cost was 90 billion USD, equivalent to 7 percent of Russia's annual GDP. See *Russian Federation Systemic Country Diagnosis: Pathways to Inclusive Growth,* World Bank, 2016, p. 38. On the early anti-crisis measures, see Panov, Kuvshinova, Shpigel, and Pis'mennaya (2008).

38 The size of additional budgetary spending targeting the financial sector alone was 3.3 percent of GDP. See *Russian Economic Report – 18,* World Bank, 2009, p. 9. Additionally, the Russian government took measures to slow down the depreciation of the ruble in order to help Russian banks and corporations pay back their dollar-denominated debt.

39 The government identified 295 nationally important and 1148 regionally important companies eligible for financial support valued at 600 billion rubles (about 16 billion USD). For details of the package see "Programma Antikrizisnykh Mer Pravitel'stvo RF na 2009 god," Regnum.

40 In 2009, corporate income tax was reduced from 24 percent to 20 percent.

41 President Medvedev announced an increase in pensions by 30 percent and 45 percent in 2009 and 2010, respectively. See *Russian Economic Report – 19,* World Bank, 2009, p. 11.

42 Gurvich (2016) pp. 175–6.

43 These two indicators are highly significant, though they are also imperfect measures. With the increased propensity of the Russian government to resort to quasi-fiscal measures after 2008, the non-oil balance tends to underestimate actual government spending. Likewise, the oil price balancing the budget tends to fluctuate widely along with changes in the value of the ruble.

44 "Russian Federation: 2010 Article IV Report," *IMF Country Report,* 2010, p. 8.

45 Up from 52 USD/barrel in 2008, according to IMF estimates. Corresponding figures for the federal budget were 49 USD/Barrel in 2008 and 92 USD/barrel in 2009.

46 The Russian economy recorded growth of 3.1 percent and 5.2 percent during the first and second quarters of 2010, respectively. *Russian Economic Report – 23,* World Bank, 2010, p. 6.

47 Ibid., p. 12.

48 "Russian Federation: Article IV Report," *IMF Country Report,* 2011, pp. 9–11.

49 *Russian Economic Report – 27,* World Bank, April 2012, p. 23.

50 The decrees were issued on 7 May 2012 and consisted of 13 distinct documents. See Presidential Decrees, 7 May 2012.

51 "Russian Federation: 2010 Article IV Report," p. 17.

52 "Dve Voennykh Petiletki …," *Lenta.ru,* 2011.

53 The IMF noted increased infrastructure spending as a major novelty compared with previous periods. "Russian Federation: 2014 Article IV Report," IMF, 2014, p. 7.

54 On Russia's relative neglect of infrastructure development in its budgets, see Drobyshevsky and Sinelnikov-Murylev (2012), pp. 4–24; Knobel and Sokolov (2012), pp. 23–32.

55 Russia's GDP growth rate dropped from 3.4 percent in 2012 to 1.3 percent in 2013. By the first quarter of 2014, the growth rate was down to 0.9 percent. Ibid., p. 3.

56 The size of the anti-crisis package was estimated at 2.4 trillion rubles. Yet, only a small part of this involved a budgetary expansion; 1 trillion rubles were secured through issuing treasury bonds to recapitalize banks. State guarantees constituted another quasi-fiscal measure. See *Russia Economic Report – 33,* World Bank, 2015, p. 18.

57 In 2015, defense spending increased by 18.8 percent in real terms. See *Russia Economic Report – 35,* World Bank, 2016, pp. 25–6.

58 Ibid., p. 51.

59 Mau (2016), p. 15.

60 Gurvich (2016), p. 176.

61 This sale brought the government 382 billion rubles (6.1 billion USD) in 2016. See *Russia Economic Report – 36,* World Bank, 2016, p. 24.

62 The oil price assumption in the 2010 budget had been the first one since the late 1990s to assume a price that was above the predicted oil futures prices at the time of the budgetary approval. See "Russian Federation – Concluding Statement for the 2010 Article IV Consultation," IMF, 2010.

63 For instance, the mid-term budget for 2017–19 assumed 40 USD/barrel as the oil price. See *Russia Economic Report – 37,* World Bank, 2017, pp. 7–8.

64 Fortescue notes that recipients of budgetary revenues are unsurprisingly expected to fight over budget allocations. See Fortescue (2017b), p. 528. Meanwhile, it is common to observe fights that reflect bureaucratic competition across government agencies. See Butrin (2016b).

65 There is no single definition of "fiscal prudence," though the IMF has provided a general guide, suggesting that fiscal policies are prudent if they lead to a sustainable fiscal position and do not endanger a fiscal crisis. See Mauro, Romeu, Binder, and Zaman (2013), p. 4.

66 Furthermore, as the author argues, a society as complex and modern as Russia's can hardly be "run purely on the basis of closed, informal and personalist" rule. Fortescue (2017a), pp. 451–2.

67 See the transcript of a roundtable discussion by Russian academics on the fate of various economic programs: "Sud'ba Ekonomicheskikh Programm i Reform v Rossii" (2017), *Voprosy Ekonomiki*, pp. 22–44.

68 Jakobson (2017), p. 495.

69 Gel'man and Starodubtsev (2016), p. 107.

70 Cooper (2012).

71 The process is briefly described in the history section of the Center for Strategic Research. www.csr.ru/istoriya-tssr/ – accessed on 30 March 2018.

72 Rather than formally adopting the Gref Program, the cabinet approved it as a document to form the basis of further policy discussions. Subsequently, it approved several medium-term programs that were based on the Gref Program. The first major one was the 2002–4 medium-term program approved in 2001, soon followed by another one for the 2003–5 period. See "Ekonomicheskaia Politika Federal'nogo Tsentra," 2003.

73 Aslund (2007), p. 215.

74 Smirnov (2000).

75 For an interview with Viktor Ishayev in 2001, see Zubkov (2001).

76 Information on the Gref Program can be found at the website of the Center for Strategic Research (www.csr.ru/document/original_436.stm – accessed 30 March 2018). Some of the details of the program were presented in an interview with Gref in Golovachev (2000). For details on Ishayev's draft, see Korabel'nikova (2001); Tennenbaum (2001).

77 Additional measures included reforming natural monopolies and the banking system, and reducing trade barriers.

78 For the views of a large number of Russian policy-makers and scholars on both Gref's Program and Ishaev's Program, see "Kakaia Strategia Luchshe? ...," *RF Segodnia*, 2001.

79 There were additional proposals, though they never led to the same scale of discussions and a formal proposal. Some Russian economists proposed prioritizing large businesses on the assumption that they were better equipped to foster innovation. Others focused on the need to prioritize the depreciation of the ruble. This policy discussion became more intense as large oil revenues started flowing into state coffers. According to Popov, preventing the ruble's appreciation could have been at the center of an alternative economic strategy for Russia. However, Russia failed to benefit from this strategy during the 2000s. Personal interview with Popov, 2007.

80 The term "liberal" did not imply a political ideology in Russia's case. Instead, it broadly referred to adherence to market reforms launched since the early 1990s.

81 Reportedly, Kasyanov exercised little control over key appointments. Instead Putin and Dmitry Kozak managed this process. See Shevchenko (2004), p. 169.

82 Hedlund (2000), p. 402.

83 Other key personalities include Oleg Viugin, who assumed a top position within the Russian Central Bank, and Dmitry Kozak, who became deputy head of the Presidential Administration.

84 Personal interview with Deliagin, 2007.

85 Personal interview with Zudin, 2007.

86 Personal interview with Stanislav Belkovski, Moscow, 26 June 2007.

87 Personal interviews with Lev Freinkman, World Bank, Washington, DC, 23 May 2007; Salin, 2007.

88 They included professionals from the Gaidar Institute and the Center for Strategic Research as well as liberal economists from the Academy of the National Economy and the Higher School of Economics. Personal interview with Gurvich, 2007.

89 Personal interview with Voloshin, 2007.

90 This point was corroborated by several economists in personal interviews in Moscow in June 2007.

91 Yeltsin, under pressure from the opposition, fired key liberal reformists Yegor Gaidar and Anatoly Chubais. Huskey (2001), pp. 39–40.

92 These include Putin's key annual speeches from late 1999 until the end of 2004. These speeches, such as the annual budget address, prepared after a long process of consideration by the president's staff, signal his thinking on key economic matters.

93 See President Putin's address to the Federal Assembly, 8 July 2000.

94 According to Tompson, Putin's support to liberals at this point "helped to create an elite consensus – or at least the appearance of one, given the reluctance of much of the elite to oppose Putin openly – on the need for reform and a sense of inevitability about it." See Tompson (2002), p. 948.

95 See "Ekonomicheskaia Politika Federal'nogo Tsentra," *CCPR*, 2003.

96 See President Putin's address to the Federal Assembly, 16 May 2003.

97 Menshikov (2001).

98 Yasin (2001).

99 Ibid.

100 Observed by Fish (2005), p. 261.

101 For example, in a speech in November 2005, Putin asserted: "The favorable economic conditions in today's Russia allow us to make large investments in raising living standards."

102 Fish (2005), p. 262.

103 Deliagin (2001).

104 President Putin's address to the Federal Assembly, 8 July 2000.

105 President Putin's address to the Federal Assembly, 18 April 2002.

106 President Putin's address to the Federal Assembly, 16 May 2003.

107 President Putin's address to the Federal Assembly, 26 May 2004.

108 See Yasin (2001) and Tompson (2002).

109 Tompson (2002), pp. 949–50.

110 Point noted during interviews in Moscow. (Personal interviews with Salin, Zudin, Gurvich, 2007.)

111 About half of the growth in the 2000–8 period has been estimated to have come from the booming oil sector and higher oil prices. See Kudrin and Gurvich (2015).

112 Such statements often came from deputy prime minister and former Gosplan head Yuri Maslyukov.

113 Personal interview with Evsey Gurvich, Moscow, 14 April 2017.

114 Their major representative within the cabinet after the May 2000 reshuffle was Valentina Matvienko, the deputy prime minister in charge of social policy. She lobbied intensively for more social spending. See "Ekonomicheksaia Politika Federal'nogo Tsentra," *CCPR*, April 2001.

115 Following the May 2000 cabinet reshuffle, Deputy Prime Minister Ilya Klebanov was among the chief proponents of an industrial policy requiring more government spending. Ibid.

116 In 2003, Primakov proposed the creation of a special fund to support the revival of Russian industry. RUIE members came up with similar requests. See "Komentarii or Redaktsii: Sreda Zaela," *Vedomosti*, 2004; Ilina and Redichkina (2002).

117 This conclusion is based on interviews with over 20 experts and officials conducted in 2007. About half of the interviewees were officials from the World Bank and the IMF who were involved in negotiations with the Russian government. Other officials included Russian economists, political scientists, and business representatives. All gave the most credit to Kudrin for Russia's fiscal discipline, save one oil executive who believed Gref should get at least equal credit.

118 Personal interview with Deliagin, 2007.

119 Personal interview with a World Bank official, 2007.

120 Another significant pick by Putin was Andrey Illarionov as his economic advisor. However, he lacked the institutional clout of Kudrin and Gref, who occupied ministerial positions, and his fiscal proposals were often found to be "ultraliberal." For some of his proposals see Illarionov and Pivovarova (2002), pp. 18–45; Viktorov and Bardin (2001).

121 This criticism is widespread among Russian politicians and economists. Several Russian economists voiced the same criticism during interviews. Personal interviews with Nikolaev, Popov, Deliagin, 2007.

122 Personal interview with Arkady Dvorkovich, Head of Experts Department of the President, Moscow, 27 June 2007.

123 President Putin's address to the Federal Assembly, 26 May 2004.

124 Personal interview with Freinkman, 2007.

125 This does not necessarily mean that ministries were devoted to a countercyclical policy, however, as they often questioned its rationale.

126 Personal interview with Dvrokovich, 2007.

127 Personal interview with Gurvich, 2007.

128 See President Putin's annual budgetary address on 24 May 2005: www.kremlin.ru /text/appears/2005/05/88533.shtml.

129 Personal interview with Andrey Movchan, Moscow, 13 April 2017.

130 Some Duma members openly accused Kudrin's ministry of deliberately understating expected government revenues. "Ekonomicheskaia Politika Federal'nogo Tsentra," *CCPR*, 2 September 2001.

131 For recurring discrepancies between the ministry's forecasts and actual budgetary parameters, see Gurvich (2006), p. 6.

132 Government spending for "national defense" increased from 1.9 percent of GDP in 2000 to 2.52 percent of GDP in 2005. Similarly, spending on "national security and law enforcement" consistently increased from 1.05 percent of GDP to 1.95 percent of GDP during the same period. (Source: IMF.)

133 "Putin Orders 20 Percent Wage Hike for Military, Police," *RFE/RL Newsline*, 2000.

134 Personal interview with Litwack, 2007.

135 "Kasyanov to Cut Taxes, Improve Investment Climate," *RFE/RL Newsline*, 2000.

136 According to Vladimir Milov, Prime Minister Kasyanov was particularly active in calling for reduced taxes. Personal interview with Milov, 2017.

137 In essence economy-wide tax cuts were replacing subsidies and tax exemptions to specific companies and sectors. This made them broadly appealing to liberal reformists.

138 Ishayev's alternative economic program, for instance, was largely in line with the Gref Program on cutting taxes.

139 Personal interview with Stanislav Voskresensky, Expert Department of the President, Moscow, 27 June 2007.

140 On the MEDT's role in tax reform, see Kamyshev and Bagrov (2000). The MEDT's outstanding role during this period was noted by former insiders during personal interviews as well. (Personal interviews with Litwack and Gurvich, 2007.)

141 Luong and Weinthal (2004), pp. 148–9.

142 "Arkadii Dvorkovich o Naprevlaniakh …," *WPS – Economic Teledigest*, 2002.

143 Bekker (2002b).

144 Milov notes that Kudrin fought successfully against more ambitious tax cut proposals by Gref and other government figures such as Prime Minister Fradkov. Personal interview with Milov (2017).

145 "Old Habits Die Hard in Russia," *Transition* 2002, pp. 33–44.

146 VAT appeared as the largest source of revenue for the federal government in the 1994–2004 period. (Source: IMF.)

147 Some Duma members, for example, hoped to set the VAT rate at 10 percent. MEDT officials were keen to set it at 15 percent. "Kto i Kogda Obeshtal Snizhat' Nalogi," *Kommersant*, 2002.

148 On Putin's warnings, see ibid.; Lapunova (2003).

149 Personal interviews with Voskresensky and Gurvich, 2007.

150 Personal interview with Oleg Ignatov, Center for Current Policy, Moscow, 13 April 2017.

151 Until an amendment in the Budget Code in 2007, the federal budget bill had to pass through four readings. With this amendment, the number of readings was reduced to three.

152 For the period from 1994 to 1999, I rely on an extensive study on the Duma's budgetary voting patterns by Troxel. See: Troxel (2003), pp. 138–51. For the period after 1999, I rely on roll call data from the "Perechni Zakonoproektov i Proektov Postanovlenii," State Duma's website: sozd.duma.gov.ru (accessed 30 March 2018).

153 Ibid., p. 147.

154 Ibid., p. 149.

155 Regarding the recurring problem of "unrealistic" budgets, see Sokolowski (2001), pp. 541–72.

156 Putin's first encounter with the Duma's resistance on approving the budget occurred during the 2000 budget negotiations. The budget bill was overwhelmingly rejected during the first reading. "Duma Rejects Budget," *RFE/RL Newsline*, 1999. The budget passed only after concessions to KPRF on more federal spending. See: "New Budget Allocates More for Defense," *RFE/RL Newsline*, 1999.

157 Sergey Satiukov, leader of Unity in Arkhangelsk, quoted in a personal interview by Steven Fish in May 2001. See Fish (2005), p. 261.

158 Compared to other "parties of power" in the past such as Russia's Choice and Our Home Is Russia, the proportion of partylist-based deputies belonging to Unity was substantially higher. See Smith (2002), pp. 566–8.

159 Remington (2001), pp. 293–5.

160 Smith (2002), p. 567.

161 For the 16 roll call votes (one for each of the four readings for the 2001–4 budgets), an average of 98.6 percent of Unity faction members voted "yes."

162 During the Third Duma, the four factions could pass the 226 votes threshold only once: they delivered 228 "yes" votes for the second reading of the 2002 budget bill.

163 On average, only 78 percent of the members of this faction voted "yes" for the 2000–4 budget bills (data based on the 16 roll call votes taken during each budget reading during the Third Duma).

164 The 2000 budget bill had assumed a deficit, though in reality, Russia witnessed its first surplus for an entire fiscal year.

165 OVR member Vyacheslav Volodin praised the government for raising spending on defense, agriculture, and health services. Thus, OVR decided to support the budget during the second reading. See "Budget Expected to Sail through Second Reading," *RFE/RL Newsline*, 2000.

166 Remington (2004), p. 41.

167 "Unity Wants More for Defense," *RFE/RL Newsline*, 2001.

168 Remington (2006), p. 287.

169 "Duma Approves Budget in Third Reading," *RFE/RL Newsline*, 2004.

170 Personal interview with Ignatov, 2017.

171 Bohlen (2000).
172 Pavlov, Skhors, and Westin (2000).
173 During the Fourth Duma, owing to United Russia's overwhelming success in the 2003 elections, passing almost any bill became easier.
174 For instance, the government proposed to eliminate the Road Tax, which accrued to regions. It agreed to postpone the process while compensating regions for lost revenues with the new Transportation Tax. It also promised additional direct federal transfers. See Granik (2002).
175 For alternative proposals by Duma members, see Lapunova (2003).
176 For instance, in 2003, the Finance Ministry fought successfully against Duma proposals demanding more drastic cuts for VAT and the unified social tax (ESN). Ibid.
177 A confrontation arose over the government's proposal to cut the profit tax rate in 2001. Both sides agreed to reduce the tax rate, but the Finance Ministry pressed to eliminate tax exemptions associated with the profit tax in exchange. Lapunova (2001a).
178 Granik (2002).
179 Kizilova (2001).
180 The Duma's alternative tax proposal called for reducing the VAT by 4 percent, while the government called for a 2 percent reduction. See Petrov (2003).
181 Regional interests are represented not only by regional authorities and the upper chamber, but also by the Duma. For example, all three players bargain with the executive on the size of federal transfers to regional budgets or on the provision of subsidies to the agricultural sector. Thus, it is difficult to disaggregate their individual contributions to particular legislative outcomes.
182 The Federation Council exhibits one major weakness during the approval process: it can reject the budget bill, but unlike the Duma, it cannot introduce its own amendments to the bill. It has to either approve the bill, or reject it and call for the creation of a reconciliation committee with the lower chamber and the executive.
183 Soderlund (2006), pp. 71–85.
184 "Hostile" electorate refers to regions where opposition parties or leaders obtained relatively larger percentages of votes. See Treisman (1998), pp. 893–906.
185 Revenues for Russia's extrabudgetary funds are not part of this calculation. Data for regional budgets include federal transfers. Based on data from the IMF.
186 Ibid.
187 Thus, the number of regions witnessing a deficit in their budgets rose from 42 in 2001 to 63 in 2002. Nearly two-thirds of Russia's regions could not make ends meet without federal support. "Regional Budgets Wind Up in Deficit," *RFE/RL Newsline*, 2003.
188 Based on data from the IMF.
189 Wetzel (2004).

190 "New Changes to Budget Code …," *RFE/RL Russia Report*, 2004.

191 Putin's annual budget address in 2002 outlined multiple objectives regarding interbudgetary relations to be achieved by 2005. The speech was widely seen as a call for radically curtailing regional financial independence. "President Urges Tighter Control over State Revenues," *RFE/RL Newsline*, 2002.

192 The average rate of approval stood at 62 percent during the 1994–9 period. This share rose to 77 percent during the 2000–6 period. (Source: Voting data from the Federation Council.)

193 As noted in chapter 2, the upper chamber's approval rate increased with regard to all federal legislation following Putin's "centralization" reforms during 2000.

194 On at least three occasions (in the 2001, 2005, and 2006 budgets) the Duma would have had the power to override any veto from the upper chamber.

195 Chaisty (2012), pp. 92–101.

196 Dmitry Skrypnik, a Russian economist, suggests that this lack of consensus in policy-making circles was highly complicated. Thus, for instance, proponents of major fiscal expansion opposed the government's fiscally conservative stance, but disagreed on the precise extent of state involvement. Personal interview with Dmitry Skrypnik, Russian Academy of Sciences, Moscow, 12 April 2017.

197 On the rise of several development agencies see Simachev, Kuzik, and Ivanov (2012), pp. 4–29.

198 From an interview with Kudrin in Pis'mennaya (2013), p. 134.

199 Ironically, this new policy direction was much more in line with proposals from veto players that the government had managed to consistently ignore.

200 Personal interviews with Movchan, Gurvich, 2017.

201 Gaddy and Ickes (2010), p. 288.

202 Gryzlov praised the recently launched Investment Fund and four national projects. Gryzlov (2006).

203 Abramov, Radygin, and Chernova (2017), p. 9.

204 The Russian leader has continuously received advice from members of the executive as well as experts with often diverging views on a policy matter. Yet, according to Russian economist Andrey Movchan, he has never delegated full authority on key policies, acting as the ultimate decision-maker. Personal interview with Movchan, 2017.

205 Based on analysis of Putin's annual address to the Federal Assembly between 2006 and 2008.

206 From an interview with Kudrin. Pis'mennaya (2011).

207 It is less clear whether such reformists shifted away from their fiscally conservative approach owing to pressure from Putin or to a genuine shift in their thinking about the economy.

208 For instance, one of MEDT's projections referred to the oil price rising to 75 USD/barrel in 2007. Petrachkova, Bekker, and Tutushkin (2006).

209 It involved other parties of the executive branch, as well as representatives of regional governments and businesses. "Pravitel'stvo RF Rassmotrit Kontsepsiiu …," *Ria Novosti*, 1 October 2008.

210 The text of the program accessed at: http://government.ru/info/6217/ (11 February 2018).

211 For instance, the profile and the fate of one of the rising stars behind the preparation of KDR 2020, Andrey Belousov, was telling. A proponent of state-led development (albeit not aligned with statists such as Glazev), he became one of Gref's deputies in 2006, and was brought in by Putin to lead economic and financial policy within the government apparatus after 2008, eventually returning to the MEDT as minister in 2012. Dabrowska and Zweynert (2015), pp. 529–30.

212 Igor Shuvalov was another prominent reformist from the early days of Putin's presidency who became a proponent of more active state involvement in the economy.

213 According to Russian economist Andrey Yakovlev, the replacement of Kasyanov with Fradkov could be regarded as an early sign of Russia's upcoming shifts in fiscal and economic policies. Personal interview with Yakovlev, 2017.

214 Some authors have put him in the *siloviki* camp. See Aslund (2007), p. 244.

215 Stenin and Tumanov (2008).

216 Hanson and Teague (2013), p. 13.

217 Pis'mennaya (2013), pp. 174–81. Storchak was acquitted in 2011 for lack of evidence. See "Storchaka Priznali Nevinovnym," *Rossiiskaya Gazeta*, 2011.

218 For an interview with Kudrin explaining the growing pressure to raise public spending after 2005. See Pis'mennaya (2013), p. 166.

219 Periodic reports on the Russian economy issued by the World Bank and the IMF between 2006 and 2008 include repeated warnings against abandoning fiscal prudence, highlighting a vulnerability to oil price shocks.

220 The legislation (FZ 122, also widely known as the "Law on Monetization") was approved by the Duma on 5 August 2004, and was signed by the president on 22 August 2004.

221 Grinkevich (2009).

222 Polls indicated about 80 percent of military staff opposed the reform. Ibid.

223 Pis'mennaya (2013), pp. 149–51.

224 Personal interviews reveal that Russian scholars have been divided on the impact of Ukraine's Orange Revolution on Putin's economic policies.

225 A poll taken at the peak of protests in January 2005 indicated that 38 percent of respondents blamed the government, while 23 percent put the blame on President Putin. Only 5 percent blamed local authorities. See "Monetizatsia L'got: Protivniki …," Levada Center Press Office, 2005.

226 Golosov (2011), pp. 623–39.

227 Sinitsina (2009).

228 Alexandrova and Struyk (2007), pp. 153–66; Vlad Grinkevich (2009).

229 Wengle and Rasell (2008), p. 746. According to the IMF, health and education reforms were particularly affected. See "Russian Federation: 2005 Article IV Report," IMF, 2005, p. 16.

230 Pis'mennaya (2013), p. 155.

231 Sinitsina (2009).

232 A. Kudrin's speech at the Moscow Finance Forum, 8 September 2017. https://akudrin.ru/news/za-nevypolnenie-strategicheskih-zadach-v-rossii-ne-nakazyvayut-vystuplenie-na-moskovskom-finansovom-forume-8-sentyabrya-2017-goda – accessed 21 February 2018.

233 From an interview with Kudrin: Pis'mennaya (2011).

234 Sakwa (2008), p. 889.

235 Kamyshev (2005).

236 Personal interview with Belkovski, 2007.

237 According to Andrey Yakovlev, such an expansionary fiscal policy also aimed to reduce regional inequalities and counter associated risks of social unrest. Personal interview with Yakovlev, 2017.

238 Aleksashenko (2010).

239 Nemtsov (2007).

240 Noble (2017), p. 514.

241 Pis'mennaya (2013), p. 148.

242 Personal interview with Ignatov, 2017.

243 Personal interview with Movchan, 2017.

244 From an interview with Kudrin: Pis'mennaya, 2011.

245 Ibid.

246 Ibid.

247 Medvedev (2009).

248 "Russian Federation: 2010 Article IV Report." Ibid., p. 21.

249 Personal interview with Drobyshevksy, 2017.

250 Russian Economic Report – 22, World Bank, 2010, p. 12.

251 The share of state defense in total federal budgetary spending rose from 12.6 percent in 2010 to 37 percent in 2015. See: Cooper (2017), p. 477.

252 Reportedly, Kudrin proposed 13 trillion rubles, whereas the Ministry of defense asked for 36 trillion rubles. Putin and Medevedev agreed to 20 billion rubles. See ibid., p. 486.

253 From an interview with Kudrin: Pis'mennaya (2011).

254 Pis'mennaya (2011). Ben Noble notes that United Russia shifted its position on the budget to coincide with changes in the government's preferences. Thus, its populism can hardly be regarded as a factor that drove policy decisions. See Noble (2016).

255 "Ministr Finansov Rossii Pokinul Svoy Post, Kommersant, 2011.

256 From an interview with Kudrin: Pis'mennaya (2011).

257 Likewise, the parliamentary terms were also extended from four to five years.

258 Hale (2015), p. 283.

259 "Do Samykh Do Okrain …," *Lenta.ru*, 2011. For a detailed overview of Russia's protest movements in 2011–12 period, see Volkov (2012).

260 United Russia received 49 percent of the votes, down from 64 percent during the 2007 Duma elections.

261 Putin gained 65 percent of the vote in 2012, while Medvedev had recorded 70 percent of the votes during the 2008 presidential elections.

262 Reforms included installing webcams at the polling stations, liberalizing political party registrations, and restoring direct elections for regional governors. Hale (2015), pp. 286–7.

263 The three-year budget plan proposed a drop in the consolidated budget deficit to go into effect not earlier than 2014. See *Russian Economic Report – 26*, World Bank, 2011, p. 13.

264 *Russian Economic Report – 27*, World Bank, 2012, p. 23.

265 Putin (2012a).

266 Movchan notes this shift towards more optimistic forecasts about oil prices after 2010. This shift in thinking might also explain why the Russian government supported Rosneft to purchase TNK-BP in 2013 during record-high prices. Personal interview with Movchan, 2017.

267 Some of Putin's articles from 2012 included Putin (2012a), Putin (2012b), Putin (2012c).

268 For Strategy 2020, see Mau and Kuzminov (2013).

269 See Presidential Decrees, 7 May 2012. On the limitations faced during the implementation of these decrees, see: Remington (2014).

270 *Russian Economic Report – 28*, World Bank, 2012, p. 20.

271 "V. Putin: Moi Predvybornye Obeshchania …" *RBK.ru*, 2012.

272 From an interview with Kudrin: Pis'mennaya (2011).

273 Khmelnitskaya (2017), p. 458.

274 Connolly (2013), pp. 5–9.

275 Cerami notes this lack of strong veto players as a major factor shaping the way Russia's welfare policy evolved under Putin. Cerami (2009), pp. 105–20.

276 *Russia Economic Report – 36*, ibid., p. 31.

277 Abramov et al. (2017), p. 2.

278 Personal interview with Movchan, 2017.

279 The general government deficit stood at 1.3 percent of GDP in 2013, down from a surplus of 0.4 percent of GDP in 2012. See "Russian Federation: 2011 Article IV Report, ibid., p. 7.

280 Ibid., p. 36.

281 Gurvich (2012), pp. 5–7.

282 Korsunskaya (2012).

283 According to Kudrin and Gurvich, half of the growth during the first oil boom (2000–8) and the entire economic growth during the second boom were due to rising oil windfalls. Kudrin and Gurvich (2015).

284 Glazev and Fetisov (2014), pp. 63–76.

285 Khmelnitskaya (2017), p. 470.

286 The clash was mainly between the Finance Ministry and the Economy Ministry, on the one hand, and Deputy Prime Minister Olga Golodets, on the other. The latter represented the "social bloc" within the government. See Kuvshinova, Lyutova, and Papchenkova (2015).

287 One of the groups, known as Stolypin Club, opposed spending cuts for social policy, while advocating for looser monetary policy. Another group, led by Kudrin, called for substantial structural reforms as a means to revive the economy. Kudrin re-emerged in public politics when Putin assigned him to prepare a new economic strategy draft. Prime Minister Medvedev also developed an alternative proposal suggesting some structural reforms. See: Hille (2017). Key proposals by Stolypin Club can be found at its website: http://stolypinsky.club. On Kudrin's new role see Khamraev (2016).

288 Real wages and productivity grew during this period by 46 percent and 18 percent, respectively. Kuvshinova et al. (2015).

289 Maniulova (2016).

290 Henry Hale notes that Putin, in the aftermath of the Crimea crisis faced record high public support, but was also aware that such support could easily be squandered. Given his high popularity in the 2014–16 period, he did not welcome a political thaw. Instead, further restrictions on the opposition and civil society were imposed. This appears as a risk-averse decision. Within this context Putin chose fiscal restraint in the name of future fiscal stability. See Hale (2015), p. 290.

291 Butrin (2016a).

292 Khmelnitskaya (2017), p. 467.

293 *Russia Economic Report – 35*, p. 27.

294 *Russia Economic Report – 37*, p. 29.

295 President Putin's speech in Izhevsk, cited in Cooper (2017), p. 486.

6. The State as a Redistributor of Oil Rents: The Battle to Save the Windfalls

1 For an overview of oil funds and sovereign wealth funds, see Yi-chong and Bahgat (2010).

2 On this particular effect, known as the "Dutch Disease," see Corden (1984), pp. 359–80.

3 The earliest example of a sovereign wealth fund was Kuwait's Investment authority, set up in 1953. More countries started experimenting with oil funds in the 1970s. Bahgat (2009), pp. 283–93.

4 Gaidar (2007b).

5 The last quarter of 1999 recorded a minor surplus in the federal budget.

6 These three options represented competing priorities, but were not mutually exclusive.

7 The Reserve Fund received 80 percent of the savings of the Stabilization Fund, and the NWF received the rest.

8 Federal Law, no. 63 of 26 April 2007, "On the Amendments to the Budget Code of the Russian Federation …."

9 By comparison, total federal spending for 2008 stood at 7,571 billion rubles, equivalent to about 305 billion USD. *Ispolnenie Federal'nogo Biudshet* …, Ministry of Finance, 2013.

10 The fund also received any surplus in the federal budget at the end of the year.

11 The functioning of the "financial reserve" is examined in Minaev (2007).

12 Lebedinskaya (2012), p. 103.

13 "Russian Federation: 2009 Article IV Report," IMF, 2009, p. 31.

14 Russia's IMF debt stood at 15.2 billion USD in 1999. "Obzor Ekonomicheskikh …," EEG, 2006.

15 This outcome was partly due to the appreciation of the Russian currency as well.

16 The average rate of sovereign debt for the group of 25 countries stood at 50 percent of GDP. Arias and Restrepo-Echavarria (2016), pp. 1–3.

17 For estimates on the impact of oil funds, see Drobyshevksy (2011), pp. 130–58.

18 The amount transferred stood at 30 billion rubles. Ivanova (2006).

19 Zubov (2008).

20 In August 2008, gross international reserves (including gold) peaked at 598 billion USD. "Russian Federation: 2009 Article IV Report," IMF, 2009.

21 Cherniavksii (2015), pp. 10–13.

22 The last major withdrawal during the first period was in December 2010, and the first major withdrawal in the second period was in February 2015. (Source: Finance Ministry.)

23 The government placed 5.5 billion USD in Eurobonds in April 2010. This was the first international bond issue implemented by Russia since 1998. *Russian Economic Report – 22*, World Bank, 2010, p. 13.

24 "Russian Federation: 2019 Article IV Consultation Staff Report," IMF, 2019, p. 25.

25 The size of the Reserve Fund grew only marginally between 2013 and 2014 – years of high oil prices. Its holdings increased from 82.2 billion USD in February 2013 to the new peak of 91.7 billion USD in September 2014. After this, its savings declined consistently. (Source: Finance Ministry.)

26 Ulyukaev (2014).

27 Bazanova (2017).

28 Se "Fond Natsional'nogo Blagosostoyania," Ministry of Finance website. https://minfin.gov.ru/ru/perfomance/nationalwealthfund/ – accessed 10 August 2020.

29 Zolotareva, Drobyshevsky, Sinel'nikov, and Kadochnikov (2001).

30 Putin, for the first time, referred to the idea of establishing a formal mechanism in the budget to deal with fluctuations in oil revenues in his annual address to the Federal Assembly in April 2001.

31 Also known as the "2003 problem." See *Russiiskaia Ekonomika v 2006 godu ...*, Institute for the Economy in Transition, 2007, p. 9.

32 Personal interview with Gurvich, 2007.

33 Korop (2003).

34 Some proponents of these ideas within the cabinet included Deputy Prime Minister Ilya Klebanov and Deputy Prime Minister Valentina Matvienko. "Ekonomicheskaia Politika ...," *CCPR*, 2001.

35 Deputies from opposition parties, KPRF mainly, urged the government to reschedule payment of its foreign debt to the Paris Club. See "Many in Duma Oppose Paying Paris Club," *RFE/RLE Newsline*, 2001.

36 "Crushing Blow or Failed Gambit," *RFE/RL Russia Report*, 2001.

37 Pis'mennaya (2013), p. 121.

38 See Putin's address to the Federal Assembly on Russia's budgetary policy on 20 April 2001; also, Putin's address to the Federal Assembly on 13 May 2003.

39 Foreign debt payments in 2003 were commonly presented as a "strategic challenge" for the country. *Russiiskaia Ekonomika v 2006 godu ...*, ibid., p. 9.

40 The functioning of the "financial reserve" is examined in Minaev (2007).

41 The Duma was largely unsatisfied and, led by deputy head of the Budget Committee Zadornov (from Yabloko), it came up with its own proposal for the creation of a different reserve fund, whose operations would be subject to legislative approval. "Hedging Against Crisis," *Vremya MN*, 2003.

42 Personal interview with Drobyshevksy, 2017.

43 The proposal was clearly in sync with the major tax reforms in the oil sector accomplished in the 1999–2001 period: export duties and NDPI had emerged as the two key elements of the tax regime.

44 Bekker (2003).

45 This was equivalent to about 1.1 trillion rubles at the time. Shokhina (2003).

46 Voting took place on 28 November 2003. Data from Indem Foundation (accessed 10 July 2008).

47 Personal interview with Gurvich, 2017. See also Gurvich (2004), p. 25.

48 The amendment in the Budget Code authorizing the establishment of the fund explicitly stated this function. See "Budget Code of the Russian Federation, Chapter 13.1, Article 96.1."

49 Tabakh (2006).

50 Personal interviews with Movchan, Drobyshevksy, 2017.

51 At this early stage of debate on how to establish a savings fund, the discourse was still focused on specific policy issues such as debt repayment and managing the surplus in the budget. It was in later years that the functions of the fund became increasingly questioned within the executive.

52 Personal interview with Gurvich, 2017.

53 Gaidar (2007b).

54 Personal interview with Gurvich, 2017.

55 Ibid.

56 Frumkin (2004).

57 His ministry had received multiple proposals from other ministries on infrastructure development. "German Gref Khochet' Tratit' Stabfond na Investitsii," *Kommersant*, 2004.

58 Bekker and Panov (2005).

59 Calls for more spending on health and education came from some leading liberal economists as well, such as Yevgeny Yasin. See "Press Conference with HSE Head Yevgeny Yasin," 2004.

60 Personal interview with Yulia Latynina, Novaya Gazeta, Moscow, 23 June 2007.

61 "Edinaia Rossiia Vkliuchalas' v Diskussiu …," *WPS – TV and Radio Monitoring*, 2005.

62 "Luzhkov: Dengi v Stabfonde …," *Pravda.ru*, 2006.

63 "S. Mironov: Neobkhodimo Razpechatat' Stabilizatsionny Fond …," *RBK.ru*, 2006.

64 "Stabilizatsionny Fond: Kuda Potratit' Deng'gi?," *CCPR*, 2004.

65 Sokolova and Pyanykh (2004).

66 Based on a VTsIOM survey in mid-2005, 90 percent of respondents believed the Stabilization Fund's money should be spent one way or another. Only 5 percent favored accumulating oil revenues in the fund as a precaution. "Stabilization Fund Money Should Be Spent – Poll," *Tass*, 2005.

67 The poll conducted by the Levada Center revealed that 73 percent of the respondents felt that "a part of the money in the Stabilization Fund should be used for social services or investments in the economy." Thirteen percent were opposed. Cited in Tabata (2008), p. 709.

68 This position was voiced commonly by the Finance Ministry, Illarionov, and Russia's Central Bank. See "Russian President's Aide Suggests …," *RIA Novosti*, 2004; "Liberal Ministers Oppose Prime Minister's Plans," *RIA Novosti*, 2004.

69 For an extensive interview with Kudrin, see Pis'mennaya (2010).

70 Personal interview with Deliagin, 2007.

71 Dabrowska and Zweynert (2015), pp. 532–5.

72 According to IMF estimates, private external debt skyrocketed from 262 billion USD to 447 billion USD during the 2006–8 period. See "Russian Federation: 2009 Article IV Report," IMF, 2009, pp. 30–1. See also Zubov (2008).

73 Personal interview with Ignatov.

74 Sergey Witte also served eleven years as Finance Minister – from 1892 to 1903. Historian Orlando Figes refers to him as the "great reforming Finance Minister." Figes (1996), p. 41.

75 Bekker and Petrachkova (2006).

76 For a discussion on Russia's investment strategy for its oil funds see Fortescue (2010), pp. 113–31.

77 Panov (2006).

78 Zubov (2008); Fortescue (2010), p. 121.

79 Personal interview with Movchan, 2017.

80 Personal interview with Gurvich, 2017.

81 Kudrin (2007), pp. 6–26.

82 Bekker and Petrachkova (2006).

83 Morozov (2006).

84 Its nominal growth was 40 percent – a record growth since the 1998 default. See Zubov (2008).

85 New institutions created in 2006 and 2007 included Russian Venture Company, Russian Nanotechnology Corporation (Rosnano), Bank for Development and Foreign Economic Activity (Vneshekonombank), and Russian Information and Communications Technologies Investment Fund. See Simachev, Kuzik, and Ivanov (2012), pp. 4–29.

86 *Russian Economic Report – 15*, World Bank, 2007, p. 12.

87 Shapovalov (2007).

88 President Putin's Address to the Federal Assembly, 6 April 2007.

89 *Russian Economic Report – 14*, World Bank, 2007, p. 11.

90 President Putin's Address to the Federal Assembly, 6 April 2007.

91 President Putin's Address on the Budget Policy for 2008–2010, 9 March 2007.

92 Kuvshinova and Ivanitskaya (2007).

93 For a detailed account of the fiscal rule, see Tabata (2008).

94 The fiscal rule stipulated that the size of the transfer of oil and gas revenues to the annual federal budget would be capped at 3.7 percent of the GDP. Kudrin (2013), pp. 4–19.

95 For an interview with Kudrin, see Pis'mennaya (2011).

96 Personal interview with Yakovlev, 2017.

97 Based on personal interviews with officials from the World Bank and the IMF in 2007. Also, see *Russian Economic Report – 16*, World Bank, 2008, p. 17.

98 Author's translation from Evgeniya Pis'mennaya's interview with Kudrin (2010).

99 Personal interviews with Ignatov, Movchan, 2017.

100 In 2009, amid intense debate, the Finance Ministry insisted on keeping the fiscal deficit at 6 percent of the GDP in 2010. Minister Nabiullina argued for a 10 percent deficit. Putin took the final decision, involving a compromise that set the deficit at 8 percent. Pis'mennaya (2010).

101 Milov (2009).

102 Aleksashenko (2010).

103 Personal interview with Milov, 2017.

104 Chevrier (2009), p. 79.

105 Federal Law no. 314 of 17 December 2009 amended the legislation: "On the Federal Budget for 2010, and the Planned Period of 2011 and 2012." See Drobyshevsky (2011), p. 138.

106 Cherniavksii (2015).
107 Kudrin left the Finance Ministry in part owing to his disagreements with President Medvedev on the rapid growth of military spending. Pis'mennaya (2011).
108 Expenditure in the budget was capped based on the ex ante projection of the sum of the following: non-oil-and-gas revenues; oil and gas revenues calculated on the average price of oil for the preceding ten years (initially set as five years), and net financing of 1 percent of GDP. See "Russian Federation: 2013 Article IV Report," *IMF Country Report*, 2013, pp. 51–4.
109 Unlike earlier, only half of the additional revenues would accrue to the NWF, while the rest would be used to support infrastructure and other important projects.
110 "Russian Federation: 2014 Article IV Report," *IMF Country Report*, 2014, p. 7.
111 In 2015, the NWF invested 440 billion rubles (about 7.3 billion USD) in domestic financial assets. Most of this amount was used to purchase bonds and shares of major state-owned companies, such as Russian Railways and Atomenergoprom, and support a gas development project in Yamal. See *Russia Economic Report – 35*, World Bank, 2016, p. 26.
112 The collapse in the price of oil exposed a shortcoming in the fiscal rule. The rule had represented an attempt to set an objective benchmark for the price of oil. But, as the benchmark was based on the average price of the previous several years, it delivered an excessively optimistic oil price projection. See "Russian Federation: Selected Issues," *IMF Country Report,* 2017, pp. 23–35.
113 *Russian Economic Report – 36*, World Bank, 2016, p. 49.

7. The Oil Sector as a Redistributor of Rents

1 Gaddy and Ickes (2005), pp. 560–1.
2 For instance, in 2010, Russian consumers ranked as the world's third-largest fossil fuel subsidy beneficiaries, despite the absence of oil subsidies based on the definition adopted by the International Energy Agency. *World Energy Outlook 2011*, p. 515.
3 Vatansever (2010).
4 This has been due to the different rates set for crude oil versus petroleum products, allowing refineries to benefit from depressed crude oil prices while selling products at relatively higher prices. Kalyukov (2014).
5 The size of forgone revenues is unknown owing to confidentiality of agreements with traders.
6 Guriev (2012), pp. 24–5.
7 Vasil'ev (2016).
8 In 2012, Gunvor accounted for only 15 percent of long-term contracts signed with Russian oil producers. Ibid.

9 "Treider Lukoila …," *RBK Daily*, 2017.

10 According to Russian journalist Yulia Latynina, Surgutneftegaz's trade deals with Gunvor helped the company survive amid a hostile takeover. Personal interview with Latynina, 2007. Also in Korchagina (2004).

11 Belton and Buckley (2008).

12 Polukhin (2005).

13 Harding (2007a).

14 Tutushkin, Mazneva, and Repka (2008).

15 Harding (2007b).

16 Belton (2011).

17 For several revealing interviews with oil traders, see "Oil Traders: Pipeline exports to Europe …," *WikiLeaks,* 24 November 2008.

18 Personal interview with Moscow-based expert (consultant for Russian oil companies), Moscow, April 2017.

19 Rosneft Trading AS was set up in Geneva in 2011. Ratnikov (2015).

20 Ibid.

21 Hume and Sheppard (2016).

22 Slobodian (2014).

23 Klimenteva and Raybman (2014).

24 His company, Stroytransgaz, was among the winners of a bid to build sections of the Power of Siberia gas pipeline. Lossan (2016).

25 See "Oil and Gas Quarterly: Odd One Out," *Troika Dialog,* 2009, pp. 23–4.

26 In 2008, they accounted 53 percent and 10 percent of Rosneft's transportation expenses, respectively. Ibid.

27 "Transneft," *Troika Dialog Research*, 2003, pp. 18–19.

28 "Oil and Gas Quarterly: Odd One Out," p. 24.

29 "Transneft: Fair Value Raised to $3,000," *Troika Dialog*, p. 1.

30 Transneft does not face export duties and NDPI. Its main tax expense is the corporate profit tax.

31 Derbilova (2004).

32 Transneft paid 189 million USD to charities in 2010. Mazneva (2011).

33 According to Navalny, Transneft disbursed over 15 billion rubles between 2005 and 2008. Lapshin (2016).

34 Solodovnikova, Mel'nikov, and Samokhina (2013).

35 Andrianov (2013), pp. 16–20.

36 Starinskaya (2015).

37 On the surplus capacity, see Vatansever (2017), p. 4.

38 Tokarev (2015).

39 In the gas sector, Gazprom has also been commonly in the spotlight for building pipelines at excessive cost. Bradshaw (2006), p. 740.

40 Gaddy and Ickes (2005), pp. 566–7.

41 Haldevang (2017).
42 Timchenko acquired control over the company in December 2007. "Vektor: Toropitsia Ne Obezatel'no," *Vedomosti*, 8 July 2009.
43 In 2013, oil accounted for 56 percent of freight handled in Russian ports. Chelpanova (2014).
44 Weaver (2011).
45 Frynas (2009), p. 194.
46 Dobers and Halme (2009), p. 242.
47 Poussenkova and Nikitina (2016), pp. 3–7.
48 Henry, Nysten-Haarala, Tulaeva, and Tysachniouk (2016), p. 1346.
49 For VCIOM survey results from 2008 see "Pomoch po Russki," *Vedomosti*, 25 March 2008.
50 Veksler and Tul'chinsky (2006), pp. 220–4.
51 Henry et al. (2016), p. 1341.
52 Chistyakova and Tauseneva (2014), pp. 353–7.
53 This is according to a study by the Russian Union of Industrialists and Entrepreneurs (RSPP) examining the 2000–12 period. See Nikolaeva (2012).
54 Nekhoda, Kolbysheva, and Makoveeva (2015), pp. 1–6.
55 Kelman, Loe et al. (2016), p. 164.
56 Personal interviews with Zudin, 2007. Also in Maleva and Dubrovina (2005).
57 Yakovlev (2006), p. 1054.
58 Personal interviews with Miriam Elder, *Moscow Times*, Moscow, 18 June 2007; Vladislav Inozemtsev, Center for Post-Industrial Societies, Moscow, 27 June 2007; Elena Panfilova, Transparency International, Moscow, 28 June 2007.
59 Butrin (2009).
60 Gaysina (2011), pp. 1368–71; Mordiushenko, Dhusoiti, and Vedeneeva (2016).
61 Personal interview with Valery Nesterov, Troika Dialog, Moscow, 22 June 2007; see also Rebrov (2004).
62 "Blagotvritel'ny Fond Yukosa …," 2004. Silaev (2004).
63 Crotty (2016), p. 842.
64 Golyashev (2015), pp. 10–14.
65 Personal interview with Zudin, 2007.
66 Personal interview with an executive at TNK-BP, Moscow, April 2007.
67 Personal interview with Latynina, 2007.
68 Clover (2013).
69 Personal interview with a former official of the Russian government, Moscow, April 2007.
70 For a list of potential indicators see Heinrich, Lis, and Pleines (2005), p. 8.
71 Adachi (2013), pp. 65–89. Similar problems existed in the rest of the economy as well. Adachi (2010).
72 Heinrich (2005), pp. 3–9.
73 Koriukin and Tutushkin (2004).
74 Dvortsov (2014). "Russian Oil and Gas: Till Debt Do Us Part," 2012, p. 6.
75 Dvortsov (2014).
76 Devitt (2017).

77 Belton and Buckley (2008).

78 Ibid.

79 Transparency International has reported exceptionally low levels of transparency among several companies providing construction and transportation service for the oil sector (e.g., Transoil, StroyTransNeftegaz, and Neftetransservis). *Transparency in Corporate Reporting ...*, 2017.

80 *Transparency and Disclosure by Russian State-owned Enterprises,* 2005, p. 11. On Bashneft, see Mokrousova and Vasilieva (2015).

81 Zhanov (2013).

82 "Mevedev Poruchil do Iulia Vyvesti Ministrov ..."

83 *Stenogramma: Zasedanie Pravitel'stvo,* 51, 25 December 2014; Korostikov (2015).

84 "Effekt Rosnefti," *News.ru,* 19 June 2014.

85 Kiselev (2014).

86 "Russian Oil and Gas: If Unborn Wells ...," 2010, pp. 23–36.

87 "Russian Oil and Gas: Two Weddings and a Funeral ...," 2014, p. 59.

88 Sanctions have made it more likely that Russian rather than foreign companies would benefit from this development. The Russian government has brought new requirements for oil companies to adopt import substitution measures.

89 Personal interview with Drebentsov, 2017.

90 "Russian Oil and Gas: If Unborn Wells Could Talk," p. 37–41.

91 Personal interview with head of Moscow-based research center (consultant for Russian oil companies), London, May 2017.

92 Personal interview with Milov, 2017.

93 Heinrich (2005), pp. 3–9.

94 "Russian Oil and Gas: Two Weddings and a Funeral ...," pp. 35–43.

95 Tovkaylo (2012).

96 "Sechin Pozhalovalsia ...," *Interfax,* 27 September 2012.

97 Tovkaylo and Gavshina (2012).

98 The amounts corresponded to about 2.7 billion USD and 8.5 billion USD, respectively. See Dmitrenko (2012); Papchenkova (2017).

99 Papchenkova and Vorobev (2016).

100 Sechin stepped down briefly for several months during 2011 and 2012.

101 Tovkaylo and Gavshina (2012).

102 "Neftegazovye Kompanii Mogut ...," *Vedomosti,* 4 October 2015.

103 Papchenkova and Vorobev (2016).

104 "Pravitelstvo Utverdilo Proekty ...," *Vedomosti,* 2016; "Rosnefegaz Pozhertvoval ...," *Vedomosti,* 2014.

105 Papchenkova and Starinskaia (2017).

106 In this particular case, TEK Mosenergo, owned by Rotenberg brothers, won the contract. See Alina Fadeeva (2014).

107 Rogers (2012); Rogers (2015).

108 Vatansever (2010).

109 Mordiushenko and Pavlova (2016).

110 Andrianov (2013).

111 Ledeneva (2013), p. 278.

112 Henry et al. (2016), p. 1347; p. 1361.

113 Gaddy and Ickes (2005), p. 571.

114 According to the International Property Rights index, there was only a very marginal improvement in the "protection of physical property" between 2007 and 2017. Russia's score rose from 3.6 to 4.3 (on a scale of 10). In 2017, Russia still ranked 84th among 125 countries. See www.internationalpropertyrightsindex.org/country/russia (accessed 1 October 2018).

115 World Governance Indicators of the World Bank have ranked Russia's "rule of law" in the bottom quartile during the 2001–8 period, recording marginal though irregular improvement after 2009. https://datacatalog.worldbank.org/dataset/worldwide-governance-indicators – accessed 21 October 2018.

116 By contrast, formal paths for diverting rents from the oil sector, such as tariffs by Transneft and export duties, cannot be associated with the weak rule of law.

117 Putin's presidency started with 2.1 points (out of 10, which is for least corrupt) in 2000. It reached its best score of 2.8 in 2004, followed by nearly consistent deterioration by 2010, when Russia's score dropped to 2.1. There were some marginal improvements after 2012: Russia had scored 29 points (out of 100 for least corrupt) between 2015 and 2017 (annual reports from Transparency International). Freedom House provides an alternative measure, suggesting that corruption initially declined in Putin's Russia, but was consistently on the rise after 2005. The country remained in the ranks of the most corrupt throughout the Putin era (Freedom House – Nations in Transit annual reports).

118 According to Freedom House, the highest score of 4.25 (out of 7, which is for the least independent judiciary) of the Putin era was achieved in 1999. Russia's score deteriorated progressively, reaching 6.75 in 2018. (Source: Freedom House – Nations in Transit Score: https://freedomhouse.org/report/nations-transit/2018/russia – accessed 3 September 2018.)

119 Andrews and Montinola (2004), p. 56.

120 A minor portion of these rents is captured by the state budget. This is the case when a portion of dividends from state-owned companies ends up in the federal or regional budgets. Additionally, oil companies have occasionally made direct contributions to regional government budgets.

121 Ledeneva (2013), p. 252.

122 Hale (2005).

123 There has been a noteworthy increase in the number of Russian businessmen appearing in the annual *Forbes* list of billionaires during the Putin era. Many of them could be identified from sectors benefiting from contracts with the oil industry, such as transportation and steel production.

124 A new generation of billionaires emerged during the Putin era. For many, the growth of their business empires has been largely facilitated through contracts awarded by oil producers and Transneft.

125 A key example is the battle over Rosneftegaz's dividends. Despite a government regulation requiring state-owned companies to transfer a designated share of their profits to the state as dividends, Sechin was able to prevent this from happening after 2013.

126 Ledeneva (2006), p. 13.

127 This vulnerability is not limited to transactions with oil company rents, as the government can also redistribute its own financial resources through shady transactions.

128 This is in line with Robinson, Torvik, and Verdier (2006), pp. 447–68.

129 This relates to what Michael Ross refers to as the "group formation effect" of being rich in natural resources. Namely, an oil-rich government employs the resources at its disposal to prevent the formation of social groups independent of the state. See Ross (2001), pp. 325–61.

130 Ledeneva (2013), p. 253.

Conclusion

1 Bjorvaten and Farzanegan (2014).

2 Robinson, Torvik and Verdier (2006).

Bibliography

Books, Academic Articles, Policy Papers, and Industry Reports

2006 Oil *and Gas Yearbook*. Moscow: Renaissance Capital, 2006.

Abramov, Alexander, Alexander Radygin, and Maria Chernova. (2017). "State-Owned Enterprises in the Russian Market: Ownership Structure and Their Role in the Economy." *Russian Journal of Economics*, 3, pp. 1–23. https://doi.org/10.1016/j.ruje.2017.02.001.

Acosta, Andres, Maria Araujo, Anibal Perez-Linan, and Sebastian Saiegh. (2006). "Veto Players, Fickle Institutions and Low-Quality Policies: The Policymkaing Process in Ecuador: 1979–2005." Washington, DC: Inter-American Development Bank.

Adachi, Yuko. (2010). *Building Big Business in Russia: The Impact of Informal Governance Practices*. New York: Routledge.

Adachi Yuko. (2013). "The Ambiguous Effects of Russian Corporate Governance Abuses of the 1990s." *Post Soviet Affairs*, 22/1, pp. 65–89. https://doi.org/10.2747/1060-586X.22.1.65.

Ahrend, Rudiger, and William Tompson. (2006). "Realizing the Oil Supply Potential of the CIS: The Impact of Institutions and Policies." OECD Working Paper, 12.

Akerman, Ella. (2004). "The Development of the Oil and Gas Industries in Russia," in Leo McCann, *Russian Transformations: Challenging the Global Narrative*." London: Routledge-Curzon.

Alekperov, Vagit. (2011). *Oil of Russia: Past, Present and Future*. Minneapolis: East View Press.

Alexandrova, Anastassia, and Raymond Struyk. (2007). "Reform of In-Kind Benefits in Russia: High Costs for a Small Gain." *Journal of European Social Policy*, 17/2, pp. 153–66. https://doi.org/10.1177/09589287070170020501.

Alexeev, Mikhail, and Robert Conrad. (2009a). "The Elusive Curse of Oil." *Review of Economics and Statistics*, 91/3, August, pp. 586–98. https://doi.org/10.1162 /rest.91.3.586.

Alexeev, Mikhail, and Robert Conrad. (2009b). "Russian Oil Tax Regime in Comparative Perspective." *Eurasian Geography and Economics*, 50/1, pp. 93–104. https://doi.org/10.2747/1539-7216.50.1.93.

Almond, Gabriel. (1988). "The Return to the State." *The American Political Science Review*, 82/3, September, pp. 853–74. https://doi.org/10.2307/1962495.

Ambrosio, Thomas. (2006). "A Reply to McFaul and Vacroux." *Post-Soviet Affairs*, 22/1, pp. 34–6. https://doi.org/10.2747/1060-586X.22.1.34.

Andreson, Jorgen Juel, and Silje Aslaksen. (2013). "Oil and Political Survival." *Journal of Development Economics*, 100/1, pp. 89–106. https://doi.org/10.1016 /j.jdeveco.2012.08.008.

Andrews, Josephine, and Gabriella Montinola. (2004). "Veto Players and the Rule of Law in Emerging Democracies." *Comparative Political Studies*, 37/1, pp. 55–87. https://doi.org/10.1177/0010414003260125.

Andrianov, Valery. (2013). "Va-Bank Transnefti." *Neftegazovaya Vertikal*, 1/1, pp. 16–20.

Appel, Hilary. (2008). "Is It Putin or Is It Oil? Explaining Russia's Fiscal Recovery." *Post-Soviet Affairs*, 24/4, pp. 301–23. https://doi.org/10.2747/1060-586X.24.4.301.

Appel, Hilary. (2011). *Tax Policy in Eastern Europe: Globalization, Regional Integration and the Democratic Compromise*. Ann Arbor: University of Michigan Press.

Arendt, Hannah. (1969). *On Violence*. New York: Harcourt, Brace and World.

Arias, Maria, and Paulina Restrepo-Echavarria. (2016). "Sovereign Default and Economic Performance in Oil-Producing Economies." *Economic Synopses*, 20, pp. 1–3. https://doi.org/10.20955/es.2016.20.

Ascher, William. (1999). *Why Governments Waste Natural Resources*. Baltimore: John Hopkins University Press.

Aslund, Anders. (2005). "Russian Resources: Curse or Rents?" *Eurasian Geography and Economics*, 46/8, pp. 610–17. https://doi.org/10.2747/1538-7216.46.8.610.

Aslund, Anders. (2007). *Russia's Capitalist Revolution: Why Market Reform Succeeded and Democracy Failed*. Washington DC: Peterson Institute for International Economics.

Auty, Richard. (1990). *Resource-based Industrialization: Sowing the Oil in Eight Developing Countries*. New York: Oxford University Press.

Auty, Richard, ed. (2001). *Resource Abundance and Economic Development*. Oxford: Oxford University Press.

Bahgat, Gawdat. (2009). "Oil Funds: Perils and Opportunities." *Middle Eastern Studies*, 45/2, pp. 283–93. https://doi.org/10.1080/00263200802697399.

Balassone, Fabrizio. (2005). *Measuring Fiscal Performance in Oil-Rich Countries*. Rome: Bank of Italy; Washington, DC: IMF.

Balzer, Harley. (2005a). "The Putin Thesis and Russian Energy Policy." *Post-Soviet Affairs*, 21/3, pp. 210–25. https://doi.org/10.2747/1060-586X.21.3.210.

Balzer, Harley. (2005b). "Vladimir Putin on National Energy Policy." *The National Interest*, November. http://nationalinterest.org/article/vladimir-putin-on-russian -energy-policy-600 – accessed 23 April 2018.

Balzer, Harley. (2006). "Vladimir Putin's Academic Writings and Russian Natural Resources Policy." *Problems of Post-Communism*. January–February, pp. 46–54. https://doi.org/10.2753/PPC1075-8216530105.

Barnett, Steven, and Ossowski, Rolando. (2003). "What Goes Up ...Why Oil Producing States Must Husband Their Resources." *Finance and Development*, 40/1, March.

Bayulgen, Oksan. (2010). *Foreign Investment and Political Regimes: The Oil Sector in Azerbaijan, Russia and Norway*. New York: Cambridge University Press.

Beblawi, Hazem. (1987). "The Rentier State in the Arab World," in Hazem Beblawi and Giacomo Luciani (eds.), *The Rentier State*, 49–62. London: Croom Helm.

Beblawi, Hazem, and Giacomo Luciani, eds. (1987). *The Rentier State*. London: Croom Helm.

Berezinskaia, O., and V. Mironov. (2006). "Otechestvenny Neftegazovy Kompleks: Dinamika Konkurentnosposobnosti i Perspektivy Finansirovaniia." *Voprosy Ekonomiki*, no 8. https://doi.org/10.32609/0042-8736-2006-8-137-153.

Bjorvatn, Kjetil, and Mohammed Reza Farzanegan. (2014). "Resource Rents, Power and Political Stability." CESIFO Working Paper 4727, March. www.cesifo-group .de/DocDL/cesifo1_wp4727.pdf – accessed 1 December 2017.

Bladel, Joris Van, I. (2008). *The Dual Structure and Mentality of Vladimir Putin's Power Coalition: A Legacy for Medvedev*. Stockholm: Swedish Defense Research Agency.

Blokhina, Tatiana, Oksana Karpenko, and Andrey Gurnskiy. (2016). "The Relationship between Oil Prices and Exchange Rate in Russia." *International Journal of Energy Economics and Policy*, 6/4, pp. 721–6. https://EconPapers.repec .org/RePEc:eco:journ2:2016-04-08.

Bosquet, Benoit. (2002). "The Role of Natural Resources in Fundamental Taz Reform in the Russian Federation," *Policy Research Working Paper*, Washington DC: The World Bank.

BP Statistical Review of World Energy 2019. London: British Petroleum, 2019.

Bradshaw, Michael. (2006). "Observations on the Geographical Dimensions of Russia's Resource Abundance." *Eurasian Geography and Economics*, 47/6, pp. 724–46. https://doi.org/10.2747/1538-7216.47.6.724.

Bremmer, Ian. (2003). "The Russian Roller Coaster." *World Policy Journal*, 20/4, pp. 22–9. https://doi.org/10.2307/40209886.

Bremmer, Ian, and Samuel Charap. (2006). "The Siloviki in Putin's Russia: Who They Are and What They Want." *The Washington Quarterly*, 30/1, pp. 83–92. https://doi .org/10.1162/wash.2006-07.30.1.83.

Buzdalov, I. (2004). "Prirodnaia Renta kak Kategoriia Rynachnoi Ekonomiki." *Voprosy Ekonomiki*, 3. https://doi.org/10.32609/0042-8736-2004-3-24-35.

Calder, Jack. (2010). "Resource Tax Administration: Functions, Procedures and Institutions," in Philip Daniel (ed.), *The Taxation of Petroleum and Minerals – Principles, Problems and Practice*, pp. 340–77. Oxon: Routledge.

Caselli, Francesco. (2006). "Power Struggle and the Natural Resource Curse." LSE Working Paper. http://eprints.lse.ac.uk/4926 – accessed 1 December 2017.

Cerami, Alfio. (2009). "Welfare State Developments in the Russian Federation: Oil-Led Social Policy and the 'Russian Miracle.'" *Social Policy and Administration*, 43, pp. 105–20. https://doi.org/10.1111/j.1467-9515.2009.00650.x.

Chaisty, Paul. (2012). "The Federal Assembly and the Power Vertical," in Graeme Gill and James Young (eds.), *Routledge Handbook of Russian Politics and Society*, pp. 92–102. New York: Routledge.

Chaisty, Paul, and Petra Schleiter. (2002). "Productive but Not Valued: The Russian State Duma, 1994–2001." *Europe-Asia Studies*, 54/5, pp. 701–24. https://doi.org/10.1080/09668130220147010.

Cheeseman, Nic, and Blessing-Miles Tendi. (2010). "Power Sharing in Comparative Perspective: The Dynamics of Unity Government in Kenya and Zimbabwe." *Journal of Modern African Studies*, 48/2, pp. 203–29. https://doi.org/10.2307/40864715.

Cherniavksii, Andrey. (2015). "Kak Nam Potratit FNB." *Komentarii o Gosudarstvo i Biznese*, 105, 25 November–14 December, pp. 10–13. https://dcenter.hse.ru/data/2015/12/16/1134345775/KGB_105.pdf – accessed 27 July 2017.

Chevrier, Clelia. (2009). "Sovereign Wealth Funds in Russia." *Revue d'économie financière* (English ed.), Special Issue, pp. 73–81. https://www.persee.fr/docAsPDF/ecofi_1767-4603_2009_hos_9_1_5493.pdf.

Chistyakova, Galina, and Maria Tauseneva. (2014). "Social'naya Otvetsvennost' na Predpriatiakh Toplivo-Energeticheskogo Kompleksa," in V. Plenkina (ed.), *Innovatsii v Upravlenii Regional'nym i Otraslevym Razvitiem*, pp. 353–7. Tyumen: TGNU.

Colton, Timothy. (1995). "Superpresidentialism and Russia's Backward State." *Post-Soviet Affairs*, 11/2, pp. 144–8. https://doi.org/10.1080/1060586X.1995.10641399.

Colton, Timothy, and Stephen Holmes (eds.). (2006). *The State after Communism – Governance in the New Russia*. Lanham: Rowman and Littlefield Publishers.

Colton, Timothy, and Michael McFaul. (2000). "Reinventing Russia's Party of Power: 'Unity' and the 1999 Duma Elections." *Post-Soviet Affairs*, 16/3, pp. 201–24. https://doi.org/10.1080/1060586X.2000.10641486.

Connolly, Richard. (2013). "Economic Growth and Strategies for Economic Development." *Russian Analytical Digest*, 133, pp. 5–9. https://www.files.ethz.ch/isn/167341/RAD-133.pdf.

Connolly, Richard. (2018). *Russia's Response to Sanctions: How Western Economic Statecraft Is Reshaping Political Economy in Russia*. Cambridge, UK: Cambridge University Press.

Cooper, Julian. (2012). *Reviewing Russian Strategic Planning: The Emergence of Strategy 2020*. Rome: NATO Defense College. www.ndc.nato.int/download /downloads.php?icode=338 – accessed 11 Nov. 2017.

Cooper, Julian. (2017). "The Russian Budgetary Process and Defence: Finding the 'Golden Mean.'" *Post-Communist Economies*, pp. 476–90. https://doi.org/10.1080 /14631377.2017.1333793.

Coote, Bud. (2018). "Impact of Sanctions on Russia's Energy Sector." Atlantic Council Issue Brief.

Corden, Max. (1984). "Booming Sector and Dutch Disease Economics: Survey and Consolidation." *Oxford Economic Papers*, 36/3, pp. 359–80.

Cox, Garry, and Mathew McCubbins. (2001). "The Institutional Determinants of Economic Policy Outcomes," in Stephan Haggard and Mathew McCubbins (eds.), *President, Parliament and Policy*. Cambridge: Cambridge University Press.

Crotty, Jo. (2016). "Corporate Social Responsibility in the Russian Federation: A Contextualized Approach." *Business and Society*, 55/6, pp. 825–53. https://doi .org/10.1177/0007650314561965.

Dabrowska, Ewa, and Joachim Zweyner.t (2015). "Economic Ideas and Institutional Change: The Case of the Russian Stabilization Fund." *New Political Economy*, 20/4, pp. 518–44. https://doi.org/10.1080/13563467.2014.923828.

Dauderstadt, M. (2006). "Introduction," in M. Dauderstadt and A. Schildberg (eds.), "Dead Ends of Transition: Rentier Economies and Protectorates." Frankfurt am Main: Campus Verlag.

David, Jeffrey, Rolando Ossowski, James Daniel, and Steven Barnett. (2001). "Oil Funds: Problems Posing as Solutions." *Finance and Development*, 38/4, pp. 56–9. https://www.imf.org/external/pubs/ft/fandd/2001/12/davis.htm.

Desai, Padma. (2006). *Conversations on Russia: Reform from Yeltsin to Putin*. Oxford University Press.

Dittrick, Paula. (2014). "IHS: Western Sanctions Indirectly Could Hinder Russian Oil, Gas Revenues."27 *Oil and Gas Journal*, March. https://www.ogj.com/general -interest/economics-markets/article/17270258/ ihs-western-sanctions-indirectly-could-hinder-russian-oil-gas-revenues.

Dobb, M. (1973). *Theories of Value and Distribution since Adam Smith*. Cambridge: Cambridge University Press.

Dobers, Peter, and Minna Halme. (2009). "Corporate Social Responsibility and Developing Countries." *Corporate Social Responsibility and Environmental Management*, 16/2, pp. 237–49. https://doi.org/10.1002/csr.212.

Drobyshevksy, Sergey. (2011). "Russian Sovereign Wealth Funds," in *Sovereign Wealth Funds – New Challenges for the Caspian Countries*, pp. 130–58. Baku: Revenue Watch.

Drobyshevsky, S., and S. Sinelnikov-Murylev. (2012). "Makroekonomicheskie Predposylki Realizatsii Novoi Modeli Rosta." *Voprosy Ekonomiki*, 9, pp. 4–24. https://doi.org/10.32609/0042-8736-2012-9-4-24.

Easter, Gerald. (2006). "Building Fiscal Capacity," in Timothy Colton and Stephen Holmes (eds.), *The State after Communism: Governance in the New Russia*. Lanham: Rowman and Littlefield Publishers.

Eaton, Kent. (2000). "Review: Parliamentarism vs. Presidentialism in the Policy Arena." *Comparative Politics*, 32/3, pp. 355–76. https://doi.org/10.2307/422371.

"Ekonomicheksaia Politika Federal'nogo Tsentra." *CCPR – Russian Economic Policy*, 1 April 2001.

"Ekonomicheskaia Politika Federal'nogo Tsentra." *CCPR – Russian Economic Policy*, 2 September 2001.

"Ekonomicheskaia Politika Federal'nogo Tsentra." *CCPR – Russian Economic Policy*, 24 February 2003.

Fish, Steven. (2005). *Democracy Derailed in Russia: The Failure of Open Politics*. New York: Cambridge University Press.

Figes, Orlando. (1996). *A People's Tragedy: The Russian Revolution 1891–1924*. New York: Penguin Books.

Fjaertoft, Daniel, and Lars Lunden. (2015). "Russian Petroleum Tax Policy – Continuous Manoeuvring in Rocky Waters." *Energy Policy*, 87, pp. 553–61. https://doi.org/10.1016/j.enpol.2015.09.042.

Fortescue, Stephen. (2007). *Russia's Oil Barons and Metal Magnates: Oligarchs and the State in Transition*. Houndmills: Palgrave Macmillan.

Fortescue, Stephen (2010). "Russia's SWFs: Controlled by a Domestic Agenda," in Xu Yi-chong and Gawdat Bahgat (eds.), *The Political Economy of Sovereign Wealth Funds*, 113–31. New York: Palgrave Macmillan.

Fortescue, Stephen. (2017a). "Russian Federal Budget Formation: Introduction." *Post-Communist Economies*, 29/4, pp. 449–56. https://doi.org/10.1080/14631377.2017.1333795.

Fortescue, Stephen. (2017b). "The Role of the Executive in Russian Budget Formation." *Post-Communist Economies*, 29/4, pp. 523–37. https://doi.org/10.1080/14631377.2017.1333790.

Frantz, Erica, and Natasha Ezrow. (2011). *The Politics of Dictatorship: Institutions and Outcomes in Authoritarian Regimes*. Boulder CO: Lynne Rienner.

Franzese, Robert. (2002) *Macroeconomic Policies of Developed Democracies*. Cambridge: Cambridge University Press.

Freedom in the World Reports. http://freedomhouse.org/report/freedom-world/2016/russia – accessed 1 Sept. 2018.

Frynas, Jedrzej. (2009). *Beyond Corporate Social Responsibility: Oil Multinationals and Social Challenges*. Cambridge: Cambridge University Press.

Fukuyama, Francis. (2004). "The Imperative of State Building. *Journal of Democracy*, 15/2, April, pp. 17–31.10.1353/jod.2004.0026.

Gaddy, Clifford. (2004). "Perspectives on the Potential of Russian Oil." *Eurasian Geography and Economics*, 45/5, pp. 346–51. https://doi.org/10.2747/1538-7216.45.5.346.

Gaddy, Clifford, and Barry Ickes. (2002). *Russia's Virtual Economy*. Washington DC: Brookings Institution Press.

Gaddy, Clifford, and Barry Ickes. (2005). "Resource Rents and the Russian Federation." *Eurasian Geography and Economics*, 46/8, pp. 559–83. https://doi.org /10.2747/1538-7216.46.8.559.

Gaddy, Clifford, and Barry Ickes. (2010). Russia after the Global Financial Crisis." *Eurasian Geography and Economics*, 51/3, pp. 281–311. https://doi.org/10.2747 /1539-7216.51.3.281.

Gaidar, Yegor. (2007a). "The Soviet Collapse: Grain and Oil." *AEI On the Issue*, April. www.aei.org/wp-content/uploads/2011/10/20070419_Gaidar.pdf – accessed 1 Sept. 2018.

Gandhi, Jennifer. (2008). *Political Institutions under Dictatorship*. New York: Cambridge University Press.

Ganghof, Steffen. (2003). "Promises and Pitfalls of Veto Player Analysis." *Swiss Political Science Review*, 9/2, pp. 1–25. https://doi.org/10.1002/j.1662-6370.2003.tb00411.x.

Gel'man, Vladimir, and Andrey Starodubtsev. (2016). "Opportunities and Constraints of Authoritarian Modernisation: Russian Policy Reforms in the 2000s." *Europe-Asia Studies*, 68/1, pp. 97–117. https://doi.org/10.1080/09668136 .2015.1113232.

Glazev, S., and G. Fetisov. (2014). "On a Strategy for a Steady Development of the Russian Federation." *Problems of Economic Transition*, 56/12, pp. 63–76.

Goldman, Marshall. (2004). "Putin and the Oligarchs." *Foreign Affairs*, Nov.–Dec., pp. 33–44. https://doi.org/10.2307/20034135.

Goldman, Marshall. (2008). *Petrostate: Putin, Power and the New Russia*. New York: Oxford University Press.

Goldsworthy, Brenton, and Daria Zakharova. (2010). "Evaluation of the Oil Fiscal Regime in Russia and Proposal for Reform." IMF Working Paper, 10/33.

Golosov, Grigorii. (2011). "Regional Roots of Electoral Authoritarianism in Russia." *Europe-Asia Studies*, 63/4, pp. 623–39. https://doi.org/10.1080/09668136.2011 .566427.

Golyashev, Alexander. (2015). "Sotsial'naia Otvetsvennost Nefetgazovogo Biznesa: Peredovye Pozitsii v Rossii." *Energeticheskii Biulleten*, 30, Nov. 2015. https://ac.gov .ru/archive/files/publication/a/7047.pdf.

"Gossudarstvennoe Regulirovanie Rossiiskogo Nefetgazovogo Kompleksa: Itogi 2003 Goda, Perspektivy na 2004." *Center for Current Politics in Russia – Analytical Reports*, 18 January 2004.

Gurvich, E., E. Vakulenko, and P. Krivenko. (2009). "Tsiklicheskie Svoistva Biudzhetnoi Politiki v Neftedobyvaiushchikh stranakh." *Voprosy Ekonomiki*, 2, pp. 51–70. https://doi.org/10.32609/0042-8736-2009-2-51-70.

Gurvich, Evsey. (2004). "Makroekonomicheskaia Otsenka Roli Rossiiskogo Neftegazovogo Kompleksa." *Voprosy Ekonomiki*, 10, pp. 4–31. https://doi.org/10 .32609/0042-8736-2004-10-4-31.

Gurvich, Evsey. (2006). "Naskol'ko Tochnye Makroekonomicheskie i Biudzhetnye Prognozy." *Voprosy Ekonomiki*, 9. https://doi.org/10.32609/0042-8736-2006 -9-4-20.

Gurvich, Evsey. (2012). "A New Step in Russia's Budget Policy." *Russian Analytical Digest*, 121, pp. 5–7. https://www.files.ethz.ch/isn/157225/Russian_Analytical _Digest_121.pdf.

Gurvich, Evsey. (2016). Evolyutsia Rossiiskoi Makroekonomicheskoi Politiki ve Trekh Krizisakh. *Zhurnal NEA*, 29/1, pp. 174–81. http://www.eeg.ru/files/lib/2016 /NEA-29.pdf.

Gustafson, Thane. (1989). *Crisis amid Plenty: The Politics of Soviet Energy under Brezhnev and Gorbachev*. Princeton: Princeton University Press.

Gustafson, Thane. (2012). *The Wheel of Fortune: The Battle for Oil and Power in Russia*." Cambridge, MA: Harvard University Press.

Hagen, J., and I. Harden. (1995). "Budget Processes and Commitment to Fiscal Discipline." *European Economic Review*, 39, pp. 771–9. https://doi.org/10.1016 /0014-2921(94)00084-D.

Hale, Henry. (2005). "Regime Cycles: Democracy, Autocracy and Revolution in Post-Soviet Eurasia." *World Politics*, 58/1, pp. 133–65. https://doi.org/10.2307/40060127.

Hale, Henry. (2015). *Patronal Politics: Eurasian Regime Dynamics in Comparative Perspective*. New York: Cambridge University Press.

Hallerberg, Mark, and Scott Basinger. (1998). "Internationalization and Changes in Tax Policy in OECD Countries: The Importance of Domestic Veto Players." *Comparative Political Studies*, 31/3, pp. 321–52. https://doi.org/10.1177/00104140 98031003003.

Hanson, Philip. (2009). "The Resistible Rise of State Control in the Russian Oil Industry." *Eurasian Geography and Economics*, 50/1, pp. 14–27. https://doi.org /10.2747/1539-7216.50.1.14.

Hanson, Philip, and Elizabeth Teague. (2013). *Liberal Insiders and Economic Reform in Russia*. London: Chatham House.

Haspel, Moshe, Thomas Remington, and Steven Smith. (2006). "Lawmaking and Decree Making in the Russian Federation: Time, Space, and Rules in Russian National Policymaking." *Post-Soviet Affairs*, 22/3, pp. 249–75. https://doi.org /10.2747/1060-586X.22.3.249.

Hedlund, Stefan. (2000). "Path Dependence in Russian Policy-making: Constraints on Putin's Economic Choice." *Post-Communist Economies*. 12/4, pp. 389–406. https://doi.org/10.1080/14631370050216470.

Heinrich, Andreas. (2005). "Why Corporate Governance in the Russian Oil and Gas Industry Is Improving." *Corporate Governance: The International Journal of Business in Society*, 5/4, pp. 3–9. https://doi.org/10.1108/14720700510616550.

Henisz, Witold. (2000). "The Institutional Environment for Economic Growth." *Economics and Politics*, 12/1, pp. 1–31. https://doi.org/10.1111/1468-0343.00066.

Henry, Laura, Soili Nysten-Haarala, Svetlana Tulaeva, and Maria Tysachniouk. (2016). "Corporate Social Responsibility and the Oil Industry in the Russian Arctic: Global Norms and Neo-Paternalism." *Europe-Asia Studies*, 68/8, pp. 1340–68. https://doi.org/10.1080/09668136.2016.1233523.

Hill, Fiona, and Florence Fee. (2002). "Fueling the Future: The Prospects for Russian Oil and Gas," *Demokratizatsia*, pp. 462–87. https://demokratizatsiya.pub /archives/10-4_HillFee.PDF.

Holmes, Stephen. (1993). "Superpresidentialism and Its Problems." *East European Constitutional Review*, 3, Fall/Winter, pp. 123–6. https://www.ucis.pitt.edu /nceeer/1994-808-05-2-Holmes.pdf.

Huskey, Eugene. (1999). *Presidential Power in Russia*. New York: M.E. Sharpe.

Huskey, Eugene. (2001). "Overcoming the Yeltsin Legacy: Vladimir Putin and Russian Political Reform," in Archie Brown (ed.), *Contemporary Russian Politics: A Reader*. Oxford: Oxford University Press.

Hyde, Matthew. (2001). Putin's Federal Reforms and Their Implciations for Presidential Power in Russia." *Europe-Asia Studies*, 53/5, pp. 719–43. https://doi .org/10.1080/09668130120060242.

Illarionov, A,. and N. Pivovarova. (2002). "Razmery Gosudarstvo i Ekonomicheskii Rost." *Voprosy Ekonomiki*, 9, pp. 18–45. http://www.iea.ru/article/publ/vopr/2002_9.pdf.

Ispolnenie Federal'nogo Biudsheta i Biudzhetov Biudzhetnoy Sistemy Rossiiskoy Federatsii v 2012 Godu. Moscow: Ministry of Finance, 2013.

Jakobson, Lev. (2017). "Russian Experts: Missing Actors of the Budget Process." *Post-Communist Economies*, 29/4, pp. 491–504. https://doi.org/10.1080/14631377 .2017.1333792.

Karl, Terry Lynn. (1997). *The Paradox of Plenty: Oil Booms and Petro-States*. Berkeley: University of California Press.

Kauffman, Daniel, Aart Kraay, and Massimo Mastruzz.i (2007). "Governance Matters VI: Governance Indicators for 1996–2006." World Bank Policy Research Paper 4280.

Kelman, Ilan, Julia Loe, Elana Rowe, Emma Wilson, Nina Poussenkova, Elena Nikitina, and Daniel Fjaertoft. (2016). "Local Perceptions of CSR for Arctic Petroleum in the Barents Region." *Arctic Review on Law and Politics*, 7/2, pp. 152–78. https://doi.org/10.17585/arctic.v7.418.

Khmelnitskaya, Marina. (2017). "The Social Budget Policy Process in Russia at a Time of Crisis." *Post-Communist Economies*, pp. 457–75. https://doi.org/10.1080 /14631377.2017.1333794.

Knight, Amy. (2000). "The Enduring Legacy of the KGB in Russian Politics." *Problems of Post-Communism*, 47/4, pp. 3–15. https://doi.org/10.1080/10758216 .2000.11655889.

Knobel, A., and I. Sokolov. (2012). "Otsenka Biudzhentoi Politiki RF na Srednosrochnuyu Perspektivu." *Ekonomicheskoe Razvitie Rossii*, 12, pp. 23–32.

https://www.iep.ru/files/persona/knobel/Ocenka_bjudzhetnoj%20_politik_RF
_na_srednesrochnuju_perspektivu.pdf.

Korostikov, Mikhail. (2015). "Leaving to Come Back: Russian Senior Officials and State-Owned Companies." *Russia.Nei.Visions*, 87, August.

Korppoo, Anna. (2016). "Who Is Driving Russian Climate Policy? Applying and Adjusting Veto Players Theory to a Non-Democracy." *International Environmental Agreements*, 16, pp. 639–53. https://doi.org/10.1007/s10784-015-9286-5.

Krasner, Stephen. (1978). *Defending the National Interest: Raw Material Investment and US Foreign Policy*. Princeton: Princeton University Press.

Kryshtanovskaya, Olga, and Stephen White. (2003). "Putin's Militocracy." *Post-Soviet Affairs*, 19/4, Oct.–Dec., pp. 289–306. https://doi.org/10.2747/1060-586X.19.4.289.

Kryukov Veleriy, and Arild Moe. (2016). "Oil Industry Structure and Developments in the Resource Base: Increasing Contradictions," in Jaub Godzimirski (ed.), *Russian Energy in a Changing World*, 35–55. New York: Routledge.

"Kto i Kak Delit Rossiiskii TEK?" *Center for Current Politics in Russia – Analytical Reports*, 11 July 2005.

Kudrin, Alexei. (2007). "Stabilization Funds: International and Russian Experience." *Problems of Economic Transition*, 50/1, May, pp. 6–26. https://doi.org/10.2753/PET1061-1991500101.

Kudrin, Alexei. (2013). "Vliyanie Dokhodov na Exporta Neftegazovykh Resurosov na Denezhno-Kreditnuiu Politiku Rossii." *Voprosy Ekonomiki*, 3, pp. 4–19. https://doi.org/10.32609/0042-8736-2013-3-4-19.

Kudrin, Alexei, and Evsey Gurvich. (2015). "A New Growth Model for the Russian Economy." BOFIT Policy Paper 1.

Kurtz, Heinz, and Neri Salvadori. (2001). "Classical Economics and the Problem of Exhaustible Resources." *Metroeconomica*, 52/3, pp. 282–96. https://doi.org/10.1111/1467-999X.00120.

Kusznir, Julia. (2007). "Economic Actors in Russian Regional Politics: The Example of the Oil Industry," in Graeme Gill (ed.), *Politics in the Russian Regions*. Houndmills: Palgrave Macmillan.

Lane, David. (1999). *The Political Economy of Russian Oil*. Lanham: Rowman and Littlefield Publishers.

Lebedinskaya, Elena. (2012). "Rol Nefetgazovykh Fondov v Rossii." *Voprosy Ekonomiki*, 3, pp. 98–119. https://doi.org/10.32609/0042-8736-2012-3-98-119.

Ledeneva, Alena. (2006). *How Russia Really Works*. Ithaca, NY: Cornell University Press.

Ledeneva, Alena. (2013). *Can Russia Modernise? Sistema, Power Networks and Informal Governance*. Cambridge, UK: Cambridge University Press.

LeVan, Carl. (2015). *Dictators and Democracy in African Development: The Political Economy of Good Governance in Nigeria*. New York: Cambridge University Press.

Lijphart, Arendt, ed. (1992). *Parliamentary vs. Presidential Government*. New York: Oxford University Press.

Lockman, Conway. (1976). "The Classical Base of Modern Rent Theory." *The American Journal of Economics and Sociology*, 35/3. https://doi.org/10.1111/j.1536 -7150.1976.tb03013.x.

Lowry, Anna. (2014). "Between Neopatrimonalism and Developmentalism: Exploring the Causes of Nationalization in Russia." Doctoral dissertation, Indiana University.

Luciani, Giacomo. (1987). "Allocation vs. Production States: A Theoretical Framework," in Hazem Beblawi and Giacomo Lucinia (eds.), *The Rentier State*. London: Croom Helm.

Lunden, Lars. (2014). "Rossiiskaya Nalogovaya i Litsenzionnaya Politika v Otnoshenii Shelfovykh Proektov." *EKO Vserosiiskii Ekonomicheskii Zhurnal*, 3, pp. 30–55. https://publications.hse.ru/mirror/pubs/share/folder/vpr37s9t4w /direct/119978144.

Luong, Pauline Jones, and Erika Weinthal. (2004). "Contra Coercion: Russian Tax Reform, Exogenous Shocks, and Negotiated Institutional Change." *American Political Science Review*, 98/1, pp. 139–52. https://www.jstor.org/stable/4145302.

Luong, Pauline Jones, and Erika Weinthal. (2006). "Rethinking the Resource Curse: Ownership Structure, Institutional Capacity and Domestic Constraints." *Annual Review of Political Science*, pp. 241–63. https://doi.org/10.1146/annurev.polisci .9.062404.170436.

Lynch, Allen. (2005). *How Russia Is Not Ruled – Reflections on Russian Political Development*. Cambridge, MA: Cambridge University Press.

MacIntyre, Andrew. (2001). "Institutions and Institutions and Investors: The Politics of the Financial Crisis in Southeast Asia." *International Organization*, 55/1, pp. 81–122. https://www.jstor.org/stable/3078598.

Mahdavy, H. (1970). "The Patterns and Problems of Economic Development in Rentier States: The Case of Iran," in M. Cook (ed.), *Studies in the Economic History of the Middle East*. London: Oxford University Press.

Maleva, O., and N. Dubrovina. (2005). "Dobrovol'naya Pomoshch Ili Obiazatel'naya Blagotvoritel'nost." *Ekonomika i Zhizn*, Dec. 9.

Martyn, L., and G. Vanberg. (2011). *Parliaments and Coalitions: The Role of Legislative Institutions in Multiparty Governance*. Oxford: Oxford University Press.

Maslovskiy, Mikhail. (2013). "Social and Cultural Obstacles of Russian Modernisation." *Europe-Asia Studies*, 65/10, pp. 2014–22. https://doi.org/10.1080 /09668136.2013.848657.

Mau, Vladimir. (2016). "Anti-Crisis Measures or Structural Reforms: Russian Economic Policy in 2015." *Russian Journal of Economics*, 2/1, March, pp. 1–22. https://doi.org/10.1016/j.ruje.2016.04.001.

Mau, Vladimir, and Yaroslav Kuzminov. (2013). *Strategia 2020: Novaya Model' Rosta – Novaya Sotsial'naya Politika*. Moscow: Delo.

Mauro, Paolo, Rafael Romeu, Ariel Binder, and Asad Zaman. (2013). "A Modern History of Fiscal Prudence and Profligacy." IMF Working Paper.

Mazalov, Ivan, and Polina Bolshakova. (2000). "Oil Sector Report." *Troika Dialogue Research* (Moscow), March.

McFaul, Michael. (1995). "State Power, Institutional Change, and the Politics of Privatization in Russia." *World Politics*, pp. 210–43. https://www.jstor.org /stable/2950651.

McFaul, Michael. (1999). "Authoritarian and Democratic Reponses to the Financial Meltdown in Russia." *Problems of Post-Communism*, July/Aug., pp. 22–32. https:// doi.org/10.1080/10758216.1999.11655842.

McFaul, Michael. (2000). "Russian Democracy: Still Not a Lost Cause." *Washington Quarterly*, 23/1, pp. 161–72. https://doi.org/10.1162/016366000560629.

McFaul, Michael, and Nikolai Petrov. (2004). "Russian Democracy in Eclipse – What the Elections Tell Us." *Journal of Demcoracy*, 15/3, July, pp. 20–31.

"The Mechanism of Lobbying Oil and Gas Companies' Interests at the Federal Level." *Center for Current Politics in Russia – Analytical Reports*, 30 June 2004.

Metke, Jorg. (2007). "The Rise and Fall of the Drunken Czar." *Spiegel International*, 24 April. www.spiegel.de/international/world/0,1518,479096-2,00.html – accessed 6 Feb. 2008.

Migdal, Joel, Atul Kohli, and Vivienne Shue, eds. (2004). *State Power and Social Forces – Domination and Transformation in the Third World*. Cambridge: Cambridge University Press.

"Neftegazovy Kompleks v Rossiiskoi Politike: Itogi 2000 i Perspektivy 2001 Goda." *Center for Current Politics in Russia – Analytical Reports*, 1 February 2001.

Nekhoda, E., Y. Kolbysheva, and V. Makoveeva. (2015). "Corporate Social Policy – Problems of Institutionalization and Experience of Russian Oil and Gas Companies." *IOP Conference Series: Earth and Environmental Science*, 27, pp. 1–6.

Nikolaev, Igor. (2003). "Prirodnaia Renta: Tsena Vorposa (na Primyere Neftianoi Otrasli)," *Obshchestvo i Ekonomika*, 12. https://www.fbk.ru/upload/images/renta _final.pdf.

Noble, Ben. (2017). "Amending Budget Bills in the Russian State Duma." *Post-Communist Economies*, 29/4, pp. 505–22. https://doi.org/10.1080/14631377.2017 .1333791.

Nordlinger, Eric. (1981). *On the Autonomy of the Democratic State*. Cambridge, MA: Harvard University Press.

North, Douglas, Joseph Wallis, Steven Webb, and Barry Weingast. (2007). "Limited Access Orders in the Developing World: A New Approach to the Problem of Development." World Bank Policy Research Paper.

Novaia Struktura Rossiiskogo Neftianogo Sektora: Nekatorye Itogi. Institute of Energy Policy, Moscow, July 2004.

"Oil and Gas Industries as a Field for Elite Groups' Fighting." *Center for Current Politics in Russia – Analytical Reports*, 20 April 2004.

"Oil and Gas Quarterly: Odd One Out." *Russia Oil and Gas*, Moscow: Troika Dialog, July 2009.

Oil and Gas Yearbook 2011. Otrkitie Kapital, Moscow, 21 July 2011.

"Old Habits Die Hard in Russia." *Transition*, October–November–December 2002, pp. 33–44. (Published by the World Bank.)

Orlov, Viktor, and Yulia Nemeriuk. (2001). "Renta v Novoi Sisteme Nalogooblazheniia," *Ekonomika i Upravlenie*, 3, pp. 34–41.

Orttung, Robert, and Peter Reddaway (eds). (2004). *Dynamics of Russian Politics: Putin's Reform of Federal-Regional Relations*, Lanham: Rowman and Littlefield.

Parrish, Scott. (1998). "Presidential Decree Authority in Russia, 1991–1995," in J. Carey and M. Shugart (eds.), *Executive Decree Authority*, 62–102. Cambridge, UK: Cambridge University Press.

Pavlov, Georgii, Khun Skhors, and Peter Westin. (2000). "Ekonomicheskie Programmy i Ekonomicheskaia Politika: Kuda Poidet Rossia?" *Russian Economic Trends Monthly*, January.

"Peredel Sobstvennosti v Rossiiskom Nefetgazovom Komplekse." *Center for Current Politics in Russia – Analytical Reports*, 3 May 2003.

Pis'mennaya, Evgenia. (2013). *Sistema Kudrina: Istoria Klyuchevogo Ekonomista Putinskoy Rossii*. Moscow: Mann Ivanov & Ferber.

Popova, Tatiana, and Merja Tekoniemi. (1998). "Challenges to Reforming Russia's Tax System." *Review of Economies in Transition*, 1, pp. 13–30. http://urn.fi/URN: NBN:fi:bof-201408113022.

Poussenkova, Nina. (2006). "Rosneft as a Mirror of Russia's Evolution." *Pro Et Contra*, 10/2–3. https://carnegieendowment.org/files/Rosneft.pdf.

Poussenkova, Nina, and Elena Nikitina. (2016). "Petroleum CSR in Russia: Affordable Luxury or Basic Necessity." *Russian Analytical Digest*, 181, pp. 3–7. https://ethz.ch/content/dam/ethz/special-interest/gess/cis/center-for-securities -studies/pdfs/RAD181.pdf.

Putin, V.V. (1999). "Mineral'no-Syrevye Resursy v Strategii Razvitiia Rossiiskoi Ekonomiki." *Zapiski Gornogo Instituta*, 144, pp. 3–9.

Radygin, Alexander. (2004). "Rossia v 2000–2004 Godakh: Na Puti k Gosudarstvennomu Kapitalizmu." *Voprosy Ekonomiki*, 4, pp. 42–65. https://doi .org/10.32609/0042-8736-2004-4-42-65.

Reddaway, Peter. (2001). "Will Putin Be Able to Consolidate Power? *Post-Soviet Affairs*, 17/1, pp. 23–44. https://doi.org/10.1080/1060586X.2001.10641493.

"Redistribution of Property in Oil and Gas Sector: Charting a New Russian 'Oil and Gas Map.'" *Center for Current Politics in Russia – Analytical Reports*, 18 January 2005.

Remington, Thomas. (2000). "The Evolution of Executive-Legislative Relations in Russia since 1993." *Slavic Review*, 59/3, Fall, pp. 499–520. https://www.jstor.org /stable/2697343.

Remington, Thomas. (2001). "Putin and the Duma." *Post-Soviet Affairs*, 17/4, pp. 285–308. https://doi.org/10.1080/1060586X.2001.10641505.

Remington, Thomas. (2002). "Democratization and the Problem of Governance." Paper presented at Miami University, 7–8 April 2002. http://citeseerx.ist.psu.edu /viewdoc/download?doi=10.1.1.522.4405&rep=rep1&type=pdf – accessed on 1 March 2018.

Remington, Thomas. (2003). "Majorities without Mandates: The Russian Federation Council since 2000." *Europe-Asia Studies*, 55/5, pp. 667–91. https://doi.org/10.1080/0966813032000086828.

Remington, Thomas. (2004). "Putin, the Duma and Political Parties," in Dale Herspring (ed.), *Putin's Russia: Past Imperfect, Future Uncertain*, Rowman and Littlefield Publishers.

Remington, Thomas. (2005). "Parliamentary Politics in Russia," in Stephen White, Zvi Gitelman, and Richard Sakwa (eds.), *Developments in Russian Politics*. Durham: Duke University Press.

Remington, Thomas. (2006). "Democratization, Separation of Powers, and State Capacity," in Timothy Colton and Stephen Holmes (eds.), *The State after Communism – Governance in the New Russia*, Lanham: Rowman and Littlefield Publishers.

Remington, Thomas. (2014). *Presidential Decrees in Russia: A Comparative Perspective*. New York: Cambridge University Press.

Remington, Thomas, and Steven Smith. (1996). "The Early Legislative Process in the Russian Federal Assembly." *Journal of Legislative Studies*, 2/1, pp. 161–92. https://doi.org/10.1080/13572339608420463.

Remington, Thomas, Steven Smith, and Moshe Haspel. (1998). "Decrees, Laws and Inter-Branch Relations in the Russian Federation." *Post-Soviet Affairs*, 14/4, pp. 287–322. https://doi.org/10.1080/1060586X.1998.10641455.

Reuter, Ora John, and Graeme Robertson. (2009). "Legislation, Cooptation and Social Protests in Contemporary Authoritarian Regimes." *Journal of Politics*, 77/1, pp. 235–48. http://dx.doi.org/10.1086/678390.

Rivera, Sharon Werning, and David Rivera. (2006). "The Russian Elite under Putin: Militocratic or Bourgeois?" *Post-Soviet Affairs*, 22/2, pp. 125–44. https://doi.org/10.2747/1060-586X.22.2.125.

Robinson, James, Ragnar Torvik, and Thierry Verdier. (2006). "Political Foundations of the Resource Curse." *Journal of Development Economics*, 79, pp. 447–68. https://doi.org/10.1016/j.jdeveco.2006.01.008.

Rogers, Douglas. (2012). "The Materiality of the Corporation: Oil, Gas and Corporate Social Technologies in the Remaking of a Russian Region." *American Ethnologist*, 39/2, pp. 284–96. https://doi.org/10.1111/j.1548-1425.2012.01364.x.

Rogers, Douglas. (2015). *The Depths of Russia: Oil, Power and Culture after Socialism*. Ithaca: Cornell University Press.

Ross, Michael. (1999). "The Political Economy of the Resource Curse." *World Politics*, 51/2, pp. 297–322. https://www.jstor.org/stable/25054077.

Ross, Michael. (2001). "Does Oil Hinder Democracy." *World Politics*, 53/3, pp. 325–61. https://www.jstor.org/stable/25054153.

Ruschemeyer, Dietrich. and Peter Evans (1985). "The State and Economic Transformation: Toward an Analysis of the Conditions Underlying Effective Intervention," in Peter Evans, Dietrich Ruschemeyer, and Theda Skocpol (eds.), *Bringing the State Back In*. New York: Cambridge University Press.

Russia Energy Survey 2002. Paris: International Energy Agency, 2002.

"Russia: Mission Concluding Statement on the 2008 Article IV Consultation." Washington, DC: IMF, 9 June 2008. www.imf.org/en/News/Articles/2015/09 /28/04/52/mcs060108 – accessed 12 February 2018.

Russian Economic Report – 12. Moscow: World Bank, April 2006.

Russian Economic Report – 14. Washington DC: World Bank, June 2007.

Russian Economic Report – 15. Washington DC: World Bank, November 2007.

Russian Economic Report – 16, Washington DC: World Bank, June 2008.

Russian Economic Report – 17. Moscow: World Bank, 2008.

Russian Economic Report – 18. Moscow: World Bank, March 2009.

Russian Economic Report – 19. Moscow: World Bank, June 2009.

Russian Economic Report – 22. Moscow: World Bank, June 2010.

Russian Economic Report – 23. Moscow: World Bank, November 2010,

Russian Economic Report – 26. Moscow: World Bank, September 2011.

Russian Economic Report – 27. Moscow: e World Bank, April 2012.

Russian Economic Report – 28. Moscow: World Bank, Autumn 2012.

Russia Economic Report – 32. Moscow: World Bank, September 2014.

Russia Economic Report – 33. Moscow: World Bank, April 2015.

Russia Economic Report – 35. Moscow: World Bank, April 2016.

Russia Economic Report – 36. Moscow: World Bank, November 2016.

Russia Economic Report – 37. Moscow: World Bank, May 2017.

"Russian Federation – Concluding Statement for the 2010 Article IV Consultation." Washington, DC: International Monetary Fund, 28 June 2010.

"Russian Federation: 2005 Article IV Consultation Staff Report." *IMF Country Report*. Washington, DC: International Monetary Fund, October 2005.

"Russian Federation: 2006 Article IV Consultation Staff Report." *IMF Country Report*. Washington, DC: International Monetary Fund, December 2006.

"Russian Federation: 2008 Article IV Consultation Staff Report." *IMF Country Report*. Washington, DC: International Monetary Fund, September 2008.

"Russian Federation: 2009 Article IV Consultation Staff Report." *IMF Country Report*. Washington, DC: International Monetary Fund, August 2009.

"Russian Federation: 2010 Article IV Consultation Staff Report." *IMF Country Report*. Washington, DC: International Monetary Fund, July 2010.

"Russian Federation: 2011 Article IV Consultation Staff Report." *IMF Country Report*. Washington, DC: International Monetary Fund, September 2011.

"Russian Federation: 2013 Article IV Consultation Staff Report." *IMF Country Report*. Washington, DC: International Monetary Fund, October 2013.

"Russian Federation: 2014 Article IV Consultation Staff Report." *IMF Country Report*. Washington, DC: International Monetary Fund, July 2014.

"Russian Federation: 2019 Article IV Consultation Staff Report." *IMF Country Report*. Washington, DC: International Monetary Fund, August 2019.

"Russian Federation – Selected Issues." *IMF Country Report*, 5/379, October 2005, pp. 49–61.

"Russian Federation: Selected Issues." *IMF Country Report*, Washington, DC: International Monetary Fund, October 2015.

"Russian Federation: Selected Issues." *IMF Country Report*, Washington, DC: International Monetary Fund, July 2017.

Russian Federation Systemic Country Diagnosis: Pathways to Inclusive Growth. Washington, DC: World Bank, 2016.

"Russian Oil and Gas: If Unborn Wells Could Talk." *Russia Oil and Gas.* Moscow: Troika Dialog, October 2010.

"Russian Oil and Gas: The Anglo-Saxon Age of Gas." *Russia Oil and Gas.* Moscow: Sberbank Investment Research, August 2014.

"Russian Oil and Gas: Till Debt Do Us Part." *Russia Oil and Gas.* Moscow: Troika Dialog, April 2012.

"Russian Oil and Gas: Too Big to Fail." *Russia Fixed Income.* Moscow: Sberbank Investment Research, May 2014.

"Russian Oil and Gas: Two Weddings and a Funeral." *Russia Oil and Gas.* Moscow: Sberbank Investment Research, February 2014.

Russiiskaia Ekonomika v 2006 godu – Tendencii i Pespektivy, 27. Institute for the Economy in Transition, Moscow, March 2007.

Rutland, Peter. (2000). "Putin's Path to Power." *Post-Soviet Affairs*, 16/4, pp. 313–54. https://doi.org/10.1080/1060586X.2000.10641490.

Sachs, Jeffrey, and Andrew Warner. (1995). "Natural Resource Abundance and Economic Growth." NBER Working Paper 5398.

Sagers, Matthew, Valeriy Kryukov, and Vladimir Shmat. (1995). "Resource Rents from the Oil and Gas Sector in the Russian Economy." *Post-Soviet Geography*, 36/7, pp. 401–10. https://doi.org/10.1080/10605851.1995.10640999.

Sagers, Matthew, and Adnan Vatansever. (2002). "Russian Oil Companies Expanding into Eastern Europe's Downstream Oil Business: Strategy or Merely Opportunity." CERA Private Report. Cambridge, MA: Cambridge Energy Research Associates.

Sakwa, Richard. (2008). "Putin's Leadership: Character and Consequences." *Europe Asia Studies*, 60/6, pp. 879–97. https://doi.org/10.1080/09668130802161132.

Sakwa, Richard. (2014). *Putin and the Oligarch: The Khodorkovsky-Yukos Affair.* New York: I.B. Tauris & Co.

Samoylenko, Vladimir. (2004). "Government Policies for Internal Tax Havens in Russia." *Tax Notes International*, 5 April, pp. 84–5.

Samuels, David, and Scott Mainwaring. (2004). "Strong Federalism in Brazil," in Edward Gibson (ed.), *Federalism and Democracy in Latin America*, 85–130. Baltimore: Johns Hopkins University Press.

Schumpeter, Joseph. (1954). *History of Economic Analysis.* New York: Oxford University Press.

Shafer, Michael. (1994). *Winners and Losers: How Sectors Shape the Development Prospects of States.* London: Cornell University Press.

Shevchenko, Yulia. (2004). *The Central Government of Russia: From Gorbachev to Putin*. Ashgate Press.

Shugart, Matthew. (1996). "Executive-Legislative Relations in Post-Communist Russia." *Transition*, 13, pp. 6–11.

Shugart, Matthew, and Carey, John. (1992). *President and Assemblies: Constitutional Design and Electoral Dynamics*. New York: Cambridge University Press.

Sim, Li-Chen. (2008). *The Rise and Fall of Privatization in the Russian Oil Industry*. New York: Palgrave Macmillan.

Simachev, I., M. Kuzik, and D. Ivanov. (2012). "Rossiiskie Finansovye Instituty Razvitiia: ernoi Dorogoi?" *Voprosy Ekonomiki*, 7, pp. 4–29. https://doi.org /10.32609/0042-8736-2012-7-4-29.

Sinitsina, Irina. (2009). "Experience in Implementing Social Benefits Monetization Reform in Russia." *CASE Network Studies and Analysis*, July, 381. www.case -research.eu/files/?id_plik=2173 – accessed 18 February 2018.

Skocpol, Theda. (1985). "Bringing the State Back In: Strategies of Analysis in Current Research," in Peter Evans, Dietrich Ruschemeyer, and Theda Skocpol (eds.), *Bringing the State Back In*, 3–40. New York: Cambridge University Press.

Smith, Regina. (2002). "Building State Capacity from the Inside Out: Parties of Power and the Success of the President's Reform Agenda in Russia." *Politics and Society*, 30/4, December, pp. 555–78. https://doi.org/10.1177/003232902237826.

Soderlund, Peter. (2006). *The Dynamics of Federalism in Russia*. Biskopsgatan, Finland: Abo Akademi University Press.

Sokolowski, Alexander. (2001). "Bankrupt Government: Intra-Executive Relations and the Politics of Budgetary Irresponsibility in Eltsin's Russia." *Europe-Asia Studies*, 53/4, pp. 541–72. https://doi.org/10.1080/09668130120052881.

Sokolowski, Alexander. (2003). "Institutional Determinants of Chronic Policy Failure in Yeltsin's Russia." *Demokratizatsiya*, 11/3, Summer, pp. 412–39. https:// demokratizatsiya.pub/archives/11-3_Sokolowski.PDF.

"Stabilizatsionny Fond: Kuda Potratit' Deng'gi?" *Center for Current Politics in Russia – Russian Economy*, 27 June 2004. (Center for Current Politics in Russia's newsletter, accessed via www.securities.com 25 July 2006.)

"State Regulation of the Oil and Gas Complex – the 2002 Results." *Center for Current Politics in Russia – Analytical Reports*, 20 December 2002.

Steedman, Ian. (1982) "Marx on Ricardo," in Ian Bradley and Michael Howard (eds.), *Classical and Marxian Political Economy*. London: Macmilla, pp. 115–56.

Stegen, Karen. (2011). "Deconstructing the 'Energy Weapon': Russia's Threat to Europe as a Case Study." *Energy Policy*, 39, pp. 6505–13. https://doi.org/10.1016 /j.enpol.2011.07.051.

Stepan, Alfred. (2004). "Electorally Generated Veto Players in Unitary and Federal Systems," in Edward Gibson (ed.), *Federalism and Democracy in Latin America*. Baltimore: Johns Hopkins Press.

"Sud'ba Ekonomicheskikh Programm i Reform v Rossii." (2017). *Voprosy Ekonomiki*, 6, pp. 22–44. https://doi.org/10.32609/0042-8736-2017-6-22-44.

Tabata, Shinichiro. (2008). "The Russian Stabilization Fund and Its Successor: Implications for Inflation." *Eurasian Geography and Economics*, 48/6, pp. 699–712. https://doi.org/10.2747/1539-7216.48.6.699.

Tennenbaum, Jonathan. (2001). "The Ishaev Report: An Economic Mobilization Plan for Russia." *Executive Intelligence Review*, March. www.larouchepub.com/other /2001/2809ishayevreportintro.html – accessed 30 March 2018.

Tompson, William. (2002). "Putin's Challenge: The Politics of Structural Reform in Russia." *Europe-Asia Studies*, 54/6, pp. 933–57. https://doi.org/10.1080/096681302 2000008465.

Tompson, William. (2004). "The Russian Economy under Vladimir Putin," in Cameron Ross (ed.), *Russian Politics under Putin*. Manchester: Manchester University Press.

Tompson, William. (2005a). "The Political Implications of Russia's Resource-Based Economy." *Post-Soviet Affairs*, 21/4, pp. 335–59. https://doi.org/10.1080/1060586X .2005.12049785.

Tompson, William. (2005b). "Putin and the Oligarchs: A Two-Sided Commitment Problem," in Alex Pravda (ed.), *Leading Russia – Putin in Perspective: Essays in Honor of Archie Brown*. New York: Oxford University Press.

"Transneft: Fair Value Raised to $3,000." *Troika Dialog – Russia Oil and Gas*, 10 January 2006.

"Transneft." *Troika Dialog Research*, October 2003.

Transparency and Disclosure by Russian State-owned Enterprises. New York: Standard and Poor's, 2005.

Transparency in Corporate Reporting: Assessing Russia's Largest Companies. Moscow: Transparency International, 2017.

Travin, Dmitry, and Otar Marganiya. (2010). "Resource Curse: Rethinking the Soviet Experience," in Vladimir Gelman and Otar Marganiya (eds.), *Resource Curse and Post-Soviet Eurasia: Oil, Gas and Modernisation*, pp. 23–48. Lanham: Lexington Books.

Treisman, Daniel. (1998). "Deciphering Russia's Federal Finance: Fiscal Appeasement in 1995 and 1996." *Europe-Asia Studies*, 50/5, July, pp. 893–906. https://doi.org /10.1080/09668139808412571.

Treisman, Daniel. (1999). "Russia's Tax Crisis: Explaining Falling Revenues in a Transitional Economy." *Economics and Politics*, 11/2, July, pp. 145–69. https://doi .org/10.1111/1468-0343.00056.

Troxel, Tiffany. (2003). *Parliamentary Power in Russia – 1994–2001*. Oxford: Macmillan.

Truex, Rory. (2016). *Making Autocracy Work: Representation and Responsiveness in Modern China*. New York: Cambridge University Press.

Tsebelis, George. (1995). "Decision-Making in Political Systems: Veto Players in Presidentialism, Parliamentarism, Multicameralism and Multipartism. *British Journal of Political Science*, 25, pp. 289–325. https://www.jstor.org/stable/194257.

Tsebelis, George. (2002). *Veto Players: How Political Institutions Work*. Princeton: Princeton University Press.

Tsebelis, George, and Eric Chang. (2004). "Veto Players and the Structure of Budgets in Advanced Industrialized Countries." *European Journal of Political Research*, 43/3, pp. 449–76. https://doi.org/10.1111/j.1475-6765.2004.00161.x.

Tsebelis, George, and Tatiana Rizova. (2007). "Presidential Conditional Agenda Setting in the Former Communist Countries." *Comparative Political Studies*, 40/10, October, pp. 1155–82. https://doi.org/10.1177/0010414006288979.

Varga, Mihai. (2004). "Putin Running the Duma: A Quest for Stability Regardless of Democratization." *Romanian Journal of Political Science*, 4/2, pp. 47–70.

Vatansever, Adnan. (2010). "Russia's Oil Companies Feeling the Heat on Domestic Prices for Petroleum Products: Are They Too High?" *IHS CERA Insight*, 5 January.

Vatansever, Adnan. (2017). "Is Russia Building Too Many Pipelines? Explaining Russia's Oil and Gas Strategy." *Energy Policy*, 108, pp. 1–11. https://doi.org/10.1016/j.enpol.2017.05.038.

Veksler, A., and G. Tul'chinsky. (2006). *Zachem Biznesu Sponsorstvo i Blagotvorotel'nost*. St. Petersburg: Vershina.

Volkov, Denis. (2012). *Protestnoe Dvizhenie v Rossii v Kontse 2011–2012 gg: Istoki, Dinamika, Rezul'taty*. Moscow: Levada Center.

Vygon, G., A. Rubtsov, and S. Ezhov. (2017). *Osnovnye Napravlenia Nalogovoi Reformy Neftianoi Otrasli*. Moscow: Vygon Consulting.

Vygon, G., A. Rubtsov, S. Klubkov, and S. Ezhov. (2015). *Nalogovaia Reforma Neftianoi Otrasli: Osnovnie Razvilki*. Moscow: Vygon Consulting.

Waller, Michael. (1995). "The KGB Legacy in Russia." *Problems of Post-Communism*, 42/6, pp. 3–10.

Wengle, Susanne, and Michael Rasell. (2008). "The Monetisation of L'goty: Changing Patterns of Welfare Politics and Provision in Russia." *Europe Asia Studies*, 60/5, pp. 739–56. https://doi.org/10.1080/09668130802085125.

Wetzel, Deborah. (2004). "Fiscal Federalism in Russia: Progress and Challenges." *World Bank Policy Notes*, June.

White, Stephen, Zvi Gitelman, and Richard Sakwa. (2005). *Developments in Russian Politics*. Durham: Duke University Press.

Wick, Katharina, and Erwin Bulte. (2006). "Contesting Resources – Rent Seeking, Conflict and the Natural Resource Curse." *Public Choice*, 128/3–4, September, pp. 457–76. https://doi.org/10.2307/25487568.

Worcester, D.A., Jr. (1946). "Reconsideration of the Theory of Rent." *American Economic Review*, 36, pp. 258–77. https://www.jstor.org/stable/1801836.

World Energy Outlook 2011. Paris: International Energy Agency, 2011.

Yakovlev, Andrey. (2006). "The Evolution of Business-State Interaction in Russia: From State Capture to Business Capture?" *Europe-Asia Studies*, 58, pp. 1033–56. https://doi.org/10.1080/09668130600926256.

Yasin, Yevgeny. (2001). "Putin's Undercover Liberalism." *Project Syndicate*, 4 May. www.project-syndicate.org/commentary/yasin1 – accessed 30 March 2018.

Yates, Douglass. (1996). *The Rentier State in Africa*. Trenton, NJ: Africa World Press.

Yergin, Daniel. (2011). *The Quest: Energy, Security and the Remaking of the Modern World*. London: Penguin Books.

Yermakov, Vitaly, James Henderson, and Bassam Fattouh. (2019). "Russia's Heavy Fuel Oil Exports: Challenges and Changing Rules Abroad and at Home." OIES Paper, April.

Yi-chong, Xu, and Gawdat Bahgat, eds. (2010). *The Political Economy of Sovereign Wealth Funds*. New York: Palgrave Macmillan.

Zolotareva, A., S. Drobyshevsky, S. Sinel'nikov, and P. Kadochnikov. (2001). *Perspectivy Sozdaniia Stabilizatsionnogo Fonda v RF*. Moscow: Institute for the Economy in Transition.

Zubanov, Alexander. (2006). "Neft: Oblomki Yukosa." *Novoe Vremia*, 5 July.

Zweynert, Joachim. (2007). "Conflicting Patterns of Thought in the Russian Debate on Transition: 1992–2002." *Europe-Asia Studies*, 59/1, pp. 47–69. https://doi.org/10.1080/09668130601072621.

Newspapers, Conference Papers, and Websites

"25 Samykh Rentabel'nykh Kompanii." *Finans*, 4 October 2004.

"AFK Sistema Dogovorilas' o Kompensatsii s Prodavtsom Bashnefti." *Interfax*, 19 March 2015. www.interfax.ru/business/430918 – accessed 28 April 2018.

"Alaska ne Nauchit – Prirodnaia Renta ne Reshit Problemy Nashego Blagosostoyaniya." *UralPolit.Ru – Economic and Political Reviews*, 27 October 2003.

Aleksashenko, Sergey. (2010). "Sokrashchat Raskhody v Rossii Pridetsia Sil'no." *Vedomosti*, 17 May.

Alexandrovich, Sergey. (2000). "Ministerstvo Topless." *Neft i Kapital*, no. 6.

"All Inclusive: Comprehensive Tax and Legal Overhauls Planned." *Nefte Compass*, 27 October 2005.

"Andrey Illarionov: Politika – Eto Vsegda o Den'gakh." *Novaia Gazeta*, 15 April 2004.

"Arkadii Dvorkovich o Naprevlaniakh i Tempakh Nalogovoi Reformy." *WPS – Economic Teledigest*. 15 December 2002.

Aslund, Andres. (2017). "The Achilles Heel of Putin's Regime." *Project Syndicate*, 22 April. www.project-syndicate.org/commentary/russia-crony-capitalism-achilles -heel-by-anders-aslund-2017-08 – accessed 1 August 2017.

Babich, Dmitry. (2006). "A 'Conservative' Prosecutor General Dismissed." *Russia Profile*, 2 June.

Bagrov, Andrey. (1999). "Neftianiki Pereigrali Putina." *Kommersant,* 7 September.

Bazanova, Elizaveta. (2017). "Biudzhetnoe Blagosostoyanie." *Vedomosti,* 3 July.

Bazanova, Elizaveta, and Vitaly Petlevoy. (2018). "Pravitel'stvo Soglasilos Podderzhat' Neftianikov." *Vedomosti,* 5 October.

Bazina, G. (2003). "Budut Bit'." *Rodnaia Gazeta,* 21 November.

Bekker, Alexander. (2002a). "Interviu: Viktor Khristenko, Vitse-Prem'er." *Vedomosti,* 25 March.

Bekker, Alexander. (2002b). "Nalogovaia Reforma Vernetsia v Ianvare." *Vedomosti,* 6 December.

Bekker, Alexander. (2003). "Stabfond Pokhudel."*Vedomosti,* 21 June.

Bekker, Alexander, and Andrey Panov. (2005). "Tsena Otsechenia Uvelichena do $27." *Vedomosti,* 31 March.

Bekker, Alexander, and Alexandra Petrachkova. (2006). "Neftedollary Ne Nuzhny." *Vedomosti,* 28 February.

Belton, Catherine. (2002). "Result of Slavneft's 'One-Horse" Auction Faces Criticism" *St. Petersburg Times,* 20 December.

Belton, Catherine. (2011). "Putin Denies Aiding Oil Trader." *Financial Times,* 28 September.

Belton, Catherine, and Neil Buckley. (2008). "On the Offensive: How Gunvor Rose to the Top of Russian Oil Trading." *Financial Times,* 14 May.

"Bez Gosodarstvo v Rossii Dolgo ne Zhivut: Reshenie o Sozdanii Natsional'noi Neftianoi Kompanii Uzhe Priniato, Delo za Eio Polnomochiiami i Rukovoditelem." *Kompaniia,* 12 April 1999, no. 13.

"Blagotovritel'ny Fond Yukosa Ishchet Zamenu Khodorkovskomy." *Lenta.ru,* 30 June 2004. https://lenta.ru/news/2004/06/30/leader/ – accessed 21 August 2018.

Blakkisrud, Helge. (2005). "The Appointed Governors: The End of Russian Federalism?" Paper presented at the 9th Annual Association for the Study of Nationalities Convention, Harriman Institute, Columbia University, 15–17 April.

Bohlen, Celeste. (2000). "Putin's Team Hammers Out a Plan to Untwist, Level and Streamline Russia's Economy." *New York Times,* 2 April.

Borozdina, S., and A. Litvinov. (2003). "Rentu Podeliat v Kremle." *Gazeta,* 9 December.

Borozdina, Svetlana. (2003). "Kak i Skol'ko Vziat s Neftianikov?" *Gazeta,* 30 October.

Budget Code of the Russian Federation, Chapter 13.1, Article 96.1. http://www1.minfin .ru/ru/stabfund/legislation/ – accessed 4 August 2008.

"Budget Committee Recommends Passage of Tax Code Section on Subsurface Resources," *Interfax Petroleum Report,* 10/47, 6–12 July 2001.

"Budget Expected to Sail through Second Reading." *RFE/RL Newsline,* 20 October 2000.

"Budget Passes Second Reading by Larger Margin." *RFE/RL Newsline,* 23 October 2000.

Butrin, Dmitri. (2004). "Skandal Novogo Tipa." *Gazeta,* 4 October.

Butrin, Dmitri. (2009). "Dorogaya Neft Podderzhala Delovoi Klimat." *Kommersant,* 10 April.

Butrin, Dmitri. (2016a). "God Dobrovol'noi Bednosti."*Kommersant,* 10 May.

Butrin, Dmitri. (2016b). "Strukturny Profitsit Vsemu Golova." *Kommersant,* 15 June.

Butrin, Dmitri, Petr Netreba, and Oleg Sapozhkov. (2011). "Krupneishie Dostizheniia Alekseia Kudrina." *Kommersant,* 7 October.

Chelpanova, Milana. (2014). "Glavnym Gruzom dlia Rossiiskikh Portov Ostaetsia Neft.'" *Vedomosti,* 2 December.

"The Clash: Gazprom, Rosneft Clash Over a Merger Plan." *Nefte Compass,* 7 October 2004.

Clover, Charles. (2013). "Russian Puzzle Proves Hard to Crack." *Financial Times,* 23 October.

"Crushing Blow or Failed Gambit." *RFE/RL Russia Report,* 26 February 2001.

Deliagin, Mikhail. (2001). "Novaia Oligarkhia." *Vedomosti,* 12 March.

Demchenko, Vladimir. (2005). "Dmitry Kozak: Iskorenit' Klanovost' vo Vlasti Neobhkodimo." *Izvestiia,* 21 January.

Derbilova, Ekaterina. (2004). "Industria/Energoresursy – Bez Blagtvoritel'nosti." *Vedomosti,* 8 April.

Devitt, Polina. (2017). "Declare Offshore Wealth? Russia Tycoons Would Rather Ship Themselves Off Shore." *Reuters,* 6 June. https://uk.reuters.com/article/us-russia -economy-tax-insight/declare-offshore-wealth-russia-tycoons-would-rather-ship -themselves-off-shore-idUKKBN18X0XJ – accessed 21 August 2018.

Dmitrenko, Dmitri. (2012). "Dvorkovich Poruchil 'Rosnefegazu' Otdat' Tret' Nakoplenii v Biudzhet." *Vedomosti,* 5 October.

"Do Samykh Do Okrain: Mitingi Protesta 10 Dekabria Proshli v 99 Gorodakh Rossii." *Lenta.ru,* 11 December 2011. https://lenta.ru/articles/2011/12/10/world protest/ – 27 February 2018.

"Duma Approves Budget in Third Reading." *RFE/RL Newsline,* 29 November 2004.

"Duma Rejects Budget." *RFE/RL Newsline,* 29 September 1999.

Duma voting data: sozd2.duma.gov.ru.

"Dve Voennykh Petiletki: Minoborony Rasskazalo o Planakh Perevooruzhenia Rossii." *Lenta.ru,* 25 February 2011. https://lenta.ru/articles/2011/02/25/prog/ – accessed 30 March 2018.

Dvortsov, Alekei. (2014). "Gazprom Neft: As Russia Adjusts Its Corporate Law, Companies Must Adapt." *World Finance,* 11 August. www.worldfinance.com /strategy/gazprom-neft-as-russia-adjusts-its-corporate-law-companies-must -adapt – accessed 21 August 2018.

Dziadko, Timofey. (2013). "Timchenko Upakoval Vse Aktivy v Volga Group." *Vedomosti,* 21 June.

"Edinaia Rossiia Vkliuchalas' v Diskussiu ob Ispol'zovanii Stabilizatsionnogo Fonda." *WPS – TV and Radio Monitoring,* 26 June 2005. www.securities.com – accessed 10 August 2008.

"Effekt Rosnefti." *News.ru*, 19 June 2014. www.newsru.com/finance/19jun2014
/rutransparency.html – accessed 21 August 2018.

Fadeeva, Alina. (2014). "Struktura Rotenbergov Postroit GRES Dlia Rosgidro za 17
.4 Mlrd Rub." *Vedomosti*, 27 January.

"Federal'ny Zakon No 57 'O Poriadke Osuschestvlenia Innostrannykh Investicii
v Khoziaystvennye Ohschestva, Imeiushcie Strategicheskoe Zhachenie dlia
Obespechenia Oborony Strany i Bezopasnosti Gosudarstvo." 29 April 2008. http://
base.garant.ru/12160212/ – accessed 2 June 2019.

"Fond Natsional'nogo Blagosostoyania." Ministry of Finance website. https://minfin
.gov.ru/ru/perfomance/nationalwealthfund/ - accessed 10 August 2020.

Frumkin, K. (2004). "Chinovniki Deliat Stabfond." *Gazeta*, 18 October.

Gaidar, Yegor. (2007b). "Vernutsia k Privatizatsii." *Vedomosti*, 22 March.

Gaysina, L. (2011). "Sotsial'naia Ustoychivost' Rossiiskikh Nefetgazovykh Kompanii
v Usloviakh Krizisa." *Vestnik Bashkirksogo Universiteta*, 16/4, pp. 1368–71.

"German Gref Khochet' Tratit' Stabfond na Investitsii." *Kommersant*, 11 October
2004.

"German Gref: Ekonomicheskaia Svoboda Neobkhodima kak Vozdukh." *Trud*,
23 March 2000.

"German Gref: Politicheskaia Elita Ustala ot Stabil'nosti." *Vedomosti*, 21 August
2002.

"Giant Steps: BP and TNK Tie the Knot." *Nefte Compass*, 11 February 2003.

Glazov, Andrey. (2004). "Giant Step: Gazprom Swallows Rosneft to Create New State
Colossus." *Nefte Compass*, 16 September.

Glazov, Andrey. (2005). "Black Hole: Kremlin Scraps Gazprom-Rosneft Merger. *Nefte
Compass*, 19 May.

Golovachev, Vitalii. (2000). "German Gref: Ekonomicheskaia Svoboda Neobkhodima
kak Vozdukh." *Trud*, 23 March.

Golubkova, Katya, Dmitri Zhannikov, and Stephen Jewkes. (2017). "How Russia Sold
Its Oil Jewel: Without Saying Who Bought It." *Reuters*, 24 January. www.reuters
.com/article/us-russia-rosneft-privatisation-insight/how-russia-sold-its-oil-jewel
-without-saying-who-bought-it-idUSKBN1582OH – accessed 21 August 2018.

"Governors Question Constitutionality of Resource Bill." *Petroleum Report*,
11 August 2004.

"Gref Obeshtaet Ne Peresmatrivat' Privatizatsiu." *BBC Newsletter*, 21 July 2003.
http://news.bbc.co.uk/hi/russian/russia/newsid_3083000/3083717.stm – accessed
30 April 2018.

"Gref Urges Oil Tax Changes." *Energy in East Europe*, 2 September 2005. (Accessed
via Lexis-Nexis 21 March 2008.)

Granik, Irina. (2002). "Na Puti Biudzheta Vozniklo Novoe Prepiatstvie."
Kommersant, 24 June.

Granik, Irina. (2003). "Nalog na Dobychu Poleznykh Iskopaemykh Stanet Rentoi
Perspektivy." *Kommersant*, 2 December.

Grinkevich, Vlad. (2009). "Monetizatsia L'got: Itogy Piatiletnei Reformy." *Ria Novosti*, 20 August.

Grozovskii, Boris. (2003). "Interviu: Mikhail Motorin." *Vedomosti*, 24 March.

Gryzlov, Boris. (2006). "Po Puti Razvitiia." *Vedomosti*, 18 July.

Guk, Sergey. (2001). "Uproshchennoe Nalogooblozhenie ili Podarok Oligarkhom." *Vremya MN*, 8 June.

Guriev, Sergey. (2012). "U Nas Po Moemu Politicheskikh Zakliuchennykh Net." *New Times*, 13 February, pp. 24–5. https://dlib.eastview.com/browse/doc/26606121 – accessed 1 June 2018.

Haldevang, Max de. (2017). "How the Family of Vladimir Putin's US-Sanctioned Ally Uses British Companies to Burnish Its Reputation." *Quartz*, 26 July. https://qz.com/1037549/how-the-family-of-vladimir-putins-us-sanctioned-ally-uses-british-companies-to-burnish-its-reputation/ – accessed on 29 September 2018.

Harding, Luke. (2007a). "Secretive Oil Firm Denies Putin Has Any Stake in Its Ownership." *The Guardian*, 22 December.

Harding, Luke. (2007b). "Putin, the Kremlin Power Struggle and the $40 Billion Fortune." *The Guardian*, 20 December.

"Hedging against Crisis." *Vremya MN*, 2 July 2003. (Accessed via Lexis-Nexis 10 August 2008.)

Heinrich, Andreas, Alexandra Lis, and Heiko Pleines. (2005). "Corporate Governance in the Oil and Gas Industry: Cases from Poland, Hungary, Russia and Ukraine in Comparative Perspective." KICES Working Paper 3, December.

Hille, Kathrin. (2017). "Kremlin Gathers Experts to Tackle Russia's Growth." *Financial Times*, 31 May.

Hume, Neil, and David Sheppard. (2016). "Gunvor Boss Used $1 Billion Payout to Sever Ties with Russian Oligarch." *Financial Times*, 31 May.

Hume, Neil, and David Sheppard. (2018). "Energy Trader Gunvor Profits Fall 48% after Challenging Year." *Financial Times*, 3 May.

"Interviu: Mikhail Motorin, Zamestitel' Ministra Finansov." *Vedomosti*, 24 March 2003.

Ispolnenie Federal'nogo Biudsheta i Biudzhetov Biudzhetnoy Sistemy Rossiiskoy Federatsii v 2012 Godu. Moscow: Ministry of Finance, 2013. www.minfin.ru/common/upload/library/2013/04/Ispolnenie.compressed.pdf – accessed 6 September 2017.

"Istoria." *Trasneft.ru*. www.transneft.ru/about/story/ – accessed 10 August 2020.

Ivanov, Nikolai. (2001). "Simuliatsiia: Gosudarstvo i Neftianiki Igraiut v Nalogovuiu Reformu." *Vek*, 18 May.

Ivanov, Vitaly. (2003). "Kasyanov Zastupilsia za Yukos." *Vedomosti*, 9 July.

Ivanova, Svetlana. (2006). "Dyrka of Pensii." *Vedomosti*, 3 March.

Jack, Andrew, and Arkady Ostrovsky. (2003). "Russia Threatens Yukos with $5 bn Bill." *Financial Times,* 3 December.

Joachem, Sven. (2003). "Veto Players or Veto Points: The Politics of Welfare State Reform in Europe." Conference paper presented at the 2003 annual meeting of the American Political Science Association, Philadelphia, pp. 1–41.

"Kakaia Strategia Luchshe? Mnenia Uchenykh i Politikov, Vystupivshikh na Parlamentskikh Slushaniakh." *RF Segodnia*, no. 9, 2001.

Kalyukov, E. (2014). "Zakon o Nalogovom Manevre v Neftianoi Otrasli Podpisan Putinym." *RBK Daily*, 25 November.

Kaminarskaya, Natalia. (2013). "Pravila Igry: Naladit' Partnerstva i Raziasnit' Smysly." *Vedomosti*, 20 November.

Kamyshev, Dmitri. (2005). "Gladkiy Putenok." *Kommersant Vlast*, 21 November.

Kamyshev, Dmitri, and Andrey Bagrov. (2000). "Polgoda pod Kremlem." *Kommersant*, 25 July.

"Kasyanov to Cut Taxes, Improve Investment Climate." *RFE/RL Newsline*, 11 May 2000.

Katasonov, Valentin. (2013). "Kolonizatorskaya 'Sdelka Veka.'" *Svobodnaya Pressa*, 29 March. http://svpressa.ru/economy/article/66138/ – accessed 24 April 2018.

Khamraev, Viktor. (2016). "Alexei Kudrin Gotovit Predlozhenia Vysokoi Stepeni Soglosovannosti." *Kommersant*, 6 June.

Khamraev, Viktor. (2001). "Edinaia Partia – Edinaia Fraktsia." *Vremia Novostei*, 9 November.

Kimel'man, Semen. (2001). "Mezhdu Nalogom i Rentnymi Platezhami." *Nezavisimaia Gazeta*, 22 May.

Kiselev, Sergey. (2014). "Obshchestvennaia Palata Zanialas' Offshorami." *Nezavisimaya Gazeta*, 25 April.

Kizilova, Lyubov. (2001). "Zanimatel'naia Arifmetika: Nalogovaia Diskusia Obostriaetsia." *Izvestiia*, 19 June.

Klimenteva, Lyudmila, and Natalia Raybman. (2014). "Timchenko Gotov Zavtra Zhe Predat' Svoi Aktivy Gosudarstvu." *Vedomosti*, 4 August.

"Komentarii or Redaktsii: Sreda Zaela." *Vedomosti*, 20 January 2004.

Korabel'nikova, Olga. (2001). "Strategiia dlia Rossii: Predlozhenie Gubernatora Ishaeva Obsuzhdaiut Rossiiskie Uchenye." *Trud*, 10 February.

Korchagina, Valeria. (2004). "Forbes Editor Klebnikov Shot Dead." *Moscow Times*, 12 July.

Koriukin, Kirill, and Alexander Tutushkin. (2004). "Neftianikov Pooshchrili." *Vedomosti*, 16 January.

Korop, Elena. (2003). "Stabilizatsionny Fond: Kakim on Dolzhen Byt?" *Finansovye Izvestia*, 4 February.

Korsunskaya, Daria. (2012). "Interviu: Minfin Sovetuet Shtedremu Putinu Prekhodit' k Ekonomii." *Reuters*, 27 February. https://ru.reuters.com/article/businessNews /idRURXE81Q0RX20120227?sp=true – accessed 1 March 2018.

Kravchenko, E. (2002). "Neftianikov Poshadiat." *Finansovye Izvestia*." 25 April.

"Kto i Kogda Obeshtal Snizhat' Nalogi." *Kommersant,* 26 September 2002.

Kudrin's speech at the Moscow Finance Forum, 8 September 2017. https://akudrin.
ru/news/za-nevypolnenie-strategicheskih-zadach-v-rossii-ne
-nakazyvayut-vystuplenie-na-moskovskom-finansovom-forume-8-sentyabrya
-2017-goda – accessed 21 February 2018.

Kuvshinova, Olga, and Nadezhda Ivanitskaya. (2007). "Neravnie Chasti Stabfonda."
Vedomosti, 20 December.

Kuvshinova, Olga, Margarita Lyutova, and Margarita Papchenkova. (2015).
"Pravitel'stvo Podderzhalo Predlozhenia Minfina po Sokrashteniu Indeksatsii
Sotsial'nykh Razkhodakh." *Vedomosti,* 25 June.

Kuznetsova, Vera, and Vladimir Gurevich. (2002). "Bol'she Ambitsii." *Vremia
Novostei,* 9 April.

Lapshin, Andrey. (2016). "Alexei Navalny – Vechny Istets." *Forbes,* 3 February. www
.forbes.ru/311105-vechnyy-istec – accessed 1 July 2018.

Latynina, Yulia. (2003) "Alexander Stalievich Makiavelli." *Novaya Gazeta,*
30 October.

Lavitskii, Vladimir. (2001). "Nalogovy Kodeks Podpravili." *Delovoi Peterburg,* 9 July.

Lapunova, Galina. (2001a). "Rasstroistvo Nalogovoi Reformy." *Kommersant,* 4 June.

Lapunova, Galina. (2001b). "Skol'ko Stoiat Novye Nalogi." *Kommersant,* 23 July.

Lapunova, Galina. (2003). "Reformenny Obman," *Kommersant-Vlast,* 28 April.

Lapunova, Galina, and Irina Reznik. (2001). "Rossiiskie Nedra Priravniali k
Zarubezhnym." *Kommersant,* 27 April.

"Leonid Nevzlin Obvinil v Razvale Yukosa Medvedeva, Kudrina i Abramovicha,"
Lenta.ru, 18 April 2005. www.lenta.ru/news/2005/04/18/nevzlin/ – accessed on
30 April 2018.

"Liberal Ministers Oppose Prime Minister's Plans." *RIA Novosti,* 11 November 2004.

Logvinov, M. (2003). "Vseobshtee Blago za \$17." *Russkii Kur'er,* 6 December.

Lolaeva, Svetlana. (2001). "Nalogovy Rai. Fiskal'nye Novshestva Vse Bol'she
Nraviatsia Vlastiam." *Vremia Novostei,* 9 July.

Lossan, Alexei. (2016). "Why Is Russia's Biggest Gas Pipeline Being Built on an
Uncompetitive Basis? *Russia Beyond,* 2 June. www.rbth.com/business/2016/06/02
/why-is-russias-biggest-gas-pipeline-being-built-on-an-uncompetitive-basis
_599621 – accessed 1 July 2018.

"Luzhkov: Dengi v Stabfonde Nado Vkladyvat' v Oboronu." *Pravda.Ru,* 5 May 2006.

Makarkin, Alexei. (2004). "Nakanune Pravitel'stvu Nuzhno Bol'she Neftedollarov."
Neft i Kapital, no. 4.

Maksimov, Vladimir. (2003). "Aliaska Ne Nauchit – Prirodnaia Renta Ne Reshit
Problemy Nashego Blagosostoyaniya." *Moskovskie Novosti,* 27 October.

Malkova, I. (2010). "Eksportnaia Poshlina na Vostochnusibirskuiu Neft' Budet
Povyshena." *Vedomosti,* 26 March.

Maniulova. (2016). "Zarplatny Manevr." *Kommersant,* 10 May.

"Many in Duma Oppose Paying Paris Club." *RFE/RLE Newsline,* 14 February 2001.

Mazneva, Elena. (2011). "Gazprom Pomagaet." *Vedomosti*, 1 June.

Mazneva, Elena, and Anna Repka (2008). "Navalny Proigral." *Vedomosti*, 21 August.

Medvedev, Dmitry. (2009) "Go Russia."10 September. http://en.kremlin.ru/events
/president/news/5413 – accessed 27 February 2018.

Menshikov, Stanislav. (2001). "No Confidence Vote Was Not Exactly a Farce: And the
Government's Troubles Are Far from Over." *Moscow Tribune*, 15 March.

"Mevedev Poruchil do Iulia Vyvesti Ministrov iz Sovetov Goskompanii." *Ria Novosti*,
30 March 2011. https://ria.ru/politics/20110330/359349325.html – accessed
21 August 2018.

Milov, Vladimir. (2009). "Stabfond i Vyplata Gosdolga Navredili Rossii." *Vedomosti*,
9 December.

Minaev, Sergey. (2007). "Utroenie Stabil'nosti." Kommersant Vlast'. 21 May.

"Minenergo Predlozhit Kabminu Vybor iz Shesti Mer po Stimulirovania Dobycha
Nefti." *TASS*, 3 October 2018.

"Ministr Finansov Rossii Pokinul Svoy Post. *Kommersant*, 26 September 2011.

Mokrousova, Irina, and Elena Vasilieva. (2015). "Fiasko: Prem'iernaia po Stanovka."
Forbes.ru, 3 January. www.forbes.ru/forbes/issue/2015-01/275607-fiasko-premer
naya-po-stanovka – accessed 21 August 2018.

"Monetizatsia L'got: Protivniki Poka Preobladaiut." Levada Center Press Office,
3 March 2005. http://polit.ru/article/2005/03/03/lgoty/ – accessed 18 February 2018.

Mordiushenko, Olga, Afsati Dhusoiti, and Anastasia Vedeneeva. (2016). "Dlia
Bashneft Dorozhe Vsego Khokkei." *Kommersant*, 25 August.

Mordiushenko, Olga, and Natalia Pavlova. (2016). "Bashkiria Khochet Ostat'sia pri
Nefti." *Kommersant Daily*, 29 July.

Morozov, Alexander. (2006). "Byudzhet: Igra v Priatki." *Vedomosti*, 6 October.

Movchan, Andrey. (2015). "Just an Oil Company? The True Extent of Russia's Oil
Dependency on Oil and Gas." *Carnegie Moscow Center Commentary*,
14 September. https://carnegie.ru/commentary/61272 – accessed 30 April 2018.

Murtazin, Irek. (2016). "Voyna Dvukh Vyshek."21 November. https://irek-murtazin
.livejournal.com/1807216.html – accessed 1 July 2018.

"Nagruzka na Neftianuiu Otrasl' Snizhena na 500 Mlrd Rublei." *Kommersant*,
12 February 2009.

"Nalogooblazhenie Ispol'zovania Prirodnykh Resursov." *ABCentre – Russian
Economy State Regulation*, 21 April 2001.

"Nalogovaia Reforma Prodolzhaetsia." *Rossiiskaia Biznes Gazeta*, 12 November 2002.

Natalia Ilina, and Olga Redichkina. (2002). "Putinu Predlozhili 18% Rosta." *Gazeta*,
16 October.

"Natsional'naia Neftianaia Mozhet Stat' Kompaniei #1." *Kommersant*, 20 February
1999.

"Nedra Dolzhny Prinosit' Dokhody Gosudarstvu." *Segodnia*, 22 July 1998.

"Nedra Razdora." *Infomaker – Russian Focus*, 16 December 2002.

"Neft'! Novy Lozung Vladimira Putina." *Kommersant-Daily*, 2 September 1999.

"Neftegazovye Kompanii Mogut Sokratit Dividenty." *Vedomosti*, 4 October 2015.

"Neftianiki Protestuiut Protiv Povysheniia Eksportnykh Poshlin na Neft'." *WPS – TV and Radio Monitoring*, 31 August 1999.

Nemtsov, Boris. (2007). "Zhit' Stalo Luchshe, no Protivneye." *Vedomosti*, 18 July.

Nenarokov, V. (2003). "Prirodnaia Renta Kak Predvyborny Piar." *Vostochno-Sibirskaia Pravda (Irkutsk)*, 25 November.

"New Budget Allocates More for Defense." *RFE/RL Newsline*, 4 October 1999.

"New Changes to Budget Code to Tighten Center's Control Over Money Flows." *RFE/RL Russia Report*, 4 August 2004.

"New Look – MVK Replaced by New Federal Commission." *Nefte Compass*, 9 November 2000.

Nikol'skii A., and A. Shterbakova. (2002). "Nedra – v Moskvu." *Vedomosti*, 25 April.

Nikolaeva, Anna, Irina Reznik, Ekaterina Derbilova, and Mikhail Overchenko. (2004). "The President's People." *Vedomosti*, 22 December.

Nikolaeva, Daria. (2012). "Krizis Sotsial'nuyu Otvetstvennost' Biznesa Ne Usugubil." *Kommersant*, 14 February.

Noble, Ben. (2016). "Authoritarian Legislatures and Intra-Executive Constraints." Paper presented at the annual conference of the Midwest Political Science Association, Chicago, 7–10 April.

"Obzor Ekonomicheskikh Pokazatelei." EEG, Ministry of Finance, January 2006. www.eeg.ru/downloads/obzor/rus/pdf/2006_01.pdf – accessed 1 July 2018.

Orlov, Dmitri. (2003). "Uzda Dlia Oligarkhov." *Vremya MN*, 4 July.

"Oil Traders: Pipeline Exports to Europe Still Opaque." *Wikileaks*, 24 November 2008. https://wikileaks.org/plusd/cables/08MOSCOW3380_a.html – accessed 1 July 2018.

"On the Amendments to the Budget Code of the Russian Federation in Terms of Regulating the Budgetary Process and Bringing Legislative Acts in Line with the Budget Legislation." www.consultant.ru/document/cons_doc_LAW_58942/ – accessed 11 July 2017.

"Opasenie Nestabil'nosti Ostaiotsia." *Ekonimika i Vremia*, 26 June 2000.

"Osnovnye pokazateli raboty neftepererabotyvayuschchei otrasli." *Infotek*, November 2000.

Ostrovsky, Arkady. (2003). "Russia Threatens Yukos with $5 bn Bill." *Financial Times*, 3 December.

Ostrovsky, Arkady. (2005). "Gazprom Buys Sibneft Stake for $13.1bn." *Financial Times*, 28 September.

Panov, Andrey. (2006). "Stabfond Teryaet v Vese." *Vedomosti*, 25 January.

Panov, Andrey, Olga Kuvshinova, Maria Shpigel, and Yevgenia Pis'mennaya. (2008). "Dve Treti Biudzheta." *Vedomosti*, 21 October.

Papchenkova, Margarita. (2017). "Chinovniki Podbiraiutsia k Dengam Rosneftegaza." *Vedomosti*, 9 May.

Papchenkova, Margarita, and Galina Starinskaya. (2015). "Minfin Khochet Zastavit' Neftianikov Podelit'sia Deval'vatsionnoi Pribyliu." *Vedomosti*, 20 September.

Papchenkova, Margarita, and Galina Starinskaia. (2017). "Finansy Rosneftegaz Zakryty Poka i Dlia Pravitel'stvo." *Vedomosti*, 26 June 2017.

Papchenkova, Margarita, and Alexander Vorobev. (2016). "Valdimir Putin: Rosneftegaz – Eto Esche Odin Biudzhet Pravitel'stvo." *Vedomosti*, 26 December.

"Partnership with Rosneft." British Petroleum website. www.bp.com/en_ru/russia /about-bp-in-russia/business.html – accessed 1 November 2018.

"Perechni Zakonoproektov i Proektov Postanovlenii." State Duma's website: sozd .duma.gov.ru – accessed 30 March 2018.

Petlevoi, V., and G. Starinskaia. (2014). "L'goty pod Ugrozoi." *Vedomosti*, 23 January.

Petrachkova, Alexandra, Alexander Bekker, and Alexander Tutushkin. (2006). "$35 za Barrel." *Vedomosti*, August.

Petrov, Andrey. (2003). "Duma Ustupila Pravitel'stvo Nalog s Prodazh." *Kommersant*, 16 June.

Petrova, Natalia. (2004). "Novye Marsrhuty po Starym Koridoram." *Neft i Kapital*, no. 4.

Pis'mennaya, Evgeniya. (2010). "Zhivu s Chustvom Viny za Krisiz – Alexei Kudrin, Zamestitel' Predsetadel' Pravitel'stva." *Vedomosti*, 18 May.

Pis'mennaya, Evgeniya. (2011). "Ne Stal By Nas s Putinym Nazyvat' Edinomyshlennikami." *Vedomosti*, 12 December.

Polukhin, Alexei. (2005). "Rosneft' v Taige." *Novaya Gazeta*, 2 December.

"Pomoch po Russki." *Vedomosti*, 25 March 2008.

"Poshlina na Neft' Budet Uvelichena do 7,5 Evro za Tonnu." *Segodnia*, 9 September 1999.

"Pravitel'stvo RF Rassmotrit Kontsepsiiu Razvitiia Strany do 2020 Goda." *Ria Novosti*, 1 October 2008. https://ria.ru/economy/20081001/151746239.html – accessed 11 February 2018.

"Pravitelstvo Utverdilo Proekty Finansiruemye za Schet Rosneftegaza." *Vedomosti*, 27 December 2016.

President Putin's Address to the Federal Assembly, 8 July 2000.

President Putin's Address to the Federal Assembly, 20 April 2001.

President Putin's Address to the Federal Assembly, 18 April 2002.

President Putin's Address to the Federal Assembly, 16 May 2003.

President Putin's Address to the Federal Assembly, 26 May 2004.

President Putin's aAnual Budgetary Address, 24 May 2005.

President Putin's Address on the Budget Policy for 2008–10, 9 March 2007. http:// base.consultant.ru/cons/cgi/online.cgi?req=doc;base=LAW;n=66865;fld=134;dst= 4294967295;rnd=0.3150732693843719 – accessed 3 August 2017.

President Putin's Address to the Federal Assembly, 6 April 2007. http://base .consultant.ru/cons/cgi/online.cgi?req=doc;base=LAW;n=67870;fld=134;dst=4294 967295;rnd= 0.4393070399188872 – accessed 3 August 2017.

Presidential Decree No. 1403, 17 November 1992. "On Special Considerations for the Privatization and Reorganization as Joint Stock Companies of State Enterprises and Production and Scientific Production Associations of the Oil and Oil Processing Industry and Oil Product Supply."

Presidential Decree No. 314, 9 March 2004. www.rg.ru/2004/03/11/federel-dok.html – accessed 29 June 2017.

Presidential Decrees No. 594, 596, 597, 598, 599, 600, 601, 602, 603, 604, 605, 606. 7 May 2012. www.rsr-online.ru/doc/2012_06_25/6.pdf – accessed 23 October 2017.

"President Urges Tighter Control over State Revenues." *RFE/RL Newsline*, 3 June 2002.

Press Conference with Higher School of Economics Head Yevgeny Yasin." Official Kremlin International News Broadcast, 24 August 2004. (Accessed via Lexis-Nexis 10 August 2008.)

"Prognozy Dnia: Budet li Snizhenie Eksportnykh Poshlin na Neft' Kompensirovano za Schet Neftianikov." *Vedomosti*, 19 February 2001.

"Programma Antikrizisnykh Mer Pravitel'stvo RF na 2009 god." Regnum Information Agency. https://regnum.ru/news/1139580.html – accessed 21 October 2017.

Putin, Vladimir. (2012a). "Nam Nuzhna Novaya Ekonomika." *Vedomosti*, 30 January.

Putin, Vladimir. (2012b). "Rossia Sosredotachivaetsia – Vyzovy na Katorye My Dolzhny Otvetit.'" *Izvestia*, 16 January.

Putin, Vladimir. (2012c). "Spravedlivoe Ustroistvo Obschestvo, Ekonomiki." *Komsomol'skaya Pravda*, 13 February.

"Putin Nazhal na Krasnuiu Knopku." *Izvestia*, 27 December 2001.

"Putin Orders 20 Percent Wage Hike for Military, Police." *RFE/RL Newsline*, 25 August 2000.

"Putin Podpisal Zakon O L'gotakh pri Dobyche Trudnoizvlekaemoi Nefti." *Ria Novosti*, 4 December 2012.

"Putin's Approval Rating." Yuri Levada Analytical Center. www.levada.ru/en/ratings/ – accessed 1 September 2019.

Ratnikov, Alexander. (2015). "Treider Po Predoplate." *RBK Daily*, 8 July.

Rebrov, Denis. (2004). "Yukos – Dva Protsenta: Opal'naia Neftianaia Kompania 'S Ponimaniem' Otnositsia k Blagotvorotel'nosti." *Vremia Novostei*, 64, 14 April.

"Regional Budgets Wind Up in Deficit." *RFE/RL Newsline*, 5 February 2003.

Reshul'skii, S. (2002). "Duma Oberegaet Koshel'ki Oligarkhov." *Sovetskaia Rossiia*, 15 June.

Ritchie, Michael. (2004). "Iron Curtain: Russia Closes Door on Western Majors in Yukos Aftermath." *Nefte Compass*, 22 July.

"Rosnefegaz Pozhertvoval Pochti $200 mln Agenstvu Strategicheskikh Initsiativ." *Vedomosti*, April 2014.

"Rossia Sosredotachivaetsia – Vyzovy na Katorye My Dolzhny Otvetit.'" *Izvestia*, 16 January 2012.

"Ruble's Continued Weakness Provides a Respite for Russia's Oil Sector." *Russian Petroleum Investor*, February 1999.

"Russia May Approve New Scale for Oil Export Duties." *Interfax Petroleum Report*, 10/17–18, 27 April–10 May 2001.

"Russia Raises Oil Export Duty to 15 Euros per Tonnes." *Interfax Petroleum Report*, 10–16 December 1999.

"Russian President's Aide Suggests to Spend Petrodollars for Advanced Payments of Foreign Debt." *RIA Novosti*, 8 November 2004.

Rybal'chenko, Irina. (2003). "Gosudarstvennaia Duma Otreguliruet Nedra." *Kommersant*, 24 December.

"Sale Power – Crude Export Bonanza on the Cards." *Nefte Compass*, 1 February 2001.

Samokhina, Sofia. (2013). "Deputaty Vybivaiut Opory iz-pod Transnefti." *Kommersant*, 11 April.

Sands, David. (2006). "Researchers Peg Putin as a Plagiarist over Thesis." *Washington Times*, 25 March.

Sanko, Vladimir. (2002). "Neefektivnoe i Nerachitel'noe Nedropol'zovanie." *Nezavisimaia Gazeta*, 23 March.

Sapsay, Alexander. (2004). "Gde Skryvaiutsia Nalogi." *Rossiiskaia Gazeta*, 17 November.

"Pozhalovalsia Putinu na Medvedeva." *Interfax*, 27 September 2012.

"Shans dlia Malykh Neftianykh Kompanii." *TEK Rossii*, November 2014.

Shapovalov, Alexei. (2007). "German Gref Ukhodit ot Konkurentsii." *Kommersant*, 26 March.

Sharushkina, Nelli. (2005). "No Laughter Matter: Gazprom-Rosneft Merger Descends into Farce." *Nefte Compass*, 10 March.

Sharushkina, Nelli, and Carter Tellinghuisen. (2005). "Makeover: Gazprom Buys Sibneft in Biggest Russian Takeover." *Nefte Compass*, 29 September.

Shokhina, E. (2003). "Stabilizatsiony Fond Vmesto Snizhenia Nalogov," *Ekspert*, 24 February.

Shokhina, E., I. Reznik, and B. Grozovskii. (2006). "Profil Gazrpoma." *Vedomosti*, 8 June.

Shokhina, E., E. Rudneva, F. Sterkin, S. Ivanova, and A. Kornia. (2006). "Porabotali na Slavu." *Vedomosti*, 10 July.

Silaev, Nikolai. (2004). "Chem Zanimalsia Yukos Pomimo Nefti." *Profil*, 21 June.

Sivakov, Dmitry. (2003). "Vlast' Bol'shoi Nefti." *Ekspert*, 3 Feburary.

Skliarova, Irina. (2004). "Stavka na Vyshku." *Vremia Novostei*, 26 April.

Slobodian, Elena. (2014). "Chem Izvesten Gennady Timchenko?" *Argumenty i Fakty*, 11 June. www.aif.ru/dontknows/file/1376242 – accessed 1 July 2018.

"S. Mironov: Neobkhodimo Razpechatat' Stabilizatsionny Fond i Napravit' Sredstva na Povyshenie Rozdhaemosti." *RBK.ru*, 10 May 2006.

Smirnov, Konstantin. (2000). "Zhizh' i Smert' Programmy Grefa." *Kommersant*, 4 July.

"Sobytiia i Komentarii – Prostye Pravila Prezidenta." *Trud*, 19 December 2003.

Sokolova, Viktoria, and Dyna Pyanykh. (2004). *TASS*, 16 November.

Solodovnikova, Anna, Mel'nikov, Kirill, and Sofia Samokhina. (2013). "Deputaty Vybivaiut Opory iz-pod Transnefti," *Kommersant*, 11 April.

"Sovladelets AFK Sistema Yevtushenkov Osvobozhden iz-pod Domashnego Aresta." *Ria Novosti*, 17 December 2014.

"Spravedlivoe Ustroistvo Obschestvo, Ekonomiki." *Komsomol'skaya Pravda*, 13 February 2012.

"Stabilization Fund Money Should Be Spent – Poll." *Tass*, 12 July 2005. (Accessed via Lexis-Nexis 10 August 2008.)

Starinskaya, G. (2015). "Shchiotnaya Palata Nashla Narushenia v Transneft." *Vedomosti*, 18 March.

Starinskaya, G., and M. Papchenkova. (2014). "Opasny Nalog." *Vedomosti*, 2 September.

Stenin, Andrey, and Grigory Tumanov. (2008). "Storchak Vyshel Rabotat.'" *Gazeta.ru*, 21 October. www.gazeta.ru/social/2008/10/21/2861947.shtml – accessed 15 February 2018.

Stenogramma Zasedanii Gosudarstvennoi Dumy, 20 June 2003. http://wbase.duma .gov.ru/steno/nph-sdb.exes – accessed on 21 April 2008.

Stenogramma: Zasedanie Pravitel'stvo, 51, 25 December 2014. http://government.ru /meetings/16314/stenograms/ – accessed 21 August 2018.

Stoiber, Michael. (2006). *Different Types of Veto Players and the Fragmentation of Power*. Paper presented at the 64th annual meeting of the Midwest Political Science Association, Chicago.

Stoliarov, Bulat. (2002). "Kreml' Khochet Zabrat' Nedra." *Vedomosti*, 26 July.

"Storchaka Priznali Nevinovnym." *Rossiiskaya Gazeta*, 1 February 2011.

"Stroitelstvo Nefteprovodov v Obkhod Belarusi Mozhet Nachatsia Uzhe v Aprele." *Belorusskiy Partizan*, 13 March 2007.

Tabakh, Anton. (2006). "Stabfond: Zanachka, Kopilka, Resurs." *Vedomosti*, 16 March.

Tokarev, Nikolay. (2015). "100 Milionov Ton Uspekha." *Rossiiyskaya Gazeta*, 7 April.

Topalov, Alexei. (2018). "Kak Pomoch Nezavisimym." *Neftegazovaya Vertikal*, 8, pp. 60–3.

Tovkaylo, Maksim. (2012). "Dividenty Goskompanii Opredelit Zakon." *Vedomosti*, 12 September.

Tovkaylo, Maksim. (2013). "Pravitel'stvo Riskuet Poteriat' Kontrol' nad Rosneftiu." *Vedomosti*, 19 February.

Tovkaylo, Maksim, and Oksana Gavshina. (2012). "Sechin Ne Khochet Pomoch Medvedevu Vypolnit Predvybornie Obeshchania Putina." *Vedomosti*, 24 September.

"Treider Lukoila Sokhranil Liderstvo v Reitinge Forbes." *RBK Daily*, 30 April 2017.

Tutushkin, Alexander, Elena Mazneva, and Anna Repka. (2008). "Navalny Proigral." *Vedomosti*, 21 August.

"Uglevodorody – Narodu!" *Kommersant-Vlast*, 16 February 2004.

Ulyukaev, Alexei. (2014). "Ekonomicheskaya Politika: Kak Sokhranit' Bogatstvo." *Vedomosti*, 7 August.

"United Russia List." *The Moscow Times*, 5 December 2003.

"Unity Wants More for Defense." *RFE/RL Newsline*, 24 October 2001.

Vardul, Nikolai. (2004). "The Three Prime Minister Government – Mikhail Fradkov Gets a Cabinet." *Kommersant*, 12 March.

Vasil'ev, Ivan. (2016). "Kak Trafigura Pomagaet Rosnefti v Usloviyakh Sanktsii Prodavat' Neft' na Zapad." *Vedomosti*, 19 June.

"Vektor: Toropitsia Ne Obezatel'no." *Vedomosti*, 8 July 2009.

Viktorov, Sergey, and Vadim Bardin. (2001). "Kopilka dlia Prezidenta." *Kommersant Vlast*, 12 June.

Vinogradova, Olga. (2007). "Otralsevy Puting: Pro i Contra." *Neftegazovy Vertikal'*, no. 15.

Visloguzov, Vadim. (2003). "Deputat Barrelia." *Kommersant-Vlast*, 8 December.

Visloguzov, Vadim. (2004). "Sverkhdokhody Iziali Sverkhprovodimost'iu." *Kommersant*, 26 April.

"Vladimir Putin Preodolel Vekhu – 6602 Dnia." *Rambler.ru*, 20 September 2017. https://news.rambler.ru/other/37946899-vladimir-putin-preodolel-vehu-6-602 -dnya-samyy-prodolzhitelnyy-srok-pravleniya-posle-stalina/?updated – accessed 1 October 2019.

"Voloshina i Kasyanova Mogut Otpravit' v Otstavku," *Delovaia Pressa*, 12 August 12 2003. www.businesspress.ru/newspaper/article_mId_33_aId_273631.html – accessed 29 April 2018.

Vostretsova, Yulia. (2004). "Neefektivny Iaitsa Faberzhe." *Ural'skii Rabochii (Ekaterinburg)*, 2 March.

"V. Putin: Moi Predvybornye Obeshchania ne Zavisiat ot Tsen na Neft.'" *RBK.ru*, 11 April 2012.

"Vstupaiut v Silu L'goty po NDPI na Neft' s Malykh Mestorozhdenii." *Ria Novosti*, 1 January 2012.

Vyhuloeva, Ekaterina. (2004). "U Neftianikov Poiavitsia Porog Rentabil'nosti." *Izvestiia*, 4 March.

"Warrants Issued for 10 Yukos Executives." *RFE/RL Newsline*, 24 January 2004.

Weaver, Courtney. (2011). "Russia's Richest Man Buys Freight Rail Stake." *Financial Times*, 28 October.

"Yukos Khochet Stat Osnovnym Sobstvennikom Nefteprovoda Angarsk-Dacin." *Neft i Kapital*, 10 December 2002.

"Yukos Seeks Damages from Yugansk Sale." *Nefte Compass*, 6 January 2005.

Zagorodnaia, Elena, and Elena Korop. (2003). "Pochemu on Tak Skazal." *Izvestia*, 8 July.

Zateychuk, M., and F. Sterkin. (2008). "Nalogovy Otdykh," *Vedomosti*, May 15.

Zhanov, Alexander. (2013). "Osobennosti Upravleniia v Kompaniakh Gozudarstvennym Uchastiem: Mirovoi Opyt," Ekonomika i Zhizn', August 23.

Zhavaronkova, E. (2015). 'Analiz Nalogovoi Nagruzki v Neftionoi Otrasli v Razreze Krupneyshikh Rossiiskikh i Inostrannykh Neftianykh Kompanii', *Gosudarstvennoe Upravlenie Elektronny Vestnik*, June.

Zubkov, Valentin (2001). "Vremennoe Okno dlia Rossii Mozhet Zakhlopnutsia," *RF Segodnia* www.voskres.ru/interview/ishaev.htm – accessed 30 March 2018.

Zubov, Valery. (2008). "Perestroika: Iskushenie Izobiliem," *Vedomosti*, April 24.

Index

property rights: as institutional quality, 21, 74–5; in Russia, 41, 75, 82, 83, 90, 126, 146, 216, 223, 225, 290n114
public approval (Putin), 46–7, 174, 178, 181
public protests: against monetization reform, 163, 166–7, 180, 278n225; as a political risk, 144, 234, 241, 237n279; after 2011, 174
Putin, Vladimir: academic writings of, 76–7; approach to oil sector organizational setup, 66, 71, 76–7, 88–92; approach to oil tax policy, 96, 106–8, 111, 123, 129; and awareness of resource dependence, 18, 165; benefits from historic oil windfalls, 60–4; and consolidation of power, 11, 45–7, 47–55; emphasis on growth, 152, 155, 165, 255n72, 256n75; and fiscal centralization, 53, 119, 162, 219; on fiscal prudence, 132, 151–2, 155, 163, 165, 174, 178–9; and longevity, 3, 37–8, 60, 238–9; and oil funds, 194, 197–9, 202–3; and rule of law, 75, 223–4, 231; on sovereign debt, 192, 196; and state-led development, 150–4, 163, 167–9, 175–6, 195, 199, 239; style of governance, 145, 147–50, 151, 155, 165, 173, 177–9, 204, 225; on tax cuts, 156–7, 161, 176; and Yukos Affair, 78, 80–7. See also elections

rent collection: Putin and transformation of, 9, 94–100, 106–8, 112; as a stage in rent allocation, 5, 6, 40. See also tax reform (oil)
rent generation model: elements of continuity in the, 87–9, 126, 232; factors behind the transformation of the, 77–81, 90–2, 231, 238; key players in transforming Russia's, 81–7; Putin's stance on the, 76–7, 90; Russia's unique, 13, 59–60, 64–70, 105; and its transformation under Putin, 70–3, 74–6, 122, 225–6

rent-seeking, 21, 80, 221, 239. See also resource rents
rentier state, 16–17, 18, 244n8, 245n37
rents. See resource rents
Reserve Fund: depletion of, 190, 191, 203, 204; and economic crises, 188–9, 201; establishment of, 184, 198; replenishing the, 189, 202; savings of, 185–6, 188–9, 198, 282nn7, 25
resolute state: definition of, 11, 32
resource curse: Russian awareness of, 18; theories about, 15, 18–22, 37, 42, 245n36; and USSR collapse, 18, 184
resource rents: definition of, 106, 243n5; as a distributional problem, 15–16, 41–2, 240; implications of, 21, 37, 238, 248n104; methodological problems in measuring of, 106; in the spotlight in Russian politics, 104–6, 113–16, 262n52, 263n66. See also rent collection; state-led development
Road Tax, 136, 276n174
Rodina (party), 113, 115, 117, 159, 160
Rosnanotech, 198
Rosneft: acquires Bashneft, 72, 78, 80, 257n100; acquires TNK-BP, 72, 255n59, 259n137; acquires Yuganskneftegaz, 72, 77, 85–9, 164, 231; avoids privatization, 65, 67, 70–1, 253n27; as a national oil champion, 70, 72, 88–92, 126, 210, 231; and oil trading, 209–10, 223, 226, 287n19; as a redistributor of rents, 211, 218, 223, 287n26; and tax reform, 122, 126–7; undergoes partial privatization, 72, 74, 77, 255nn63, 64, 256n84, 257n94. See also Rosneftegaz
Rosneftegaz, 216; as an extrabudgetary fund, 217, 220, 223, 225, 227; and the federal budget, 217, 221, 222–3, 291n125
Rotenberg brothers, 289n106
ruble appreciation, 185, 187, 196, 197, 271n79, 282n15